New Perspectives on

Microsoft®

FrontPage® 98

INTRODUCTORY

The New Perspectives Series

The New Perspectives Series consists of texts and technology that teach computer concepts and microcomputer applications (listed below). You can order these New Perspectives texts in many different lengths, software releases, custom-bound combinations, CourseKits™ and Custom Editions®. Contact your Course Technology sales representative or customer service representative for the most up-to-date details.

The New Perspectives Series

Computer Concepts

Borland® dBASE®

Borland® Paradox®

Corel® Presentations™

Corel® Quattro Pro®

Corel® WordPerfect®

DOS

HTML

Lotus® 1-2-3®

Microsoft® Access

Microsoft® Excel

Microsoft® FrontPage®

Microsoft® Internet Explorer

Microsoft® Office Professional

Microsoft® PowerPoint®

Microsoft® Windows® 3.1

Microsoft® Windows® 95

Microsoft® Windows NT® Server 4.0

Microsoft® Windows NT® Workstation 4.0

Microsoft® Word

Microsoft® Works

Microsoft® Visual Basic® 4 and 5

Netscape Navigator™

Netscape Navigator™ Gold

New Perspectives on
Microsoft®
FrontPage® 98

INTRODUCTORY

Roger Hayen
Central Michigan University

COURSE
TECHNOLOGY

ONE MAIN STREET, CAMBRIDGE, MA 02142

an International Thomson Publishing company I(T)P®

Cambridge • Albany • Bonn • Boston • Cincinnati • London • Madrid • Melbourne • Mexico City
New York • Paris • San Francisco • Singapore • Tokyo • Toronto • Washington

New Perspectives on Microsoft FrontPage 98—Introductory is published by Course Technology.

Associate Publisher	Mac Mendelsohn
Series Consulting Editor	Susan Solomon
Senior Product Manager	Donna Gridley
Developmental Editors	Janice Jutras, Jessica Evans
Senior Production Editor	Catherine DiMassa
Text and Cover Designer	Ella Hanna
Cover Illustrator	Douglas Goodman

© 1998 by Course Technology—I(T)P®

For more information contact:

Course Technology
One Main Street
Cambridge, MA 02142

ITP Europe
Berkshire House 168-173
High Holborn
London WCIV 7AA
England

Nelson ITP, Australia
102 Dodds Street
South Melbourne, 3205
Victoria, Australia

ITP Nelson Canada
1120 Birchmount Road
Scarborough, Ontario
Canada M1K 5G4

International Thomson Editores
Seneca, 53
Colonia Polanco
11560 Mexico D.F. Mexico

ITP GmbH
Königswinterer Strasse 418
53227 Bonn
Germany

ITP Asia
60 Albert Street, #15-01
Albert Complex
Singapore 189969

ITP Japan
Hirakawacho Kyowa Building, 3F
2-2-1 Hirakawacho
Chiyoda-ku, Tokyo 102
Japan

ISBN 0-7600-5417-7

Printed in the United States of America

1 2 3 4 5 6 7 8 9 10 BM 02 01 00 99 98

At Course Technology we have one foot in education and the other in technology. We believe that technology is transforming the way people teach and learn, and we are excited about providing instructors and students with materials that use technology to teach about technology.

Our development process is unparalleled in the higher education publishing industry. Every product we create goes through an exacting process of design, development, review, and testing.

Reviewers give us direction and insight that shape our manuscripts and bring them up to the latest standards. Every manuscript is quality tested. Students whose backgrounds match the intended audience work through every keystroke, carefully checking for clarity and pointing out errors in logic and sequence. Together with our own technical reviewers, these testers help us ensure that everything that carries our name is error-free and easy to use.

We show both how and why technology is critical to solving problems in college and in whatever field you choose to teach or pursue. Our time-tested, step-by-step instructions provide unparalleled clarity. Examples and applications are chosen and crafted to motivate students.

As the New Perspectives Series team at Course Technology, our goal is to produce the most timely, accurate, creative, and technologically sound product in the entire college publishing industry. We strive for consistent high quality. This takes a lot of communication, coordination, and hard work. But we love what we do. We are determined to be the best. Write to us and let us know what you think. You can also e-mail us at *newperspectives@course.com*.

The New Perspectives Series Team

Joseph J. Adamski	Kathy Finnegan	Scott MacDonald
Judy Adamski	Dean Fossella	Mac Mendelsohn
Roy Ageloff	Marilyn Freedman	William Newman
Tim Ashe	Robin Geller	Dan Oja
David Auer	Kate Habib	David Paradice
Dirk Baldwin	Donna Gridley	June Parsons
Rachel Bunin	Roger Hayen	Harry Phillips
Joan Carey	Cindy Johnson	Sandra Poindexter
Patrick Carey	Charles Hommel	Ann Shaffer
Sharon Caswell	Janice Jutras	Karen Shortill
Barbara Clemens	Chris Kelly	Susan Solomon
Rachel Crapser	Mary Kemper	Susanne Walker
Kim Crowley	Stacy Klein	John Zeanchock
Melissa Dezotell	Terry Ann Kremer	Beverly Zimmerman
Michael Ekedahl	John Leschke	Scott Zimmerman
Jessica Evans	Melissa Lima	

Preface The New Perspectives Series

What is the New Perspectives Series?

Course Technology's **New Perspectives Series** is an integrated system of instruction that combines text and technology products to teach computer concepts and microcomputer applications. Users consistently praise this series for innovative pedagogy, creativity, supportive and engaging style, accuracy, and use of interactive technology. The first New Perspectives text was published in January of 1993. Since then, the series has grown to more than 100 titles and has become the best-selling series on computer concepts and microcomputer applications. Others have imitated the New Perspectives features, design, and technologies, but none have replicated its quality and its ability to consistently anticipate and meet the needs of instructors and students.

What is the Integrated System of Instruction?

New Perspectives textbooks are part of a truly Integrated System of Instruction: text, graphics, video, sound, animation, and simulations that are linked and that provide a flexible, unified, and interactive system to help you teach and help your students learn. Specifically, the *New Perspectives Integrated System of Instruction* includes a Course Technology textbook in addition to some or all of the following items: Course Labs, Course Test Manager, Online Companions, and Course Presenter. These components— shown in the graphic on the back cover of this book—have been developed to work together to provide a complete, integrative teaching and learning experience.

How is the New Perspectives Series different from other microcomputer concepts and applications series?

The **New Perspectives Series** distinguishes itself from other series in at least four substantial ways: sound instructional design, consistent quality, innovative technology, and proven pedagogy. The applications texts in this series consist of two or more tutorials, which are based on sound instructional design. Each tutorial is motivated by a realistic case that is meaningful to students. Rather than learn a laundry list of features, students learn the features in the context of solving a problem. This process motivates all concepts and skills by demonstrating to students *why* they would want to know them.

Instructors and students have come to rely on the high quality of the **New Perspectives Series** and to consistently praise its accuracy. This accuracy is a result of Course Technology's unique multi-step quality assurance process that incorporates student testing at at least two stages of development, using hardware and software configurations appropriate to the product. All solutions, test questions, and other supplements are tested using similar procedures. Instructors who adopt this series report that students can work through the tutorials independently with minimum intervention or "damage control" by instructors or staff. This consistent quality has meant that if instructors are pleased with one product from the series, they can rely on the same quality with any other New Perspectives product.

The **New Perspectives Series** also distinguishes itself by its innovative technology. This series innovated Course Labs, truly *interactive* learning applications. These have set the standard for interactive learning.

How do I know that the New Perspectives Series will work?

Some instructors who use this series report a significant difference between how much their students learn and retain with this series as compared to other series. With other series, instructors often find that students can work through the book and do well on homework and tests, but still not demonstrate competency when asked to perform particular tasks outside the context of the text's sample case or project. With the **New Perspectives Series**, however, instructors report that students have a complete, integrative learning experience that stays with them. They credit this high retention and competency to the fact that this series incorporates critical thinking and problem-solving with computer skills mastery.

How does this book I'm holding fit into the New Perspectives Series?

New Perspectives applications books are available in the following categories:

Brief books are typically about 150 pages long, contain two to four tutorials, and are intended to teach the basics of an application.

Introductory books are typically about 300 pages long and consist of four to seven tutorials that go beyond the basics. These books often build out of the Brief editions by providing two or three additional tutorials. The book you are holding is an Introductory book.

Comprehensive books are typically about 600 pages long and consist of all of the tutorials in the Introductory books, plus four or five more tutorials covering higher-level topics. Comprehensive books also include two Windows tutorials and three or four Additional Cases.

Advanced books cover topics similar to those in the Comprehensive books, but go into more depth. Advanced books present the most high-level coverage in the series.

Office books are typically 800 pages long and include coverage of each of the major components of the Office suite. These books often include tutorials introducing the suite, exploring the operating system, and integrating the programs in the suite.

Custom Books The New Perspectives Series offers you two ways to customize a New Perspectives text to fit your course exactly: *CourseKits*™, two or more texts packaged together in a box, and *Custom Editions*®, your choice of books bound together. Custom Editions offer you unparalleled flexibility in designing your concepts and applications courses. You can build your own book by ordering a combination of titles bound together to cover only the topics you want. Your students save because they buy only the materials they need. There is no minimum order, and books are spiral bound. Both CourseKits and Custom Editions offer significant price discounts. Contact your Course Technology sales representative for more information.

New Perspectives Series Microcomputer Applications

■ Brief Titles or Modules	■ Introductory Titles or Modules	■ Intermediate Tutorials	■ Advanced Titles or Modules	□ Other Modules
Brief	**Introductory**	**Comprehensive**	**Advanced**	**Custom Editions**
2 to 4 tutorials	6 or 7 tutorials, or Brief + 2 or 3 more tutorials	Introductory + 3 to 6 more tutorials. Includes Brief Windows tutorials and Additional Cases	Quick Review of basics + in-depth, high-level coverage	Choose from any of the above to build your own Custom Editions® or CourseKits™

In what kind of course could I use this book?

This book can be used in any course in which you want students to learn the most important topics of FrontPage 98, including creating, changing, maintaining, and publishing a Web site. It is particularly recommended for a full-semester course on FrontPage 98. This book assumes that students have learned basic Windows 95 or Windows NT navigation and file management skills from Course Technology's *New Perspectives on Microsoft Windows 95—Brief, New Perspectives on Microsoft Windows NT Workstation 4.0—Introductory*, or an *equivalent* book.

This book has been approved by Microsoft as courseware for the Microsoft Office User Specialist program. After completing the tutorials and exercises in this book, you will be prepared to take the Expert level MSOUS Exam for Microsoft FrontPage 98. By passing the certification exam for a Microsoft software program you demonstrate your proficiency in that program to employers. MSOUS exams are offered at participating test centers, participating corporations, and participating employment agencies. For more information about certification, please visit the MSOUS program World Wide Web site at **http://www.microsoft.com/office/train_cert/**

How do the Windows 95 editions differ from the Windows 3.1 editions?

Sessions We've divided the tutorials into sessions. Each session is designed to be completed in about 45 minutes to an hour (depending, of course, upon student needs and the speed of your lab equipment). With sessions, learning is broken up into more easily assimilated portions. You can more accurately allocate time in your syllabus, and students can better manage the available lab time. Each session begins with a "session box," which quickly describes the skills students will learn in the session. Furthermore, each session is numbered, which makes it easier for you and your students to navigate and communicate about the tutorial. Look on page FP 1.5 for the session box that opens Session 1.1.

Quick Checks Each session concludes with meaningful, conceptual Quick Check questions that test students' understanding of what they learned in the session. Answers to the Quick Check questions in this book are provided on pages FP 6.63 through FP 6.68.

New Design We have retained the best of the old design to help students differentiate between what they are to *do* and what they are to *read*. The steps are clearly identified by their shaded background and numbered steps. Furthermore, this new design presents steps and screen shots in a larger, easier to read format. Some good examples of our new design are pages FP 1.14 and FP 1.16.

What features are retained in the Windows 95 editions of the New Perspectives Series?

"Read This Before You Begin" Page This page is consistent with Course Technology's unequaled commitment to helping instructors introduce technology into the classroom. Technical considerations and assumptions about software are listed to help instructors save time and eliminate unnecessary aggravation. See page FP 1.2 for the "Read This Before You Begin" page in this book.

Tutorial Case Each tutorial begins with a problem presented in a case that is meaningful to students. The problem turns the task of learning how to use an application into a problem-solving process. The problems increase in complexity with each tutorial. These cases touch on multicultural, international, and ethical issues—so important to today's business curriculum. See page FP 1.3 for the case that begins Tutorial 1.

Step-by-Step Methodology This unique Course Technology methodology keeps students on track. They enter data, click buttons, or press keys always within the context of solving the problem posed in the tutorial case. The text constantly guides students, letting them know where they are in the course of solving the problem. In addition, the numerous screen shots include labels that direct students' attention to what they should look at on the screen. On almost every page in this book, you can find an example of how steps, screen shots, and labels work together.

TROUBLE?

TROUBLE? Paragraphs These paragraphs anticipate the mistakes or problems that students are likely to have and help them recover and continue with the tutorial. By putting these paragraphs in the book, rather than in the Instructor's Manual, we facilitate independent learning and free the instructor to focus on substantive conceptual issues rather than on common procedural errors. Some representative examples of TROUBLE? paragraphs appear on page FP 3.23.

Reference Windows Reference Windows appear throughout the text. They are succinct summaries of the most important tasks covered in the tutorials. Reference Windows are specially designed and written so students can refer to them when doing the Tutorial Assignments and Case Problems, and after completing the course. Page FP 1.40 contains the Reference Window for viewing HTML code.

Task Reference The Task Reference contains a summary of how to perform common tasks using the most efficient method, as well as references to pages where the task is discussed in more detail. It appears as a table at the end of the book.

Tutorial Assignments, Case Problems, and Lab Assignments Each tutorial concludes with Tutorial Assignments, which provide students with additional hands-on practice of the skills they learned in the tutorial. See page FP 1.43 for examples of Tutorial Assignments. The Tutorial Assignments are followed by four Case Problems that have approximately the same scope as the tutorial case. In the Windows 95 applications texts, the last Case Problem of each tutorial typically requires students to solve the problem independently, either "from scratch" or with minimum guidance. See page FP 1.44 for examples of Case Problems. Finally, if a Course Lab accompanies a tutorial, Lab Assignments are included after the Case Problems.

Exploration Exercises The Windows environment allows students to learn by exploring and discovering what they can do. Exploration Exercises can be Tutorial Assignments or Case Problems that challenge students, encourage them to explore the capabilities of the program they are using, and extend their knowledge using the Help facility and other reference materials. Page FP 2.46 contains Exploration Exercises for Tutorial 2.

What supplements are available with this textbook?

Course Test Manager: Testing and Practice at the Computer or on Paper
Course Test Manager is a powerful testing and assessment package that enables instructors to create and print tests from Testbanks designed specifically for Course Technology titles. In addition, instructors with access to a networked computer lab (LAN) can administer, grade, and track tests on-line. Students can also take on-line practice tests, which generate customized study guides that indicate where in the text students can find more information on each question.

Figures on CD-ROM: This lecture presentation tool allows instructors to create electronic slide shows or traditional overhead transparencies using the figure files from the book. Instructors can customize, edit, save, and display figures from the text in order to illustrate key topics or concepts in class.

Online Companions: Dedicated to Keeping You and Your Students Up-To-Date When you use a New Perspectives product, you can access Course Technology's faculty sites and student sites on the World Wide Web. You can browse this text's password-protected Faculty Online Companion to obtain an online Instructor's Manual, Solution Files, Student Files, and more by visiting Course Technology at http://www.course.com. Please see your Instructor's Manual or call your Course Technology customer service representative for more information.

Instructor's Manual New Perspectives Series Instructor's Manuals contain instructor's notes and solutions for each tutorial. Instructor's notes provide tutorial overviews and outlines, technical notes, lecture notes, and extra Case Problems. Solutions include answers to Tutorial Assignments, Case Problems, and Lab Assignments.

Student Files Student Files contain all of the data that students will use to complete the tutorials, Tutorial Assignments, and Case Problems. A Readme file includes technical tips for lab management. See the inside covers of this book and the "Read This Before You Begin" page for more information on Student Files.

Solution Files Solution Files contain every file students are asked to create or modify in the tutorials, Tutorial Assignments, and Case Problems.

The following supplements are included in the Instructor's Resource Kit that accompanies this textbook:

- Electronic Instructor's Manual
- Solution Files
- Student Files
- Course Test Manager Test Bank
- Course Test Manager Engine
- Figures on CD-ROM

Some of the supplements listed above are also available over the World Wide Web through Course Technology's password-protected Faculty Online Companions. Please see your Instructor's Manual or call your Course Technology customer service representative for more information.

Acknowledgments

I would like to thank the many individuals who contributed to the successful completion of *New Perspectives on Microsoft FrontPage 98—Introductory*.

Thanks to Joe Dougherty and Mac Mendelsohn for their support and to Donna Gridley for keeping everything coordinated and on schedule. Janice Jutras and Jessica Evans performed editing magic to deliver a truly remarkable book for learning FrontPage. I want to thank Catherine DiMassa and the production department for turning the manuscript into a colorful, well-designed book. And to all the people at Course Technology who contributed to the overall success of this project in ways too numerous to recount, I extend my sincere thanks. I would also like to thank the following reviewers—Jenny Alvis, Virginia Highlands Community College; Stephanie Low, The College of Charleston; Thomas A. Larkin, Rennselaer Polytechnic Institute; and Mark Westlund, Green River Community College—who offered valuable comments, suggestions, and criticisms that helped to shape this book. Thanks also to the quality assurance testers—Seth Freeman and Catherine DiMassa—for their excellent work. I am also grateful for the many suggestions and valuable insights provided by my colleagues, and especially to Terry Arndt, dean of the College of Business Administration, who provided motivation in pursuing this project.

And last but certainly not least, I would like to thank my family. During this project, the "book" overshadowed many family activities, but their encouragement, support and most of all perseverance enabled me to complete this project.

Roger Hayen

Brief Contents

Table of **Contents**

NEW
PERSPECTIVES
S E R I E S

Microsoft®
FrontPage® 98

LEVEL I

TUTORIALS

Read This **Before You Begin**

STUDENT DISKS

To complete FrontPage Tutorials 1–6 and the end-of-tutorial assignments in this book, you need three Student Disks. Your instructor will either provide you with Student Disks or ask you to make your own.

To make your own Student Disks, you will need three blank, formatted high-density disks. You will need to copy a set of folders from a file server or standalone computer onto your disks. Your instructor will tell you which computer, drive letter, and folders contain the files you need. The following table shows you which folders go on each of your disks, so that you will have enough disk space to complete all the tutorials, Tutorial Assignments, and Case Problems.

Student Disk	Write this on the disk label	Put these folders on the disk		
1	Student Disk 1: Tutorial 1	wwwroot	Tutorial.01	
2	Student Disk 2: Tutorials 2 through 6	wwwroot	Tutorial.03	Tutorial.05
		Tutorial.02	Tutorial.04	Tutorial.06
3	Student Disk 3: Tutorials 2 through 6, Case Problems only	wwwroot	Tutorial.03	Tutorial.05
		Tutorial.02	Tutorial.04	Tutorial.06

When you begin each tutorial, be sure you are using the correct Student Disk. See the inside front or inside back cover of this book for more information on Student Disk files, or ask your instructor or technical support person for assistance.

WINDOWS 95 INSTALLATION INSTRUCTIONS

Before installing FrontPage, use the Network Control Panel to make sure the TCP/IP network protocol is installed and Access Control is set to user-level. Also, you should have a Web browser installed (preferably Internet Explorer 4.0 or higher).
1. Run "Setup.exe" from the FrontPage CD.
2. Install the Microsoft Personal Web Server. (You will need to restart the computer after installing the server.)
3. Install FrontPage. Choose the "Typical" install when prompted. You can now access FrontPage from the Start menu.

WINDOWS NT INSTALLATION INSTRUCTIONS

Before installing FrontPage, use the Network Control Panel to make sure the TCP/IP network protocol is installed and the Microsoft Peer Web Server network service is installed. Also, you should have a Web browser installed (preferably Internet Explorer 4.0 or higher).
1. Run "Setup.exe" from the FrontPage CD.
2. Install FrontPage. Choose the "Typical" install when prompted. You can now access FrontPage from the Start menu.

USING YOUR OWN COMPUTER

If you are going to work through this book using your own computer, you need:

■ **Computer System** Windows 95, FrontPage 98, and Microsoft Internet Explorer 3.02 or higher (Internet Explorer 4.0 is preferred) must be installed on your computer. This book assumes a Typical installation of FrontPage 98.

■ **Student Disks** Ask your instructor or lab manager for details on how to get the Student Disks. You will not be able to complete the tutorials or end-of-tutorial assignments until you have Student Disks. The Student Files may also be obtained electronically over the Internet.

VISIT OUR WORLD WIDE WEB SITE

Additional materials designed especially for you are available on the World Wide Web. Go to **http://www.course.com**.

To complete FrontPage Tutorials 1–6 and the end-of-tutorial assignments, your students must use a set of files on three Student Disks. These files are included in the Instructor's Resource Kit, and they may also be obtained electronically over the Internet. Follow the instructions in the Readme file to copy the files to your server or standalone computer.

Once the files are copied, you can make Student Disks for the students yourself, or you can tell students where to find the files so they can make their own Student Disks.

Please note: Students must use Internet Explorer 4.0 or higher to use dynamic, active elements and FrontPage components on a Web page. Earlier versions of Internet Explorer can be used with this book but students will not see the dynamic elements taught in Tutorials 4, 5, and 6.

COURSE TECHNOLOGY STUDENT FILES

You are granted a license to copy the Student Files to any computer or computer network used by students who have purchased this book.

TUTORIAL 1

Introducing FrontPage 98

Exploring the Sunny Morning Products Web Site

OBJECTIVES

In this tutorial you will:

▨ Learn what the Internet and the World Wide Web (WWW) are and how they work

▨ Start Internet Explorer to explore a Web site

▨ Print a Web page

▨ Learn what FrontPage is and how it works

▨ Learn how the FrontPage Explorer and FrontPage Editor tools work

▨ Start and exit FrontPage Explorer and FrontPage Editor

▨ Open a FrontPage Web to explore a Web site

▨ View HTML code for Web pages

CASE

Sunny Morning Products

Sunny Morning Products is an international bottler and distributor of Olympic Gold brand fresh orange juice and thirst-quencher sports drink. Olympic Gold products are sold in grocery stores, convenience stores, and many other outlets. Located in Garden Grove, California, the company was established in 1909 by Edwin Towle. Edwin's grandson, Andrew Towle, now serves as the chairman of the board. To better accommodate the customers and visitors who often tour the citrus groves of Sunny Morning Products, Andrew opened the Sunshine Country Store in 1951. In addition to selling Olympic Gold juice products, the Country Store also sells its fresh produce, such as oranges and grapefruits. In 1987, Andrew expanded the Country Store to include mail orders of citrus products.

Amanda Bay has been working for Sunny Morning Products for two years as an assistant marketing manager. Her main responsibility is to assist Andrew in promoting and marketing Sunny Morning Products. One of Amanda's latest projects was to create a Web site for Sunny Morning Products to reach new and existing customers online. Because of the overwhelming success of this initial Web site, Andrew decided to expand the company's Web activities into other areas of the business. He assigned Amanda the task of training employees in Web site development.

In response, Amanda prepared a Web site development training program that utilizes the Microsoft FrontPage 98 program. During most of the training program, participants explore the current Sunny Morning Products Web site in order to build Web development skills. Upon completing the training program, employees are either ready to assist in maintaining the current Web or work on new Web development projects in other departments.

As a management intern in the marketing department, you will participate in Amanda's training program. Once you've completed the program, you will assist Amanda in maintaining and updating the current Sunny Morning Products Web site and in helping to train others. Although you've used the Internet for e-mail purposes, you are inexperienced when it comes to directly working with Web sites. Amanda assures you that by the end of the training, you will have mastered the process of creating and designing a Web site. But first, you need an introduction to the Internet and the World Wide Web in order to understand how FrontPage 98 is used to develop and maintain Web sites.

Using the Tutorials Effectively

These tutorials are designed to be used at a computer. Each tutorial is divided into sessions. Watch for the session headings, such as "Session 1.1" and "Session 1.2." Each session is designed to be completed in about 45 minutes, but take as much time as you need. When you've completed a session, it's a good idea to exit the program and take a break. You can exit the Microsoft FrontPage 98 program by clicking the Close button in the top-right corner of the program window.

Before you begin, read the following questions and answers. They are designed to help you use the tutorials effectively.

Where do I start?

Each tutorial begins with a case, which sets the scene for the tutorial and gives background information to help you understand the tutorial activities. Read the case before you go to the lab. Once you are in the lab, begin with the first session of the tutorial.

How do I know what to do on the computer?

Each session contains steps that you will perform on the computer to learn how to use Microsoft FrontPage. The steps are numbered and are set against a colored background. Read the introductory text, and then read each step carefully and completely before you try it.

How do I know if I did the step correctly?

As you work, compare your computer screen with the corresponding figure in the tutorial. Don't worry if your screen display is somewhat different from the figure. The important parts of the screen display are labeled in each figure. Check to make sure these parts are on your screen.

What if I make a mistake?

Don't worry about making mistakes; they are part of the learning process. Paragraphs labeled "TROUBLE?" identify common problems and explain how to get back on track. Follow the steps in a TROUBLE? paragraph only if you are having the problem described. If you run into other problems, carefully consider the current state of your system, the position of the pointer, and any messages on the screen.

How do I use the Reference Windows?

Reference Windows summarize the procedures you learn in the tutorial steps. Do not complete the actions in the Reference Windows when you are working through the tutorial. Instead, refer to the Reference Windows while you are working on the assignments at the end of the tutorial.

How can I test my understanding of the material I learned in the tutorial?

At the end of each session, you can answer the Quick Check questions. If necessary, refer to the Answers to Quick Check Questions to check your work.

After you have completed the entire tutorial, you should complete the Tutorial Assignments and Case Problems. These exercises are carefully structured to review what you have learned and then help you apply your knowledge to new situations.

What if I can't remember how to do something?

You should refer to the Task Reference at the end of the book; it summarizes how to accomplish commonly performed tasks.

Now that you've seen how to use the tutorials effectively, you are ready to begin.

In this session you will learn what the Internet and World Wide Web (WWW) are and how they work. You will start the Internet Explorer Web browser and learn the various components that make up both the Internet Explorer window and a Web page. Finally, you will print a Web page.

The Internet

The **Internet** is a large computer network consisting of smaller, interconnected networks. A **network** consists of two or more computers connected to one another for purposes of shared communication and resources. Within each network, one computer is designated as the network **server**, or **host**, which functions as the network's central computer that stores and distributes information and resources across the network to individual computers. The Internet is not a single, massive computer but rather, millions of connected computers so a variety of information can be exchanged. The Internet allows you to communicate and share data with people in the next office, across the street, or around the world. Today, the Internet is the largest and most widely used computer network in the world.

Each Internet host is a network server that is connected to the Internet and permits people around the world to access its files. Every host is attached to a major connection called a **backbone**, which moves information quickly on the Internet over long distances.

The Internet's resources are organized in a client/server architecture, where the **server** stores the information that is accessed and shared using a **client** computer that receives and displays the requested information. Each request for information is transferred as a file. When a client requests information from the server, the server finds the information and sends back the requested file. This file travels over the Internet from one computer to another. The various computers that make up the backbone of the Internet forward data from one computer to another until the data reaches the intended destination.

To access the Internet, you need an account with a commercial information service provider, commonly called an Internet Service Provider. An **Internet Service Provider (ISP)** is a service company that provides you with a user account on a host computer that has access to the Internet backbone. These providers range from small electronic bulletin boards that run on a single microcomputer to large enterprises such as Microsoft Network and America Online. Many colleges, universities, and large businesses have their own direct connection to the Internet and are, in effect, their own ISP. Most individuals and smaller businesses use an ISP for their Internet connection.

The World Wide Web (WWW)

The **World Wide Web (WWW),** or simply **the Web,** is a global information-retrieval system that makes finding information and navigating the Internet easier. The Web organizes the Internet's vast resources in a common way so that information is easily stored, transferred, and displayed among the various types of computers that make up the Internet. Hundreds of thousands of businesses regularly use the Web for everything from advertising to distributing software.

Each electronic document of information on the Web, known as a **Web page,** contains different types of information, ranging from simple text to complex multimedia items. A **Web site** is a related set of Web pages available from a Web server, where they are stored. A **Web server** is an Internet host for Web pages. Each individual Web server can have multiple Web sites. For example, a college or university might have a single Web server, while each faculty member or student maintains a separate Web site with his or her collection of related Web pages residing on that single Web server.

Most Web sites consist of a series of documents that are linked together, rather than a single Web page. **Hypertext,** or **hypertext links,** are keywords, phrases, or images in a document that you select to connect to another related document. The process of connecting through hypertext is called **linking,** and hypertext links are commonly referred to simply as **links. Hypermedia** is hypertext that contains links to multimedia, such as graphic images, photographs, and sound clips. By selecting a link, or clicking it with your mouse pointer, you retrieve that file from the specified Web server, which can be either the same Web server or any other server connected to the Internet, and display it using the client's Web browser. A **Web browser** is the software program that requests, retrieves, interprets, and displays the content of a Web page on a user's computer screen. A browser can locate a Web document on a server anywhere in the world. Microsoft Internet Explorer, commonly called **Internet Explorer**, is a powerful and easy-to-use Web browser capable of accessing Web documents. You will learn more about Internet Explorer later in this session. Figure 1-1 shows how the Internet and WWW work together.

Figure 1-1
How the Internet and World Wide Web (WWW) work together

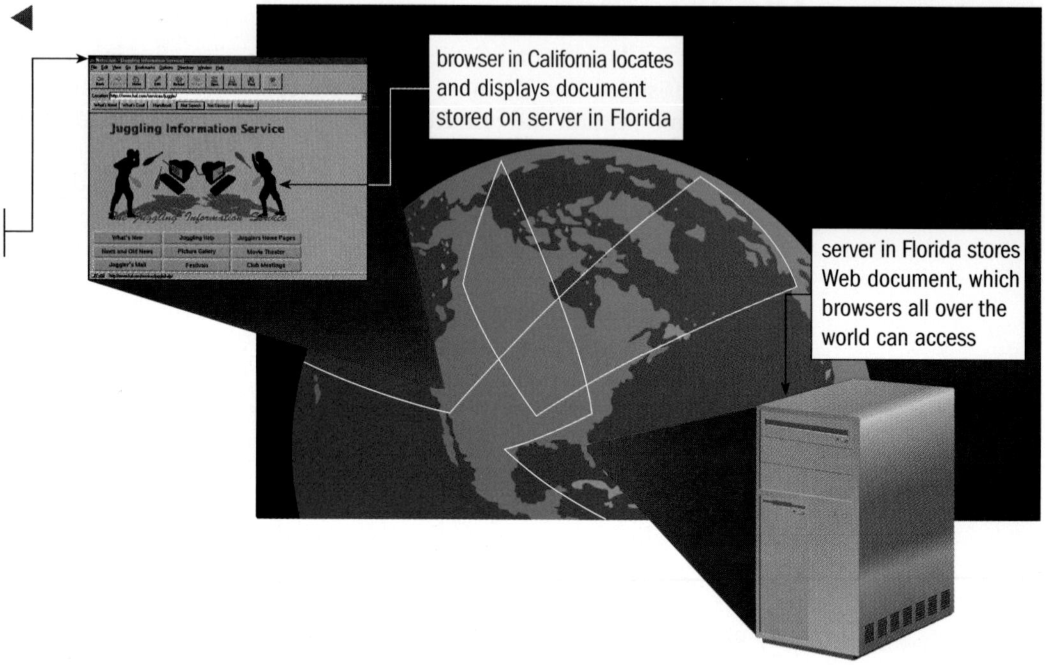

Internet Explorer browser

browser in California locates and displays document stored on server in Florida

server in Florida stores Web document, which browsers all over the world can access

Understanding HTML

The WWW must work across many different computer platforms. Because each computer connected to the Internet and/or the WWW differs in terms of what, if any, formats it can display, it is the Web browser's role to determine how text is displayed on a user's screen by translating the Web page file into a formatted page. This portability frees Web developers from attempting to make their documents compatible with the large variety of computers and operating systems on the Internet. The most common method of storing information for transfer and display on the various computers that are connected to the Internet is a **hypertext document**. These documents are prepared using a special language known as **hypertext markup language (HTML)**; hypertext documents are often referred to as **HTML documents**. These documents use only a standard character set that is recognized by all computers. Each HTML document contains special codes that a Web browser interprets in order to display data in the desired format on your client computer. A Web page is, in fact, nothing more than an HTML document that is stored on a server. You will learn more about HTML later in this tutorial.

Microsoft Web Servers

In order to function as a Web server, a computer connected to the WWW needs special software that works with the computer's operating system, such as Windows 95, to receive and carry out requests for Web pages. Microsoft provides three different versions of Web server software: the FrontPage Personal Web Server, the Microsoft Personal Web Server, and the Internet Information Server. The FrontPage Personal Web Server is used with either Windows 95 or Windows NT 4.0. The Microsoft Personal Web Server is used only with Windows 95, whereas the Internet Information Server is used with Windows NT Server 4.0. Personal Web servers satisfy less-demanding programs and are adequate for developing and testing Web sites, whereas the Internet Information Server is designed for use with commercial Web sites.

Many Web pages can be developed and tested using a **disk-based Web** that utilizes the Web pages on your computer's disk drive. The testing of several more advanced features of a Web site, such as user-defined forms and searches, requires a **server-based Web** that uses Web server software, although they might be installed on the same computer. A disk-based Web is accessed using a drive letter and backslashes, such as a:\wwwroot\sun.morn, whereas a server-based Web is accessed using an "http:" protocol and forward slashes, such as http://mypc/sun.morn.

The Web site that Amanda created for Sunny Morning Products can be examined as either a disk-based Web or as a server-based Web; therefore, you will work with both Webs in these tutorials. However, all the examples in Tutorial 1 utilize a disk-based Web, which doesn't allow you to obtain a response when processing any of the Web forms. In order to interact with a Web form, a server-based Web is required. (You will use a server-based Web in later tutorials.) Consult with your instructor or technical support person concerning the use of an access method that is different from the ones described previously.

Getting Started with Internet Explorer

Recall that Internet Explorer is a Web browser that allows you to view HTML documents. As part of the FrontPage program, Internet Explorer is provided on the same CD-ROM with other FrontPage software. This book uses Internet Explorer 4.0 as the default Web browser. Your computer might have Internet Explorer 3.02 as the default Web browser, which is not a problem. Your output should look the same.

Unlike some software programs, Internet Explorer does not always open with a standard start-up screen. A **Start page** is the first page that loads when you start a Web browser, such as Internet Explorer, and is the default **universal resource locator (URL)** set as the navigation option for the browser. A URL is simply an address of an Internet server. If you cannot access a specific URL, then a default Web page, usually BLANK.HTM, opens from your computer's hard drive. If the Start page is to a Web site, then a home page for that Web site opens. A **home page** is the first page that usually opens for a Web site. It often contains information about the host computer or sponsoring organization, links to other Web sites, and corresponding graphics and sounds. Figure 1-2 provides an example of a home page for Edmund's Automobile Buyer's Guides accessed using Internet Explorer. Note that this figure identifies the key components of the Internet Explorer window. Figure 1-3 describes some of these Internet Explorer components in more detail. For example, the Address box shows the URL of the current Web page displayed in the browser window, while the status bar might display messages that describe current actions, such as "Done" or "Web site found. Waiting for reply."

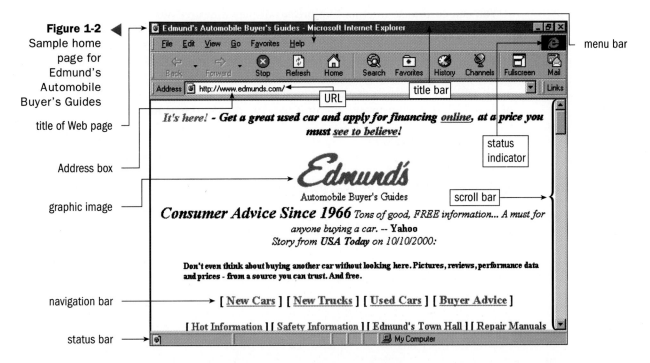

Figure 1-2 ◄
Sample home page for Edmund's Automobile Buyer's Guides

title of Web page

Address box

graphic image

navigation bar

status bar

menu bar

Figure 1-3 ◀
Components of
the Internet
Explorer window

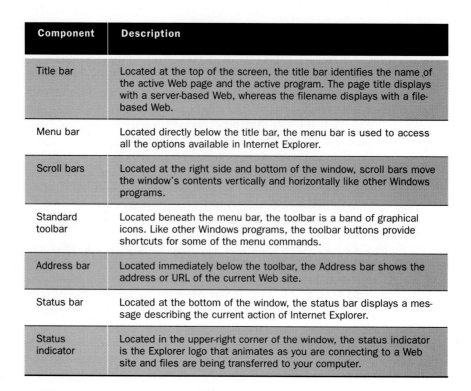

Component	Description
Title bar	Located at the top of the screen, the title bar identifies the name of the active Web page and the active program. The page title displays with a server-based Web, whereas the filename displays with a file-based Web.
Menu bar	Located directly below the title bar, the menu bar is used to access all the options available in Internet Explorer.
Scroll bars	Located at the right side and bottom of the window, scroll bars move the window's contents vertically and horizontally like other Windows programs.
Standard toolbar	Located beneath the menu bar, the toolbar is a band of graphical icons. Like other Windows programs, the toolbar buttons provide shortcuts for some of the menu commands.
Address bar	Located immediately below the toolbar, the Address bar shows the address or URL of the current Web site.
Status bar	Located at the bottom of the window, the status bar displays a message describing the current action of Internet Explorer.
Status indicator	Located in the upper-right corner of the window, the status indicator is the Explorer logo that animates as you are connecting to a Web site and files are being transferred to your computer.

Starting Internet Explorer

You start Internet Explorer just like any other program. When you start Internet Explorer, you might see any one of the following:

- Microsoft home page
- Your educational institution's home page
- A home page that your technical support person set as the default
- A blank page

You can customize Internet Explorer to display a desired Web page as the Start page. For example, when Amanda starts Internet Explorer from her office, she sees the Home Page for Sunny Morning Products because this has been set as her default Start page.

You are ready to begin exploring the Sunny Morning Products Web site as the first phase of your training in learning how to develop a Web site. Once you have a better understanding of different Web pages that can be used with a Web site, you can learn how to create one of these HTML documents using FrontPage. You decide to start Internet Explorer.

To start Internet Explorer:

1. Make sure Windows 95 is running on your computer and the Windows 95 desktop appears on your screen with the taskbar displayed. See Figure 1-4.

Figure 1-4
Windows 95
Desktop

Internet Explorer
desktop icon (your
icon might look
different)

Internet Explorer
taskbar icon

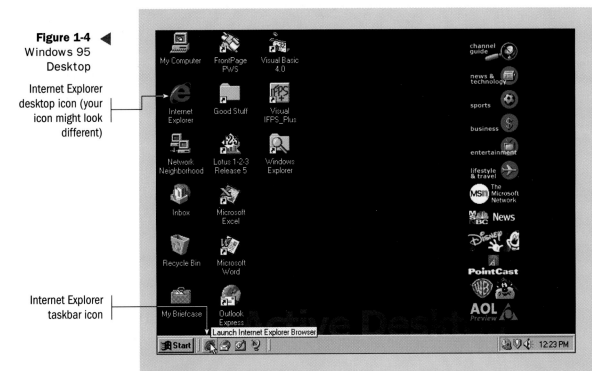

TROUBLE? You might not see the Internet Explorer toolbar on your taskbar. This is not a problem; go to Step 2.

2. Click the **Launch Internet Explorer** button [e] on the taskbar to start the program. If you do not see the Internet Explorer toolbar on your taskbar, double-click the **Internet Explorer** icon on the desktop. The Start page selected when Internet Explorer was installed displays. In this example, it is the Home Page for Sunny Morning Products. See Figure 1-5. This figure identifies the key components of a home page.

TROUBLE? Don't worry if your Start page is different from the Home Page for Sunny Morning Products. Another Start page will display in your window unless your copy of Internet Explorer has been installed to display this specific Start page. If Internet Explorer cannot locate a Web site, then a blank page (BLANK.HTM) displays using a disk-based file that is stored with Internet Explorer. Continue with Step 3.

TROUBLE? If you're uncertain whether you started Internet Explorer, check the title bar at the top of the window; it should display "Microsoft Internet Explorer." If it doesn't, you might have selected the wrong icon. Click File on the menu bar, and then click Close to close the program and return to the Windows desktop. Repeat Step 2.

TROUBLE? If you do not see the Internet Explorer toolbar on your taskbar or the Internet Explorer icon on the desktop, ask your instructor or technical support person for help to start the Internet Explorer program.

Figure 1-5
Home Page for
Sunny Morning
Products

Web home page and
program name listed
in title bar

image

background

text

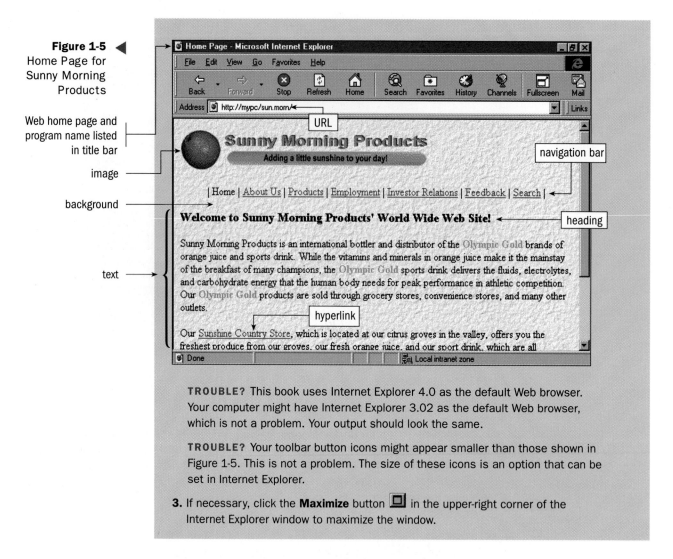

TROUBLE? This book uses Internet Explorer 4.0 as the default Web browser.
Your computer might have Internet Explorer 3.02 as the default Web browser,
which is not a problem. Your output should look the same.

TROUBLE? Your toolbar button icons might appear smaller than those shown in
Figure 1-5. This is not a problem. The size of these icons is an option that can be
set in Internet Explorer.

3. If necessary, click the **Maximize** button in the upper-right corner of the
Internet Explorer window to maximize the window.

Figure 1-6 describes some of the key elements of a home page that are identified in
Figure 1-5. For example, the navigation bar, located at the top of every Sunny Morning
Products Web page, makes it easy for you to move through the various pages in the Web.
Clicking a link on the navigation bar allows you to easily move to a new page or return to
a previous one.

Figure 1-6 ◀
Components of
a home page

Component	Description
Title	Identifies the name of the active Web page and/or program located in the title bar.
Text	Located in the body of the document as a narrative description.
Heading	Provides heading text in the document.
Hyperlink	Provides links to other Web pages. Hyperlinks are indicated by different color and underlining. Hyperlinks may be inline text or a separate line of text.
Image	A graphic on a Web page; may or may not be a hyperlink.
Background	Enhances the appearance of a Web page through different colors and textures. Text and images appear on top of the background.
Navigation bar	Represents a convenient use of hyperlinks to other Web pages. It is located at the top of the document for ease of use. This is a frequently used Web page design feature.

Opening a Location with a URL

One of the earliest methods of identifying computers on the network was through the use of Internet Protocol addresses. An **Internet Protocol (IP)** address is a uniquely assigned address that identifies an individual computer on the network. Typically, an IP address consists of a long string of numbers, such as 141.209.151.119. Because IP addresses were often difficult to memorize, however, a more user-friendly addressing system was developed featuring URLs. A URL identifies a file on the WWW so that client computers can find and retrieve the page. A URL can be broken down as follows:

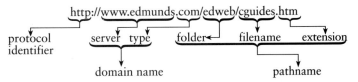

Networked computers use standardized procedures, called **protocols**, to transmit files over the Web. HTML documents travel between Web sites using the **HyperText Transfer Protocol (HTTP)**; hence, every URL for a Web page begins with "http://" to identify this protocol. Other protocols used on the Internet include File Transfer Protocol (FTP), news, and Gopher.

A **domain name**, which acts as a synonym for an IP address, identifies the exact address of the Internet server and the type of organization that owns and operates it. For example, in the domain name "www.edmunds.com," "www" indicates that the server is a Web server on the WWW; "edmunds" indicates the name of the organization that owns the server; and ".com" indicates that it is a commercial-type server. Other common types of servers in the United States are education (.edu), organization (.org), and government (.gov). For municipal governments and servers outside North America, a two-letter state or country code is used. For example, ".uk" indicates that a server is located in Great Britain.

Finally, all files stored on a Web server must have a unique pathname, just like files stored on a disk. A **pathname** includes the folder that the file is stored in as well as the filename and extension. The extension for all Web pages is either ".html" or ".htm," both of which indicate an HTML file. The ".html" extension is used with computers that run the UNIX operating system, whereas the ".htm" extension is used most frequently with computers that run Microsoft Windows operating systems. Internet Explorer processes files with either of these extensions as HTML documents.

To access a particular Web site, or open a location, you simply type its URL in the Address box. Internet Explorer connects to the server the URL specifies, sends a request for information based on the address, and accepts the information. It then displays this information on your screen and automatically terminates the connection to this site.

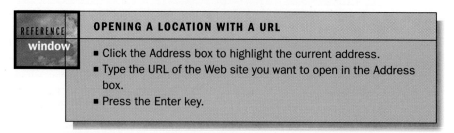

REFERENCE window

OPENING A LOCATION WITH A URL

- Click the Address box to highlight the current address.
- Type the URL of the Web site you want to open in the Address box.
- Press the Enter key.

Amanda wants you to examine the Sunny Morning Products Web site to familiarize yourself with the basic features of a Web page. Later, you will use FrontPage to create your own Web pages. *Don't be concerned if you can't remember all the details of this Web site.* All of the elements you are introduced to in this overview of the Sunny Morning Products Web site will be reinforced throughout the tutorials as you progress through Amanda's training course. Now you access the Sunny Morning Products Web site that Amanda created.

To open a location with a URL:

1. Make sure the Internet Explorer window is open and your Student Disk is in drive A or the appropriate disk drive.

2. Click the **Address box** to select the current text.

3. Type **a:\wwwroot\sun.morn\index.htm** in the Address box. See Figure 1-7. The wwwroot folder is the default folder used for storing Webs with several of the Web servers, including the Microsoft Personal Web Server and the Internet Information Server. In this example, it is used to identify your disk-based Web; however, the default folder could be any folder and is not limited to wwwroot. As you type the Web address, the Explorer's AutoComplete feature might suggest a match for you if you have visited the Web site before. The suggested match is highlighted in the Address box.

Figure 1-7 ◀
Opening a
location with a
URL

URL for
disk-based Web

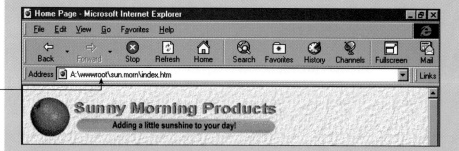

TROUBLE? If your instructor provides you with a different access method than the one described in Step 3, use that method.

TROUBLE? If you are using your own computer, make sure the sun.morn Web is available on your Student Disk or is installed in the wwwroot\sun.morn directory of your Web server.

4. Press the **Enter** key. The Home Page for Sunny Morning Products opens. If your computer is equipped for multimedia and your speakers are turned on, a background sound plays.

5. If desired, click the **Stop** button 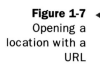 on the toolbar to stop the music. The sound is terminated either by clicking the Stop button or by opening another Web page.

Next you continue with your Web development training by examining the various hyperlinks on the Sunny Morning Products Home Page.

Linking to a Web Page

A hypertext link on the Internet, like a link in a chain, connects two end points. The Sunny Morning Products Home Page you are currently viewing contains several underlined links. Each link is a set of directions that tells Internet Explorer the path to follow in order to bring you to a file at that site. You follow a hyperlink by clicking it. A link can bring you to another link within that specific Web page or connect you to a different Web page or Web site entirely.

Because you will create and test Web page links while you learn how to develop a Web site, Amanda wants you to practice using hyperlinks to move from one Web page to another.

To link to a Web page:

1. Place your mouse pointer on the **Products** hyperlink in the navigation bar. Note that the pointer changes from a ⬦ to a ⬦ to indicate that you are pointing to a hypertext link. In addition, a description of the link appears in the status bar. However, because of the overall length of the pathname to the file, only part of the pathname is visible.

2. Place your mouse pointer on the **Sunshine Country Store** hyperlink. The link to the PRODUCTS.HTM file that is partially listed in the status bar is the same one that appeared for the "Products" hyperlink. You can have more than one hyperlink to the same Web page.

3. Click the **Employment** hyperlink in the navigation bar to initiate the link to that Web page. The Employment Web page, which contains a bulleted list that is a series of hyperlinks within the Web page, appears. See Figure 1-8.

Figure 1-8 ◄
Employment
Web page

bulleted list with
hyperlinks

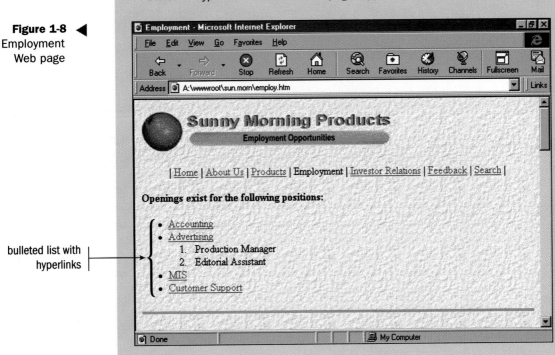

Next Amanda wants you to examine a link to another location within the same Web page. The hyperlink text and the anchor name for the referenced location may be the same or may consist of different text. A common feature used with Web page design is to provide a link that allows you to easily return to the top of a Web page, rather than using the vertical scroll bar. This is particularly useful with long Web pages, such as the Employment Web page that currently appears in your window. By using this type of internal page link, you can jump to the named anchor location by selecting the hyperlink text or return to the top of the Web page.

To link to a location within a Web page:

1. Place your mouse pointer on the **MIS** link. Note that the description of the link appears in the status bar. Again the filename is only partially visible.

2. Right-click the **MIS** link to display the Shortcut menu, and then click **Properties** to open that dialog box. The HTM#MIS File type indicates this is an internal link to the MIS anchor on the current EMPLOY.HTM page. See Figure 1-9.

Figure 1-9 ◀
Properties
dialog box

MIS anchor on
current page

complete URL with
filename and anchor

right-click to display
the Shortcut menu for
selected hyperlink

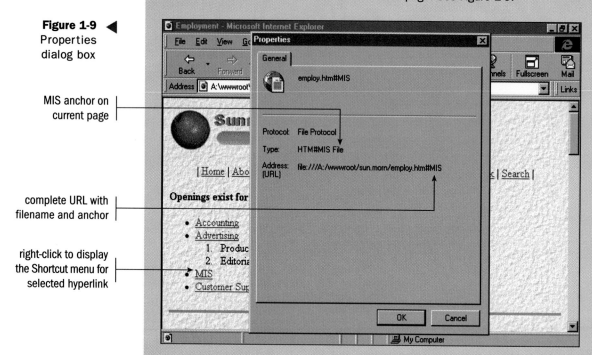

3. Click the **OK** button to close the Properties dialog box.

4. Click the **MIS** link. See Figure 1-10. The Employment Web page automatically scrolls to the place on the page where the MIS anchor name—the internal page reference—is located. Note that the Address box displays the anchor name on the Employment Web page.

Figure 1-10 ◀
MIS location
within
Employment
Web page

MIS anchor location

hyperlink to another
anchor location

Customer Support
anchor location

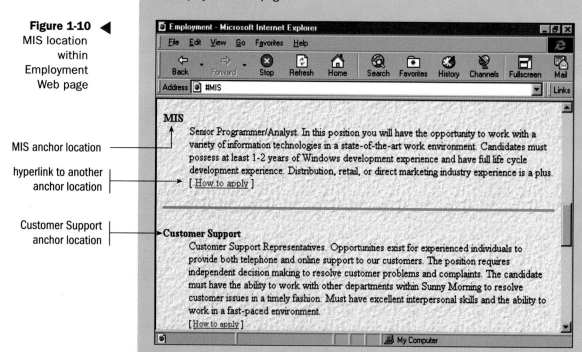

5. Click the **How to apply** link at the end of the MIS job description. The Employment Web page automatically moves to the place where this internal reference information is located. Clicking any of the various "How to apply" links on this Web page jumps you to this same location. In addition to referencing a location in the same Web page, you can establish a similar hyperlink for sending e-mail.

6. Click the **down** arrow on the vertical scroll bar until you see the Top of Page link at the bottom of the Employment Web page. See Figure 1-11.

Figure 1-11
Bottom of
Employment
Web page

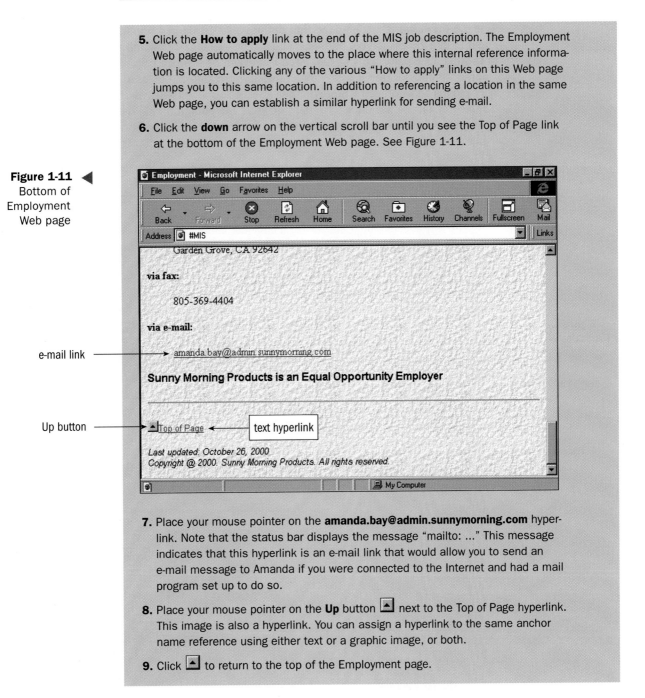

e-mail link

Up button

7. Place your mouse pointer on the **amanda.bay@admin.sunnymorning.com** hyperlink. Note that the status bar displays the message "mailto: ..." This message indicates that this hyperlink is an e-mail link that would allow you to send an e-mail message to Amanda if you were connected to the Internet and had a mail program set up to do so.

8. Place your mouse pointer on the **Up** button ▲ next to the Top of Page hyperlink. This image is also a hyperlink. You can assign a hyperlink to the same anchor name reference using either text or a graphic image, or both.

9. Click ▲ to return to the top of the Employment page.

The pages in the Sunny Morning Products Web that you have viewed so far were all single pages. Now that you've examined several individual Web pages, Amanda wants you to explore a special Web page feature that enables you to have multiple pages open on your screen at one time. This capability makes it easier to view different pages of related information.

Examining a Frame Set

Rather than displaying only a single Web page, the Internet Explorer window can be divided into several different window panes, or regions, with a different Web page displayed in each region. This allows you to display a new page in one region while the other pages remain unchanged. For example, one pane can continuously display a table of contents while a second pane displays a page selected from that table of contents. This type of multidisplay allows you to easily select other pages from the table of contents because it remains displayed. This division of a Web page into several windows is known as a frame set. A **frame set** is a Web page that defines a set of named windows in which other Web pages can be displayed. A **frame** is a single element or window of a frame set where another Web page is displayed. Each frame can be scrolled up or down if the Web page is larger than the frame's size. A hyperlink in one frame can be used to change the Web page displayed in another frame. Amanda uses a frame set with the Products Web page for Sunny Morning Products. As part of your introduction to Web site features, Amanda wants you to examine the frame set that is used to furnish potential customers with product information.

To examine a frame set:

1. Click the **Products** link to display that Web page. See Figure 1-12. Note that the Products Web page is divided into three panes that indicate this Web page is a frame set. The top frame, called the **banner frame**, contains the Sunny Morning Products logo and navigation bar. The left frame, called the **contents frame**, contains a bulleted menu while the right frame, called the **main frame**, contains a detailed page that you can scroll through. The Drink Gift Packs Web page currently appears in the main frame.

Figure 1-12 ◀
Products Web
page frame set

title of frame set ——

banner frame ——

contents frame ——

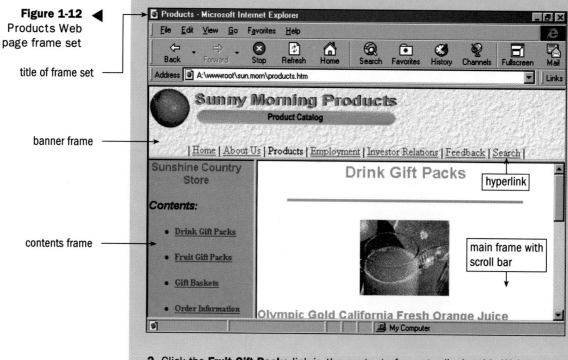

2. Click the **Fruit Gift Packs** link in the contents frame to display this Web page in the main frame. See Figure 1-13.

Figure 1-13 ◀
Fruit Gift Packs
Web page in
frame set

URL references same
Web page frame set

new Web page
replaces Drink Gift
Packs Web page in
main frame

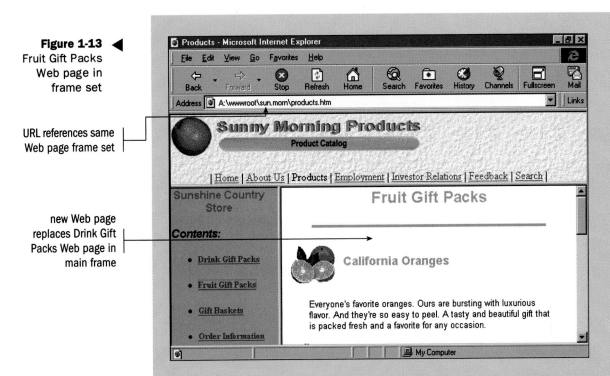

3. Scroll down to view the contents of the Fruit Gift Packs Web page. Notice that this Web page does not use a background image but, instead, utilizes color. The page includes a centered heading, a horizontal rule, and an image.

4. If necessary, scroll up the page until the **California Oranges** image is visible, and then place your mouse pointer on this image.

   The text "Oranges" appears in a box for a moment and then disappears. This indicates that this link contains **alternative text**. If your Web browser could not find this image, then the alternative text "Oranges" is all that would appear. Since no shortcut appears in the status bar, this image is not a hyperlink.

5. Click the **Gift Baskets** link in the contents frame to display this Web page, and then scroll down until you see a table listing available products and their prices. See Figure 1-14. Tables are frequently used with Web pages to control the arrangement of information on a page. Tables are discussed in more detail in Tutorial 4.

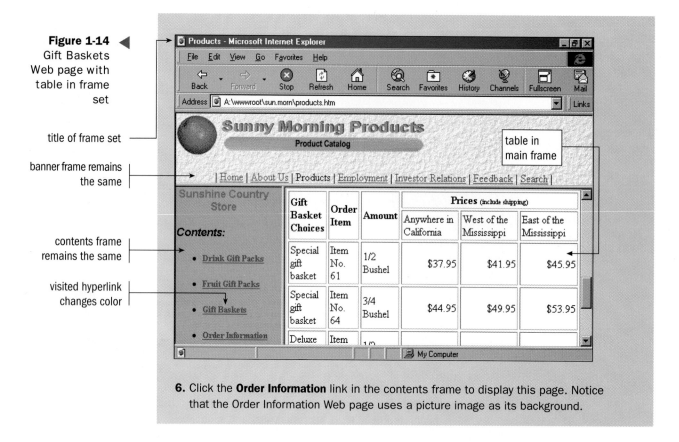

Figure 1-14 ◀
Gift Baskets
Web page with
table in frame
set

title of frame set ──

banner frame remains
the same

contents frame
remains the same

visited hyperlink
changes color

6. Click the **Order Information** link in the contents frame to display this page. Notice that the Order Information Web page uses a picture image as its background.

Using WebBots

So far in this tutorial, all of the Sunny Morning Products Web pages you have viewed have been static. A **static Web page** is a Web page requested from the server and displayed using your browser. However, Web pages also can be interactive. An **interactive**, or **dynamic**, **Web page** is a Web page that doesn't already exist as a file on the server, but rather is created based on data entered by the user. For example, a user who wants to complete a survey questionnaire on the Web would enter specific responses to the various queries and send that information through his browser to the server for processing. The server would process the data and return a response in the form of a Web page, which now would contain some or all of its content based on the user's specific request. Using FrontPage, processing these types of user requests on the server is handled by a feature known as WebBots. A **WebBot** is a prewritten program that carries out a particular processing function. FrontPage contains a number of WebBots that are readily included in Web pages for implementing various server processing activities. For example, the Search WebBot performs a search across all the pages of a Web based on a search request entered by the user.

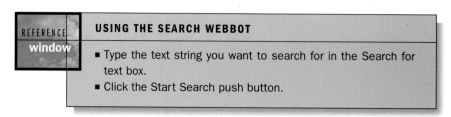

REFERENCE
window

USING THE SEARCH WEBBOT

- Type the text string you want to search for in the Search for text box.
- Click the Start Search push button.

The Sunny Morning Products Web site contains a Search WebBot that enables users to easily locate matching keywords or information throughout any of the Sunny Morning Products Web pages. Amanda wants you to try out the Search WebBot so you can see the effectiveness of this type of WebBot when designing a Web site. Keep in mind, however, that you are using a disk-based Web in this tutorial, so you won't receive a response based on your search request.

To use the Search WebBot:

1. In the banner frame at the top of the window, click the **Search** link in the navigation bar to display this Web page.

   Note that the Search Web page replaces the entire frame set page in the browser.

2. Scroll down the page until the Start Search and Clear push buttons are visible. See Figure 1-15.

Figure 1-15 ◄
Search
Web page

internal page
hyperlink to
instructions
for search

click this push button
to initiate search

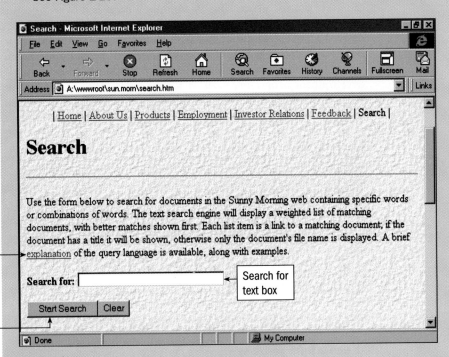

3. Click in the Search for text box, and then type **MIS** to specify the text string Web you want to find.

4. Click the **Start Search** push button to search all the Web pages in the Sunny Morning Products Web site. The FrontPage Run-Time Component Page opens in the Web browser. See Figure 1-16. This page indicates that a Web server is required to process the request because the search is carried out on the server.

Figure 1-16 ◄
FrontPage
Run-Time
Component
Page

message indicates
need for server

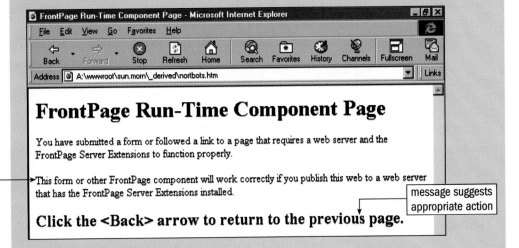

5. Click the **Back** button 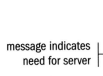 on the toolbar to return to the Search page.

If a search using this WebBot was performed using a server-based Web, instead of a disk-based Web, a search confirmation page would appear, indicating all the Web pages with a match for the MIS text string you entered. You will perform these types of searches using a server-based Web with the FrontPage Server Extensions in Tutorial 6.

Using a Form Web Page

Often, Web pages are forms that are completed by a user and submitted to the server at the Web site for processing. A **form Web page** is a Web page used to gather input from users and subsequently save the results to a text file or Web page on the server. Its name is derived from the fact that the Web page contains a number of form objects, such as text boxes and check boxes, that allow users to input information that is then sent to the server for processing. These objects are similar to those used with other object-oriented development programs, such as Visual Basic. Two of the Sunny Morning Products Web pages are organized as form Web pages—the customer order form and the feedback form. A FrontPage WebBot is used to process these forms on the server.

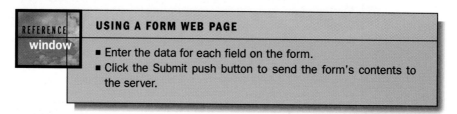

REFERENCE window

USING A FORM WEB PAGE

- Enter the data for each field on the form.
- Click the Submit push button to send the form's contents to the server.

Amanda's Web site for Sunny Morning Products contains two forms. One is used to gather general feedback from customers, and the other is used to process customer orders. As part of your training, Amanda wants you to understand the significance of using form Web pages because they will be a key component in future Web sites you develop.

To use a form Web page:

1. With the Search Web page displayed in your window, scroll up until you see the navigation bar for the Sunny Morning Products Web, and then click the **Feedback** link to display this Web page.

2. Scroll down the Feedback Web page until you see several form objects, including option buttons, a drop-down menu, and a scrolling text box. See Figure 1-17.

Figure 1-17 ◀
Form objects of Feedback Web page

option buttons

drop-down menu

scrolling text box

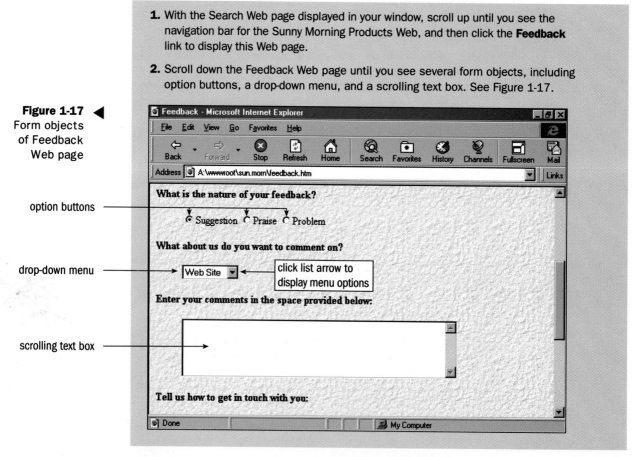

3. Click the **Praise** option button to select it.

4. Click the **list arrow** to display the menu options, and then click **Products**.

5. Click in the scrolling text box, and then type the following message: **Your Olympic Gold sports drink is great stuff. It really gives me the extra energy I need to keep going during our slow pitch softball games. Without it, we wouldn't have won the company trophy. The new lemon-mango-strawberry flavor is super.**

6. Scroll down until you see additional form objects at the bottom of the page. See Figure 1-18. This part of the form uses several text boxes, a check box, and two push buttons.

Figure 1-18 ◄
Additional
form objects
of Feedback
Web page

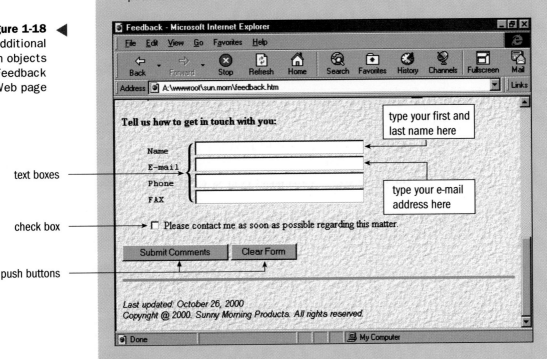

7. Click in the Name text box, and then type your first and last name (leave a space between them).

8. Press the **Tab** key to move to the E-mail text box, type your e-mail address, and then press the **Tab** key.

   TROUBLE? If you don't have an e-mail address, you can enter the one for your school, or skip this box by pressing the Tab key and skipping to Step 9.

9. Click the **Please contact me** check box to select it. The data entry for this form is now complete.

10. Click the **Submit Comments** push button to submit the form to the server. The FrontPage Run-Time Component Page opens because you are using a disk-based server, so there is no server to process your submission. Click the **Back** button on the Internet Explorer toolbar to return to the feedback form.

When a form is submitted using a server-based Web, a default confirmation Web page displays in your window and your results are stored in a file on the server. In Tutorial 6, you will use a form Web page to complete a form using a server-based Web.

Printing a Web Page

At times, you'll want to print a specific Web page, such as when you want to keep a hard copy of the information you have viewed or if you want to give this information to someone who doesn't have access to the Internet. Also, when you visit other Web sites and find an interesting page, you might want to print a copy so it is available for your reference as you design your own Web pages. Any Web page that you display can be printed for your use. You continue your training by printing the Investor Relations Web page and giving it to Amanda.

To print a Web page:

1. Scroll up to the top of the Feedback Web page, click the **Investor Relations** link in the navigation bar to display that page, and then scroll down the window until you see two tables containing summary information. See Figure 1-19.

Figure 1-19 ◄
Investor
Relations
Web page

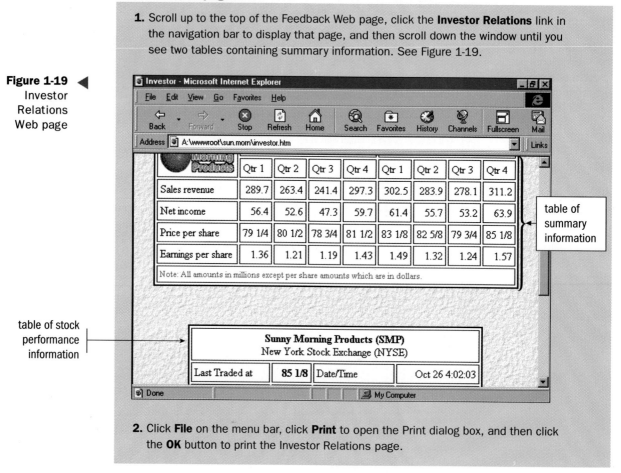

2. Click **File** on the menu bar, click **Print** to open the Print dialog box, and then click the **OK** button to print the Investor Relations page.

You have successfully examined several Web pages and printed the Investor Relations page. The FrontPage Explorer keeps track of the pages you have opened so you can easily reopen them.

Using the History List

Internet Explorer 4.0 tracks the Web pages you opened by maintaining a **History list,** which is a list of the URLs of pages you have opened, including URLs you visited in prior sessions. You can display a list of the pages you visited in a separate pane of the Internet Explorer 4.0 window known as the **Explorer bar**. This list is separate from the list of the last five visited pages that appears on the File menu, and it restarts every time you start Internet Explorer. You will view the History list in the Explorer bar next.

To view the History list in the Explorer bar:

1. Click the **History** button 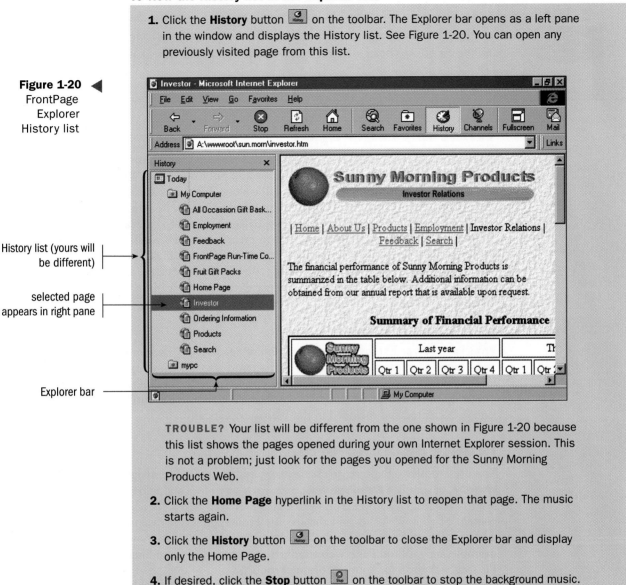 on the toolbar. The Explorer bar opens as a left pane in the window and displays the History list. See Figure 1-20. You can open any previously visited page from this list.

Figure 1-20
FrontPage
Explorer
History list

History list (yours will be different)

selected page appears in right pane

Explorer bar

TROUBLE? Your list will be different from the one shown in Figure 1-20 because this list shows the pages opened during your own Internet Explorer session. This is not a problem; just look for the pages you opened for the Sunny Morning Products Web.

2. Click the **Home Page** hyperlink in the History list to reopen that page. The music starts again.

3. Click the **History** button on the toolbar to close the Explorer bar and display only the Home Page.

4. If desired, click the **Stop** button on the toolbar to stop the background music.

Quick Check

1. What is the difference between the Internet and the World Wide Web (WWW)?

2. How do a Web browser and a Web server work together to provide you with information?

3. The _____ is a pathname that identifies the server and desired document from the WWW.

4. A(n) _____ is a keyword, phrase, or image in a Web document that you select to connect to another related document.

5. A Web _____ is a set of related Web pages that are available from a Web server.

6. In a few sentences, describe the difference between a disk-based Web and a server-based Web.

7. The _____ page is usually the first page you access from a Web site.

You have completed the first part of your training by examining the main features of the existing Sunny Morning Products Web site. Now you will explore these Web pages using FrontPage.

SESSION

1.2

In this session you will learn what FrontPage is and its role in the development of a Web page. You will learn about FrontPage Explorer and FrontPage Editor. Also, you will learn how to open a FrontPage Web site and to examine a Web page using FrontPage Editor.

What is FrontPage?

FrontPage is an integrated set of programs that are used for authoring and publishing Web sites. FrontPage simplifies the development and publishing of a Web site because you can use the program to develop professional-looking Web sites for the Internet even if you have little or no HTML knowledge. FrontPage consists of two main tools: FrontPage Explorer and FrontPage Editor. **FrontPage Explorer** is used to view and manage your entire Web site, while **FrontPage Editor** is used to create new Web pages and edit existing ones. FrontPage also includes other features that make Web site creation easy, such as templates for creating Web pages, as well as the WebBot components that help you complete complex tasks without programming experience. Finally, a **Tasks List** tracks the necessary tasks involved in creating a Web page and keeps you up to date on what tasks are completed and/or outstanding.

Creating a FrontPage Web on a WWW server is easy as long as you have the proper FrontPage Server Extensions installed. **FrontPage Server Extensions** are a set of programs and scripts that support FrontPage and extend the functionality of the Web server for interactive Web processing. These extensions are used by the WebBots in performing their pre-programmed tasks. Whenever you create a Web using FrontPage, these server extensions are created and included in the Web automatically.

FrontPage Explorer

You use FrontPage Explorer to create, view, and maintain FrontPage Web sites. A **FrontPage Web site**, or simply a **FrontPage Web**, contains a set of files and folders that you can open and test in FrontPage Explorer. This Web consists of Web pages, files, and folders that form the content of your Web site, and the specific FrontPage server extension support files. These additional support files provide FrontPage Explorer with its powerful functionality. For example, only a FrontPage Web supports automatic form handling with WebBots, such as the feedback form for Sunny Morning Products.

FrontPage Explorer's graphical interface is used to create and publish FrontPage Web sites either on your computer, on a local area network, or on the Internet. A **local area network**, or **LAN**, is a group of computers located in a specific area that are connected in order to share data, files, and software. The computers in the offices of Sunny Morning Products are an example of a LAN. FrontPage Explorer contains commands for various tasks such as administering a FrontPage Web site, testing and repairing hyperlinks, viewing the files and folders that make up a Web site, importing and exporting files, and starting FrontPage Editor and other programs to create and edit the contents of your FrontPage Web. If you rename or move any file in your FrontPage Web, FrontPage Explorer updates all hyperlink references to that file within the FrontPage Web. FrontPage Explorer functions similarly to Windows Explorer. The FrontPage Explorer screen represents a desktop, which is a workspace for you to use to manipulate the pages that make up a Web site.

Starting FrontPage Explorer

FrontPage Explorer is started in the same manner as other Windows programs. When you start FrontPage Explorer, the sun.morn folder that contains the index.htm Web page, or the home page, is displayed in Explorer's right pane. You are now ready to continue with your training by starting FrontPage and examining some of the tools and features used to create the Sunny Morning Products Web site.

To start FrontPage Explorer:

1. Click the **Start** button, click **Programs**, and then click **Microsoft FrontPage** to start this program and open FrontPage Explorer.

   The Getting Started dialog box opens. See Figure 1-21.

Figure 1-21 ◀
Getting Started
dialog box

click to select
existing Web (your list
might differ)

click to select from
other Webs

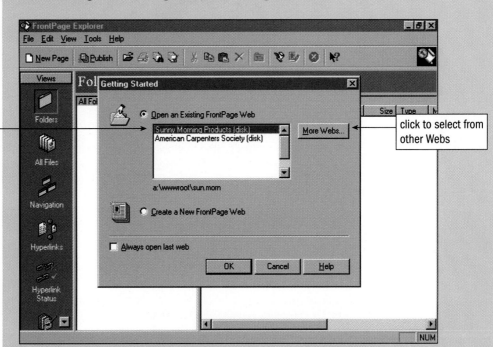

TROUBLE? If Microsoft FrontPage does not appear on the Programs menu, press the Esc key to close the Programs menu, and then look for a FrontPage icon on the desktop and double-click it. Continue with Step 2.

TROUBLE? If the Getting Started dialog box does not open, click the Open FrontPage Web button 📂 on the toolbar to open the Getting Started dialog box and then go to Step 2.

2. Click the **Open an Existing FrontPage Web** option button, click **Sunny Morning Products (disk)**, and then click the **OK** button and skip to Step 7.

3. If the Sunny Morning Products (disk) choice does not appear in the list, click the **More Webs** button to open the Open FrontPage Web dialog box. See Figure 1-22. The highlighted text in the Select a Web server or disk location text box indicates the location of the disk-based Web.

   TROUBLE? Don't worry if the highlighted text in your Select a Web server or disk location text box differs from what is shown in Figure 1-22. The current text reflects the location of the last Web opened using your computer.

Figure 1-22 ◄
Open
FrontPage Web
dialog box

indicates location of
disk-based Web
(your location might
be different)

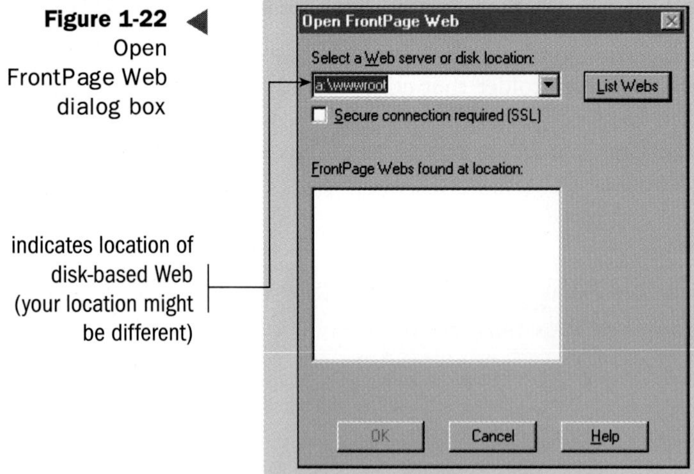

4. If necessary, type **a:\wwwroot** in the Select a Web server or disk location text box to specify the location for your disk-based Web.

TROUBLE? If you are using a different disk drive other than A for your Student Disk, then type the appropriate letter for that drive.

5. Click the **List Webs** button to display a list of available Webs in the Open FrontPage Web dialog box. See Figure 1-23. This list always contains the <Root Web> as well as any other Webs included in the wwwroot folder. As you create other Webs, their names will be added to this list.

Figure 1-23 ◄
List of available
FrontPage
Webs

existing Webs in
wwwroot folder

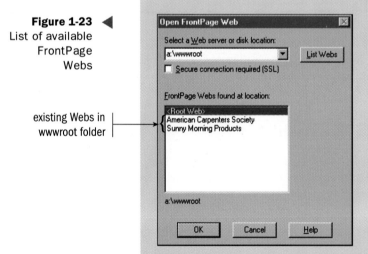

6. Click **Sunny Morning Products** in the FrontPage Webs found at location text box, and then click the **OK** button to open this Web. The message "Loading Sunny Morning Products (/sun.morn) web ..." appears in the status bar while the Web is being opened. After a few minutes, the Web opens in FrontPage Explorer. See Figure 1-24.

Figure 1-24
Folders view in
FrontPage
Explorer
window

title bar

toolbar

Views bar

folder displayed in
right pane

left pane

status bar

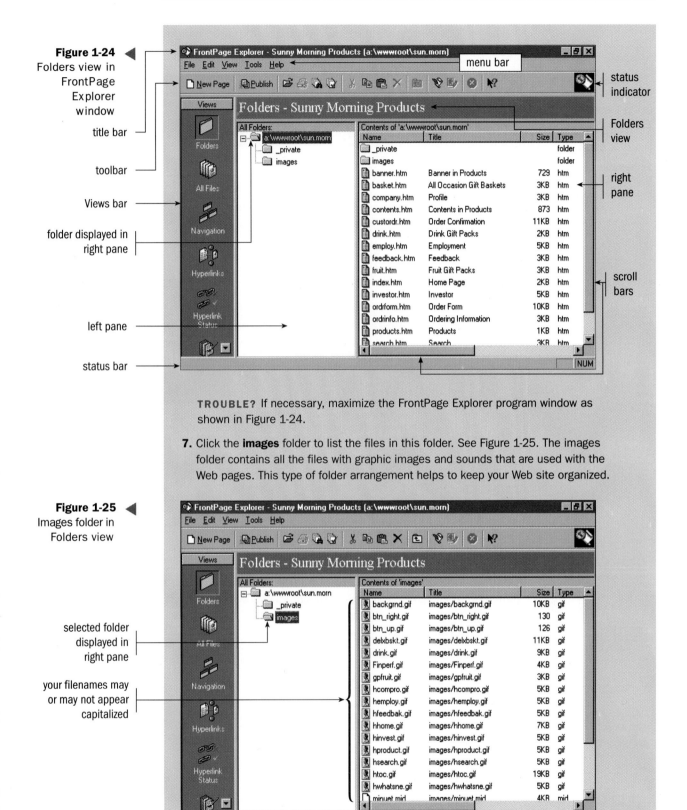

TROUBLE? If necessary, maximize the FrontPage Explorer program window as shown in Figure 1-24.

7. Click the **images** folder to list the files in this folder. See Figure 1-25. The images folder contains all the files with graphic images and sounds that are used with the Web pages. This type of folder arrangement helps to keep your Web site organized.

Figure 1-25
Images folder in
Folders view

selected folder
displayed in
right pane

your filenames may
or may not appear
capitalized

The various components of the FrontPage Explorer window that are displayed in Figure 1-24 are described in detail in Figure 1-26.

Figure 1-26 ◀
Components of
the FrontPage
Explorer window

Component	Description
Title bar	Located at the top of the screen, displays the name of the open Web.
Menu bar	Located directly below the title bar, used to access all the options available in FrontPage Explorer.
Scroll bars	Located at the right side and bottom of the window, these bars are used to scroll the window vertically and horizontally like other Windows programs.
Toolbar	Located below the menu bar, consists of a band of graphical icons. Like other Windows programs, the toolbar buttons provide shortcuts for some of the menu commands.
Views bar	Located at the left of the document window. the buttons on the Views bar let you switch to different views of your FrontPage Web, such as Folders view or Hyperlinks view.
Left pane	Displays an outline of the Web as either Web page documents or the folders that comprise the Web.
Right pane	Displays a diagram of the hyperlinks, the files in a folder of the Web, or another view.
Status bar	Located at the bottom of the window, displays a message that describes the current action of FrontPage Explorer and provides a description of a toolbar button when you position the pointer on top of a button.
Status indicator	Located in the upper-right corner of the window, this is the Explorer logo that animates as you are loading a Web.

Using Views

Views in FrontPage Explorer provide different ways of looking at the information in your FrontPage Web so you can effectively manage your Web site. The buttons on the Views bar allow you to switch between the different views of your FrontPage Web, such as Folders view or Hyperlinks view. There are seven different ways to view your FrontPage Web, as described in Figure 1-27.

Figure 1-27 ◄
FrontPage
Explorer views

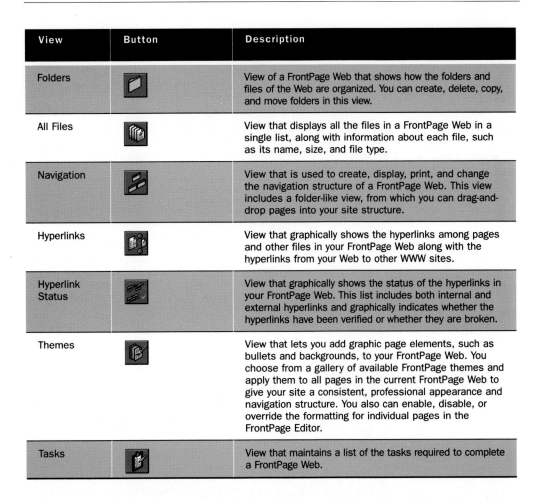

View	Button	Description
Folders		View of a FrontPage Web that shows how the folders and files of the Web are organized. You can create, delete, copy, and move folders in this view.
All Files		View that displays all the files in a FrontPage Web in a single list, along with information about each file, such as its name, size, and file type.
Navigation		View that is used to create, display, print, and change the navigation structure of a FrontPage Web. This view includes a folder-like view, from which you can drag-and-drop pages into your site structure.
Hyperlinks		View that graphically shows the hyperlinks among pages and other files in your FrontPage Web along with the hyperlinks from your Web to other WWW sites.
Hyperlink Status		View that graphically shows the status of the hyperlinks in your FrontPage Web. This list includes both internal and external hyperlinks and graphically indicates whether the hyperlinks have been verified or whether they are broken.
Themes		View that lets you add graphic page elements, such as bullets and backgrounds, to your FrontPage Web. You choose from a gallery of available FrontPage themes and apply them to all pages in the current FrontPage Web to give your site a consistent, professional appearance and navigation structure. You also can enable, disable, or override the formatting for individual pages in the FrontPage Editor.
Tasks		View that maintains a list of the tasks required to complete a FrontPage Web.

Using Folders View and Hyperlinks View

Folders view allows you to view and navigate the folders in your FrontPage Web. Simply clicking a folder using Folders view lists the folder's contents, along with valuable information about each file, such as its size, type, and title. Folders view is very similar to using Windows Explorer to examine files. You can easily switch between Folders view and Hyperlinks view, depending on the information you need to see when creating, modifying, or testing a Web. In **Hyperlinks view,** your FrontPage Web appears graphically as a hierarchical picture of the hyperlinks that connect the files of your Web, including multimedia files contained in the Web.

As you switch views and examine the files and folders that make up a Web, you will find that some of these names appear in upper-case letters, lower-case letters, or mixed-case letters. Each file and folder is uniquely identified by its name, regardless of the case of the letters. As you continue working with FrontPage and create your own files and folders, copy Webs, and perform other tasks, you may find that lower-case names change to upper-case. This is a function of FrontPage and your computer's operating system. When you compare your screens to those illustrated in the figures in these tutorials, it is important that the names of the files match, not the case of the letters for the filenames.

You continue with Amanda's training course by accessing both Folders and Hyperlinks views of the Sunny Morning Products Web in order to gain a clearer idea of the information presented in each view. Because Hyperlinks view can show only part of the entire Web at one time, you need to adjust the page in order to view its other areas. You can do this in one of two ways: by using the scroll bars or by using the mouse to drag the page. To use the mouse method, click and hold down the mouse button on a blank area of the right pane. The mouse pointer changes to a hand shape, and then you drag it to reposition the contents of the pane. Since you are currently using Folders view, you switch to Hyperlinks view.

To switch to Hyperlinks view:

1. Click the **Hyperlinks** button 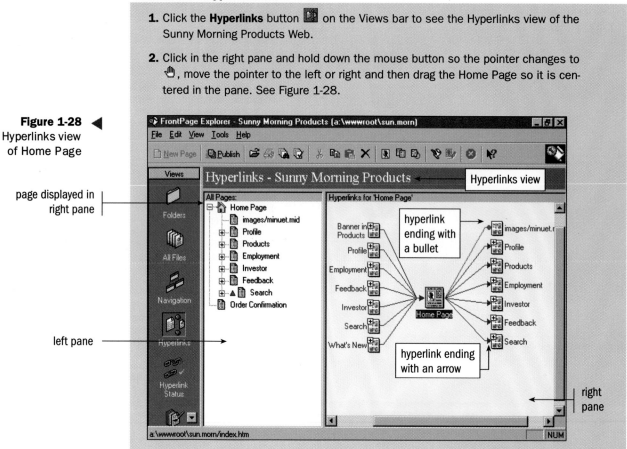 on the Views bar to see the Hyperlinks view of the Sunny Morning Products Web.

2. Click in the right pane and hold down the mouse button so the pointer changes to 🖑, move the pointer to the left or right and then drag the Home Page so it is centered in the pane. See Figure 1-28.

Figure 1-28 ◄
Hyperlinks view
of Home Page

page displayed in right pane

left pane

right pane

Notice in Figure 1-28 that some of the hyperlinks end with an arrow, whereas others end with a bullet. An arrow indicates a hyperlink to another Web document, whereas a bullet indicates that the item is included as part of the currently selected Web page that appears in the right pane. Also, the design of the navigation bar creates a circular reference arrangement so that for a selected page, another Web page has a reference both to and from that page. For example, notice in Figure 1-28 that the Home Page has a link to and from the Employment page.

Switching Pages

Although the default Web page in Hyperlinks view is the Sunny Morning Products Home Page (displayed in Explorer's right pane), you can easily switch to another page in the Web. The selected page then becomes the center focus of Hyperlinks view. When you maintain and create Webs, you frequently examine the various pages that make up that Web. FrontPage Explorer makes it easy for you to move from one page to the next in an organized manner as you follow the links from one page to the next. To switch pages, you simply select the page you want to view in the left pane in order to display it. You continue with your training using FrontPage Explorer by switching pages.

To switch pages:

1. Click **Products** in the left pane. The Products page, along with its hyperlinks, displays in the right pane. See Figure 1-29. This current Hyperlinks view of the Products pane is especially useful for determining the origination and destination of each link on a Web page.

Figure 1-29 ◀
Products
page in
Hyperlinks view

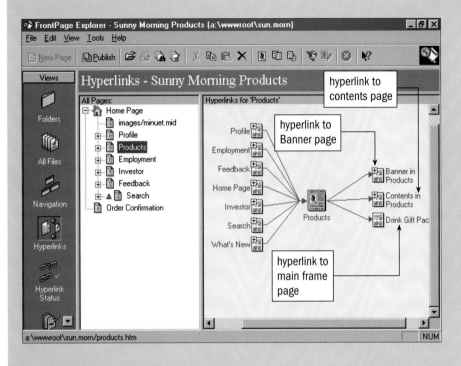

2. Click **Home Page** in the left pane to display this page again, along with its hyperlinks, in the right pane.

Selecting and Using Navigation View

Navigation view allows you to display your Web site as a diagram that shows the navigation structure like an organization chart. This view includes a folder-like view that allows you to drag and drop pages into your site structure. You can size Navigation view to fit the right pane so it is easier to examine this diagram. You also can change the arrangement of the view to rotate the objects, or you can print the Navigation view. You select Navigation view in the same manner as displaying other views of your Web.

To switch to, print, and rotate Navigation view:

1. Click the **Navigation** button 📇 on the Views bar to show the Navigation view of the Sunny Morning Web.

2. Click the **Size to Fit** button 🅰 on the Standard toolbar. Navigation view is sized to fit the right pane. See Figure 1-30.

Figure 1-30 ◀
Navigation view
of Sunny
Morning
Products Web

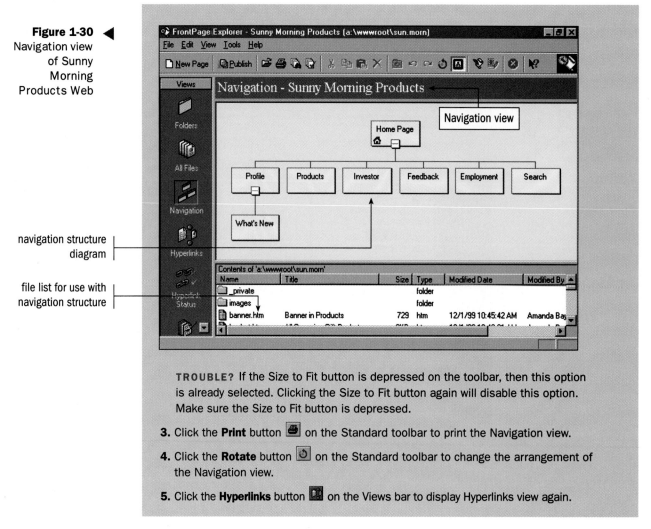

navigation structure
diagram

file list for use with
navigation structure

TROUBLE? If the Size to Fit button is depressed on the toolbar, then this option is already selected. Clicking the Size to Fit button again will disable this option. Make sure the Size to Fit button is depressed.

3. Click the **Print** button on the Standard toolbar to print the Navigation view.

4. Click the **Rotate** button on the Standard toolbar to change the arrangement of the Navigation view.

5. Click the **Hyperlinks** button on the Views bar to display Hyperlinks view again.

Now you know how to change the Navigation view of your Web and print it. As you perform various activities in the tutorials in this book, you will use views to create and explore your Web sites.

Using Hyperlinks in FrontPage Explorer

You can create hyperlinks easily using a point-and-click interface. Clipart graphics, obtained from a large library of buttons, icons, background images, and other images, are easily inserted in a Web page and assigned a hyperlink. If you rename or move a file in your FrontPage Web, FrontPage Explorer updates all hyperlink references to that file within the FrontPage Web. In order to examine the hyperlinks of your Web, you use FrontPage Explorer to provide a hyperlink diagram.

Following a Hyperlink

You can follow the hyperlinks from one document to another by using the plus (+) or minus (-) symbol in the upper-left corner of the document's icon to expand (show) or contract (hide) the hyperlinks displayed in Hyperlinks view.

You continue with Amanda's training by examining hyperlinks in FrontPage Explorer, specifically by following the hyperlinks from the Products page.

To follow a hyperlink:

1. With the Sunny Morning Products Web displayed in your window and the Home Page as the center focus, click the **plus** (+) symbol in the Products icon to expand this hyperlink and display the pages used with the Products frame set.

2. Click the **plus** (+) symbol in the Contents in Products icon to expand this hyperlink. The pages referenced by all the hyperlinks in the content frame are included in the diagram.

3. Click the **plus** (+) symbol in the Ordering Information icon to expand this link. See Figure 1-31.

Figure 1-31 ◀
Expanded links
in Hyperlinks
view

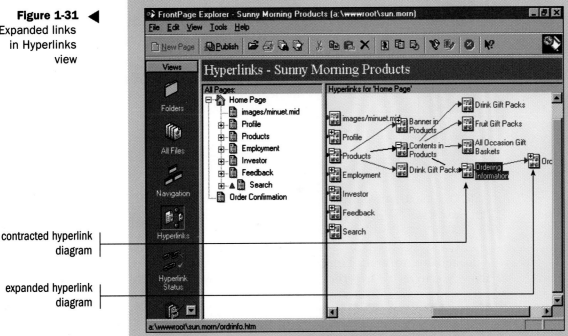

contracted hyperlink diagram

expanded hyperlink diagram

Displaying a Repeated Hyperlink

Sometimes a Web page contains more than one hyperlink to the same page in order to provide users with options in accessing pages. When more than one hyperlink to the same page appears, these links are called **repeated hyperlinks**. In order to examine the hyperlinks of your Web, you use FrontPage Explorer to access a Hyperlinks view of your Web. This enables you to determine if you have defined all your hyperlinks among the pages of your Web.

Recall that the Sunny Morning Products Home Page contains two different hyperlinks to the Products page. You continue your training by viewing the repeated hyperlinks on the home page.

To display repeated hyperlinks:

1. Click the **Repeated Hyperlinks** button 🔲 on the Standard toolbar to display the repeated hyperlinks for the Products page. See Figure 1-32. The Repeated Hyperlinks button now appears depressed on the toolbar, which indicates this feature is turned on.

   TROUBLE? If the Repeated Hyperlinks button doesn't appear depressed, it means the toggle was already turned on. Repeat Step 1 to display the correct view.

Figure 1-32 ◀
Repeated
hyperlinks of
the Products
Web page in
FrontPage
Explorer

depressed Repeated
Hyperlinks button

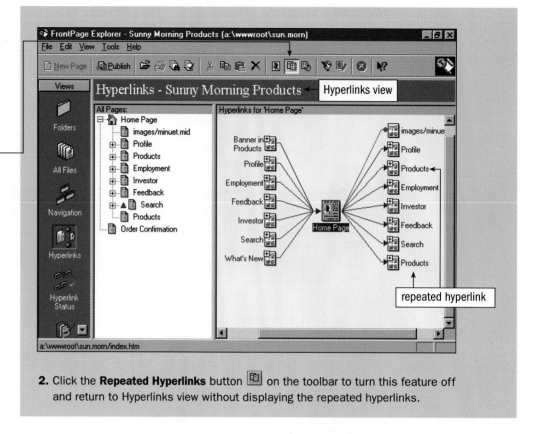

2. Click the **Repeated Hyperlinks** button 🔳 on the toolbar to turn this feature off
and return to Hyperlinks view without displaying the repeated hyperlinks.

In addition to using FrontPage Explorer to examine hyperlinks, FrontPage Editor allows you to review hyperlinks as well. You will learn about FrontPage Editor next.

FrontPage Editor

You use **FrontPage Editor** to create, edit, and test Web pages. As you add text, images, tables, form fields, and other elements to your page, FrontPage Editor displays them as they would appear in your Web browser window. This **WYSIWYG** (what you see is what you get) approach to creating Web pages is similar to using a word-processing program to prepare written documents. In addition, FrontPage Editor automatically creates all the HTML code for you as you add information (such as HTML tags that specify tables), create frames, and implement WebBots to your Web page. Tags are discussed in more detail in the next session.

Using a point-and-click interface, you can view any Web page in FrontPage Editor, not just the pages that you created with it. You can easily insert clipart images in a Web page and assign hyperlinks using the Editor. FrontPage Editor accommodates the use of a number of advanced features that include inserting ActiveX controls, Java applets, and Visual Basic scripts. All of these features provide you with a powerful tool for developing Web pages. Despite its robust quality, FrontPage Editor is easy to use and has a familiar, word-processing program interface.

You can start FrontPage Editor from FrontPage Explorer by clicking the Show FrontPage Editor button on the toolbar, or by double-clicking the document in the right pane of the FrontPage Explorer window. If FrontPage Editor is already running, you simply switch to it.

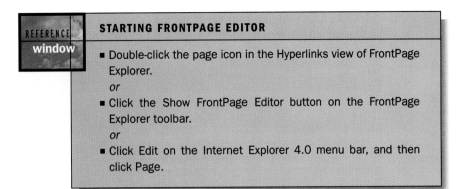

STARTING FRONTPAGE EDITOR

- Double-click the page icon in the Hyperlinks view of FrontPage Explorer.
  or
- Click the Show FrontPage Editor button on the FrontPage Explorer toolbar.
  or
- Click Edit on the Internet Explorer 4.0 menu bar, and then click Page.

Now you are ready to start FrontPage Editor to continue your training. Amanda wants you to start FrontPage Editor from the right pane of the Hyperlinks view of FrontPage Explorer.

To start FrontPage Editor:

1. Double-click the **Home Page** icon in the right pane of the FrontPage Explorer window. FrontPage Editor starts and the Sunny Morning Products Home Page displays. If necessary, maximize the FrontPage Editor program window. See Figure 1-33.

   Note that the FrontPage Editor window is similar to that of other Windows programs and contains many of the same features.

Figure 1-33 ◄
Home Page
displayed in
FrontPage
Editor

menu bar

Standard toolbar

Format toolbar

document window

Normal tab

HTML tab

Preview tab

status bar

scroll bars

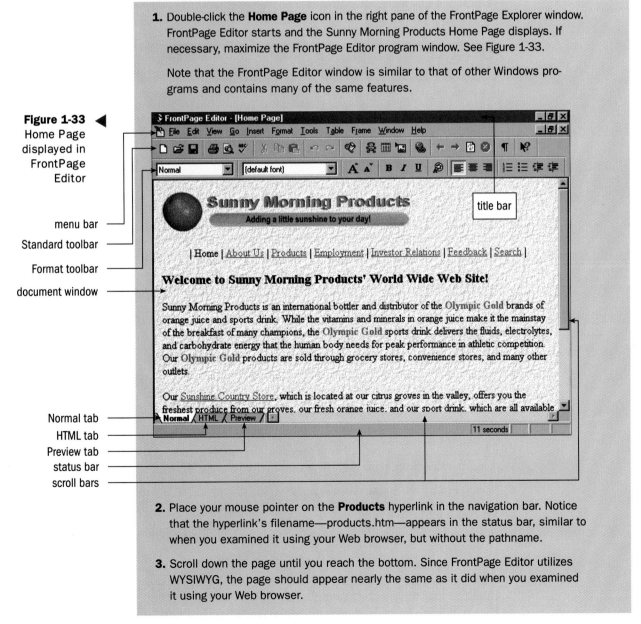

2. Place your mouse pointer on the **Products** hyperlink in the navigation bar. Notice that the hyperlink's filename—products.htm—appears in the status bar, similar to when you examined it using your Web browser, but without the pathname.

3. Scroll down the page until you reach the bottom. Since FrontPage Editor utilizes WYSIWYG, the page should appear nearly the same as it did when you examined it using your Web browser.

The key components that make up the FrontPage Editor window shown in Figure 1-33 are described in more detail in Figure 1-34.

Figure 1-34 ◀
Components of
FrontPage
Editor

Component	Description
Title bar	Located at the top of the screen, displays the name of the open Web page.
Menu bar	Located directly below the title bar, used to access all the options available in FrontPage Editor.
Scroll bars	Used to scroll the window horizontally or vertically like other Windows programs.
Toolbars	Located beneath the menu bar, this is one or more bands of graphical icons. Like other Windows programs, the toolbar buttons provide shortcuts for some of the menu commands. (Your window might have different toolbars showing.)
Document window	Displays the Web page that is being entered or revised.
Normal tab	Displays the currently active page for entering and revising a Web page using WYSIWYG editing.
HTML tab	Displays the HTML code for the currently active page and permits you to edit the HTML code in this view.
Preview tab	Allows you to quickly preview the currently active page from FrontPage Editor in the Internet Explorer browser.
Status bar	Located at the bottom of the window, displays a written message that describes the current action of FrontPage Editor. Also provides a description of a toolbar button when you position the pointer on top of the button.

You can display any one of three views in the FrontPage Editor window by clicking the tab for the view you want. The **Normal** tab is the WYSIWYG editor view where you enter and revise your Web page; this is where you will complete most of your work. The **HTML** tab displays the HTML code for you to examine, and edit, when necessary. The **Preview** tab opens the Internet Explorer browser window with the active page so you can view the window's actual browser display. However, FrontPage Editor's menu and toolbars remain displayed.

Quick Check

1 What is the main advantage of using FrontPage to create and maintain a Web site?

2 Which FrontPage tool would you use to view a Web site?

3 Which FrontPage tool would you use to edit a Web page?

4 The _____ view in FrontPage Explorer displays a graphic picture of the connections among your Web pages and other files.

5 Which FrontPage feature supports the server processing of forms?

6 What is a repeated hyperlink?

7 FrontPage Editor is very similar to which type of program?

Now that you have confirmed the WYSIWYG arrangement of FrontPage Editor, you can continue your training by examining the HTML code for a Web page. Examining HTML code will help you understand and appreciate what the FrontPage software does for you.

SESSION

1.3

In this session you will learn how HTML is used to create a Web site and how HTML tags are used to define a Web page. You will view the specific code of a Web page in order to view examples of HTML tags.

How HTML Works

Recall that HTML describes the general content of a Web page. An HTML document is similar to a document file from a word-processing program. Using a word-processing program, you can specify the appearance of text in terms of font type (such as Arial or Times Roman), an attribute (such as boldface or italics), or placement (such as a heading or bulleted list). Word-processing program document files contain special codes that represent these types of stylistic and placement features. A Web browser interprets the HTML codes that describe a file's appearance to determine how it will display the text.

Each word-processing program has its own unique set of codes. Because HTML documents must be transferred among many different types of computers, codes or specific characters can be lost in the translation. Also, since each client on the Web differs in terms of computer brand, it is rare for character sets to be identical. Because of this, HTML documents use only a standard character set that is recognized by *all* computers. Web browsers for a particular brand of client computer then can interpret these codes and display the requested HTML document file. The use of HTML in storing, transferring, and viewing document files among the many different brands and sizes of computers that make up the Internet is the key element in providing a standard method for exchanging information.

Understanding HTML Tags

HTML code that specifies a Web page contains special **tags**, or formatting codes, that the browser interprets when displaying the page. Each tag is enclosed in brackets (< >) that surround the text and usually come in pairs. The **opening tag** is the first tag, which tells the browser to turn on the feature and apply it to the subsequent document content. The browser continues to apply the feature until it encounters the **closing tag**, which indicates that it should cease applying the feature. A closing tag is identified by the slash character (/) that precedes the tag name. For example, the tags <BODY> and </BODY> specify the beginning and end of the body of a Web page, while the tags <B> and </B> indicate the beginning and end of boldface formatting. While most tags are **two-sided**, meaning that they consist of both opening and closing tags, some are **one-sided** because they require only an opening tag. For example, text appearing in a document heading might be marked with a one-sided heading code, such as <H3>, while text appearing in a bulleted list might be marked with a one-sided list code, such as <LI>.

Some of the more frequently used tags are described in Figure 1-35. The ellipse (...) in the tags indicates the place where your text information is entered, either between the pair of tags or within a tag.

Figure 1-35 ◀
Selected HTML
tag descriptions

HTML tag	Description	Use
<! ... >	Creates a comment.	Used to document HTML code and to isolate advanced features such as a Vbscript that may not be recognized by every Web browser.
<A> ... </A>	Defines a hyperlink or anchor.	Indicates link to internal or external hyperlink and specifies linking locations within a Web page.
<B> ... </B>	Boldfaces the text.	
<BGSOUND>	Specifies a background sound.	Indicates file containing the desired sound.

Figure 1-35 ◀
Selected HTML
tag descriptions
(continued)

HTML tag	Description	Use
`<BLOCKQUOTE> ... </BLOCKQUOTE>`	Indents text.	Used to set off long quotes or for other text indention.
`<BODY> ... </BODY>`	Encloses the body of the HTML document.	
` `	Forces a new line break in the text.	
`<DD> ... </DD>`	Specifies a definition within a glossary list.	Provides heading line for a definition.
`<DL> ... </DL>`	Specifies a definition or glossary list.	
`<DT> ... </DT>`	Specifies a definition term within a glossary list.	Provides font size and indentation for definition term.
`<EM> ... </EM>`	Emphasizes text, usually with italics.	
`<H1> ... </H1>` `<H2> ... </H2>` `<H3> ... </H3>` `<H4> ... </H4>` `<H5> ... </H5>` `<H6> ... </H6>`	Specifies heading and its level.	Indicates size of font for heading line with 1 as the largest.
`<HR>`	Draws a horizontal line across the page.	Provides visual break for sections of a page.
`<HTML> ... </HTML>`	Encloses the entire HTML file.	Identifies the file as one that contains HTML codes.
`<I> ... </I>`	Italicizes the text.	
`<IMG> ... </IMG>`	Specifies the appearance of an inline image in a page.	Inserts an image from a file into the document.
`<LI> ... </LI>`	Specifies an individual element in a list.	
`<OL> ... </OL>`	Specifies an ordered list of elements.	Numbers the elements in a list.
`<P> ... </P>`	Divides text into paragraphs.	
`<PRE> ... </PRE>`	Specifies preformatted text.	Keeps the spacing arrangement of text as entered in the document for use with text using special indentations or column layouts.
`<STRONG> ... </STRONG>`	Strongly emphasizes text, usually with boldface.	
`<TABLE> ... </TABLE>`	Specifies a table.	Organizes data in a row-and-column table arrangement.
`<TD> ... </TD>`	Defines data for cells in a table.	
`<TH> ... </TH>`	Creates a header row in a table.	

Figure 1-35 ◀
Selected HTML
tag descriptions
(continued)

HTML tag	Description	Use
<TITLE> ... </TITLE>	Defines the text that appears in the Web browser's title bar.	
<TR> ... </TR>	Indicates the beginning of a row in a table.	Provides rows that can hold the data for each cell.
<TT> ... </TT>	Formats text in typewriter font, usually Courier.	Applies monospaced font, used with the <PRE> tag.
<UL> ... </UL>	Specifies an unordered list of elements.	Provides bulleted elements in a list.

Just as important as the tags themselves is the order of their placement. Tags often appear in pairs, called **nested tags**. The first part of the pair, the **outside tag**, indicates that this tag is specified first, while the **inside tag** is specified after the outside tag. With nested tags, the inside tag needs to be closed before the outside tag. The opening and closing of each pair of tags is handled automatically by FrontPage Editor. You only need to be concerned with nesting the tags if you decide to make changes directly to your HTML code, which is not the recommended approach when using FrontPage Editor.

A number of the HTML tags require **properties**, or additional information, that define the appearance of the text or supply a filename for use with the document. These properties are included within the brackets (< >) that enclose the tag. Figure 1-36 shows an example of some of the HTML tags Amanda used for the Home Page of the Sunny Morning Products Web. For example, the <BGSOUND> tag indicates the use of a background sound. For this tag, the SRC property indicates the file that contains the sound, while the LOOP property specifies how many times the sound is repeated. The <BODY> tag specifies the beginning of the body of the HTML document. For this tag, the BACKGROUND property indicates the name of the file that contains an image for the background.

Figure 1-36 ◀
HTML tags for
Home Page of
Sunny Morning
Products Web

indicates hyperlink
specification

opening heading tag

closing heading tag

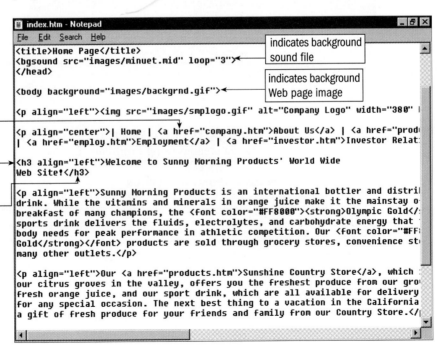

Keep in mind you can create an HTML document without using a program such as FrontPage. For example, you can use a text editor, such as the Windows Notepad program. However, since Notepad does not insert any special formatting codes into its document file, you need to know each tag's name and its parameters, which can be tedious when creating a Web page. FrontPage—specifically, the FrontPage Editor tool—is designed to insert HTML tags automatically in your Web page. This allows you to create an HTML document just as easily as you would create a document using your word-processing program. The main difference is that any HTML document you create can be **published**, or placed on a Web server, so that anyone connected to the WWW can access it.

Viewing HTML Code

Recall that tags indicate how the text and graphic files located on a particular Web page should appear. For example, the <TITLE> tag is used to specify the information that appears in the title bar when the page is displayed. By viewing the HTML code for a Web page, you can see how a particular feature has been implemented on a Web page through the use of tags. Advanced developers of Web sites often view HTML code so they can make changes directly to the code. You can examine a Web page's HTML code using either FrontPage Editor or a Web browser, such as Internet Explorer. Because you will be using FrontPage Editor to designate all the HTML tags throughout these tutorials, you won't need to adjust any codes because FrontPage Editor automatically inserts the HTML tags in your Web page.

Viewing HTML Code Using FrontPage Editor

Although you can view HTML code using either FrontPage Editor or your Web browser, you should use FrontPage Editor when you are developing a Web site. When you view HTML code using FrontPage Editor, the special HTML codes appear in different colors to help you distinguish between what you enter and what FrontPage Editor automatically creates for you.

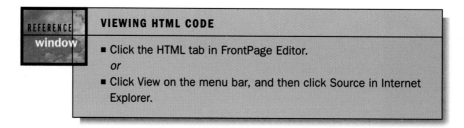

REFERENCE window

VIEWING HTML CODE

- Click the HTML tab in FrontPage Editor.
  or
- Click View on the menu bar, and then click Source in Internet Explorer.

Now you can examine the HTML code for the Home Page of the Sunny Morning Products Web that Amanda created using FrontPage Editor.

To view HTML code using FrontPage Editor:

1. Click the **HTML** tab to display the coded document. See Figure 1-37. Note that the HTML tag names appear in one color, while the parameters for the tags appear in another color.

Figure 1-37 ◀
HTML code
displayed using
FrontPage
Editor

tag name ⟶

property name ⟶

property value ⟶

text appearing in
Web browser

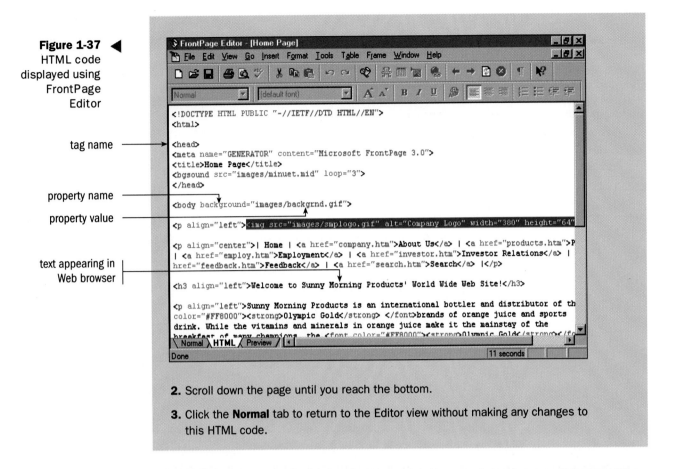

2. Scroll down the page until you reach the bottom.

3. Click the **Normal** tab to return to the Editor view without making any changes to this HTML code.

Viewing HTML Code Using Internet Explorer

The other method of viewing HTML code is by using your Web browser. This is often the most convenient method for viewing the HTML code for a Web page at a site you are just visiting and is not part of a Web that you created. In addition, viewing the HTML source code from your Web browser is useful when you are looking at Web pages from other sites and are curious to know how another designer implemented a particular Web page feature.

Once again, you view HTML tags as part of your training—this time, examining Amanda's HTML code for the Home Page of the Sunny Morning Products Web using Internet Explorer.

To view HTML code using Internet Explorer:

1. Click the **Microsoft Internet Explorer** program button on the taskbar to make this your active program.

   TROUBLE? If Internet Explorer is not running on the taskbar, start it and enter a:\wwwroot\sun.morn\index.htm as the address for your disk-based Web.

2. If necessary, click the **Home** link on the navigation bar to return to the Home Page.

3. Click **View** on the menu bar, and then click **Source** to display the HTML code in Notepad. A copy of Notepad starts automatically to display the HTML document. See Figure 1-38. Note that the HTML code is the same as what displayed in FrontPage Editor, except the color coding is missing.

Figure 1-38
HTML code
displayed in
Notepad using
Internet
Explorer

name of current page
displayed in Internet
Explorer window

HTML tag, property
name, and
property value

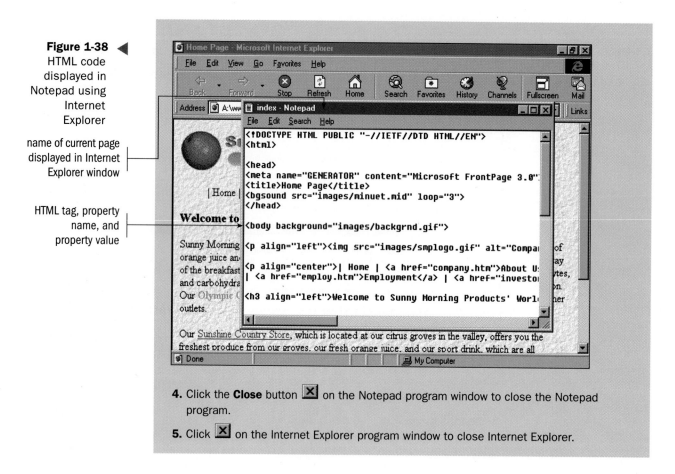

Figure 1-38
HTML code
displayed in
Notepad using
Internet
Explorer

name of current page
displayed in Internet
Explorer window

HTML tag, property
name, and
property value

4. Click the **Close** button ☒ on the Notepad program window to close the Notepad program.

5. Click ☒ on the Internet Explorer program window to close Internet Explorer.

Exiting FrontPage

You exit from FrontPage in the same manner as you close other Windows programs. Recall that you have opened two FrontPage programs— Explorer and Editor. In order to exit from FrontPage, you need to close both of these programs.

Now you have completed the first part of your training program and are ready to exit FrontPage.

To exit FrontPage:

1. Click the **FrontPage Editor** program button on the taskbar to make it the active program.

2. Click the **Close** button ☒ on the FrontPage Editor program window to close this program.

3. If FrontPage Explorer is not the active program, click the **FrontPage Explorer** program button on the taskbar to make it the active program.

4. Click ☒ on the FrontPage Explorer program window to close this program.

Quick Check

1. Which FrontPage tool automatically inserts HTML tags into your Web page?

2. Name two methods for displaying the HTML code of a Web page.

3. Which method of displaying HTML code shows the HTML tags and properties in different colors?

4   In your own words, contrast the use of opening and closing tags.

5   Which tags could you use to apply boldface formatting to Web page text?

6   Which HTML tag is used to specify a hyperlink in the navigation bar of the Home Page for Sunny Morning Products?

7   True or False: When you exit FrontPage Explorer, you also automatically exit FrontPage Editor.

Now that you have a better understanding of Microsoft FrontPage and are familiar with the Web site Amanda created for Sunny Morning Products, you can proceed with the next part of your Web site development training.

Tutorial Assignments

Amanda is pleased with the progress you are making in the Web training course she developed for Sunny Morning Products. Before you continue with your training, however, she wants you to examine some additional Web page features to increase your understanding of Web pages and Web browser usage. By practicing these related skills, you will be better prepared for developing future Web pages. If necessary, start Internet Explorer, insert your Student Disk in drive A or the appropriate disk drive, and then do the following:

1. Type a:\wwwroot\sun.morn\index.htm as the URL to access the Home Page for Sunny Morning Products.

2. Click the Fullscreen button on the toolbar to expand the size of the Internet Explorer document window. Now click the Products hyperlink to display that Web page, and then examine each of the four alternatives available in the contents frame by selecting the hyperlink and displaying the associated Web page. Note whether the page displayed in the main frame changes while the other pages displayed in the other frames remain the same.

3. Click anywhere in the banner page, except on a hyperlink, to give this frame the focus. (*Hint:* Recall that the banner page contains the navigation bar.)

4. Click the Fullscreen button on the toolbar to return to the normal size Internet Explorer document window and re-display the menu bar. Print the banner page, and then print the page that is displayed in the main frame.

5. Display the HTML source code for the Products page. Verify that the HTML code only describes the frame set and does not contain the code for any of the pages displayed using this frame set.

6. Close Notepad.

7. Right-click the page that is displayed in the main frame to display the Shortcut menu, and then click View Source to display the HTML code. Note whether this is the same code you viewed previously or if it describes the code in the main frame.

8. Close Notepad.

9. Select Order Information to display that page in the main frame, and then scroll to the bottom of the page. Click the Order Form hyperlink to display that page in the main frame.

10. Fill out the Order Form with data that you make up, and then print the completed Order Form.

11. Click the Send Order push button to simulate the action of submitting a completed Order Form. (*Hint:* If you do not enter a month number or a four-digit year number in the text boxes with the Card Number, you will not be able to complete the submit and will need to change those values before the submit is accepted.) What happens after you submit the form, and why?

12. Click the Clear Order push button to remove the data you entered from the Order Form, and then display and print the HTML code for the Order Form.

13. Close Notepad.

14. Review the printout of the Order Form code, and then circle the HTML code for the Send Order push button on the printout.

15. Click the Investor Relations hyperlink to display that Web page, and then view and print the HTML code.

16. Review the printout of the Investor Relations code, and then circle all the <A> tags on the printout.

17. Close Notepad.

18. Open the Sunny Morning Products Web in FrontPage Explorer. Click the Navigation button on the Views bar to display that view, and then click the Print button on the toolbar to print it.

19. Click the Hyperlink Status button on the Views bar. Is this view blank? What message appears in the status bar? This window displays only broken or problem hyperlinks. Are there any?

20. Click the All Files button on the Views bar. How is this view different from the Folders view?

21. Click the Hyperlinks button on the Views bar. Print the hyperlink diagram displayed in FrontPage Explorer for the Home Page. To do this, use the Print Screen key on the keyboard to capture this screen to the Windows Clipboard, and then start WordPad and paste the contents of the Clipboard into the WordPad document. Print the document.

22. Close WordPad without saving the document, and then close FrontPage and Internet Explorer.

Case Problems

1. Exploring the Web Site for the American Carpenters Society The American Carpenters Society (ACS) is a nonprofit organization that advances the common good of professional carpenters. ACS has a small headquarters staff of 15 people that supports their entire membership. Recently, you were hired by Sara Castleberry to support all of the end-user computing activities at the ACS. In addition to maintaining the daily operation of the staff computers, Sara wants you to assume responsibility for maintaining ACS's Web site. She had previously contracted EarthShare, their current ISP, to create and maintain their Web site. However, she prefers to have the ongoing development of the Web site managed in-house so it is easier to adapt to the needs of the ACS staff. Sara wants you to review the ACS Web site so you can begin to assume this job responsibility. If necessary, start Internet Explorer, insert your Student Disk in drive A or the appropriate disk drive, and then do the following:

1. Access the Web site for the American Carpenters Society located on your Student Disk.

2. Click the Membership Benefits image hyperlink to display that Web page. Examine each of the four alternatives available in the Table of Contents by selecting the hyperlink and displaying the associated Web page. Note if the page displayed in the main frame changes while the other pages displayed in the other frames remain the same.

3. Click anywhere in the banner page that contains the navigation bar of hyperlink images, but do not click any of these images.

4. Print the banner page, and then print the page displayed in the main frame.

5. Display the HTML source code for the Member Benefits Web page.

6. Print the HTML code, and then verify that the code only describes the frame set and does not contain the code for any of the pages displayed using this frame set.

7. Close Notepad.

8. Right-click the page displayed in the main frame to display the shortcut menu, and then click View Source to display the HTML code. Note if this code describes the main frame or if it is the same code you looked at in Question 5.

9. Print the HTML code, and then close Notepad.

10. Click the Become A Member hyperlink image in the banner frame to display that page. Note if the entire frame set page is replaced or if the page appears in the main frame.

11. Fill out the Become A Member form with data that you make up, and then print the completed form.

12. Click the Submit Form push button to simulate the action of submitting a completed Become A Member form to the server. What appears in the Internet Explorer document window after you submit the form? (*Note:* If you were running this with a Web server, then a Member Confirmation would appear.)

13. Click the Back button on the Internet Explorer toolbar, click the Reset Form push button to remove the data you entered from the Become A Member form, and then display and print the HTML code for the form. Close Notepad.

14. Review the HTML code, and then circle the HTML code for the Submit Form push button on the printout.

15. Click the Who's Who image hyperlink to display that Web page. Note if this page contains a table.

16. Display and print the HTML code for the Who's Who Web page. Close Notepad.

17. Review the printout of the HTML code, and then circle each <A> tag on the printout. Describe the use of the <A> tag. If the page contains a table, then also locate and circle the <TABLE> tags.

18. Print the hyperlink diagram displayed in FrontPage Explorer for the Home Page of this Web by using the Print Screen key to capture this screen to the Windows Clipboard, then start WordPad and paste the contents of the Clipboard into the WordPad document. Finally, print the document from WordPad.

19. Close WordPad, Internet Explorer, and FrontPage.

2. Examining Web Sites for Guardian Mutual Insurance Guardian Mutual Insurance (GMI) is a large, national insurance company that sells insurance for both individuals and businesses. GMI employs a staff of nearly 100 computer programmers and analysts who maintain and build its management information systems. Susan Gentry is the Human Resources manager at GMI. She recently hired Steve Michaels as a junior systems analyst and assigned him to GMI's Web development team. Susan wants you to help Steve review Web sites to obtain some ideas for developing GMI's Web site.

If necessary, start Internet Explorer and then do the following:

1. Connect to the WWW and visit at least five business-oriented Web sites. Make sure to examine Web sites that provide corporate information as well as those sites designed for doing business on the Internet.

2. While you are looking at each site, analyze the amount and type of information provided and note their overall appearance and ease of use.

3. Based on the standards described in the case introduction, identify the three Web sites you feel are the best. Print the pages for each of these Web sites (limit the number of pages you print to 10 for any one Web site).

4. For each Web site, choose one Web page and print its HTML code. Note which pages contain at least one <A> tag or <TABLE> tag.

5. Draw a diagram similar to that in the Navigation view of FrontPage Explorer for each of the three Web sites.

6. For each Web site, write a one-page report that describes its key features. Your report should include the following types of information: best and worst features, features that need improvement, suggestions for improvement, and commentary about ease of use and overall style.

7. Based on the reports you completed on the three Web sites, identify which sites you rated as the best and the worst. Defend your selections.

8. Close your Web browser and log off the Internet, if necessary.

TUTORIAL 2

Creating and Revising Web Pages

Preparing the Home Page for the Sunny Morning Products Web Site

OBJECTIVES

In this tutorial you will:

- Learn the four-step process of developing a Web site

- Create a FrontPage Web site

- Save a Web page

- Format the contents of a Web page

- View a Web page in the Internet Explorer browser window

- Spell check and print a Web page

- Add a background image and sound to a Web page

- Insert an inline image and marquee on a Web page

- Learn about the importance of META tags in marketing a Web page

Sunny Morning Products

Amanda researched many Web sites that the company's competition created before she started to develop the Sunny Morning Products Web site. She compiled a list of six sites that had a Web presence similar to the one she envisioned for Sunny Morning Products. Then she scheduled a meeting with Andrew to review these sites to help clarify the requirements for the Sunny Morning Products Web site. Amanda and Andrew discussed the type of overall design the Web site should have as well as the specific design and content of the Home Page. They agreed that Amanda would develop the Home Page first and then Andrew would review it. After that, Amanda would incorporate Andrew's input into the rest of the Web site.

In this tutorial, you continue Amanda's Web training course by exploring the four-part process she used to develop the plan for the Sunny Morning Products Web site. You learn how to create and format a Web page by re-creating the Home Page for Sunny Morning Products and applying different formatting techniques to organize the information in the Web page. Then you proceed with your training by revising the Home Page to include such features as images and multimedia.

In this session you will learn the four-part process for developing a Web site and creating your own FrontPage Web. You will learn how to insert text in a Web page that has already been created as well as add a navigation bar. Finally, you will learn how to save a Web page.

Developing a Web Site

Web sites are often created by a development team that consists of a copywriter and an editor, a graphic designer, a programmer, a systems administrator, and a marketing person. This team is coordinated by a Web design director. Figure 2-1 shows the organization of this type of team and lists some of the general responsibilities of each team member. However, these responsibilities often are assigned to a single employee, who is the so-called Web master for a company. Oftentimes, individuals who are not necessarily employees in large or small companies create and develop their own Web sites. Regardless of who is responsible for developing a Web site, FrontPage makes it easy to carry out the various activities of a development team to perform the programming and administrative functions necessary in preparing a Web site.

Figure 2-1 ◀
Web
design team

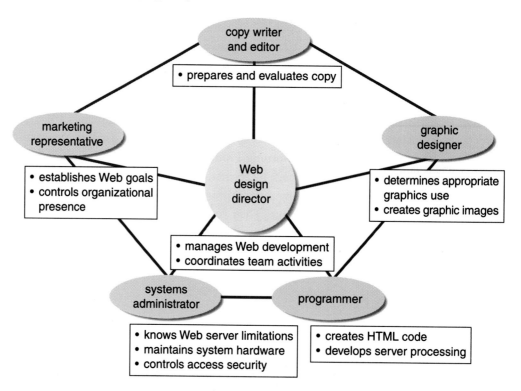

The process of developing a Web site can be divided into four major tasks: (1) analyze/define the problem, (2) design the Web site, (3) build the Web pages, and (4) review/test the Web site. Amanda is ready to explain the first step in this process—analysis.

Creating a Planning Analysis Sheet

The first step in creating a professional-looking Web site is to analyze the problem you are trying to solve. To accomplish this, you define the problem and determine what type of information the Web site should include. Then you collect the data that defines the Web's content.

As Amanda learned in her initial meeting with Andrew to discuss Web site requirements, her task was to develop a Web site that provided a corporate Web presence for Sunny Morning Products and that would assist in marketing the items sold through the Sunshine Country Store. During this meeting, Amanda obtained the preliminary information she needed to begin developing the Web site. Figure 2-2 shows a copy of her notes from this meeting.

Figure 2-2 ◀
Amanda's notes for the Sunny Morning Products Web site

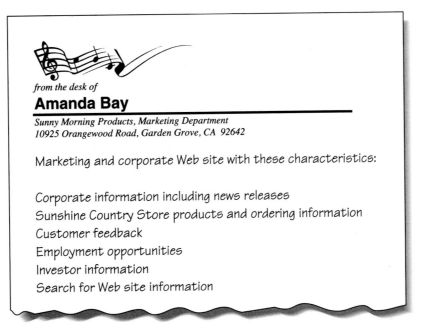

from the desk of
Amanda Bay

Sunny Morning Products, Marketing Department
10925 Orangewood Road, Garden Grove, CA 92642

Marketing and corporate Web site with these characteristics:

Corporate information including news releases
Sunshine Country Store products and ordering information
Customer feedback
Employment opportunities
Investor information
Search for Web site information

Using this preliminary information, Amanda created a planning analysis sheet. A **planning analysis sheet** is a document that contains answers to the following questions:

1. What is the goal of the Web site? The goal defines the problem you want to solve.

2. What data do you need in order to create your Web pages? This information is your **input**.

3. What results do you want to see? This information describes your **output**, or the information that your Web site should provide.

4. What type of navigation features do your Web pages need? Navigation specifies the hyperlinks that connect the Web pages to give users access to the information in your Web site.

Figure 2-3 shows Amanda's completed planning analysis sheet.

Figure 2-3
Amanda's
planning
analysis sheet

Planning Analysis Sheet

My goal:

Develop a marketing and corporate Web site that provides relevant company

information and allows users to place orders from the Sunshine Country Store.

What results do I want to see?

Web pages with the following information:

Company description

Current press releases

Product descriptions and ordering information

Employment information

Investor information

Customer feedback form

Search capability for Web content

What information do I need?

Company description

Mission statement

List of product groups and individual product descriptions and prices

List of available positions and their job descriptions

Financial performance and stock information

Designing a Web Site

The next step in developing a Web site is the design phase. Good graphic design is crucial in the commercial and competitive realm of the Web. The overall layout and images in a Web page are what make it attractive and inviting. Specific factors to consider when designing a Web page include the following:

- Primary intent. What is the purpose of the Web site?

- Short- and long-term goals. What specific goals do you want the Web site to accomplish?

- Intended audience. Who do you want/expect to visit your Web site? The quality and level of the design and the information must meet the intended audience's expectations.

- Organizational image. What message are you trying to convey about your company? Is it environmental, classic, stylish, or contemporary? What makes your organization distinct from its competitors?

Applying this list to the design of a Web site helps to draw out a plan that functions like a storyboard. The purpose of this storyboard, or sketch, is to enable you to plan the interactive relationships among Web pages before you create the pages and specify the hyperlinks. Figure 2-4 shows the rough sketch of the pages that will make up the Sunny Morning Products Web site. Amanda's sketch specifies which Web pages must be created and provides a preliminary indication of the hyperlinks needed to link the Web pages.

Figure 2-4 ◀
Amanda's preliminary sketch of the Sunny Morning Products Web site

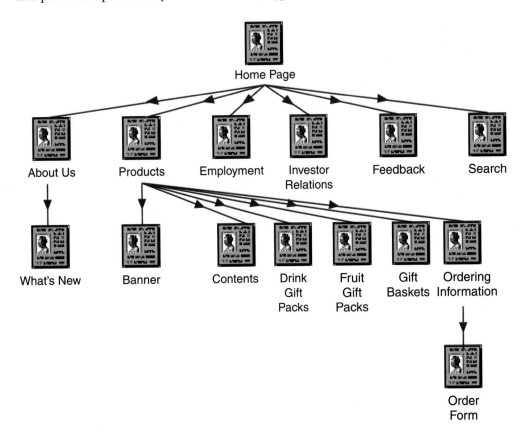

When designing a Web site, it is often helpful to complete your storyboard using a chalkboard (or a white board) so that you can easily make changes as you develop a plan for each Web page and identify its relationship to other pages in the Web site. A well-designed Web site contains an attractive entry page—usually its home page—that attracts users and "invites" them to explore the site and learn about the featured product or service. Web sites with good design usually share a few characteristics: they download quickly, they are pleasing to the eye, they organize information into well-defined areas, they allow for easy navigation, and they are easy to read. Of course, the Web site must be attractive but it also must contain enough interesting and/or informative content to make users want to stay.

Web Page Content

As part of her Web site design plan, Amanda needed to plan the content of each Web page. Content is the most fundamental aspect of Web design because the success of a Web site depends on the quality of information in it. Streamlined, appropriate language is part of any well-designed site.

You can obtain content for a Web site by collecting data about the organization from a variety of sources, including brochures and other promotional material, existing catalogs, logos, letterheads, business cards, contact information, and photos. Key questions to consider when evaluating the content of a Web site include the following:

- Is the copy complete? Does it thoroughly describe the needs of the organization and fulfill the goals of the site?

- Is the reading level appropriate? Is the copy too long or verbose? Clear ideas, written simply and to the point, are fundamental to strong Web site copy.

- Is the copy free of errors? Spelling or grammatical errors diminish the professionalism of a Web site.

Considering each of these questions helps determine the content and writing style for a Web site. After creating your Web site design, you should review it against the following standards:

- Is the balance between design and content appropriate for the audience?

- Are there any elements not pertinent to the subject matter for the intended audience?

- Is the text clear and concise? Is it free of spelling and grammatical errors?

- Do the pages download evenly and fairly quickly?

- Do all the links work?

- Does all the programming function correctly?

Once your Web design plan is in place, you can begin building the pages.

Building a Web Page

The best Web sites are visually appealing, convey information correctly and succinctly, and download quickly. There are some helpful guidelines to follow in order to build a successful Web site. Note that many of these guidelines are similar to the factors you consider when initially designing the Web site:

- Have a clear purpose. Make your goals as specific as possible. For example, do you want to market your company's products to increase sales or to increase the company's visibility? If so, how do you want to present the information?

- Keep your audience in mind. Based on the demographics of your targeted audience, how much time are visitors likely to spend at your site? For every piece of information, every graphic, and every content decision you make, consider your audience's reaction.

- Use items that download quickly. A key reason that people leave a site is that it takes too long for the information to download on their screens. Large graphics can leave potential customers waiting indefinitely. If you want to include large graphics, provide your users with the option to download them as a separate Web page.

- Make your site visually appealing. Strike a balance between a site with a simple design and one that is chaotic. Make the text large enough for easy viewing, and use color and font variation to add interest and draw the user's attention to items. However, don't attempt to use every possible font, color, and feature on every page.

- Organize your content. Arrange material in groups of related information. For example, if you are designing a Web site for a bookstore, arrange the material according to easy-to-find subject areas.

- Include appropriate navigation buttons. On every page of your Web site, provide a button that allows users to return to the home page automatically. Your goal is to make it as easy as possible for users to move through your site.

Testing a Web Site

The final step in developing a Web site involves testing it. As you complete each page, you'll need to test it by viewing it using your Web browser. Some of the aspects you'll be testing include making sure that hyperlinks work correctly and that all the images and other objects are available. A Web site should be thoroughly tested before it is published to a Web server, where users from all over the world will have access to it.

Creating a Web Site

Based on the four-step Web development process, Amanda identified a clear vision of the Web site that Sunny Morning Products needs. After reviewing her planning analysis sheet and preliminary storyboard design with Andrew and obtaining his approval, Amanda began creating the Web site.

The first step in creating the Sunny Morning Products Web site was to create the FrontPage Web that would contain the individual Web pages for the Web site. A FrontPage Web is similar to a file folder that you use in other programs. In fact, a FrontPage Web is a Windows folder. However, when you create a FrontPage Web, the additional files and folders that FrontPage uses—the FrontPage extensions—are placed in this Web. You should *always* use FrontPage to create the folder for your Web.

Now that you're familiar with the process of developing a Web site, you are ready to continue your Web training by learning how to create a Web site. You begin by starting FrontPage and creating the Sunny Morning Web.

To create a FrontPage Web:

1. Make sure your Student Disk is in drive A or the appropriate drive on your computer.

2. Start **Microsoft FrontPage Explorer**. The Getting Started dialog box opens. See Figure 2-5.

Figure 2-5 ◀
Getting Started
dialog box

last open Web
(yours may differ)

click to start
a new Web

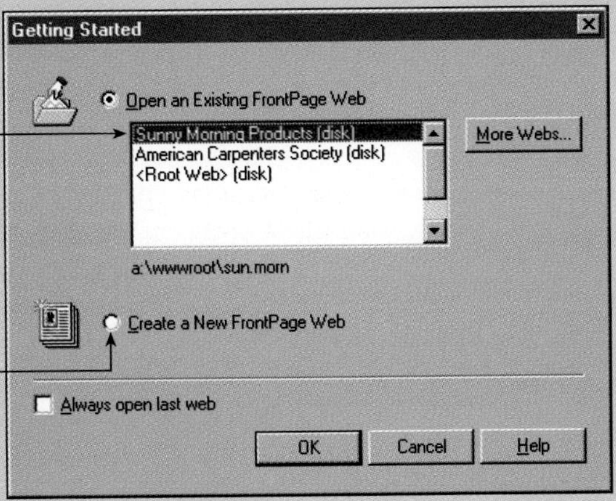

TROUBLE? If the Getting Started dialog box doesn't open, click File on the menu bar, point to New, and then click FrontPage Web to open the New FrontPage Web dialog box. Skip to Step 4.

3. Click the **Create a New FrontPage Web** option button, and then click the **OK** button to open the New FrontPage Web dialog box. See Figure 2-6.

Figure 2-6 ◄
New FrontPage
Web dialog box

click to create a Web
with a home page

enter Web title here

click to change
Web name

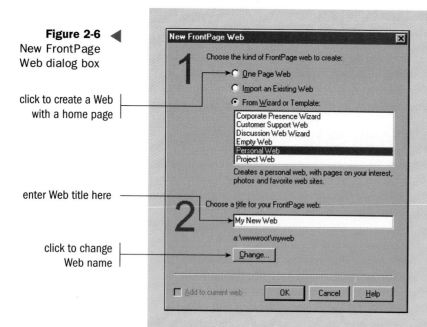

4. Click the **One Page Web** option button in the Choose the kind of FrontPage web to create section.

   Recall from Tutorial 1 that the \wwwroot folder is the location for all the Webs on your Student Disk. You need to create your new Web in this same folder.

5. Type **Sunny Morning** in the Choose a title for your FrontPage web text box. A FrontPage Web has both a title and name. The title and name may be the same or they may be different.

   Now you need to name the Web you are creating.

6. Click the **Change** button to open the Change Location dialog box. See Figure 2-7.

Figure 2-7 ◄
Change
Location
dialog box

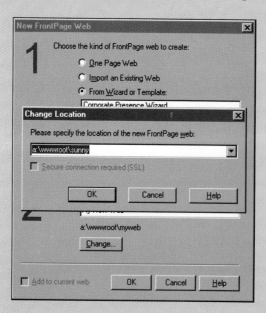

7. Type **a:\wwwroot\sunny** in the Please specify the location of the new FrontPage web text box, and then click the **OK** button to return to the New FrontPage Web dialog box. Here, *sunny* is the name of your Web and the name of the folder that contains your Web.

8. Click the **OK** button to actually create the Web. The Create New FrontPage Web dialog box opens while the new Web is created and, after a few minutes, the Home Page icon displays in the Navigation view of the FrontPage Explorer window. See Figure 2-8.

TROUBLE? If you are in Folders view, click the Navigation view button on the Views bar to switch to Navigation view.

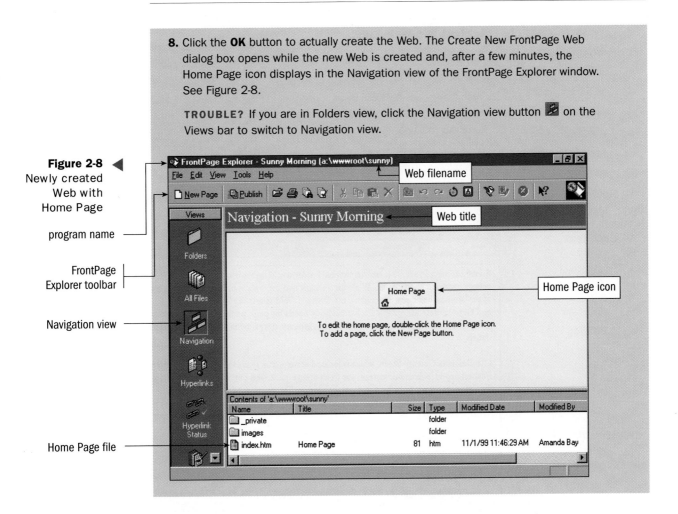

Figure 2-8
Newly created
Web with
Home Page

program name

FrontPage
Explorer toolbar

Navigation view

Home Page file

When the Sunny Morning Web is created, the filename index.htm is assigned automatically to the Home Page in the Web. The files index.htm and default.htm are usually recognized as the initial, or default, pages for a Web site. That is, when you access a Web site, this is the page that is displayed if a specific page is not requested as the URL address. This can vary among Web sites because the initial page setting can be specified during installation. However, most Web sites tend to use one of the default, initial filenames specified previously.

Creating a Web Page

After creating a Web site, you can begin creating the individual Web pages for your Web site. As the previous set of steps showed, FrontPage automatically creates the index.htm (or default.htm) home page when you create the FrontPage Web. All other new Web pages are created in FrontPage Editor. These new Web pages are automatically included in the Web that you are currently using in FrontPage Explorer.

Entering Text in a Web Page

Now that you've created the initial file for the Sunny Morning Home Page, you begin developing a Web page by re-creating the Home Page that Amanda created. With Amanda's assistance, you access the newly created Home Page and enter the information she wants it to contain.

To enter text in a Web page:

1. Double-click the **Home Page** icon in the right pane to start FrontPage Editor and display a blank Web page.

2. Type the information exactly as it appears in Figure 2-9. As with any word-processing program, you do not need to press the Enter key at the end of each line; you press the Enter key only once when advancing to a new paragraph. FrontPage automatically inserts blank space before a new paragraph; do not press the Enter key twice.

Figure 2-9 ◀
Sunny Morning Products Home Page text

program name

type text exactly as it appears (your formatting may differ)

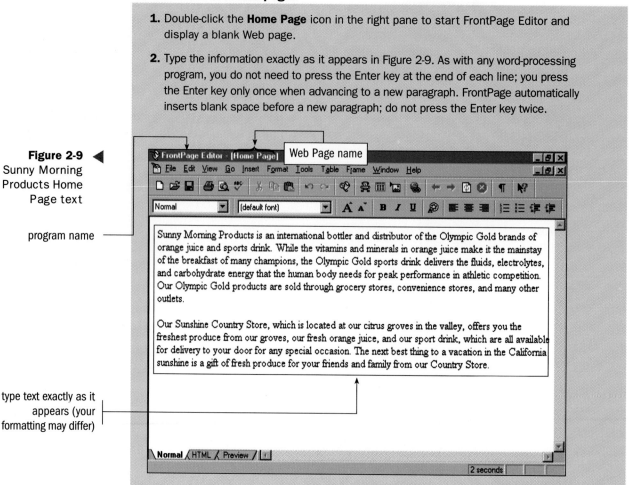

Web Page name

Sunny Morning Products is an international bottler and distributor of the Olympic Gold brands of orange juice and sports drink. While the vitamins and minerals in orange juice make it the mainstay of the breakfast of many champions, the Olympic Gold sports drink delivers the fluids, electrolytes, and carbohydrate energy that the human body needs for peak performance in athletic competition. Our Olympic Gold products are sold through grocery stores, convenience stores, and many other outlets.

Our Sunshine Country Store, which is located at our citrus groves in the valley, offers you the freshest produce from our groves, our fresh orange juice, and our sport drink, which are all available for delivery to your door for any special occasion. The next best thing to a vacation in the California sunshine is a gift of fresh produce for your friends and family from our Country Store.

Adding a Navigation Bar

Once you've created a new Web page, you'll want to begin adding key features, such as a navigation bar. A **navigation bar** is a commonly used feature that utilizes hyperlinks to easily access other Web pages. Although you can add a navigation bar before including any text information, it is often more helpful to see how the main body of your text appears on the page before including this feature.

When evaluating a Web site's design requirements, one consideration is placement of the navigation bar. Two common places for the navigation bar are at the top or the bottom of a Web page. Both locations are acceptable, depending on how you expect your users to interact with the pages of your Web site. For example, when placed at the top of the page, the navigation bar is immediately in view when the page is opened in the Web browser window. Placing the navigation bar at the bottom of the page, however, provides the reader with access to the next Web page after they have completed reading the current page.

With FrontPage, you can create a navigation bar in one of two ways. First, you can create a user-defined navigation bar by using text and/or graphics over which you have complete control. Second, you can include a navigation bar using the FrontPage navigation bar feature. The FrontPage navigation bar feature is a quick method for creating the navigation bar, but it is not as flexible as creating a user-defined navigation bar. In this tutorial, you will implement a user-defined navigation bar. In a later tutorial, you will use the FrontPage navigation bar feature.

You create a user-defined navigation bar from text that you type just like any other information entered on your Web page. Then you can separate the entries in your navigation bar in several different ways. For example, you can separate them using special characters or spaces. Special characters are used frequently because they provide a better visual separation between words. Another common method of separating entries in the navigation bar is to use either the vertical bar (|) or square brackets ([ ]) as the separator. Usually, a single vertical bar is placed between entries, whereas square brackets are used to surround each entry in the navigation bar. After entering the text for your navigation bar, you create the hyperlinks as you create the other pages to which you want to link. This is where a storyboard of a Web site is useful in providing the layout for linking the Web pages.

For the Sunny Morning Web, Amanda decided that the best location for the navigation bar is at the top of the page and she used the vertical bar character (|) as her separator. With Amanda's assistance, you create the navigation bar and insert it at the top of the Home Page.

To create a navigation bar:

1. With the Web page text you entered still displayed in FrontPage Editor, click the insertion point | before the word **Sunny** at the beginning of the first line.

2. Press the **Enter** key to insert a line before the first paragraph, and then press the **Up** arrow key ↑. The | moves to the beginning of the new line, which is where you will place the navigation bar for the Home Page.

3. Type the following navigation bar text exactly as it appears. Be sure to type the vertical bar and spacebar characters before the first entry, and then press the Spacebar, type the vertical bar, and then press the Spacebar again after each subsequent entry. The text for the navigation bar should appear on one line.

   | Home | About Us | Products | Employment | Investor Relations | Feedback | Search |

   Your completed navigation bar should match Figure 2-10.

Figure 2-10 ◀
Navigation bar
for Sunny
Morning
Products
Home Page

text entered for
navigation bar

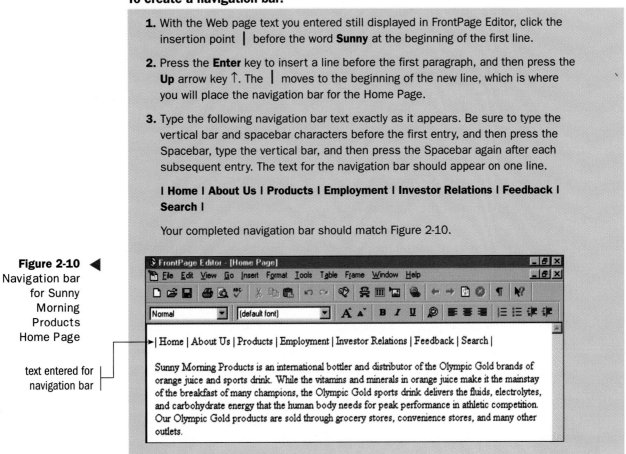

Saving a Web Page

Saving your Web page gives you access to the information even after you end your FrontPage session. It is important to save your work frequently. During the development process, your Web page is stored in the computer's RAM. If a power surge occurs or if your computer freezes, or stops working, you might lose all the information you included since you started working or since the last time you saved it. You use the Save command on the File menu or the Save button on the Standard toolbar to save the changes you have made to your Web page using the same filename. Keep in mind that using the Save command does not create a separate version of your old Web page, but rather, it replaces the old version with a new, edited Web page. If you want to save a newer version of the file under a different filename, you use the Save As command on the File menu.

SAVING A WEB PAGE

- Click the Save button on the Standard toolbar.
  or
- Click File on the menu bar, and then click Save.

Because you've already done considerable work in creating a new Web page, Amanda suggests that you save the work you have completed on the Home Page thus far.

To save a Web page:

1. Click the **Save** button 🖫 on the Standard toolbar. The file is saved in the current Web.

Quick Check

1. List the four major tasks involved in developing a Web site.

2. The goal of a Web site is defined during which major task?

3. The purpose of a storyboard is to plan the _____ relationships among Web pages.

4. True or False: Better-designed Web sites download quickly and allow for easy navigation.

5. True or False: Animated graphics are the most fundamental aspect of Web design.

6. True or False: A key reason that people leave a site is that it takes too long for information to appear on their screens.

7. A(n) _____ is the Web page that is automatically created when you create a FrontPage Web.

Amanda is pleased with your progress and she feels you're ready to apply specific formatting to the content of the Web page.

SESSION 2.2

In this session you will learn how to format the contents of a Web page by changing the style and color of text, adjusting its alignment on a Web page, and inserting special characters. You will test the appearance of your Web page by viewing it in the Internet Explorer window. Finally, you will learn how to spell check and print a Web page.

Formatting the Contents of a Web Page

One way to make your Web site more informative and visually appealing is by drawing attention to important content through the use of formatting. **Formatting** is the process of changing the appearance of text in a Web page; it does not change the Web page content. There are many ways to access FrontPage Editor's formatting options. For example, the Format menu provides access to all formatting commands, ranging from revising paragraph organization to creating numbered lists. Using a Shortcut menu provides quick access to a variety of formatting commands that you can apply to specific characters, words, or text in your Web page, such as fonts or numbered lists. Shortcut menus appear when you right-click text or objects in your document. Finally, the Format toolbar contains buttons that apply specific formatting activities to your Web page. Some of the more frequently used Format toolbar buttons include the style and alignment buttons and the Change Style and Change Font selection boxes. Figure 2-11 describes the Format toolbar buttons and their uses in more detail.

Figure 2-11 ◀
Format toolbar
buttons

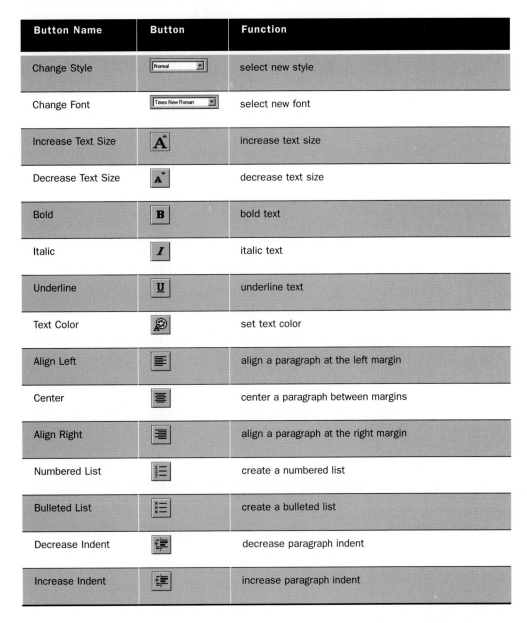

Button Name	Button	Function
Change Style	Normal	select new style
Change Font	Times New Roman	select new font
Increase Text Size	A	increase text size
Decrease Text Size	A	decrease text size
Bold	B	bold text
Italic	I	italic text
Underline	U	underline text
Text Color		set text color
Align Left		align a paragraph at the left margin
Center		center a paragraph between margins
Align Right		align a paragraph at the right margin
Numbered List		create a numbered list
Bulleted List		create a bulleted list
Decrease Indent		decrease paragraph indent
Increase Indent		increase paragraph indent

Most experienced FrontPage users develop a preference for accessing Editor's formatting options; however, most beginners find it easiest to use the Format menu. This is the method you will use most often in these tutorials.

Now that the Home Page for Sunny Morning Products contains text and a navigation bar, Amanda is ready for you to continue developing it by applying specific formatting to make it easier for users to view, interpret, and navigate the contents of the Web site.

Creating Headings

Headings in Web documents function like headings in other written documents. The selections of headings available for your Web page are limited by those defined by HTML tags. HTML provides six levels of headings that are identified as H1, H2, and so on. H1 is the heading with the largest font, whereas H6 is the heading with the smallest font. You can change the alignment of a heading before or after the heading text is entered.

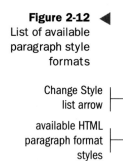

REFERENCE window

CREATING HEADINGS

- Place the pointer in the paragraph you want to use as a heading.
- Click the Style list arrow on the Format toolbar to display the list of available paragraph format styles, and then click the desired heading.

  or
- Click Format on the menu bar, click Paragraph, click the desired paragraph format style, and then click the OK button.

Amanda wants the heading for the Home Page of the Sunny Morning Web to be upbeat and welcoming. You create this heading and add it to your Web page.

To create a Web page heading:

1. If necessary, click the **Maximize** button □ on the FrontPage Editor title bar to display the entire Web page in your window.

2. If necessary, press the **End** key to move the insertion point to the end of the navigation bar, and then press the **Enter** key to insert a new line immediately below the navigation bar. Notice this new line has the same left alignment as the navigation bar.

3. Type **Welcome to Sunny Morning Products' World Wide Web Site!** as the text for your heading.

Now that you've created the heading, you'll apply a heading option to it in order to distinguish this text from the rest of the Web page.

4. Click the **Change Style** list arrow on the Format toolbar to display a list of available paragraph style formats. See Figure 2-12. These formats correspond to the HTML tags that are used to define the various paragraphs in your Web page.

Figure 2-12 ◀
List of available paragraph style formats

Change Style list arrow

available HTML paragraph format styles

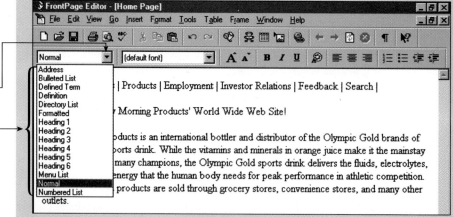

5. Click **Heading 3** to assign this format to the heading.

TROUBLE? You do not have to select (highlight) all the text in the heading before applying formatting to it, as you would in a word-processing program.

Now that you've added a heading at the top of the Web page, you'll add another heading at the bottom of the Home Page.

6. Press **Ctrl + End** to start a new line below the last paragraph of the current Web page text, and then type **Brighten your day, enjoy some of our sunshine!**

The new heading is added at the bottom of the Web page.

Aligning Text

Like any word-processing program, FrontPage Editor allows you to left-, center-, or right-align text on your Web page. The Web browser interprets the alignment tags based on the formatting you apply and displays the text accordingly.

REFERENCE window	**ALIGNING TEXT**
	▪ Click in the paragraph you want to align to select it.
	▪ Click one of the alignment buttons on the Format toolbar to apply the desired alignment.
	or
	▪ Right-click the paragraph to display the Shortcut menu, click Paragraph Properties, click the Paragraph Alignment list arrow, click the desired alignment, and then click the OK button.
	or
	▪ Click Format on the menu bar, click Paragraph, click the Paragraph Alignment list arrow, click the desired alignment, and then click the OK button.

Now that you've finished adding the headings to the Web page, you'll center the heading at the bottom of the page, and then you will center the navigation bar to balance the Web page.

To center Web page text:

1. With the heading at the bottom of the page still displayed, click anywhere in the heading to select it.

2. Click the **Center** button ▤ on the Format toolbar to center-align the heading.

3. Click the **Change Style** list arrow, and then click **Heading 3** to assign this format to the heading. See Figure 2-13.

Figure 2-13 ◀
Formatted heading

centered paragraph with Heading 3 style

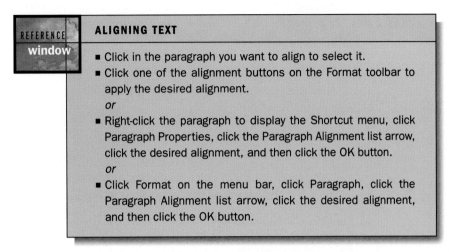

Our Sunshine Country Store, which is located at our citrus groves in the valley, offers you the freshest produce from our groves, our fresh orange juice, and our sport drink, which are all available for delivery to your door for any special occasion. The next best thing to a vacation in the California sunshine is a gift of fresh produce for your friends and family from our Country Store.

→ **Brighten your day, enjoy some of our sunshine!**

Normal ⟨ HTML ⟨ Preview ⟩ ◀

2 seconds

4. Press **Ctrl + Home** to return to the top of the Home Page, and then click anywhere on the navigation bar to select it.

5. Click ▤ on the Format toolbar to center-align the navigation bar.

Using Fonts

A **font** is a set of letters, numbers, and symbols distinguished by their typeface, point size, and style. Like a word-processing document, a Web page can have one of the following **font styles**: regular, *italic*, **bold**, or ***bold italic***. In addition, you can apply underlining to any of these font styles. You also can toggle on and off the application of these styles to a selected text string. That is, if the style is not applied, then selecting the style applies it; if the style is applied, then selecting the style removes it.

In addition to adding headings, Amanda included a footer at the bottom of the Sunny Morning Products Home Page. She applied the italic font to the footer in order to set it off from the other text on the page. You insert this footer information and apply italics to it as well.

To apply italics:

1. Press **Ctrl + End** to insert a new line after the last paragraph on the Home Page.

2. Type **Last updated: October 26, 2000**.

3. Press **Shift + Enter** to advance to a new line without starting a new paragraph.

4. Type **Copyright 2000. Sunny Morning Products. All rights reserved.**

5. If necessary, click the **Show/Hide ¶** button ¶ on the Standard toolbar so you can see the format marks.

   Your completed footer information should match Figure 2-14.

Figure 2-14 ◀
Completed
footer
information

indicates new line
in same paragraph

   Now that you've entered the footer information, you format it by applying italics.

6. Select the footer information by highlighting this paragraph.

7. Click the **Italic** button *I* on the Format toolbar. The completed footer information now appears italicized.

Inserting Special Characters

You can insert special characters or symbols, such as the copyright symbol (©), in the text of a Web page for the same purposes that these characters are used in other types of documents. In FrontPage Editor, all special characters are inserted using the Symbol dialog box. Amanda wants the copyright symbol to appear immediately after the word "Copyright" in the footer. You add this symbol to your Home Page.

To insert a special character:

1. With the italicized footer information still displayed, place the insertion point to the right of the letter **t** in the word Copyright, and then press the **Spacebar**. This is the desired location for the special character.

2. Click **Insert** on the menu bar, and then click **Symbol** to open the Symbol dialog box.

3. Click the © symbol (fourth row, tenth character from the left), click the **Insert** button, and then click the **Close** button. The Symbol dialog box closes and the copyright symbol appears in the footer. The footer information, including italics and the copyright symbol, is now complete. See Figure 2-15.

Figure 2-15
Footer
information
with copyright
symbol
inserted

special character ——————

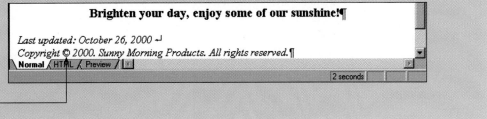

Changing Text Size and Color

Another way to adjust the appearance of a Web page is to change the current text size and/or color. You simply select the desired text in FrontPage Editor and then change the text size or apply the desired color. Oftentimes, when designing a Web page, you will need to experiment with different text sizes and colors in order to find the best one. You can adjust text size and color in any sequence you prefer; it doesn't matter which format you change first.

As part of her Web page design, Amanda wants the occurrences of the text "Olympic Gold" to have a more eye-catching, prominent appearance in the Web page than the other text information. You enhance the current brand name text by experimenting with its text size, changing its color, and applying boldface formatting.

To change text size:

1. Press **Ctrl + Home** to return to the top of the Home Page.

2. Select **Olympic Gold** in the first line of the first paragraph of the narrative.

3. Click the **Increase Text Size** button [A] on the Format toolbar once to enlarge the size of the Olympic Gold text. Each time the Increase Text button is clicked, the selected text is increased by one size.

4. Click the **Decrease Text Size** button [A] on the Format toolbar to return the text to its previous size.

Now you will change the color of the Olympic Gold text to make it even more prominent on the Web page.

To change text color:

1. With Olympic Gold still selected, click the **Bold** button [B] on the Format toolbar to boldface this text. Notice that boldface gives the text a more prominent appearance within the paragraph.

2. Click the **Text Color** button [img] on the Format toolbar to open the Color dialog box. See Figure 2-16.

Figure 2-16 ◄
Color
dialog box

click to select
orange color

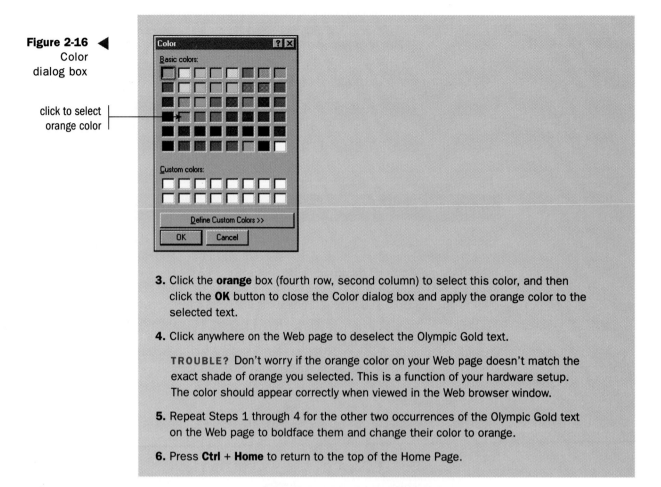

3. Click the **orange** box (fourth row, second column) to select this color, and then click the **OK** button to close the Color dialog box and apply the orange color to the selected text.

4. Click anywhere on the Web page to deselect the Olympic Gold text.

TROUBLE? Don't worry if the orange color on your Web page doesn't match the exact shade of orange you selected. This is a function of your hardware setup. The color should appear correctly when viewed in the Web browser window.

5. Repeat Steps 1 through 4 for the other two occurrences of the Olympic Gold text on the Web page to boldface them and change their color to orange.

6. Press **Ctrl + Home** to return to the top of the Home Page.

Spell Checking a Web Page

Spelling errors in any type of document make it appear unprofessional and reflect negatively on the author or creator. Checking the spelling of your Web pages should always be part of the developmental process.

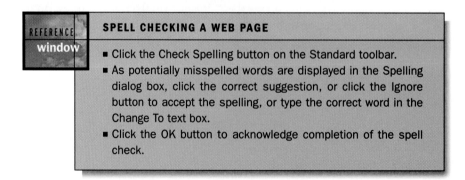

REFERENCE
window

SPELL CHECKING A WEB PAGE

- Click the Check Spelling button on the Standard toolbar.
- As potentially misspelled words are displayed in the Spelling dialog box, click the correct suggestion, or click the Ignore button to accept the spelling, or type the correct word in the Change To text box.
- Click the OK button to acknowledge completion of the spell check.

Amanda knows that spelling errors make a Web page look unprofessional. She wants you to take a few moments to review the spelling of the text that you have added thus far to the Home Page.

To spell check a Web page:

1. Click the **Check Spelling** button ☑ on the Standard toolbar.

2. When the Spelling dialog box opens with the word "bottler" selected, click the **Ignore** button. Although this word is spelled correctly, it is not in the dictionary.

   TROUBLE? If you encounter any misspelled words in your Web page before "bottler," skip to Step 3. When "bottler" appears in the Change To text box, return to Step 2.

   TROUBLE? If you do not encounter any misspelled words in your Web page, then the word "bottler" is in your dictionary. Go to Step 3.

3. If any other misspelled words are detected, they will appear in the Change To text box. Select the correct spelling of the word in the Suggestions list box, or edit the word in the Change To text box and then click the **Change** button to continue.

4. Click the **OK** button in the FrontPage Editor message box when prompted with the message "The spelling check is complete."

5. Click the **Save** button ▣ on the Standard toolbar to save your work.

With all the spelling errors corrected, Amanda is ready for you to complete the final step in developing a Web page—testing it.

Testing a Web Page Using Internet Explorer

You test the appearance of a Web page by viewing it in the Internet Explorer browser window. For example, if your hardware configuration causes a different color to be displayed in the Editor than what you selected for your Web page, opening the page in your browser window enables you to check to make sure that the desired color appears correctly. As you add other features, such as hyperlinks, to your Web pages, you confirm that they work correctly by testing them using your browser. For now, your testing is limited primarily to making sure that the appearance of the Home Page thus far in the Internet Explorer window is the same as that in FrontPage Editor. Keep in mind that in some situations, the Web page appears differently when it is displayed in the browser window than when it appears in FrontPage Editor. This is because the WYSIWYG feature of Editor does not always provide a 100% rendering of the page as it ultimately appears in the browser.

You can do the test by using either the Preview tab in FrontPage Editor or the Preview in Browser button on the Standard toolbar. When you use the Preview tab, the document window switches to the Internet Explorer window and the FrontPage Editor toolbars and window tabs remain displayed. When you use the Preview in Browser button, the application starts and switches to the Internet Explorer program window with its toolbars and menu bar.

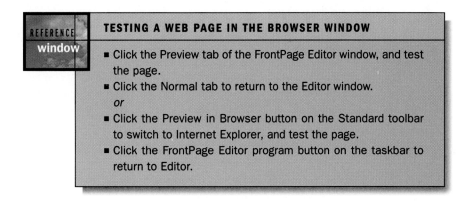

REFERENCE window

TESTING A WEB PAGE IN THE BROWSER WINDOW

- Click the Preview tab of the FrontPage Editor window, and test the page.
- Click the Normal tab to return to the Editor window.
  or
- Click the Preview in Browser button on the Standard toolbar to switch to Internet Explorer, and test the page.
- Click the FrontPage Editor program button on the taskbar to return to Editor.

Now that you have completed your initial draft of the Home Page for the Sunny Morning Web site for Amanda, you need to test it in the browser window. To do this, you use the Preview tab to display the Internet Explorer window in FrontPage Editor.

To test a Web page in the Internet Explorer window:

1. Click the **Preview** tab. The Home Page for the Sunny Morning Web displays. See Figure 2-17.

Figure 2-17 ◀
Web page
displayed in
Internet
Explorer
window

text appears in
orange color

scroll down to view
footer information at
bottom of page

your
default
font
might
be
different

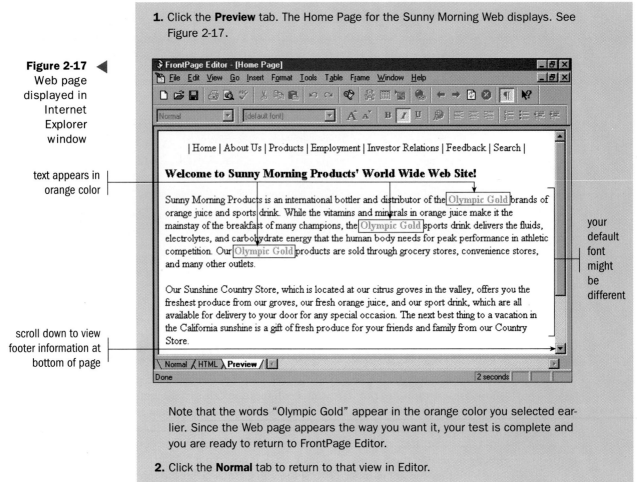

Note that the words "Olympic Gold" appear in the orange color you selected earlier. Since the Web page appears the way you want it, your test is complete and you are ready to return to FrontPage Editor.

2. Click the **Normal** tab to return to that view in Editor.

Later in the tutorial, you will use Internet Explorer to test other features you add to the Home Page of the Sunny Morning Web.

Printing a Web Page

Printing a Web page is helpful when you want a hard copy for your review. Amanda wants you to print a copy of the Home Page for the Sunny Morning Web site so that the two of you can review the work you've done thus far.

To print a Web page:

1. With the Home Page still displayed using the Normal tab in the Editor window, click the **Print** button 🖨 on the Standard toolbar. The Print dialog box opens.

TROUBLE? If the Home Page is displayed using the Preview tab, the Print button is dimmed and you are unable to print the Web page. Click the Normal tab to display the Web page for printing, and then repeat Step 1.

2. Click the **OK** button to print the Home Page.

With the printed page in hand, you are ready to review your work with Amanda.

Closing a Web Page

When you are finished working on a Web page, you can close it. This removes it from FrontPage Editor. The file remains stored on your disk according to the filename and title you saved it as. Now that you have successfully created and printed the Home Page for Sunny Morning Products, you are ready to close this Web page.

To close a Web page:

1. Click the **Close** button ☒ on the FrontPage Editor document window in which the Web page is displayed. Do *not* close the FrontPage Editor program window. You have not made any changes since the last save, so the FrontPage Editor document window simply closes without a Web page displayed.

   TROUBLE? If you made changes to the Web page since you last saved it, the FrontPage Editor message box opens. Click the Yes button to save your changes, and then the document window will close automatically.

Quick Check

1. List the three different methods that you can use to access the formatting commands in FrontPage Editor.

2. Which level of headings available for a Web page indicates the largest font size?

3. List the three alignments for text on a Web page.

4. Applying boldface or italics to text changes the font's _____.

5. True or False: A word that is spelled correctly, but is not in Editor's dictionary, appears as a misspelled word when you perform a spell check.

6. True or False: You use FrontPage Explorer to test the appearance of your Web page.

7. True or False: Closing a Web page deletes it from your open Web.

Now that you've learned how to format the contents of a Web page, you are ready to revise the existing Home Page for the Sunny Morning Products Web site to make it more interesting to potential customers.

SESSION

2.3

In this session you will learn how to revise a Web page by adding content and features to an existing page. You will learn how to change the background color, how to include both a background image and sound, how to include a graphic image as a logo, and how to add a horizontal rule and a marquee to a Web page. In addition, you will learn the significance of META tags and how to insert corresponding keywords that can be used by search engines to help users locate a Web site on the WWW.

Revising a Web Page

Once you have created a Web page, you can add, delete, or change its contents using the same text-editing features you used to create the initial Web page. Amanda had you include the basic content information in re-creating the Home Page for Sunny Morning Products. Now she wants you to revise the completed Web page by including image and sound files to give the Web page a more professional appearance. In order to begin revising the Web page, you need to open it.

Opening a Web Page

Once you have created, saved, and closed a Web page, you need to open it again before you begin revising it. You can open a Web page from FrontPage Explorer or from FrontPage Editor. Recall that you previously opened the Home Page by double-clicking the Home Page icon in FrontPage Explorer to start FrontPage Editor. If FrontPage Editor already was your active program, you could have simply opened the Web page and started working on it.

During your meeting with Amanda, you discussed additional changes that would improve the content and appearance of the current Sunny Morning Web. With her suggestions in mind, you are ready to continue working on the Home Page. Since FrontPage Editor is currently your active program, you can open the file for the Home Page and begin working.

To open an existing Web page in FrontPage Editor:

1. Make sure your Student Disk is still in drive A or the appropriate drive, the Sunny Morning Web is open, and FrontPage Editor is your active program without a Web page displayed in the document window.

   TROUBLE? If FrontPage Editor is not your active program, click the FrontPage Editor program button on the taskbar or click the Show FrontPage Editor button on the Standard toolbar in FrontPage Explorer.

2. Click the **Open** button on the Standard toolbar to open the Open dialog box. See Figure 2-18. Notice that this dialog box displays both the filename and the title of the Web page for your reference.

Figure 2-18 ◄
Open
dialog box

double-click filename
to open Web page

Web page title

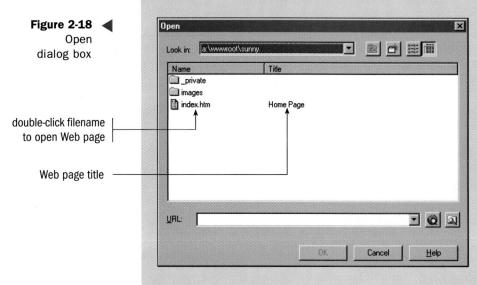

3. Double-click the **index.htm** filename to open the Home Page of the Sunny Web in FrontPage Editor.

   TROUBLE? If your Web contains the filename default.htm rather than index.htm, double-click the default.htm filename.

Changing the Background Color

Like other features of a Web page, the background color can make the page more attractive and easier to read. If you don't specify a background color in a Web page, then the default background color is gray when displaying a Web page using Internet Explorer. You specify a Web page background color using the BGCOLOR parameter within the body tag of the HTML code. The gray default background appears when no BGCOLOR tag is included in the HTML code. You can change the background color to any desired color that is available. When choosing a background color for a Web page, make sure that it coordinates with the color of the text. You might have to try several colors before you find one that provides the look you want for your Web page.

When you initially created the Home Page for Sunny Morning Products, FrontPage Editor automatically assigned the page a background color of white, rather than not specifying a color at all, which would have resulted in the default gray background. The reason for this is that a white background usually provides a better contrast than a gray one. When using FrontPage, if you want your Web page to have a background color other than white, you need to change its color.

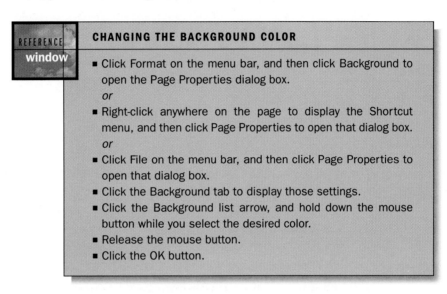

REFERENCE window

CHANGING THE BACKGROUND COLOR

■ Click Format on the menu bar, and then click Background to open the Page Properties dialog box.
or
■ Right-click anywhere on the page to display the Shortcut menu, and then click Page Properties to open that dialog box.
or
■ Click File on the menu bar, and then click Page Properties to open that dialog box.
■ Click the Background tab to display those settings.
■ Click the Background list arrow, and hold down the mouse button while you select the desired color.
■ Release the mouse button.
■ Click the OK button.

Although Amanda feels that white is a good background color, she wants you to try another color to see if it is more attractive for the Home Page.

To change the background color of a Web page:

1. Click **File** on the menu bar, and then click **Page Properties** to open the Page Properties dialog box.

2. Click the **Background** tab to display the background settings. See Figure 2-19. Notice that the background color is currently set to white.

Figure 2-19 ◄
Background
settings

current background
color

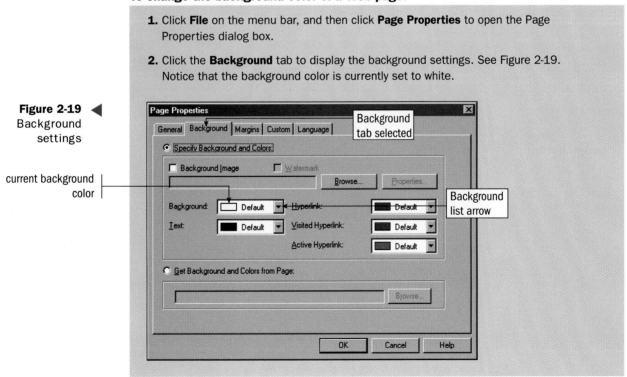

Page Properties

General | Background | Margins | Custom | Language |

○ Specify Background and Colors:

□ Background Image   □ Watermark

Browse...   Properties...

Background: □ Default   Hyperlink: ■ Default

Text: ■ Default   Visited Hyperlink: ■ Default

Active Hyperlink: ■ Default

○ Get Background and Colors from Page:

Browse...

OK   Cancel   Help

Background tab selected

Background list arrow

3. Click the **Background** list arrow and hold down the mouse button to display the list of available color selections. See Figure 2-20. You select a color by pointing to the desired color while continuing to hold down the mouse button.

Figure 2-20 ◀
List of available
background
colors

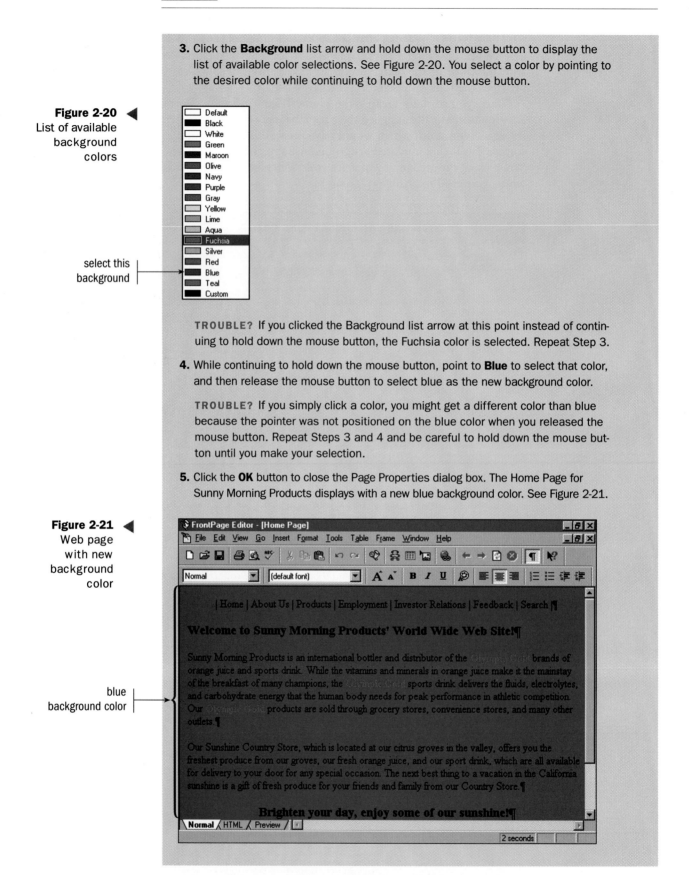

select this
background

TROUBLE? If you clicked the Background list arrow at this point instead of continuing to hold down the mouse button, the Fuchsia color is selected. Repeat Step 3.

4. While continuing to hold down the mouse button, point to **Blue** to select that color, and then release the mouse button to select blue as the new background color.

TROUBLE? If you simply click a color, you might get a different color than blue because the pointer was not positioned on the blue color when you released the mouse button. Repeat Steps 3 and 4 and be careful to hold down the mouse button until you make your selection.

5. Click the **OK** button to close the Page Properties dialog box. The Home Page for Sunny Morning Products displays with a new blue background color. See Figure 2-21.

Figure 2-21 ◀
Web page
with new
background
color

blue
background color

Although the blue background looks nice, the new color doesn't contrast enough with the black text. You could change the text to a lighter color with better contrast or choose a more appropriate background color. Another option is to select the default color. After discussing several other potential background colors with Amanda, you decide to set the background color to the default to see how it looks.

To select the default background color:

1. Click **File** on the menu bar, click **Page Properties**, and then click the **Background** tab to select those settings.

2. Click the **Background** list arrow, hold down the mouse button, point to **Default**, and then release the mouse button.

3. Click the **OK** button. The Home Page appears again with a white background color, which is the default color.

Although the text of the Web page is much easier to read with the default background color, the page lacks zest. Amanda explains that there is another way to improve the appearance of a Web page—by using a background image.

Selecting a Background Image

Another way to enhance the appearance of a Web page is to use a background image. FrontPage contains various graphic (*.GIF) files from which you can select a background image. If you have a photo or other image you want to use as a background, you can use that file instead. When FrontPage created your Sunny Morning Web, it automatically established an images folder. Recall from Tutorial 1 that the images folder is a convenient place to store all the images organized for your Web site.

REFERENCE window

SELECTING A BACKGROUND IMAGE

- Click Format on the menu bar, and then click Background to display those settings.
  or
- Right-click anywhere on the page to display the Shortcut menu, click Page Properties, and then click the Background tab.
  or
- Click File on the menu bar, click Page Properties, and then click the Background tab.
- Click the Background Image check box, and then click the Browse button to open the Select Background Image dialog box.
- Click the Clip Art button, click the Clip Art tab, and then click Web Backgrounds.
- Scroll to the desired background image, and then click it.
- Click the Insert button to return to the Page Properties dialog box, and then click the OK button.

Amanda asks you to insert the ocean themes background image to enhance the appearance of the Sunny Morning Web Home Page. Amanda instructs you to store all the images in the images folder that is provided as part of the FrontPage Web.

To select a background image:

1. Click **File** on the menu bar, click **Page Properties**, then click the **Background** tab to display those settings.

2. Click the **Background Image** check box to select it, and then click the **Browse** button. The Select Background Image dialog box opens.

   The buttons in the Select Background Image dialog box enable you to select a background image from the current FrontPage Web, another file location, or the FrontPage Clip Art collection.

3. Click the **Clip Art** button to open the Microsoft Clip Gallery 3.0 dialog box.

4. Click the **Clip Art** tab, scroll down the list until you see Web Backgrounds, and then click **Web Backgrounds** to display the available background image selections in the contents window. See Figure 2-22.

Figure 2-22 ◀
FrontPage clip
art background
image
selections

click to select
background
image from
available choices

selected background
image name

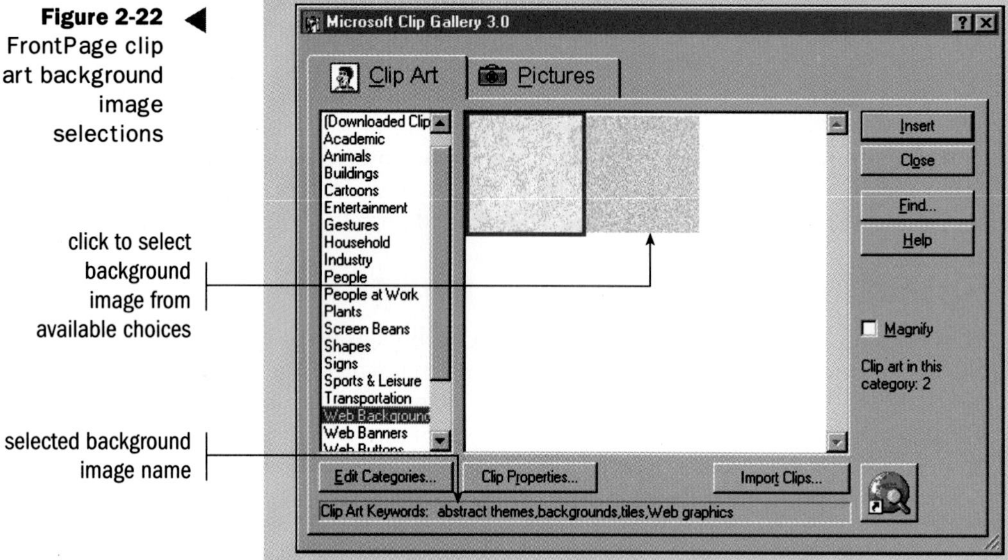

TROUBLE? Depending on your installation of FrontPage, you might see more background images than what is shown in Figure 2-22.

4. Click the **ocean themes** background, and then click the **Insert** button. The Select Background Image dialog box closes, and the Page Properties dialog box reappears.

5. Click the **OK** button to close the Page Properties dialog box. The Home Page for Sunny Morning Products reappears with the ocean themes background.

Although you are sure that Amanda would be satisfied with the professional look of this background choice, you need to ensure that this change looks good when viewed in your browser window. Before you confirm the appearance of the Web page using Internet Explorer, however, you need to place a copy of the GIF file for the background image in your Web. You do this by specifying your Web site's images folder in the Save Embedded Files dialog box. Keep in mind that you do not need to specify the entire pathname for the file, only the relative pathname within your current Web. FrontPage Explorer keeps track of the pathname that specifies the location of the current Web. You are ready to test your latest changes to the Home Page by viewing it in the Internet Explorer window.

To test background image changes using Internet Explorer:

1. Click the **Preview in Browser** button 🔍 on the Standard toolbar. The FrontPage Editor message box opens.

   Before you switch to Internet Explorer, you need to place a copy of the GIF file for your background image in the images folder of your Web.

2. Click the **OK** button to open the Save Embedded Files dialog box.

3. Click the **Change Folder** button, click the **images** folder, and then click the **OK** button. Now images/ appears as the folder name for the file WB00760_.gif, which is the filename assigned by FrontPage for the ocean themes background image. See Figure 2-23.

Figure 2-23 ◀
Save Embedded
Files dialog box

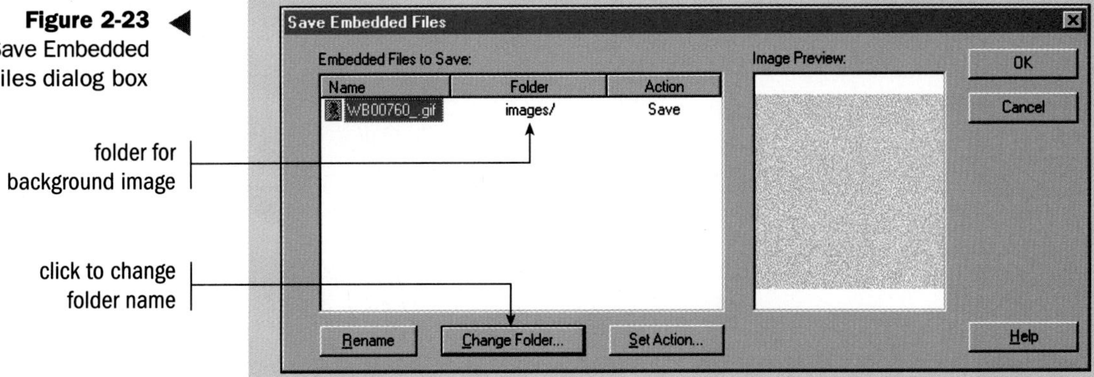

folder for
background image

click to change
folder name

TROUBLE? If the filename for your image is different, this is not a problem. FrontPage determines the filename for your selection.

4. Click the **OK** button to save the GIF file in the images folder of the Web. The Home Page opens in the Internet Explorer window. Notice the appearance of the ocean themes background.

5. Click the **FrontPage Editor** program button on the taskbar to return to the FrontPage Editor window.

Your test of the background image was a success; it appeared as you expected it to and improved the appearance of your Home Page. Now, Amanda wants you to make the background even more distinctive by adding the Sunny Morning Products logo.

Adding Inline Images

Graphic images add to the visual appearance of a Web page. These images are stored in separate files and are used with your Web pages. Two of the most popular formats for graphic images files are GIF and JPG (or JPEG). Usually, GIF files are smaller and download more quickly than JPG files, whereas JPG files usually provide a better-quality image. Most Web browsers are designed to display images that are created using either of these graphic file formats.

Graphic files are used to provide either an inline image or an external image. An **inline image** is one that appears within the text of your Web page. This is the most frequently used type of image. The Sunny Morning Products logo that you viewed in Tutorial 1 (see Figure 1-5) is an example of an inline image. In contrast, an **external image** is one in which the entire Web page displays as the image. Before you can include either image in a Web page, you must obtain the file containing the image. There are two ways to do this: you can use either the Image Composer, which is a program included with FrontPage, or a separate graphics program. Clip art is another good source of graphic images. In these tutorials you will use graphic files that have already been created for you.

REFERENCE window

ADDING AN INLINE IMAGE

- Click the location on the page where you want to place the image.
- Click the Insert Image button on the Standard toolbar.
  or
- Click Insert on the menu bar, and then click Image to open the Image dialog box.
- Select the desired image file from the appropriate source.
- Click the OK button to complete the image selection.
- Click the Save button to save the Web page and open the Save Embedded Files dialog box for a new image.
- Select images as the desired folder.
- Click the OK button to save the image file for use with the Web.

Amanda has already created a graphic image of the Sunny Morning Products logo. The logo has been saved in the Tutorial.02/images folder as an image file. Amanda wants you to add this inline image to the top of the Home Page so that users see it as soon as they open the Web site.

To add an inline image to a Web page:

1. Make sure your Student Disk is in drive A or the appropriate drive on your computer.

2. If necessary, click to the left of the **navigation bar**, press the **Enter** key to insert a new line above the navigation bar, and then click the new paragraph. The insertion point now appears at the location where you want to add the image.

3. Click the **Insert Image** button on the Standard toolbar to open the Image dialog box, and then click the **Select a file on your computer** button to open the Select File dialog box.

4. Click the **Look in** list arrow, click drive A or the appropriate drive for your Student Disk, double-click the **Tutorial.02** folder, and then double-click the **images** folder. See Figure 2-24.

Figure 2-24 ◀
Select File
dialog box

folder containing
available images

click to select
logo image

image file types

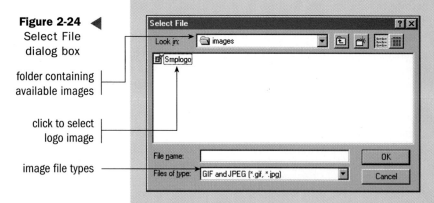

5. Click the **Smplogo.gif** file, click the **OK** button to place the logo image on the Web page, and then if necessary, click the image on the Web page to select it. See Figure 2-25. Since the logo is now located where the navigation bar was originally positioned, the current paragraph alignment—centered—is applied to the image. You prefer to have the logo located to the left of the heading.

Figure 2-25 ◀
Inline image
inserted on
Web page

logo added with
centered alignment ⎯⎯⎯⎯⎯⎯⎯⎯⎯

Image toolbar
displays when an
image is selected ⎯⎯⎯⎯⎯⎯

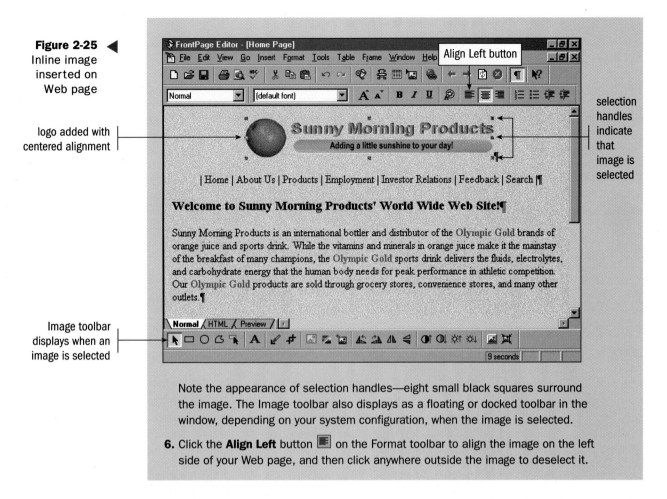

selection
handles
indicate
that
image is
selected

Note the appearance of selection handles—eight small black squares surround
the image. The Image toolbar also displays as a floating or docked toolbar in the
window, depending on your system configuration, when the image is selected.

6. Click the **Align Left** button 🖳 on the Format toolbar to align the image on the left
side of your Web page, and then click anywhere outside the image to deselect it.

Keep in mind that, depending on the transmission speed from the Web server to the
user's browser, there may be a delay before an image appears on a Web page. This is
common when the page is accessed from a remote Web server. While the image is being
transferred from the server for display in the browser window, an alternative text message
displays. **Alternative text** is a descriptive message that identifies an image on a Web page
and is an optional feature that you can include on a page. Its primary purpose is to inform
the user that an image file is being transmitted to the browser but has not yet arrived.
Alternative text also displays when you move the pointer on top of an image, after the
image is displayed in the browser window. Alternative text that you add to a Web page
consists of HTML code.

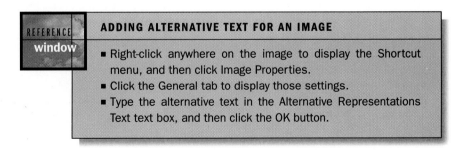

REFERENCE
window

ADDING ALTERNATIVE TEXT FOR AN IMAGE

■ Right-click anywhere on the image to display the Shortcut
 menu, and then click Image Properties.
■ Click the General tab to display those settings.
■ Type the alternative text in the Alternative Representations
 Text text box, and then click the OK button.

Amanda wants you to include alternative text for the Sunny Morning Products logo.

To add alternative text for an image:

1. Right-click the **logo image** to display the Shortcut menu, and then click **Image Properties** to open the Image Properties dialog box.

2. If necessary, click the **General** tab to display those settings. See Figure 2-26.

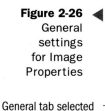

Figure 2-26
General
settings
for Image
Properties

General tab selected

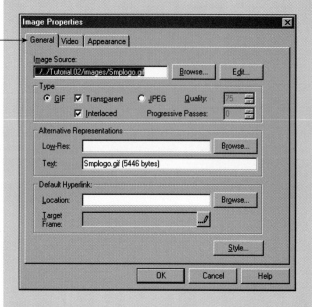

3. Select the default text in the Text box in the Alternative Representations section, type **Sunny Morning Products Logo** in the Text box, and then click the **OK** button. The Image Properties dialog box closes, and you return to the Home Page.

4. Click the **Save** button 🖫 on the Standard toolbar. The Save Embedded Files dialog box opens. You use the same method as previously used to save a background image file to save an image.

5. Click the **Change Folder** button to open that dialog box, click the **images** folder to select it, then click the **OK** button to return to the Save Embedded Files dialog box.

6. Click the **OK** button to save this GIF file in the images folder. After a few moments, the file is saved and your Web is updated.

With the image specified and saved, you are ready to test it by viewing it in the browser window.

To test inline image changes using Internet Explorer:

1. Click the **Preview** tab to switch to the Internet Explorer document window and display the Home Page with the inline image.

2. Place the pointer on the Sunny Morning Products logo. After a few moments, the alternative text—Sunny Morning Products Logo—appears. See Figure 2-27. After a moment, the alternative text disappears.

Figure 2-27
Alternative text
for logo image

pointer positioned
on top of image

alternative text box
(your text box might
look different)

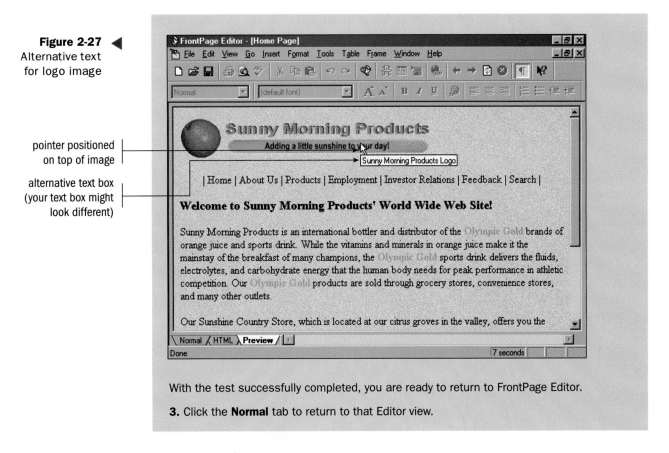

With the test successfully completed, you are ready to return to FrontPage Editor.

3. Click the **Normal** tab to return to that Editor view.

Using Horizontal Lines

Horizontal lines or rules on a Web page are often used to provide a visual break between sections of text. After inserting a horizontal line, you can change its characteristics by adjusting its length, width, and color.

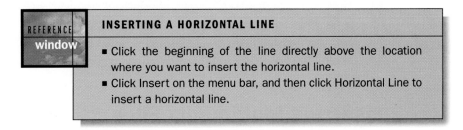

REFERENCE window	**INSERTING A HORIZONTAL LINE**
	▪ Click the beginning of the line directly above the location where you want to insert the horizontal line.
	▪ Click Insert on the menu bar, and then click Horizontal Line to insert a horizontal line.

To improve the readability of the Home Page, Amanda wants you to insert a horizontal line above the footer. This line provides a visual break between the main body of the text and the footer information.

To insert a horizontal line:

1. Press **Ctrl + End** to move to the end of the Sunny Morning Products Home Page.

2. Click before the word **Last** at the beginning of the footer information text line. The insertion point is now positioned directly above the location where you want to place the horizontal line.

3. Click **Insert** on the menu bar, and then click **Horizontal Line** to place a horizontal line on the page to separate the main body and the footer information.

With the horizontal line inserted, you want to make it appear more visible on the Home Page. You decide to make the line shorter and wider.

To change horizontal line settings:

1. Click anywhere on the **horizontal line** to select it.

2. Right-click the **horizontal line** to display the Shortcut menu, and then click **Horizontal Line Properties** to open the Horizontal Line Properties dialog box. See Figure 2-28.

Figure 2-28 ◀
Horizontal Line Properties dialog box

specifies width of horizontal line

specifies height of horizontal line

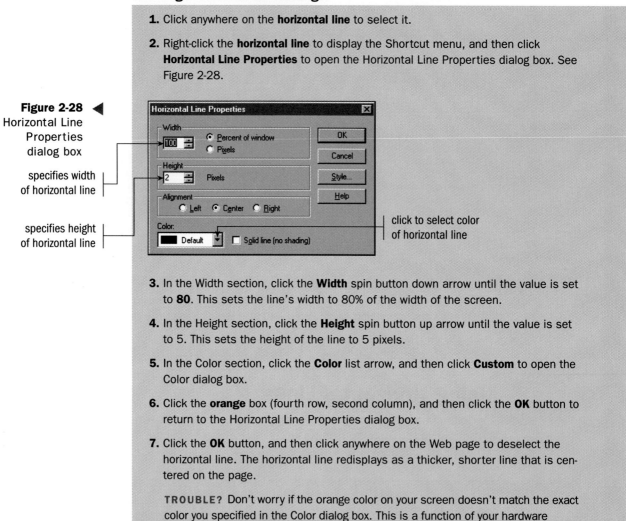

click to select color of horizontal line

3. In the Width section, click the **Width** spin button down arrow until the value is set to **80**. This sets the line's width to 80% of the width of the screen.

4. In the Height section, click the **Height** spin button up arrow until the value is set to 5. This sets the height of the line to 5 pixels.

5. In the Color section, click the **Color** list arrow, and then click **Custom** to open the Color dialog box.

6. Click the **orange** box (fourth row, second column), and then click the **OK** button to return to the Horizontal Line Properties dialog box.

7. Click the **OK** button, and then click anywhere on the Web page to deselect the horizontal line. The horizontal line redisplays as a thicker, shorter line that is centered on the page.

TROUBLE? Don't worry if the orange color on your screen doesn't match the exact color you specified in the Color dialog box. This is a function of your hardware setup. The color should appear correctly when viewed in the Web browser window.

Inserting Multimedia Files

Another way to add interest to your Web page is through the use of multimedia files. Multimedia files include graphic images, video clips, and sounds. The Sunny Morning Products logo that you added to the Home Page is an example of a multimedia file. Adding sound, such as music, to a Web page can make the page much more appealing and exciting. The disadvantage to sound files, however, is that they are often very large, which means they can take a long time to download. Two of the most popular sound file types are Wave Sound (*.WAV) and Midi Sequencer (*.MID). The WAV files usually produce a better-quality sound than the MID files do. However, the MID files are usually smaller than the WAV files and therefore download from the Web server more quickly. Like GIF and JPG image files, the multimedia files for sounds are also usually stored in the images folder of your FrontPage Web. Recall that this helps keep all the multimedia files for your Web organized in one place.

ADDING A BACKGROUND SOUND

- Click File on the menu bar, and then click Page Properties to open that dialog box.
  or
- Right-click anywhere on the page to display the Shortcut menu, and then click Page Properties to open that dialog box.
- Click the General tab.
- Click the Browse button in the Background Sound section.
- Select the desired multimedia sound file. Click the OK button to complete the file selection.
- Click the Save button to save the Web page and open the Save Embedded Files dialog box for a new image.
- Click the Change Folder button, select the images folder, and then click the OK button.
- Click the OK button to save the image file.

Amanda wants you to add a sound file that plays music when users access the Home Page of the Sunny Morning Products Web site. Since she wants to keep the time involved in downloading the sound file to a minimum, Amanda specifically suggests one that should download quickly.

To add a background sound to a Web page:

1. Click **File** on the menu bar, and then click **Page Properties** to open that dialog box and make sure that the General tab is selected.

2. Click the **Browse** button in the Background Sound section to open the Background Sound dialog box.

3. Click the **Select a file on your computer** button 🖳 to open the Select File dialog box with a list of the files and folders in the Sunny Web.

   Now select the folder where the background sound file is located.

4. Click the **Look in** list arrow, make sure that drive A or the appropriate drive for your Student Disk appears in the Look in list box, double-click the **Tutorial.02** folder, and then double-click the **images** folder.

   Notice that filenames don't appear in the File name list or text boxes. This is because the file for the Sunny Morning Web is a MID file and not a WAV file, which is the default file type.

5. Click the **Files of type** list arrow to display a list of available sound file types. See Figure 2-29.

Figure 2-29 ◀
List of available
file types for a
background
sound

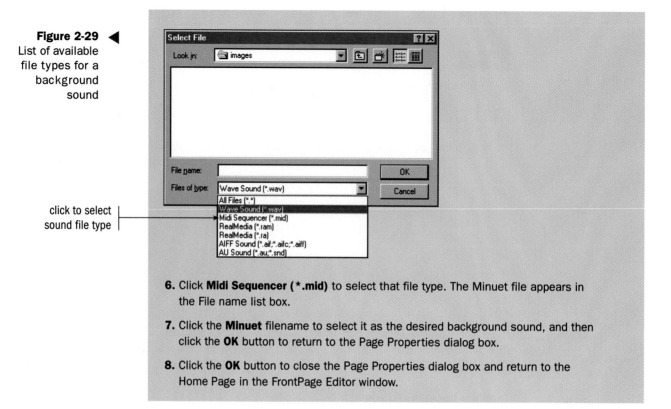

click to select
sound file type

6. Click **Midi Sequencer (*.mid)** to select that file type. The Minuet file appears in the File name list box.

7. Click the **Minuet** filename to select it as the desired background sound, and then click the **OK** button to return to the Page Properties dialog box.

8. Click the **OK** button to close the Page Properties dialog box and return to the Home Page in the FrontPage Editor window.

Note that you do not hear the desired background sound when you return to the Web page. The sound is played only when you open the page using your Web browser. You test the background sound by viewing the Home Page using Internet Explorer.

To test a background sound using Internet Explorer:

1. Click the **Preview** tab to switch to the Internet Explorer window. The Home Page opens in the window and plays the Minuet. The default is set for the background sound to play continuously, which is the infinite option.

   TROUBLE? If you do not hear the background sound, make sure that your computer is equipped with a sound card and that the speakers are turned on. If you still do not hear the sound, check with your instructor or technical support person.

   TROUBLE? Don't worry if the music sounds like it is playing too slowly on your computer. This is a function of your hardware and software setup.

2. Click the **Normal** tab to switch back to that Editor window and to stop the background sound. Because you tested the background sound using the Preview tab, the Internet Explorer's Stop button is disabled and you can't use it to stop the music.

   With this test completed successfully, you are ready to save the background sound file in the Sunny Morning Web.

3. Click the **Save** button 🖫 on the Standard toolbar to open the Save Embedded Files dialog box.

4. Click the **Change Folder** button to open that dialog box, click the **images** folder to select it, and then click the **OK** button to return to the Save Embedded Files dialog box. This places the background sound in the same Web folder as the other multimedia files.

5. Click the **OK** button to save the file and return to the Normal view in the Editor.

The sound file loop setting can be changed to specify the number of times you want to repeat a background sound. You can set this as an explicit number of times or as the default of infinite, which repeats the sound continuously. Now that you've added the background sound to the Sunny Morning Home Page, you set it to play only once.

To adjust the loop setting for a background sound:

1. Right-click anywhere on the Web page to display the Shortcut menu, click **Page Properties** to open the Page Properties dialog box, and then, if necessary, click the **General** tab to display those settings. See Figure 2-30.

Figure 2-30 ◄
General settings for page properties

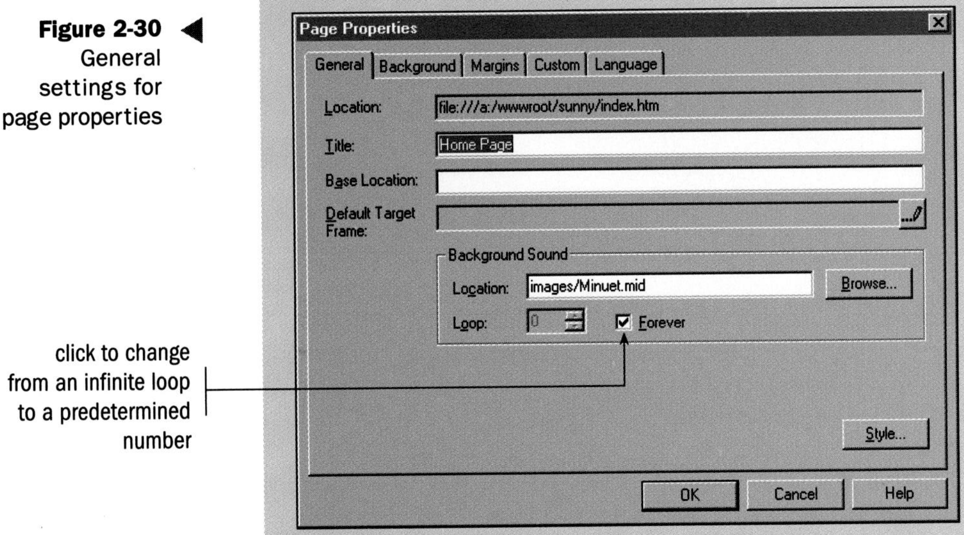

click to change from an infinite loop to a predetermined number

2. In the Background Sound section, click the **Forever** check box to deselect an infinite loop and enable the Loop text box.

3. Type **1** in the Loop text box, and then click the **OK** button to close the Page Properties dialog box.

4. Click the **Save** button 🖫 on the Standard toolbar to save the change before you test it. Now that you've adjusted the number of times the sound is played, you switch back to Internet Explorer with its toolbars to test the setting.

5. Click the **Preview in Browser** button 🗔 on the Standard toolbar to switch to Internet Explorer. The background sound plays again.

6. Click the **Refresh** button 🗔 on the Internet Explorer toolbar to reload the Home Page and repeat the sound. Whenever you refresh a Web page, it is reloaded into the Web browser and, in this example, causes the background sound to repeat.

7. Click the **Stop** button 🗔 on the Internet Explorer toolbar to stop the music.

8. Click the **FrontPage Editor** program button on the taskbar to switch back to the Editor.

Amanda is pleased with the enhancements you made to the Home Page for Sunny Morning Products using multimedia files. There is one more feature that she wants you to add to make the page more appealing.

Using a Marquee

Another way to draw the reader's attention to information on a Web page is to put specific text in motion so that it scrolls across the page. A **marquee** is a text box on a Web page that displays a horizontally scrolling message. You can create a marquee from existing text or enter new text specifically intended for the marquee. Keep in mind that scrolling marquees should be used sparingly because they can easily overpower a Web page and distract users.

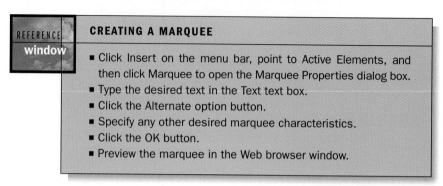

REFERENCE window

CREATING A MARQUEE

- Click Insert on the menu bar, point to Active Elements, and then click Marquee to open the Marquee Properties dialog box.
- Type the desired text in the Text text box.
- Click the Alternate option button.
- Specify any other desired marquee characteristics.
- Click the OK button.
- Preview the marquee in the Web browser window.

Amanda wants you to create a marquee that draws more attention to the phrase, "Brighten your day, enjoy some of our sunshine!" Turning this text into a marquee will cause the words to move back and forth across the screen and will draw additional attention to this vision statement.

To create a marquee:

1. Select the text **Brighten your day, enjoy some of our sunshine!**

2. Click **Insert** on the menu bar, point to **Active Elements**, and then click **Marquee** to open the Marquee Properties dialog box. See Figure 2-31. Notice that the text you selected appears in the Text text box.

Figure 2-31 ◄
Marquee
Properties
dialog box

click to move
text across screen

change current
value to go

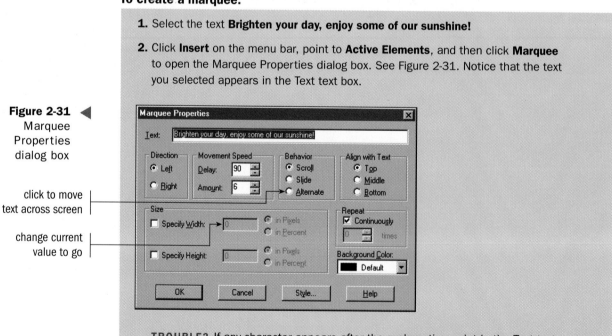

TROUBLE? If any character appears after the exclamation point in the Text text box, you should delete it. This just means that you selected the hard return at the end of the paragraph in the Web page. Continue with Step 3.

3. In the Behavior section, click the **Alternate** option button. Selecting this setting causes the text to move back and forth across your screen.

4. In the Size section, click the **Specify Width** check box to select it, click the **Specify Width** text box and type **90**, and then click the **in Percent** option button to select that option. This limits the width of the marquee to 90% of the screen width.

5. In the Background Color section, click the **Background Color** list arrow, and then click **Custom** to open the Color dialog box.

6. Select the **orange** box (fourth row, second column), click the **OK** button to return to the Marquee Properties dialog box, and then click the **OK** button again. The Page Properties dialog box closes and an orange marquee, outlined by a dashed line, surrounds the heading on the Web page. However, no movement is shown. You need to switch to Internet Explorer to test this feature.

7. Click the **Save** button 🖫 on the Standard toolbar, and then click the **Preview** tab to view the page in the Internet Explorer window.

8. Scroll to the bottom of the page to view the marquee. The text now moves back and forth in the orange marquee.

9. Click the **Normal** tab to switch back to that view in Editor.

You have finished revising the content of the Home Page for Sunny Morning Products. This completes the portion of your training devoted to developing a Web page. Both you and Amanda are pleased with the revised content and appearance of this Web page. However, Amanda wants to include some additional information that will help people using the WWW locate the Sunny Morning Products Web site.

Using META Tags

A Web site can be an effective marketing tool for a company only if users are aware that the site exists in the first place. There are many ways to promote a Web site so users will be able to find it. **Indexing** refers to the process of ensuring that a Web site is listed with WWW search engines, whereas **indexes** are the databases that Web users access to find the appropriate Web site references and resources. There are different types of indexes on the Web. Some indexes, such as Yahoo, list Web sites by category, whereas other indexes, such as Web Crawler, are search engines that "search" the Web for new URLs and Web sites and catalog their related references. Most indexes have an area, organized much like a form, in which Web designers specify the desired URL they want listed on the Web. Certain tags are commonly used to assist search engines in building their indexes. One such tag is called a META tag. A **META tag** is HTML text that signifies that a particular Web site should be added to a search engine's index. Each META tag includes several specific tag arguments, including subject, author, content, description, and keywords. The description and keywords tags are most useful in providing information for indexing purposes. META tags are placed within the HEAD tag and before the TITLE tag. FrontPage Editor automatically creates two additional META tags; one that indicates that the Web page was created using FrontPage and the other indicates that the Web page is an "http" page and specifies the character set that is used by the page. META variables do *not* change the appearance of the Web page but, rather, are available for use only by search engines.

In order to promote the Sunny Morning Web, Amanda wants you to include indexing information in the Home Page so the site can be added to the indexes of various search engines. You add the META tags for description and keywords to the Home Page.

To insert META tags:

1. Right-click anywhere on the Web page to display the Shortcut menu, click **Page Properties** to open that dialog box, and then click the **Custom** tab to display those settings.

2. In the User Variables section, click the **Add** button to open the User Meta Variable dialog box.

   TROUBLE? If you accidentally clicked the Add button in the System Variables (HTTP-EQUIV) section, that dialog box opens rather than the User Meta Variable dialog box. Click the Cancel button, and then click the Add button in the User Variables section. Continue with Step 3.

3. Type **description** in the Name text box, and then press the **Tab** key to advance to the Value text box.

4. With the insertion point in the Value text box, type **Sunny Morning Products is a leading producer of the Olympic Gold brands of orange juice and sports drink. Check out our Sunshine Country Store.** See Figure 2-32.

Figure 2-32 ◀
User Meta
Variable
dialog box

5. Click the **OK** button to return to the Page Properties dialog box. Notice that the text you just typed in the Name and Value text boxes appears under the Name and Value columns in the User Variables section. This confirms the META tags you added to your Web page.

6. Click the **Add** button to open the User Meta Variable dialog box again, type **keywords** in the Name text box, and then press the **Tab** key to advance to the Value text box.

7. Type **orange juice, sports drink, citrus products, gifts, holiday gifts, oranges, grapefruit** in the Value text box as the desired keywords.

8. Click the **OK** button to return to the Page Properties dialog box, and then click the **OK** button to close this dialog box and complete the specification.

It is helpful to view the META tags after you add them in order to better understand the exact information search engines look for to add your Web site to their indexes. Viewing META tags also allows you to confirm that the entries were correctly inserted in the HTML code because you don't see them displayed on the Web page in either the Editor or in the Internet Explorer window.

To view META tags in the HTML code:

1. Click the **HTML** tab to display the HTML code for the Sunny Morning Home Page, and then scroll to the top of the page. See Figure 2-33.

Figure 2-33
HTML META
tags for Sunny
Morning
Products
Home Page

user-defined META
tags used by
search engines

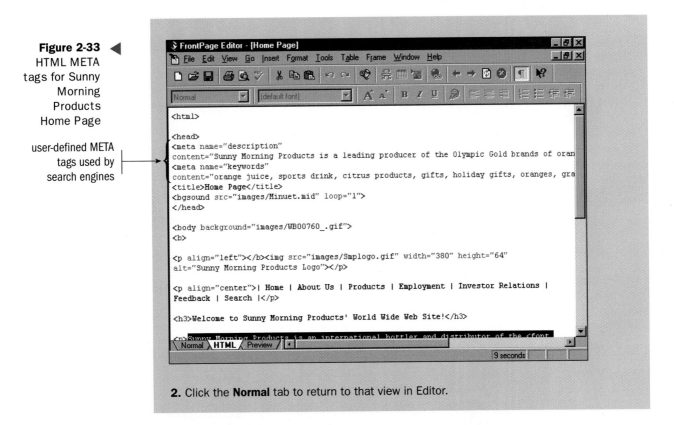

2. Click the **Normal** tab to return to that view in Editor.

You have confirmed that the META tags are included in your Web page and are available for indexing by the search engines.

Viewing HTML Code

Recall that FrontPage Editor produces the HTML code for your Web page. Your Web browser interprets this code when it displays the page. In creating the Home Page for Sunny Morning Products, you have used Editor to include a number of features that use different HTML tags. These features include using different paragraph styles, including multimedia files and using a marquee. For example, BGSOUND specifies the background sound while the ALIGN parameter of the P (paragraph) tag indicates the paragraph's alignment. The H3 tag specifies a heading and includes its alignment whereas the MARQUEE tag specifies its use on the page. FrontPage Editor selected each of these tags and their related parameters as you created this Home Page.

Amanda wants you to examine the HTML code for the Home Page so you have a better understanding of the code that FrontPage Editor created as you developed your Web page. As you learn more about HTML code, you may find that there are some options that must be entered directly as HTML code. Now you are ready to examine the HTML code created by Editor.

To view HTML code:

1. Press **Ctrl + Home** to go to the top of the Home Page.

2. Click the **HTML** tab to switch to that view in Editor and display the HTML code for the Home Page. See Figure 2-34.

Figure 2-34 ◀
Viewing the
first page of
HTML code
for the Home
Page

background sound
from specified file

logo image from
specified file

centered paragraph
for navigation bar

start of text
paragraph

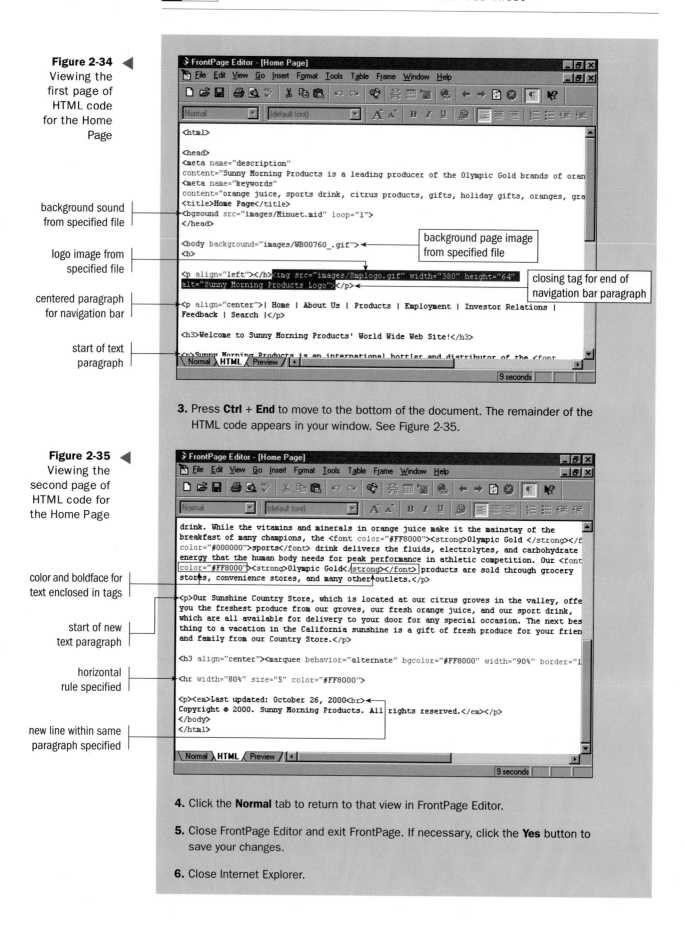

3. Press **Ctrl + End** to move to the bottom of the document. The remainder of the HTML code appears in your window. See Figure 2-35.

Figure 2-35 ◀
Viewing the
second page of
HTML code for
the Home Page

color and boldface for
text enclosed in tags

start of new
text paragraph

horizontal
rule specified

new line within same
paragraph specified

4. Click the **Normal** tab to return to that view in FrontPage Editor.

5. Close FrontPage Editor and exit FrontPage. If necessary, click the **Yes** button to save your changes.

6. Close Internet Explorer.

Quick Check

1. Describe the purpose of the images folder that is automatically created when you create a FrontPage Web.

2. The _____ color for a Web page should be coordinated with the color of the text on the page to provide good contrast.

3. True or False: FrontPage provides background images for your use.

4. A(n) _____ contains text that scrolls horizontally within the text box.

5. What is one common use of an inline image on a Web page?

6. Describe the purpose of a background sound.

7. _____ are used to supply information that is used by a search engine to make your Web site available to WWW users.

You are impressed with all of the code that FrontPage created. With the Home Page created, and its contents and features revised, you are well on your way to implementing the Web design for Sunny Morning Products. You are confident that the Home Page design meets the requirements that Andrew approved. Although the Home Page is only one page included in the Sunny Morning Web, it is the first one visitors see and it allows them to connect to the other Web pages.

Tutorial Assignments

Amanda is pleased with your development of the Home Page for the Sunny Morning Web. There are some additional tasks that she needs you to do to complete the Home Page, as well as some that will help you gain additional experience in developing future Web pages.

If necessary, start FrontPage Explorer, insert your Student Disk in drive A or the appropriate disk drive, and then do the following:

1. Start FrontPage and open the Sunny Morning Web and the new Home Page.

2. Add a horizontal line between the "Welcome to ..." heading and the first paragraph of the narrative text. Then change the line so it has the same size and color as the line you added at the bottom of the page in the tutorial.

3. Print the HTML code for the Home Page.

4. View the printed code and circle the HTML code that sets the background image and specifies the file for the background sound. (*Hint:* Reference the filenames for the multimedia files to help you find them.)

5. Locate and circle the META tags in the printout of the HTML code.

6. Reviewing your printout from Question 3, write down the HTML tag that is used with the "Welcome to ..." heading.

7. Save your changes.

8. Change the background for the Home Page to a colored background of your choice. What color did you select, and why?

9. Close the Web without saving changes, close FrontPage Editor, and then close FrontPage Explorer.

Case Problems

1. Preparing a Web Presence for Royal Hair Care Products   Royal Hair Care Products, established in 1984, has been a leader in hair-care products for women, men, and children for more than a dozen years. Current products include shampoos, conditioners, hair sprays, and styling gels. All products carry a 100% product-satisfaction guarantee. The company's newest offering is the Kuick Dry Reliable Solution that is applied to wet hair for instant drying. Kuick Dry is available in either a gel form or as a liquid spray to meet consumers' individual preferences. The product is easy to use and leaves hair feeling natural and manageable.

Recently, Nathan Dubois was hired by Valerie Suarez as an information systems intern and assigned to Royal's Web development team. Valerie wants Nathan to prepare a storyboard of their Web design and then create a Home Page for Royal Hair Care Products. Valerie and Nathan met with the rest of their Web design team members, who agreed that in addition to their Home Page, they want several other pages with the following information: (1) company profile, (2) latest company news, (3) employment opportunities, (4) customer feedback, and (5) keyword search. Valerie wants you to assist Nathan with the design and development activities for this Web page.

If necessary, start FrontPage Explorer, insert your Student Disk in drive A or the appropriate disk drive, and then do the following:

1. Prepare a planning analysis sheet for the Royal Web site.

2. Prepare a storyboard of the Web site that shows the planned Web pages and the expected hyperlinks from the Home Page.

3. Create the Royal Web site using FrontPage. Save all image and sound files included in the Web in the images folder that is created for this Web. The title of the Web is Royal Web and you will save it in the \wwwroot folder on your Student Disk.

4. Using FrontPage Editor, enter, edit, and spell check the following two paragraphs of content copy for the Home Page for the Royal Web:

   Royal Hair Care Products was established in 1984 and remains a leader in personal care products. Current products include shampoos, conditioners, hair sprays, and styling gels. We are committed to producing quality products for women, men, and children. Our products carry a 100% satisfaction guarantee. If you are not satisfied for any reason, you can return your purchase for a full refund.

   Our newest product is Kuick Dry Reliable Solution, which is applied to wet hair for instant drying. In the time it takes for you to finish your morning cup of coffee, your hair is dry, and you are on your way.

5. Create the heading "Welcome to the Royal Web Site. Join us in your quest for beautiful hair." and place it above the text you entered in Question 4. Select an appropriate font size and alignment for this heading, and make sure that the heading appears on a single line.

6. Create a navigation bar for the Home Page based on your design of the Web. Limit the navigation bar to a single line, and then center it on the Web page. Change the text in the navigation bar to bold and then change its color to blue.

7. Add footer information at the bottom of the page that includes a copyright symbol and the company name, and then on the next line, the words "Last updated" and a field that automatically updates the date and time that the Web page was last updated. (*Hint:* To add the date and time field, type the text, press the Spacebar, click Insert on the menu bar, and then click Timestamp.) Format the date as MM/DD/YY and the time with the hour and minutes. Format the footer information as bold and then change the color to blue.

8. Select an appropriate background image from those available in the Clip Art Gallery that comes with FrontPage, and then apply it to the Web page.

9. Place either the Royal01.gif or Royal02.gif file from the Tutorial.02/Royal folder as an inline image on the Web page.

10. Add at least one horizontal rule to the Web page with a length that is less than the entire width of the page and then change its color to blue.

11. Enter "The professional look for modern living!" as the slogan for Royal Hair Care Products, and place it in a scrolling marquee that is centered on the page. Select appropriate colors for the text and background of the marquee to coordinate with the logo colors.

12. Include the Quantum.mid file from the Tutorial.02/Royal folder as a background sound that repeats three times when the Web page is opened in Internet Explorer.

13. Create META descriptions and keywords and include them in the Home Page, and then save the Home Page in the Royal Web.

14. Test the Web page using the Preview tab. If necessary, return to the Normal tab and correct any errors, and then print the page.

15. Test the Web page in Internet Explorer. With the page displayed in the browser window, use the Print Screen key to capture the screen display to the Windows Clipboard. Open WordPad and use the Edit and Paste commands or Ctrl + V to paste the screen capture in WordPad, and then print this screen capture.

16. Close the WordPad document without saving it, and then close WordPad. Close Internet Explorer.

17. Use FrontPage to print the HTML code for the Home Page. Circle the META tags for the description and keywords and the tags used for the background image and sound.

18. Save your changes, and then close FrontPage Editor and FrontPage Explorer.

2. Developing a Web Site for Buffalo Trading Post Buffalo Trading Post (BTP) is a regional retail clothing business that specializes in buying, selling, and trading used clothing. The company buys all of its merchandise from customers who bring it to one of their trading post stores based on style, size, fabric, and garment condition. Although the company specializes in natural fabric clothing items, BTP also carries a limited inventory of polyester, acetate, Lycra, and other manufactured fibers to follow current styles and trends. BTP accepts clothing for resale only if it is in good condition. BTP attracts a loyal following of fashion enthusiasts and bargain hunters.

Karla Perez was recently hired by the president of the company, Donna Vargas, as a junior systems analyst and assigned to Buffalo's Web development team. Donna wants Karla to prepare a storyboard of their Web design and then create a Home Page for the BTP. Karla and Donna met with the rest of their Web design team. They agreed that in addition to their Home Page, they want several other pages with the following information about the BTP company: (1) who, (2) how, (3) what, (4) where, and (5) contact. Donna wants you to help Karla with these Web design and development activities.

If necessary, start FrontPage Explorer, insert your Student Disk in drive A or the appropriate disk drive, and then do the following:

1. Prepare a planning analysis sheet for the Buffalo Web site.

2. Prepare a storyboard of the Web site that shows the planned Web pages and the expected hyperlinks from the Home Page.

3. Create the Buffalo Web site using FrontPage. Save all image and sound files included in the Web in the images folder that is created for this Web. The title of the Web is Buffalo Web and you will save it in the \wwwroot folder on your Student Disk.

4. Using FrontPage Editor, write, enter, edit, and spell check at least two paragraphs of content copy for the Home Page for the Buffalo Web. You may use any available reference sources to help develop your content, including visiting several retail Web sites.

5. Create a heading, determine its appropriate size and alignment, and place it above the text you entered in Question 4.

6. Create a navigation bar for the Home Page, and then center it on the Web page. Change the color of the navigation bar to an appropriate color and change its style to bold.

7. Add footer information at the bottom of the page that includes copyright information with the copyright symbol, and the company name. On the next line of the footer, add the following line: "BTP™ is a registered trademark of Buffalo Trading Post." (*Hint:* Use the symbol set to insert the trademark character.) Boldface this information.

8. Change the background color of the Home Page to one that complements the text, and then apply it to the Web page.

9. Place either the Buffalo1.gif or Buffalo2.gif file from the Tutorial.02/Buffalo folder as an inline image on the Web page. Add alternative text to the logo that says "Buffalo Trading Post Logo."

10. Add at least one horizontal rule to the Web page. Its length should be less than the entire width of the page and its color should complement the rest of the Web page design.

11. Create a slogan for Buffalo Trading Post and place it in a scrolling marquee. Select appropriate colors for the marquee text and background. Format the text in the marquee as 16-point monospace font. (*Hint:* Click the Style button in the Marquee Properties dialog box, and then click the Font tab to change the marquee text font style.)

12. Use boldface, italics, and color as necessary to improve the appearance of the Web page.

13. Include either the Happy.mid or Cheers.mid file from the Tutorial.02/Buffalo folder as a background sound that repeats once when the Web page is opened in Internet Explorer.

14. Create META descriptions and keywords and include them in the Home Page.

15. Save this Home Page in the Buffalo Web.

16. Test the Web page using Internet Explorer. If necessary, return to FrontPage and correct any errors, and then print the page in Internet Explorer.

17. Use FrontPage to print the HTML code for the Home Page. Circle the META tags for the description and keywords and the tags used for the background image and sound.

18. Save your changes, and then close FrontPage Editor, FrontPage Explorer, and Internet Explorer.

3. Creating a Web Site for Pardon My Garden   Pardon My Garden is a growing chain of casual, full-service restaurants. Garden's moderately-priced menu features delicious dishes from a variety of locations around the world. Sophisticated consumer marketing research techniques are used to monitor customer satisfaction and evolving customer expectations. Pardon My Garden strives for leadership in its segment by utilizing technology as a competitive advantage. Since 1976, in-store computers have been used to assist in management of the restaurants. Restaurant support is provided from the corporate office, seven days a week, 24 hours a day. Management believes these information systems have positioned their business to support current needs as well as future growth.

A long-range information systems plan is prepared and reviewed annually with all levels of management. This plan prioritizes information systems projects based on business advantage criteria. Management's plan for the coming year includes developing a Web site. Shannon Taylor just completed her management intern orientation at the corporate offices of Pardon My Garden and was given her first job assignment working with Nolan Simmons in supporting end-user computing. Last week, Nolan's job responsibilities were increased to include managing the company's Web-development team. Nolan wants Shannon to help him prepare a storyboard of their Web design and then create a Home Page for Pardon My Garden. Nolan and Shannon just completed a meeting with the rest of their Web design team. They agreed that in addition to their Home Page, they want several other pages with the following information: (1) company profile, (2) restaurant menu, (3) franchise information, (4) employment opportunities, (5) customer feedback, and (6) keyword search. Nolan wants you to assist Shannon with their design and development activities.

If necessary, start FrontPage Explorer, insert your Student Disk in drive A or the appropriate disk drive, and then do the following:

1. Prepare a planning analysis sheet for the Garden Web site.

2. Prepare a storyboard of the Web site that shows the planned Web pages and the expected hyperlinks from the Home Page.

3. Create the Garden Web site using FrontPage. Save all image and sound files included in the Web in the images folder that is created for this Web. The title of the Web is Garden Web and you will save it in the \wwwroot folder on your Student Disk.

4. Using FrontPage Editor, enter, edit, and spell check the following content for the Home Page for the Garden Web:

   Value and variety are always on our menu! Where would you like to dine tonight? How about America, Mexico, or Italy? We've got delicious dishes from all these places, and more, each including the special Pardon My Garden touch.

   Pardon My Garden is a premier casual, full-service restaurant. Our moderately priced menu features favorite entrees from a variety of locations around the world that are sure to please you and your guests. Have a look . . . check us out . . . make a list . . . and you're ready to head to your local Garden!

5. Create the heading "Welcome to My Garden. Join us for food and fun!" and place it above the text you entered in Question 4. Change the font style to Arial by clicking the Change Font list arrow on the Format toolbar. Then select an appropriate size and alignment for this heading and a font size so the heading appears on a single line.

6. Create a navigation bar for the Home Page based on your design of the Web and limit it to a single line on your Web page. Center the bar on the Web page. Use square brackets ([ ]) to enclose your navigation items. Change the navigation bar color to purple.

7. Add footer information at the bottom of the page that includes the copyright information with the copyright symbol and the company name. On the second line add the text "Last updated" and then add a date field that identifies the date when the page was last edited. (*Hint:* To add the date field, type the text, press the Spacebar, click Insert on the menu bar, and then click Timestamp.) Format the date with the day of the week, and the full date with the month spelled out.

8. Select an appropriate background image from the Clip Art Gallery that comes with FrontPage and then apply it to the Web page.

9. Place either the Garden01.gif or Garden02.gif file from the Tutorial.02/Garden folder as an inline image after the last paragraph on the Web page. Center the image.

10. Add at least one horizontal rule to the Web page, with a length less than the entire width of the page and an appropriate color that complements the rest of the Web page.

11. Enter "Come to My Garden for food and fun!" as the slogan for Pardon My Garden and place it in a sliding marquee. Select appropriate colors for the text and background of the marquee that coordinates with the colors in the logo. Then use the Style button in the Marquee Properties dialog box to change the font of the marquee text to 16-point Century Gothic.

12. Include the Casper.mid or Castle.mid file from the Tutorial.02/Garden folder as a background sound that repeats once when the Web page is opened in the Internet Explorer.

13. Create META descriptions and keywords and include them in the Home Page, and then save this Home Page in the Garden Web.

14. Shannon and Nolan want to include a feature that will count the number of visitors to the Home Page. Use the Help system to learn more about the hit counter, and then describe the steps that you would take to add a hit counter to the Home Page.

15. Test the Web page using Internet Explorer. If necessary, return to FrontPage and correct any errors, and then print the page in Internet Explorer.

16. Use FrontPage to print the HTML code for the Home Page. Circle the META tags for the description and keywords and the tags used for the background image and sound.

17. Save your changes, and then close FrontPage Editor, FrontPage Explorer, and Internet Explorer.

4. Producing a Web Site for Replay Music Factory Replay Music Factory is a regional music store that specializes in buying, selling, and trading used compact discs. As the sale of new compact discs expands, phenomenal growth is expected in the sale of used compact discs. Unlike records and tapes, used compact discs offer quality that is comparable to that of new compact discs along with substantial savings. Replay Music buys used discs from three sources: the Internet, customers, and brokers. This gives Replay a wide variety of music for the most discriminating listener. Replay's quality control division finds a defect rate of less than 1%, so all of its products are 100% guaranteed.

Justin Stolen was recently hired by Mary Kay Falsetta as a junior systems analyst and assigned to Replay's Web development team. Mary Kay wants you to help Justin to design their Web site and then create a Home Page for it.

If necessary, start FrontPage Explorer, insert your Student Disk in drive A or the appropriate disk drive, and then do the following:

1. Prepare a planning analysis sheet for the Replay Music Web site. Determine the features and functions you feel should be included in this Web site. If you have access to the WWW, reference other Web sites for this area, keeping the number of Web pages accessed from the Home Page to between five and nine.

2. Prepare a storyboard of the Web site that shows the planned Web pages and the expected hyperlinks from the Home Page.

3. Create the Replay Web site using FrontPage. Save all image and sound files included in the Web in the images folder that is created for this Web. The title of the Web is Replay Web and you will save it in the \wwwroot folder on your Student Disk.

4. Use FrontPage Editor to write, enter, edit, and spell check at least two paragraphs of content copy for the Home Page for the Replay Web. You may use any available reference sources to help develop your content, including visiting several commercial Web sites.

5. Create a heading and place it above the text you entered in Question 4. Select an appropriate size and alignment for this heading.

6. Create a navigation bar for the Home Page, and then right-align it on the Web page. Separate the navigation bar entries with a tilde symbol (~) from the symbol set and change the color of the navigation bar.

7. Add footer information at the bottom of the page that includes the current date, copyright information with the copyright symbol, and the company name.

8. Select an appropriate background image from the Clip Art Gallery that comes with FrontPage, or from any other available source, and then apply it to the Web page.

9. Create a logo for Replay Music using appropriate graphic(s) from the Clip Art supplied with FrontPage or from any other source.

10. Save your logo as a GIF file in the Tutorial.02/Replay folder, and then place the logo as an inline image on the Web page.

11. Add at least one horizontal rule to the Web page with a length less than the entire width of the page and an appropriate color.

12. Create a slogan for Replay Music Factory and place it in a scrolling marquee. Select appropriate colors for the marquee text and background.

13. Use boldface, italics, and color to improve the appearance of your Web page by selecting complementary fonts and styles.

14. Locate a MID or WAV file on your system and include it as a background sound that repeats two times when the Web page is opened using Internet Explorer. (*Hint:* Usually sound files are saved in the Windows\Media folder on your system. If you cannot find a MID or WAV file on your system, use one from your Student Disk.)

15. Create META descriptions and keywords and include them in the Home Page, and then save this Home Page in the Replay Web.

16. Test the Web page using Internet Explorer. If necessary, return to FrontPage and correct any errors, and then print the page.

17. Review the Home Page and write a paragraph that describes at least two changes that you would like to make to this Web page and defend your choices. Base your changes on the research that you did in Question 4.

18. Use FrontPage to print the HTML code for the Home Page. Circle the META tags for the description and keywords and the tags used for the background image and sound.

19. Save your changes, and then close FrontPage Editor, FrontPage Explorer, and Internet Explorer.

Using Links, Images, and Tasks Lists

Completing the Employment Web Page

OBJECTIVES

In this tutorial you will:

- Import a Web page

- Include an RTF file in a Web page

- Create definition, bulleted, numbered, and nested lists

- Create bookmarks and links to them

- Convert a JPEG image to a GIF image with a transparent background

- Create an image hotspot and assign a hyperlink to it

- Create an e-mail link

- Prepare a Tasks list

- Complete tasks using the Tasks list

CASE

Sunny Morning Products

Amanda created a design for the Sunny Morning Products Web site including several Web pages that Andrew reviewed and approved. The navigation bar entries on the Home Page reflect the titles of these additional Web pages: About Us, Products, Employment, Investor Relations, Feedback, and Search. In addition to completing each of these pages, hyperlinks must be added in order to link each page to the Home Page. At the request of Carmen Quinn, human resources manager at Sunny Morning Products, Amanda began her Web site development by focusing on the Employment page that provides information on current employment opportunities. She created a rough draft of the Web page and then met with Carmen to review the proposed design and content. For organizational purposes, Amanda captured the meeting results in a planning analysis sheet.

In this tutorial you will continue with the development of the Sunny Morning Web site for Amanda's Web training course by completing the Employment Web page. You will learn how to use links, images, and a Tasks list to turn a partially completed Web page into a finished one. You will follow the same process that Amanda used to complete the Employment Web page.

SESSION

3.1

In this session you will learn how to import an HTML document into the current Web as well as how to include an RTF document in an HTML page. In addition, you will learn about the importance of lists in creating an organized Web page and create your own definition, bulleted, numbered, and nested lists.

Importing a Web Page

You can easily place, or **import**, an HTML page that has already been created, but is not in your current Web, into the Web you are using currently. Importing allows you to incorporate Web page information from other Webs—even for those Webs created using a different Web authoring program than FrontPage—into your current Web. That means you don't have to retype the content of a Web page from another source. When you import a Web page, a copy of the Web page is placed in your open Web.

You will begin your Web training by importing the partially completed Employment Web page that Amanda initially prepared for her meeting with Carmen. First, you refer to Amanda's planning analysis sheet as shown in Figure 3-1.

Figure 3-1 ◀
Amanda's
planning
analysis sheet

Planning Analysis Sheet

My goal:

Modify the Employment Web page to include a table of contents

and descriptions for all the position openings with links to other pages in the

corporate Web site.

What results do I want to see?

Employment Web pages with the following information:

Table of contents

Complete job descriptions

Links from table of contents to job descriptions

Links from navigation bar to other pages in Web

E-mail link

Logo to provide corporate identity to page

What information do I need?

Partially completed Employment page

Job descriptions from MIS and Customer Support

Image file for page logo

Company Profile page for inclusion in Web

This page does not currently reside in the Sunny Morning Web (a:\wwwroot\sunny). Before you can begin modifying this page, you need to open the disk-based Web that you created and then import the Web page into the Sunny Morning Web.

To open a disk-based Web:

1. Make sure your Student Disk is in drive A or the appropriate disk drive on your computer.

2. Start **FrontPage Explorer**.

3. Open the **Sunny Morning Web** (sunny) located in the a:\wwwroot folder.

With the desired Web open in FrontPage Explorer, you can import a previously created page into that Web.

REFERENCE window

IMPORTING AN EXISTING WEB PAGE

- Open the Web in FrontPage Explorer.
- Click File on the menu bar, click Import, and then click the Add File button to display a list of files.
- Select the desired file.
- Click the Open button, and then click the OK button to import the page.

Continue development of the Sunny Morning Web by importing the partially completed Employment Web page.

To import an existing Web page into the current Web:

1. Click **File** on the menu bar, and then click **Import** to open the Import File to FrontPage Web dialog box.

2. Click the **Add File** button to open the Add File to Import List dialog box.

3. Click the **Look in** list arrow, click the drive that contains your Student Disk, double-click the **Tutorial.03** folder to display the contents of that folder, click the **Files of type** list arrow, click **HTML files [*.htm, *.html]**, and then click the **employ.htm** file to select it.

4. Click the **Open** button to return to the Import File to FrontPage Web dialog box.

5. Click the **OK** button to import the Web page into the Sunny Morning Web. The Employment page icon displays in FrontPage Explorer in Folders view. See Figure 3-2.

   TROUBLE? If another view displays instead of the Folders view, click the Folders button on the Views bar to display the desired view.

Figure 3-2 ◄
Employment
Web page
imported into
Sunny Morning
Web

page icon represents
employ.htm file

title of page imported
into Web

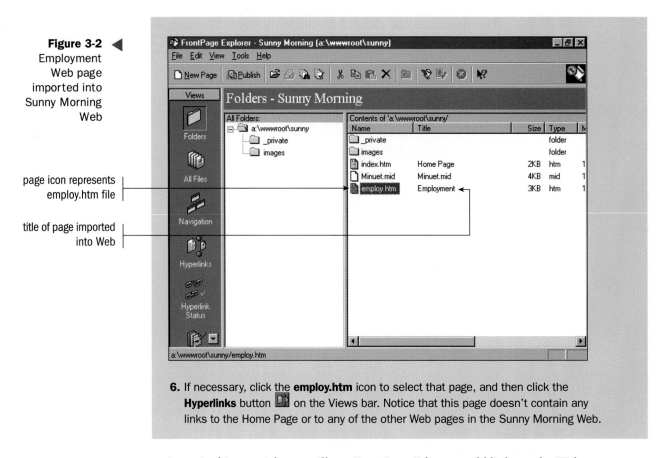

6. If necessary, click the **employ.htm** icon to select that page, and then click the **Hyperlinks** button 🖳 on the Views bar. Notice that this page doesn't contain any links to the Home Page or to any of the other Web pages in the Sunny Morning Web.

Later in this tutorial, you will use FrontPage Editor to add links to the Web page as you complete its development. Now that you've imported the Employment Web page into the Sunny Morning Web, you open it.

To open a Web page in FrontPage Editor from FrontPage Explorer:

1. Double-click the **Employment page icon** in Hyperlinks view to start FrontPage Editor. The partially completed Employment Web page opens in the Editor window. Notice that the Employment Web page appears with the default white background. See Figure 3-3.

Figure 3-3 ◄
Partially
completed
Employment
Web page

no logo on this page

list of position
openings set up for
Web page table of
contents

default background

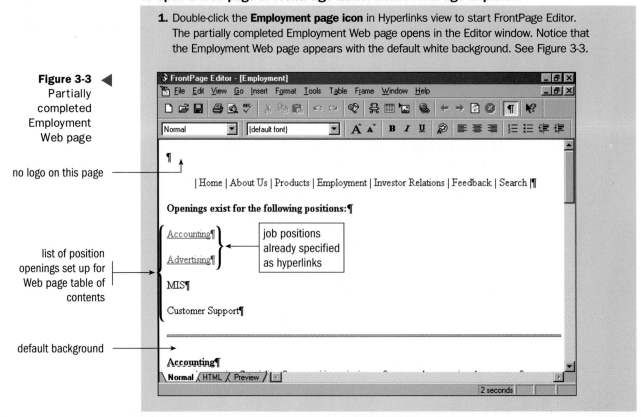

2. Scroll down the Web page until you see the job descriptions for the accounting and advertising positions. Notice that a horizontal rule separates the job descriptions for the two departments. See Figure 3-4.

Figure 3-4 ◀
Web page with completed job descriptions

default background

detailed job description

horizontal rule

Advertising department job openings

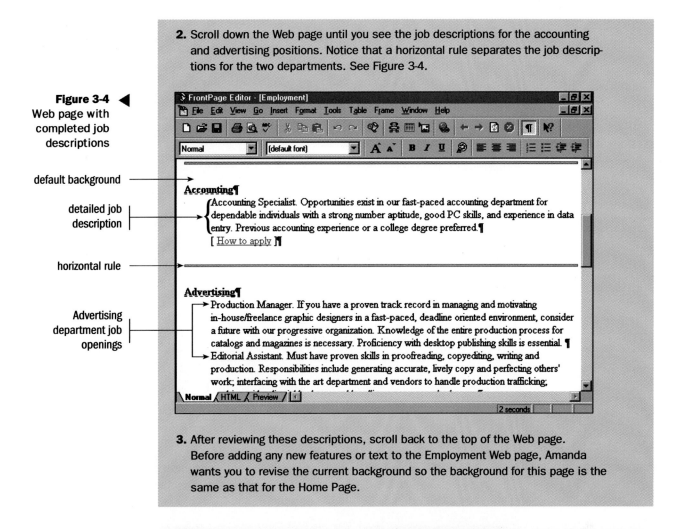

3. After reviewing these descriptions, scroll back to the top of the Web page. Before adding any new features or text to the Employment Web page, Amanda wants you to revise the current background so the background for this page is the same as that for the Home Page.

Specifying a Common Background

When designing a Web site, a common practice is to assign the same design features—color, background, and so forth—to all the Web pages that make up the site. This provides a visual cue that the pages belong to the same Web. To make the background the same for every Web page, you can use one of two methods. First, you can specify a particular background or revise the current background when creating each individual page, or, second, you can specify that you want the background for a page to be the same as another Web page. With the second method, for example, changing the background of a home page also would change the backgrounds of all the pages tied to that home page.

Rather than retaining the default background for the Employment Web page, Amanda wants you to change its background to the same one used for the Sunny Morning Web Home Page. You continue with your training by applying a common background to the Employment Web page.

To specify a background from an existing Web page:

1. Place the pointer anywhere on the Web page *except* on top of text or a horizontal rule, and then right-click to display the Shortcut menu.

2. Click **Page Properties** to open that dialog box, and then click the **Background** tab to display those settings.

3. Click the **Get Background and Colors from Page** option button, and then click the **Browse** button to open the Current Web dialog box. See Figure 3-5. Notice that the name index.htm in the file list indicates the Sunny Morning Home Page that you want to use as the source for the updated background of the Employment Web page.

Figure 3-5 ◀
Current Web
dialog box

select Home Page as
common background
source

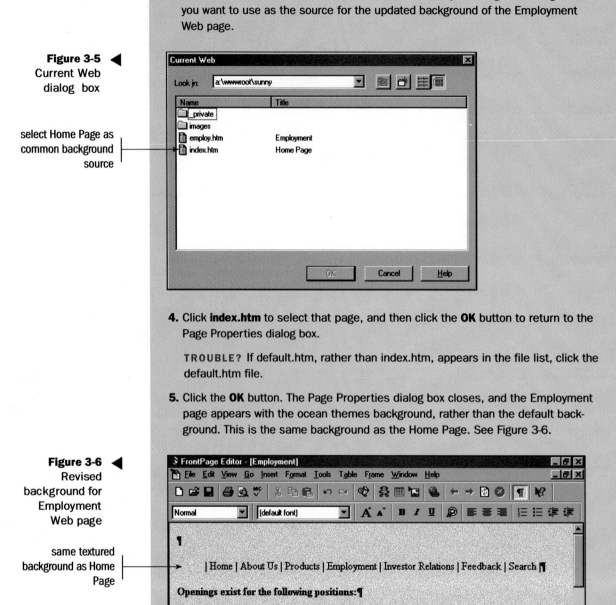

4. Click **index.htm** to select that page, and then click the **OK** button to return to the Page Properties dialog box.

TROUBLE? If default.htm, rather than index.htm, appears in the file list, click the default.htm file.

5. Click the **OK** button. The Page Properties dialog box closes, and the Employment page appears with the ocean themes background, rather than the default background. This is the same background as the Home Page. See Figure 3-6.

Figure 3-6 ◀
Revised
background for
Employment
Web page

same textured
background as Home
Page

Now that you have successfully updated the design of the Employment page by giving it a common background, you need to add additional content information to the page.

Including an RTF File in a Web Page

You can enter new content for a Web page simply by typing all the necessary text directly into FrontPage Editor. However, if the content you want to add to your Web page already exists in a different word-processing file, you can include this text directly in your Web page rather than retyping it. You accomplish this by saving a document that was created with a word-processing program as a Rich Text Format (RTF) file. An **RTF file** is a file in which all the text and formatting, such as italic or boldface font styles, is saved. Information from an RTF file can be placed anywhere on your Web page. When an RTF file is included in a Web page, FrontPage Editor automatically converts the RTF format to the HTML codes that FrontPage Editor uses. RTF files are most useful when you are creating a Web site with other individuals and you have text files to share. RTF formatting codes can be read and interpreted by other programs, including compatible Microsoft programs. Most word-processing programs allow you to save a word-processing document as an RTF file.

REFERENCE window	**INCLUDING AN RTF FILE IN A WEB PAGE**
	■ Place the insertion point where you want the text from the RTF file to appear.
	■ Click Insert on the menu bar, click File, double-click the folder that contains the file, click the Files of type list arrow, and then click Rich Text Format (*.rtf) to display a list of these files.
	■ Select the desired file, and then click the Open button to convert the file to HTML.

There might be other occasions, however, when you want to include a hyperlink from your Web page to a document in a native format, such as a Microsoft Word (.DOC) file or a text (.TXT) file. To create a link to a native document, you specify the folder and filename of the location where the document is saved on your disk-based or server-based Web. When the user clicks the hyperlink, the file will open in the native document's program window in the Internet Explorer window. Amanda considered asking you to create a link to the native file that contains the job description, but now she prefers to save the job description directly on the Web page so it is easy to read and access on the Web.

Carmen previously completed the job description for the customer support job opening and saved it as an RTF file. Rather than retyping this position information in the Employment Web page, Amanda wants you to include this RTF file in the Web page. Following the design used for the accounting and advertising job descriptions, you place the customer support job description directly underneath the customer support job title.

To include the content of an RTF file in a Web page:

1. Scroll down the Web page until you see the customer support job description title, and then click the line immediately below **Customer Support**. This is where you want to include the text from the RTF file. Recall that the job descriptions in the Employment Web page are separated by a horizontal rule.

    TROUBLE? If the Definition style does not appear in the Change Style text box, use the arrow keys to position the insertion point on the Definition paragraph under the Customer Support job title between the two horizontal rules.

2. Click **Insert** on the menu bar, and then click **File** to open the Select File dialog box.

3. Click the **Look in** list arrow, click the drive that contains your Student Disk, and then double-click the **Tutorial.03** folder to display the contents of that folder. Click the **Files of type** list arrow to display a list of available file types, and then click **Rich Text Format (*.rtf)** to display a list of the available RTF files.

4. Click the **customer.rtf** file, and then click the **Open** button to open the file and convert it from the RTF format to HTML code. The customer support job description appears on the Web page below the customer support job title. See Figure 3-7.

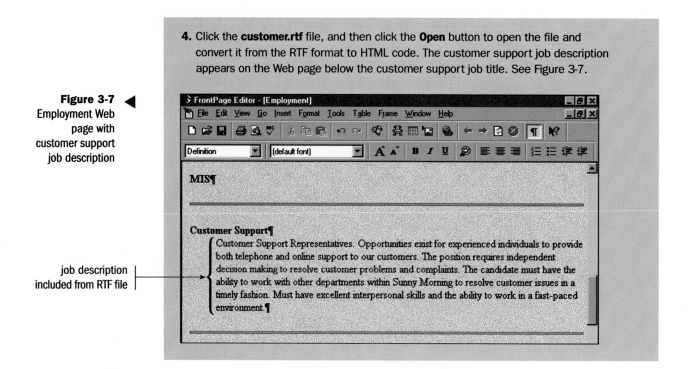

Now that you have included the customer support job description, you will continue working on the Employment Web page by creating a table of contents for the page using a list.

Creating Lists

A list is a convenient and organized way to display a series of text items on a Web page. FrontPage allows you to create several different types of lists that can be displayed when viewing a Web page. The more frequently used types of lists are bulleted, numbered, and definition lists, as well as **nested lists**, which are lists within lists. You will use all of these list types to complete the Employment Web page.

Creating a Definition List

A **definition list** consists of a defined term and its definition. A **defined term** is simply the item that is being explained. Generally, a defined term is positioned flush left with the page margin, and its definition is indented. For example, the customer support job description information you recently added is organized as a definition list. Notice in Figure 3-7 how the definition (the job description) is indented under the defined term (the customer support job title). When creating a definition list, you can specify a new paragraph as a defined term style, or you can change the paragraph style for an existing paragraph.

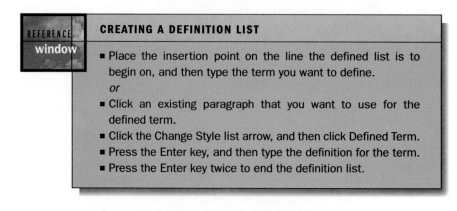

REFERENCE
window

CREATING A DEFINITION LIST

- Place the insertion point on the line the defined list is to begin on, and then type the term you want to define.
  or
- Click an existing paragraph that you want to use for the defined term.
- Click the Change Style list arrow, and then click Defined Term.
- Press the Enter key, and then type the definition for the term.
- Press the Enter key twice to end the definition list.

When Amanda created the rough draft of the Employment Web page, she entered the text for the MIS job title in anticipation of receiving the accompanying job description from Carmen. However, the MIS job title currently is formatted as a normal paragraph. Amanda asks you to change the current paragraph style to a defined term and then enter the job description (the definition) to complete the definition list.

To create a definition list:

1. If necessary, scroll up the Employment Web page until you see the MIS job title. The MIS job title is set off by horizontal rules immediately above and below it.

2. Click immediately to the right of **MIS** to place the insertion point next to this defined term. See Figure 3-8.

Figure 3-8 ◀
MIS job description area in Employment Web page

defined term ——

place insertion point here

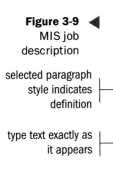

TROUBLE? If the MIS job title does not have a horizontal rule immediately above and below it, you are not in the job description area of the Web page. Scroll down the page until the MIS job title appears as shown in Figure 3-8.

3. Click the **Change Style** list arrow on the Format toolbar to display the list of available formats, and then click **Defined Term** as the desired paragraph format. Defined Term now appears in the Change Style text box.

4. Press the **Enter** key to create a new indented definition paragraph below the MIS job title. This is where you'll insert the definition for the MIS job description. However, you need to deactivate the Bold formatting currently associated with this line so that the job description appears as regular text.

5. Click the **Bold** button [B] on the Format toolbar to turn off this feature, and then type the MIS job description exactly as it appears in Figure 3-9.

Figure 3-9 ◀
MIS job description

selected paragraph style indicates definition

type text exactly as it appears

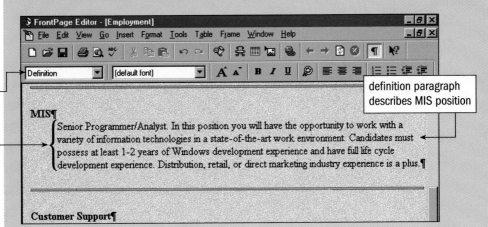

definition paragraph describes MIS position

With the two missing job descriptions added to the Employment Web page, Amanda wants you to create a table of contents for the Web page using a bulleted list.

Creating a Bulleted List

A **bulleted list,** or an **unordered list,** is not sequentially organized and can be prefixed by bullets. You specify the use of bullets with the List Properties dialog box. Generally, bulleted lists and numbered lists are displayed in your Web browser window as paragraphs separated by blank spaces. You create a bulleted list either by selecting that paragraph format style before you enter the text for an entry or by selecting the existing text and changing the paragraph style later.

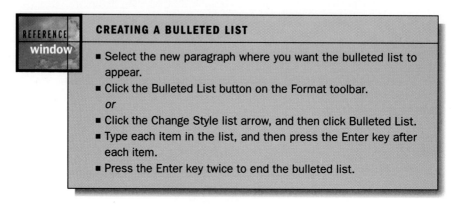

REFERENCE
window

CREATING A BULLETED LIST

- Select the new paragraph where you want the bulleted list to appear.
- Click the Bulleted List button on the Format toolbar.
  or
- Click the Change Style list arrow, and then click Bulleted List.
- Type each item in the list, and then press the Enter key after each item.
- Press the Enter key twice to end the bulleted list.

A common feature of longer Web pages is a list-style table of contents. The table of contents entries currently are set up as hyperlinks so users can link easily to any information on the Employment page. Amanda wants you to create a bulleted list table of contents at the top of the Web page that consists of the job titles for the position openings. Because the job titles already were entered as normal paragraphs, all you need to do is change them to a bulleted list.

To create a bulleted list:

1. Press **Ctrl + Home** to return to the top of the Web page, and then select the **Accounting, Advertising, MIS**, and **Customer Support** job titles. See Figure 3-10.

Figure 3-10 ◀
Creating the table of contents for the Employment Web page

current paragraph style

existing text selected for bulleted list

do not select the ¶ mark

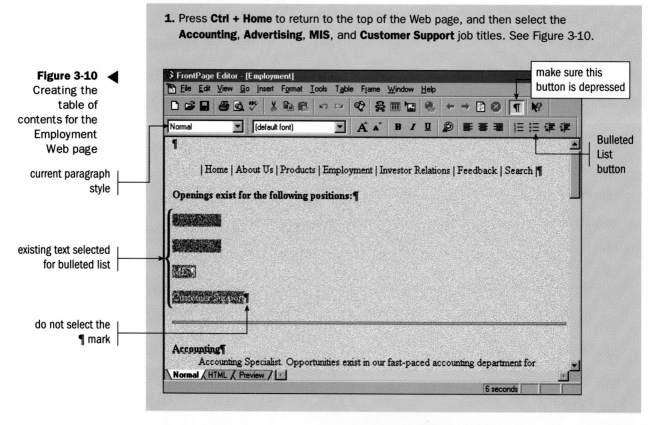

2. Click the **Bulleted List** button on the Format toolbar to organize these entries as a bulleted list, and then click **Accounting** to deselect the bulleted list. See Figure 3-11.

Figure 3-11 ◄
Completed
Employment
Web page table
of contents

revised paragraph
style

bulleted list ──────

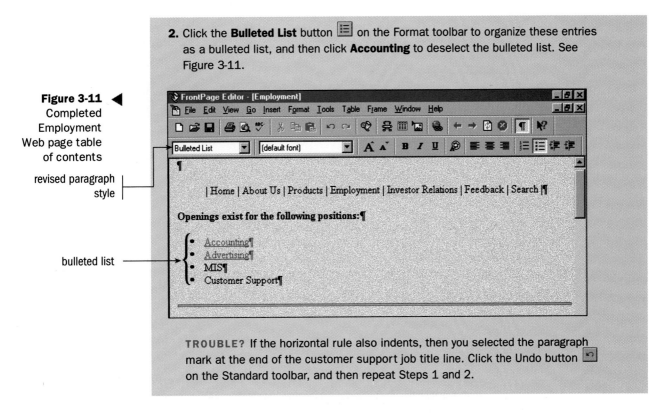

TROUBLE? If the horizontal rule also indents, then you selected the paragraph mark at the end of the customer support job title line. Click the Undo button on the Standard toolbar, and then repeat Steps 1 and 2.

Next, Amanda wants you to make the two job openings currently available in the advertising department more prominent on the Web page.

Creating a Numbered and a Nested List

A **numbered list**, or an **ordered list**, is a sequentially numbered or lettered list. A numbered list is the same as a bulleted list except that each item is prefixed by a number, rather than by a bullet. Amanda wants you to organize the advertising department job openings so they appear as a numbered list. This will help to differentiate between the two different available positions in the advertising department.

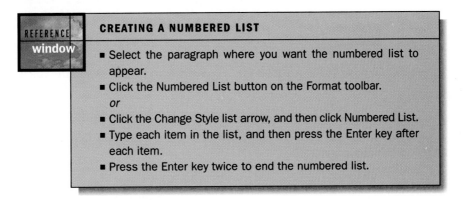

REFERENCE
window

CREATING A NUMBERED LIST

■ Select the paragraph where you want the numbered list to appear.
■ Click the Numbered List button on the Format toolbar.
  or
■ Click the Change Style list arrow, and then click Numbered List.
■ Type each item in the list, and then press the Enter key after each item.
■ Press the Enter key twice to end the numbered list.

Amanda wants this list to be numbered and placed inside the existing bulleted list of position openings. This requires that you create a nested list.

REFERENCE window

CREATING A NESTED LIST

- Insert another list paragraph where you want the nested list to appear.
- Click the Increase Indent button on the Format toolbar to nest this list.
- Click the Numbered List button or the Bulleted List button on the Format toolbar to select the desired list type.
- Type each item in the list, and then press the Enter key after each item.

Now, Amanda wants you to create a nested and numbered list for the two positions.

To create a numbered and nested list:

1. With the bulleted list displayed in your window, click immediately to the right of **Advertising**, and then press the **Enter** key to insert another bulleted list paragraph.

2. Click the **Increase Indent** button 📧 on the Format toolbar to indent this paragraph and change it to a Normal paragraph style. Notice that the top two bulleted items are now separated from the bottom two by additional space.

3. Click the **Numbered List** button 📧 on the Format toolbar to insert the number 1. This denotes the first numbered item in the nested list. (You might need to click 📧 twice to see the number 1.)

   TROUBLE? If all the position openings appear as numbered items, then you did not click the Increase Indent button before you clicked the Numbered List button. Click the Bulleted List button, and then repeat Steps 2 and 3.

4. Type **Production Manager** as the desired text for the first numbered list item, and then press the **Enter** key to create the next numbered list paragraph.

5. Type **Editorial Assistant** as the text for the second numbered list item to complete the numbered list.

6. Click the **Save** button 🖫 on the Standard toolbar to save your changes.

Quick Check

1. True or False: An RTF file is converted to HTML when the file is opened in FrontPage Editor.

2. A(n) _____ list is one that is not sequentially identified.

3. Which paragraph style would be best for a glossary that contains a list of terms with descriptions?

4. A(n) _____ list is a list within a list.

5. True or False: When entering items in a bulleted or numbered list, you press the Enter key twice to end the list.

6. To start a new list within an existing list, which button on the Format toolbar do you click to create a normal paragraph to start the new list?

You've completed the bulleted list of position openings and organized the advertising jobs as a nested and numbered list for the Employment Web page. These open positions form the Web page table of contents. Next, you'll format the MIS and customer support entries in the navigation bar as hyperlinks so users can link directly to these job descriptions.

In this session you will learn how to create a bookmark, specify a link to a bookmark, and use the different methods used to create links to other Web pages. Then you will learn how to convert a JPEG image format to a GIF image format, make a GIF image transparent, create a hotspot, and create an e-mail link. In addition, you will test hyperlinks within a Web page, between Web pages, and to an e-mail link.

Creating a Bookmark

A **bookmark**, or an **anchor**, is a named location in a document that enables a user to quickly link to that location in a Web page from any other point in the same or another Web page. Bookmarks usually consist of text that identifies a location that is the target of a hyperlink. You can place bookmarks anywhere on a Web page without associating a bookmark with a text selection. Each bookmark within a Web page is assigned a unique name. For example, the table of contents at the top of the Employment Web page is organized so that each position description can be accessed quickly using bookmarks created within the Web page.

When created in FrontPage Editor, bookmarks appear as underlined text with a dashed line, which makes their location on a Web page easily recognizable. If a bookmark is not associated with a text selection, then a bookmark icon appears in FrontPage Editor to designate the location. When you view a page with bookmarks using your browser, no underlining or other identification of the bookmark appears. You can use the suggested name assigned to the bookmark when it is created, or you can assign a different name to the bookmark by typing it in the Bookmark Name text box in the Bookmark dialog box.

Amanda designed the Employment Web page so that each of the position openings in the table of contents is associated with a bookmark. Then, a hyperlink reference can be established between the position openings and their related job descriptions. This hyperlink reference allows visitors to the Employment Web page to access any of the job descriptions from the table of contents quickly.

REFERENCE
window

CREATING A BOOKMARK

- Select the bookmark text or place the insertion point where you want the bookmark to appear.
- Click Edit on the menu bar, and then click Bookmark.
- Type the bookmark name in the Bookmark Name text box, or accept the suggested name.
- Click the OK button to create the bookmark.

In the partially completed Employment Web page, Amanda already created two bookmarks—one for accounting and the other for advertising. Next, you create the remaining two bookmarks for the MIS and customer support job descriptions.

To create a bookmark:

1. With the Employment Web page displayed in your window, scroll down until you see the MIS job description that appears between two horizontal rules.

2. Select the **MIS** job title to identify the location for the bookmark.

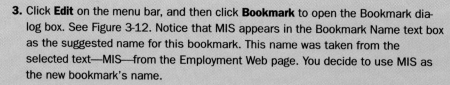

3. Click **Edit** on the menu bar, and then click **Bookmark** to open the Bookmark dialog box. See Figure 3-12. Notice that MIS appears in the Bookmark Name text box as the suggested name for this bookmark. This name was taken from the selected text—MIS—from the Employment Web page. You decide to use MIS as the new bookmark's name.

Figure 3-12 ◄
Bookmark
dialog box

text for bookmark
location (yours might
be selected)

bookmark name
taken from selected
text on Web page

4. Click the **OK** button to accept the suggested name for the bookmark and return to the Web page, and then click the **MIS** text to deselect it. MIS now appears as underlined text with a dashed line to indicate that it is a bookmark.

5. Scroll down the Web page until you see the customer support position description, select **Customer** in the customer support job title, and then repeat Steps 3 and 4 to create the **Customer** bookmark for this location.

6. Click the **Customer** text to deselect it. Your completed Web page should look like Figure 3-13.

Figure 3-13 ◄
Employment
Web page with
new bookmarks

bookmark locations
appear with a dashed
underline

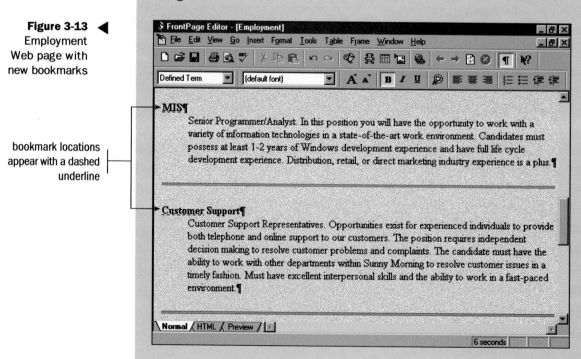

Creating a Hyperlink to a Bookmark

Now that all the bookmarks are completed, Amanda wants you to create links from the MIS and customer support job titles in the table of contents to their corresponding bookmarks. When accessed, these links will move the user to the appropriate place in the Web page using the bookmark names. Figure 3-14 illustrates how the bookmarks you created will work as a reference point for a link.

Figure 3-14 ◀
Employment
Web page with
bookmarks

hyperlink reference
to bookmark

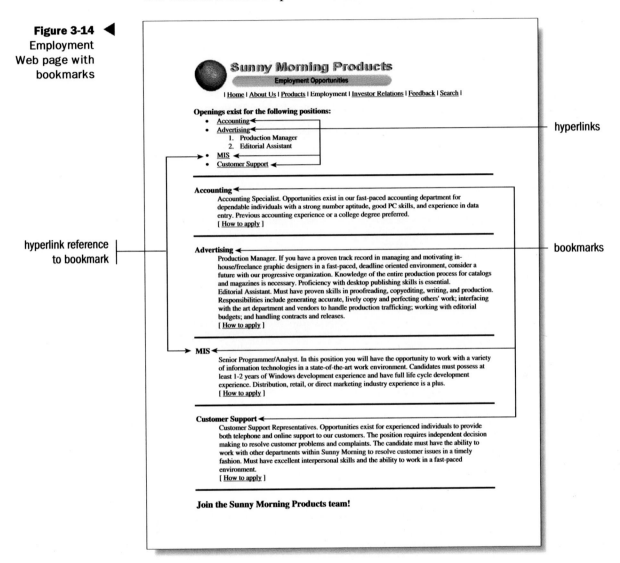

hyperlinks

bookmarks

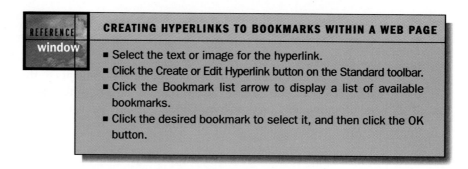

REFERENCE window

CREATING HYPERLINKS TO BOOKMARKS WITHIN A WEB PAGE

- Select the text or image for the hyperlink.
- Click the Create or Edit Hyperlink button on the Standard toolbar.
- Click the Bookmark list arrow to display a list of available bookmarks.
- Click the desired bookmark to select it, and then click the OK button.

Next, you create the necessary internal document hyperlinks so that the MIS and customer support entries in table of contents link to the bookmarks for these job descriptions.

To create a hyperlink to a bookmark within a Web page:

1. Press **Ctrl + Home** to return to the top of the Web page so you can see the table of contents.

   You begin by creating a hyperlink for the MIS bookmark.

2. Select **MIS** in the table of contents as the hypertext link.

3. Click the **Create or Edit Hyperlink** button 🔗 on the Standard toolbar to open the Create Hyperlink dialog box.

4. Click the **Bookmark** list arrow to display a list of the bookmarks for the Employment Web page. See Figure 3-15.

Figure 3-15 ◄
List of available bookmarks in the Create Hyperlink dialog box

indicates current Web page

list of bookmarks for the Employment Web page

hyperlink text (yours might be selected)

click to select target location in Employment Web page

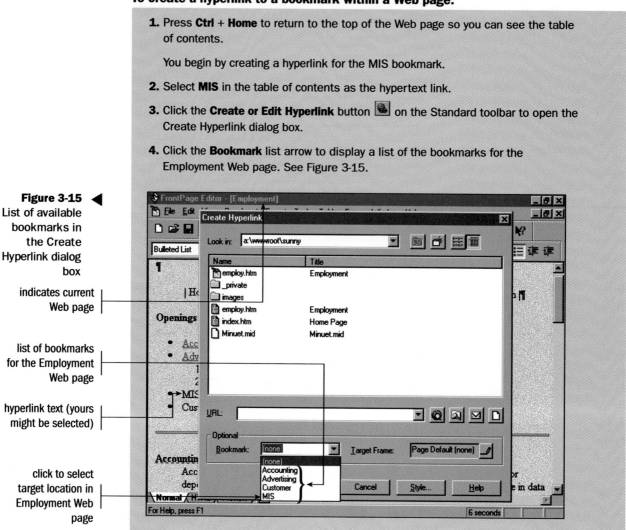

5. Click **MIS** to select that bookmark, click the **OK** button to return to the Web page, and then click **MIS** to deselect it. MIS now appears blue with a solid underline in the Web page to indicate that it is a hyperlink.

6. Select **Customer Support** in the table of contents as the next hyperlink, and then repeat Steps 3 through 5 using the **Customer** bookmark.

7. Place the pointer on top of the **Customer Support** hyperlink. Notice that the name of the hyperlink—#Customer—appears in the status bar and confirms the existence of this internal document hyperlink. See Figure 3-16.

Figure 3-16 ◀
Completed table of contents with bookmarks and hyperlinks

hyperlinks to each name reference for job descriptions

bookmark name appears as a hyperlink

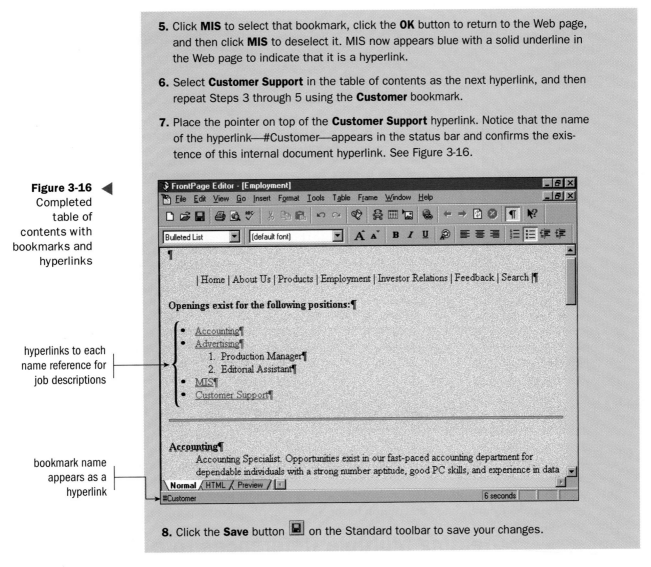

8. Click the **Save** button 🖫 on the Standard toolbar to save your changes.

Now that the hyperlinks to the bookmarks are completed, you need to make sure that they work correctly.

To test an internal document hyperlink using the Preview tab:

1. Click the **Preview** tab. The Employment Web page displays as it will in the browser.

2. Place the pointer on top of the **MIS** hyperlink. Notice that the name of the hyperlink—file:///A:wwwroot/sunny/employ.htm#MIS—displays in the status bar. Click the **MIS** hyperlink. The Web page is repositioned so the target location is at the top of the window. See Figure 3-17. Notice that the MIS bookmark does not appear underlined as it did when you created and viewed it using the Normal tab.

Figure 3-17 ◀
Web page
displayed using
Preview tab

bookmarks appear
without dashed line

job description appears
as a defined term

bookmark location
(yours might
not appear)

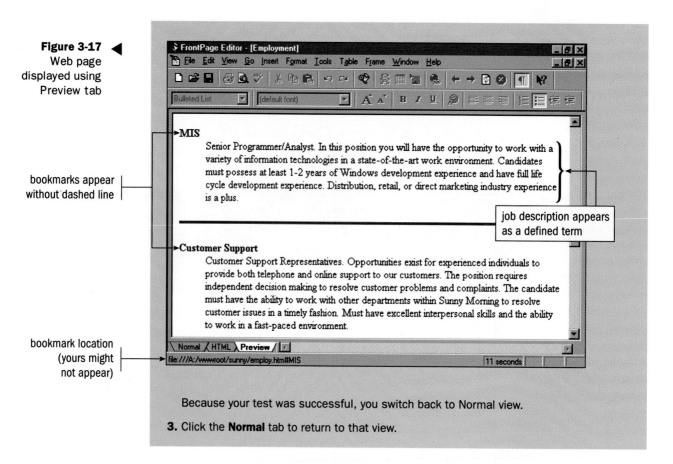

Because your test was successful, you switch back to Normal view.

3. Click the **Normal** tab to return to that view.

Now that you have completed the internal hyperlink references from the position openings in the table of contents to their respective job descriptions in the Employment page, you need to implement the next design feature. Amanda wants you to insert a link from each job description to the Sunny Morning Products contact information.

Creating Multiple References to a Bookmark

So far, the bookmarks that you created contain only one hyperlink reference. A bookmark, however, can contain numerous references from different locations within a Web page. For example, regardless of the job description in which users are interested, they need to access the same contact information to obtain additional information about the company. After creating this contact information, you need to place it in only one location on the Web page. When a bookmark contains more than one reference to a hyperlink, the bookmark has **multiple references** to it.

In designing the Employment Web page, Amanda wants to include a reference from each of the job descriptions to the contact information at Sunny Morning Products. The hyperlinks that reference this information from the accounting and advertising job descriptions already have been created. Amanda asks you to create a bookmark and then specify the hyperlinks from each of the other two job descriptions—MIS and customer support—so that they include multiple references as well. After creating these bookmarks, you use the same process to create these links as you did when you created hyperlinks earlier in this session.

To create a bookmark without any selected text:

1. Scroll down the Web page until you see the phrase, "Join the Sunny Morning Products team!" This is the beginning line for the contact information.

2. Click to the left of the **J** in **Join** (do not select the word "Join") to place the insertion point at the location where you want the new bookmark to appear.

   TROUBLE? If you selected the J in Join or the entire word "Join," repeat Step 2.

3. Click **Edit** on the menu bar, and then click **Bookmark** to open the Bookmark dialog box. Because no text was selected, a suggested name does not appear in the Bookmark Name text box.

4. Type **to_apply** in the Bookmark Name text box as the name for this new bookmark, and then click the **OK** button. A bookmark icon appears at the designated location to the left of the word "Join" on the Web page. Click to the right of the bookmark icon to deselect it. See Figure 3-18.

Figure 3-18 ◄
Contact
information for
Sunny Morning
Products

bookmark icon
specifies location
for the to_apply
bookmark

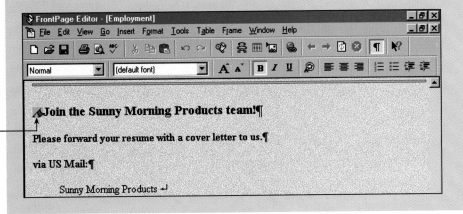

Next, you will create the hyperlink references from the job descriptions to this new bookmark. After creating the bookmark, you use the same process to create these links as you did when you created hyperlinks earlier in this session.

To create multiple hyperlinks to the same bookmark:

1. Scroll up the Web page until you see the MIS job description.

2. Click to the right of the last line in the job description to place the insertion point where you want the new hyperlink to appear.

3. Press **Shift + Enter** to create a new line within the same paragraph.

   Next, you add the text for the new hyperlink that is part of the same paragraph for the hyperlink reference.

4. Type **[How to apply]** and then select **How to apply** as the desired text for the hyperlink.

5. Click the **Create or Edit Hyperlink** button [icon] on the Standard toolbar, and then click the **Bookmark** list arrow to display the list of available bookmarks for the Employment Web page. See Figure 3-19.

Figure 3-19
List of available
bookmarks

text for hyperlink
(yours might be
selected)

name of bookmark

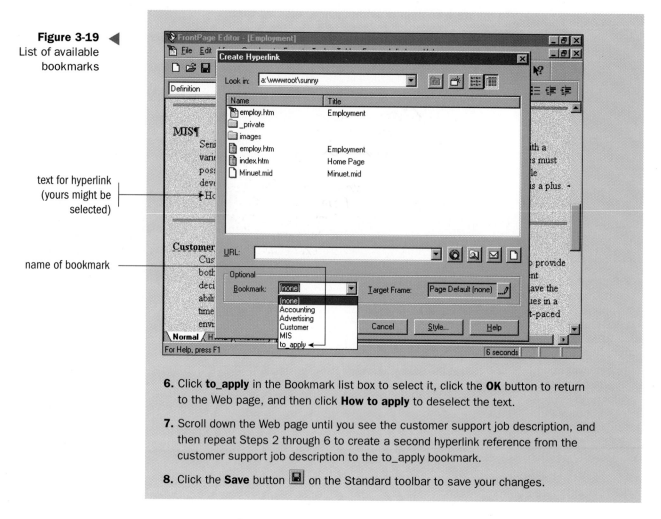

6. Click **to_apply** in the Bookmark list box to select it, click the **OK** button to return to the Web page, and then click **How to apply** to deselect the text.

7. Scroll down the Web page until you see the customer support job description, and then repeat Steps 2 through 6 to create a second hyperlink reference from the customer support job description to the to_apply bookmark.

8. Click the **Save** button 🖫 on the Standard toolbar to save your changes.

So far, you have created several hyperlinks to the bookmarks within the Employment Web page. In the next part of your training, you learn how to create links to other Web pages.

Linking to Other Web Pages

As you learned earlier in this tutorial, hyperlinks can be created that link you to other Web pages—not just to other locations on the same Web page. These links can be to another page within the same Web or to a page located at an entirely different Web site. Using FrontPage Editor, you create a link to another Web page using a similar process to the one you used to create a hyperlink within a Web page.

Creating Links to Other Web Pages

You create a hyperlink to another Web page by selecting the location on the page where you want the link to appear and then specifying the destination Web page. When creating a hyperlink to another Web page, it is helpful to select a name that provides a cue about the destination page.

CREATING A HYPERLINK TO ANOTHER WEB PAGE

- Select the text to use as the hyperlink.
- Click the Create or Edit Hyperlink button on the Standard toolbar.
  or
- Click Edit on the menu bar, and then click Hyperlink.
- Select the destination page to which you want to link.
- Click the OK button.

Amanda wants you to create a hyperlink from the Employment Web page to the Sunny Morning Home Page and also from the Home Page to the Employment Web page. These links will allow visitors to the Web site to navigate between these Web pages easily. Although she has already included the various Web page names in the navigation bar of the Home Page, hyperlinks for this text still are needed for the Sunny Morning Web.

To create a link to another Web page:

1. Press **Ctrl** + **Home** to return to the top of the Employment Web page. The partially completed navigation bar is now in view.

2. Select **Home** in the user-defined navigation bar as the text for the hyperlink.

3. Click the **Create or Edit Hyperlink** button 🔗 on the Standard toolbar to open the Create Hyperlink dialog box. (This is the same dialog box you used to create the internal page hyperlinks.) A list of the files and folders included in your current Web, including the employ.htm and index.htm Web pages, displays in the list box.

4. Click **index.htm** to select it as the Web page for the hyperlink, and then click the **OK** button to close the Create Hyperlink dialog box and return to the Web page.

   TROUBLE? If your Web contains the default.htm file rather than the index.htm file, click the default.htm filename to select the Home Page.

5. Click the **Home** text in the navigation bar to deselect it. Home now appears as a hyperlink, as indicated by the underline.

6. Place the pointer on top of the **Home** hyperlink. Notice that index.htm appears in the status bar to confirm that this is the target for the hyperlink.

7. Click the **Save** button 💾 on the Standard toolbar to save your changes.

Now that you have established a link from the Employment Web page to the Sunny Morning Web Home Page, you need to test this link by viewing the Web page in your browser.

To test a hyperlink to another Web page using Internet Explorer:

1. Click the **Preview in Browser** button 🔍 on the Standard toolbar to start Internet Explorer. The Employment Web page displays in Internet Explorer.

   TROUBLE? If the Home hyperlink does not appear with an underline, click the Refresh button 🔄 on the Internet Explorer toolbar to load the most recent version of the Employment Web page.

2. Place the pointer on top of the **Home** hyperlink. Notice that "file:////A:/wwwroot/su…" appears in the status bar to confirm that this is a hyperlink to another target Web page.

3. Right-click the **Home** hyperlink to display the Shortcut menu, and then click **Properties** to open that dialog box. Confirm that index.htm is the target address for this hyperlink, and then click the **OK** button to close the dialog box.

4. Click the **Home** hyperlink to open the Home Page for the Sunny Morning Web. Notice that the Employment entry in the navigation bar is not underlined, which indicates that this entry is not currently set up as a hyperlink. Because your test was successful, you return to the Employment Web page.

5. Click the **Back** button [icon] on the Internet Explorer toolbar to return to the Employment Web page. If the background music from the Home Page was playing, it stops now.

6. Click the **FrontPage Editor** program button on the taskbar to return to the Editor window.

Now that you have successfully established the hyperlink from the Employment Web page to the Home Page, you need to create the hyperlink from the Home Page back to the Employment Web page.

Creating Hyperlinks Using Drag and Drop

Another method of creating a hyperlink between pages in your Web is **drag and drop**, which is convenient when the pages you want to link are already open in FrontPage Editor. By default, the target's page title becomes the text for the hyperlink in the source Web page. Therefore, when you give your Web page a title, you might want to consider selecting a title that can be used as text for its hyperlink.

To use drag and drop, first open the page where you want to create the hyperlink in FrontPage Editor by selecting it as the active document window, and then switch to FrontPage Explorer. Next, select the page in FrontPage Explorer and drag the pointer on top of the FrontPage Editor program button on the taskbar. (If your taskbar is hidden, it will appear for this action.) After a short pause, Editor opens. Then you place the pointer at the location where you want to insert the hyperlink and release it to complete the drag and drop action. You create the name of the hyperlink using the page title from the original Web page to which you are linking. If you want to use a different name for the link, you can edit it after placing it on the Web page.

REFERENCE window	CREATING A HYPERLINK USING DRAG AND DROP
	■ Open the page where you want to create the hyperlink in FrontPage Editor.
	■ Click the FrontPage Explorer program button on the taskbar to switch to that program.
	■ Click the destination page in Folders view or in either pane of Hyperlinks view.
	■ Click and drag the pointer on top of the FrontPage Editor program button on the taskbar.
	■ Wait for FrontPage Editor to open, and then drag the pointer to the location where you want to insert the hyperlink.
	■ Release the mouse button to insert the hyperlink.

Next, Amanda wants you to use drag and drop to create the hyperlink from the Home Page to the Employment Web page. After you create this second hyperlink, you can use the hyperlinks to easily move between these two pages in the Sunny Morning Web.

To create a hyperlink using drag and drop:

1. Open the **Home Page** (index.htm) in FrontPage Editor.

   TROUBLE? If you have difficulty accessing the Home Page, refer to the section "Opening a Web Page" in Tutorial 2.

2. Click the **Show FrontPage Explorer** button 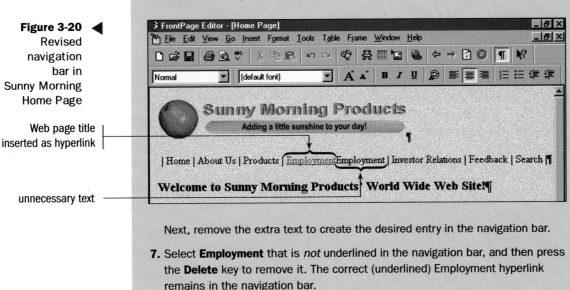 on the Standard toolbar to switch to this program. The Employment Web page opens in Hyperlinks view.

   TROUBLE? If Hyperlinks view is not displayed, then click the Hyperlinks button on the Views bar to select this view.

3. Click **Employment** in the left pane to make this page the center focus of Hyperlinks view.

4. Click and hold down the left mouse button as you drag the pointer from the **Employment** page icon to the **FrontPage Editor** program button on the taskbar. The pointer changes to ○ until it is on top of the FrontPage Editor program button (do *not* release the mouse button). After a brief pause, FrontPage Editor opens. If your taskbar is hidden, it will appear when you move the pointer to the bottom of the screen so you can locate the FrontPage Editor program button.

5. Move the pointer to the left of **Employment** in the navigation bar. The pointer changes to while it is on top of this text.

6. Release the mouse button, and then click **Employment** to deselect this text. An Employment hyperlink is inserted on the Home Page using the page title from the Employment Web page. See Figure 3-20. Notice that the text in the navigation bar is now "EmploymentEmployment" because the page title was inserted in front of the text that was already in the user-defined navigation bar. This results in extra text in the navigation bar.

Figure 3-20 ◀
Revised
navigation
bar in
Sunny Morning
Home Page

Web page title
inserted as hyperlink

unnecessary text

Next, remove the extra text to create the desired entry in the navigation bar.

7. Select **Employment** that is *not* underlined in the navigation bar, and then press the **Delete** key to remove it. The correct (underlined) Employment hyperlink remains in the navigation bar.

8. Click the **Save** button on the Standard toolbar to save your changes.

Now, test the hyperlinks between the Home Page and the Employment Web page by viewing the revised Home Page in Internet Explorer.

To test hyperlinks between Web pages using Internet Explorer:

1. Click the **Preview in Browser** button 🔍 on the Standard toolbar to switch to Internet Explorer. The Home Page displays in Internet Explorer.

2. If necessary, click the **Refresh** button 🔄 on the Internet Explorer toolbar to display the revised version of the Home Page. The Employment hyperlink is underlined.

3. Click the **Employment** hyperlink in the navigation bar to link to the Employment Web page. The page opens and its URL displays in the Address box.

4. Click the **Home** hyperlink in the navigation bar to link to the Sunny Morning Home Page. The Web page appears again in Internet Explorer.

5. Click the **Employment** hyperlink to return to that page and turn off the background music from the Home Page if it was playing.

6. Click the **FrontPage Editor** program button on the taskbar to return to that program.

You have successfully completed the hyperlink test. If you found any problems with your hyperlinks during testing, you would need to resolve them before continuing with your Web site development. You'll set up the remaining hyperlinks later. First, Amanda wants you to make some enhancements to the Employment Web page.

Converting Images to JPEG or GIF Formats

Unlike the Sunny Morning Home Page, the Employment Web page does not contain a graphic logo or banner. Similar to a common background, a logo provides a visual association among a Web site's various pages. Inserting a graphic often requires placing a separate image file into your Web page.

Graphic images you use with Web pages can be in either the JPEG or GIF format. Generally, the JPEG format provides better images with more colors, whereas a GIF image is limited to 256 colors or less. JPEG images, however, usually consist of larger files that require more storage space and longer download time. Whenever file size is a concern, use the GIF format.

FrontPage Editor allows you to convert an image saved in one format to the other without having to use a graphics program to complete this conversion. When a GIF image is converted to a JPEG image, the quality of the converted image is set as an integer from 1 to 100, with the larger number indicating a higher-quality, larger image file. As the image quality is decreased, compression increases, thereby producing a smaller image file.

Amanda already created a banner logo that she wants to include on the Employment Web page that is similar to the image used in the Home Page. She saved this file as a JPEG image. Because of the file size, she wants you to convert it to GIF format. Before you can work with an image file, you must insert it in your Web page.

To insert an image in a Web page:

1. With the Home Page still displayed in FrontPage Editor, click **Window** on the menu bar, and then click **Employment** to switch to that Web page.

2. Press **Ctrl + Home** to place and left-align the insertion point at the top of the Web page. This is the location where you want to insert the image.

3. Click the **Insert Image** button 🖼 on the Standard toolbar to open the Image dialog box, and then click the **Select a file on your computer** button 🔍 to open the Select File dialog box.

4. Make sure the drive that contains your Student Disk appears in the Look in text box, double-click the **Tutorial.03** folder, double-click the **Images** folder, click the **hemploy.jpg** file, and then click the **OK** button. The JPEG image is inserted in the Web page as a rectangular image at the top of the page. Notice the subtitle for the image is Employment Opportunities, which identifies the content of this Web page.

Your next training activity is to convert the file from JPEG to the space-saving GIF format.

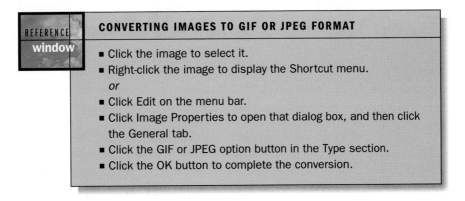

REFERENCE window

CONVERTING IMAGES TO GIF OR JPEG FORMAT

- Click the image to select it.
- Right-click the image to display the Shortcut menu.
  or
- Click Edit on the menu bar.
- Click Image Properties to open that dialog box, and then click the General tab.
- Click the GIF or JPEG option button in the Type section.
- Click the OK button to complete the conversion.

Now, convert the logo image from JPEG to GIF format.

To convert an image from JPEG to GIF format:

1. Click anywhere on the logo image to select it. Notice that eight small squares appear as selection handles at the edge of the image to indicate that it is selected, and the Image toolbar appears. See Figure 3-21.

Figure 3-21
Web page with
JPEG image

selected JPEG image

selection handles

Image toolbar

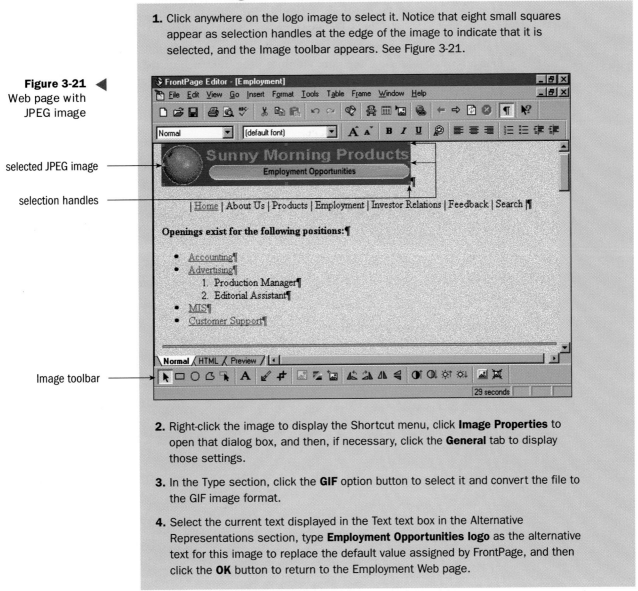

2. Right-click the image to display the Shortcut menu, click **Image Properties** to open that dialog box, and then, if necessary, click the **General** tab to display those settings.

3. In the Type section, click the **GIF** option button to select it and convert the file to the GIF image format.

4. Select the current text displayed in the Text text box in the Alternative Representations section, type **Employment Opportunities logo** as the alternative text for this image to replace the default value assigned by FrontPage, and then click the **OK** button to return to the Employment Web page.

5. Click the **Save** button 🖫 on the Standard toolbar to save both the Web page and the image. The Save Embedded Files dialog box opens with hemploy.gif listed. The GIF filename extension indicates the image was converted to the GIF format.

6. Click the **Change Folder** button, click the **images** folder to select it as the destination for the file, and then click the **OK** button to return to the Save Embedded Files dialog box.

7. Click the **OK** button to save the hemploy.gif image file in the sunny Web.

Although the rectangular logo image is effective, the blue background isn't attractive. Next, you will remove this background to improve the image's appearance.

Creating a Transparent Image

One way to enhance the appearance of an image on a Web page is to make one of the image colors transparent. **Transparency** is the quality of having one of the image colors disappear so that the Web page's background shows through. Because all inline images are rectangles, transparency allows the image to appear as a shape that is not rectangular. The Sunny Morning Products logo on the Home Page is an example of an inline image with a transparent background. In FrontPage, you can apply transparency to GIF images, but not to JPEG images, which is another advantage of converting a JPEG image to a GIF image. You could use a separate graphics program, such as the Image Composer that is included with the FrontPage 98 program, to create a transparent background for an image. Using the Image Composer to create graphics, however, is beyond the scope of these tutorials.

REFERENCE window	**MAKING AN IMAGE TRANSPARENT**
	■ Click the image to select it.
	■ Click the Make Transparent button on the Image toolbar.
	■ Click the color on the image that you want to make transparent.

Amanda asks you to make the image background transparent for the Employment Opportunities logo so that the logo will be consistent with the one on the Sunny Morning Home Page.

To make an image transparent:

1. With the Employment Web page still displayed, click anywhere on the **logo image** to select it. Selection handles appear at the edge of the image to indicate it is selected and the Image toolbar displays.

2. Click the **Make Transparent** button on the Image toolbar.

3. Place the pointer on top of the **logo image**. The pointer changes to ↘. See Figure 3-22.

Figure 3-22
Web page with
GIF image

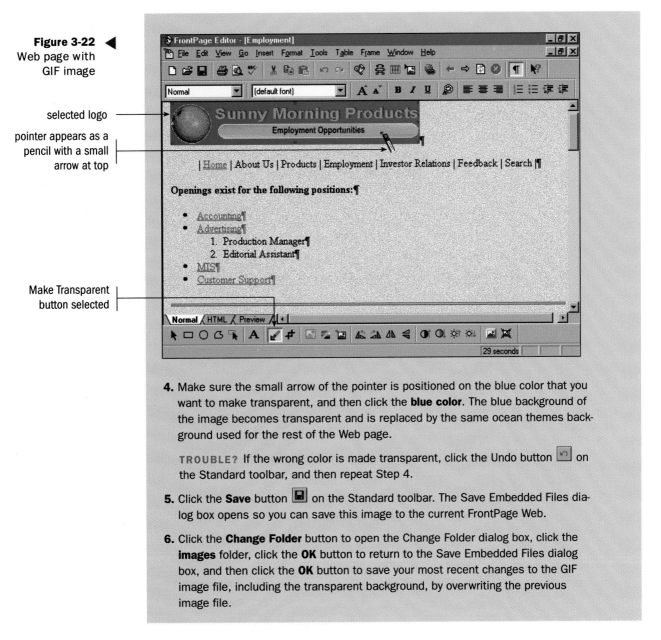

selected logo

pointer appears as a
pencil with a small
arrow at top

Make Transparent
button selected

4. Make sure the small arrow of the pointer is positioned on the blue color that you want to make transparent, and then click the **blue color**. The blue background of the image becomes transparent and is replaced by the same ocean themes background used for the rest of the Web page.

TROUBLE? If the wrong color is made transparent, click the Undo button on the Standard toolbar, and then repeat Step 4.

5. Click the **Save** button on the Standard toolbar. The Save Embedded Files dialog box opens so you can save this image to the current FrontPage Web.

6. Click the **Change Folder** button to open the Change Folder dialog box, click the **images** folder, click the **OK** button to return to the Save Embedded Files dialog box, and then click the **OK** button to save your most recent changes to the GIF image file, including the transparent background, by overwriting the previous image file.

The Employment Opportunities logo in the Web page looks more attractive with its new transparent background.

Creating Image Hotspots

Although images add visual interest to your Web pages, they can serve a functional purpose as well. For example, you can use images as hyperlinks to a bookmark or to another Web page if you create one or more hotspots on a image. A **hotspot** is an area of an image that you click to activate a hyperlink. Using FrontPage Editor, you can create one of three hotspot shapes: a rectangle, a circle, or a polygon. A number of different Web sites use hotspots as an alternative to navigation bars. The complexity of creating an image for a navigation bar with multiple hotspots, however, is beyond the scope of these tutorials.

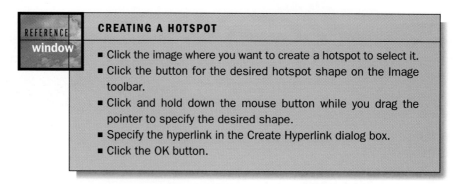

REFERENCE window

CREATING A HOTSPOT

- Click the image where you want to create a hotspot to select it.
- Click the button for the desired hotspot shape on the Image toolbar.
- Click and hold down the mouse button while you drag the pointer to specify the desired shape.
- Specify the hyperlink in the Create Hyperlink dialog box.
- Click the OK button.

Amanda wants the orange in the Employment Opportunities logo to be a hotspot with a hyperlink to the Home Page. Next, you create a circle as the shape for this hotspot.

To create a hotspot:

1. If necessary, click anywhere on the logo image to select it and display the Image toolbar.

2. Click the **Circle** button ☐ on the Image toolbar, and then place the pointer on the middle of the **orange** in the logo. The pointer changes to ✎. See Figure 3-23.

Figure 3-23 ◀
Logo image with transparent background

pointer for creating hotspot

Circle button selected

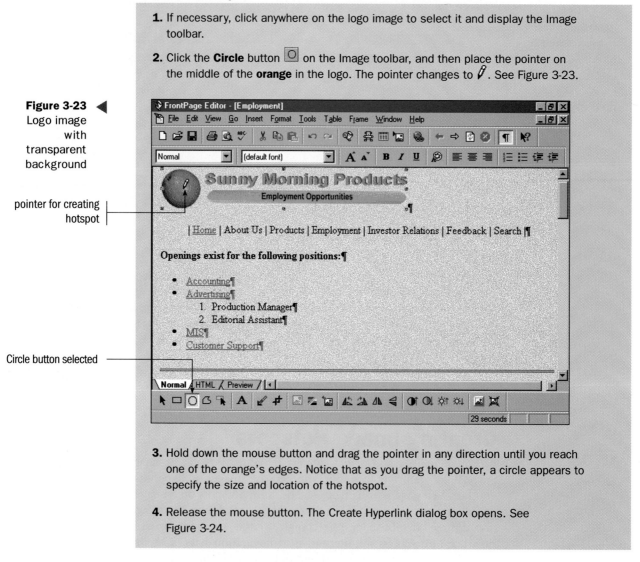

3. Hold down the mouse button and drag the pointer in any direction until you reach one of the orange's edges. Notice that as you drag the pointer, a circle appears to specify the size and location of the hotspot.

4. Release the mouse button. The Create Hyperlink dialog box opens. See Figure 3-24.

Figure 3-24 ◀
Create
Hyperlink dialog
box for logo
image

page icons indicate
pages currently open
in FrontPage Editor

page icons indicate
pages currently
open in Web

select Web page for
hyperlink to hotspot

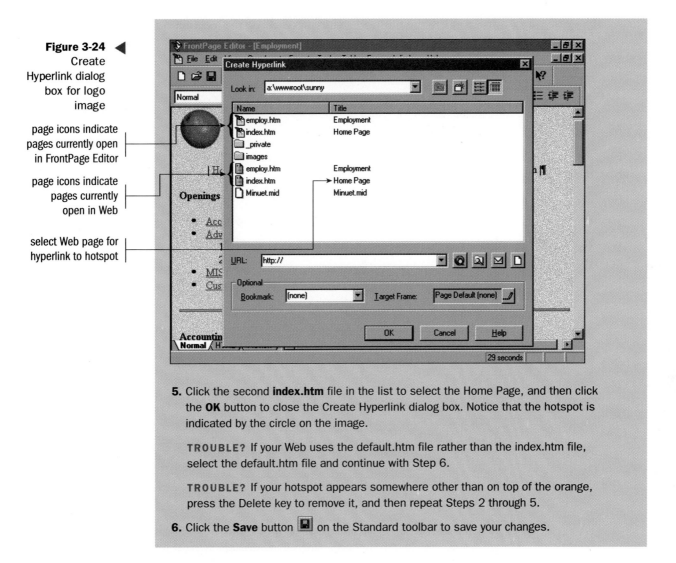

5. Click the second **index.htm** file in the list to select the Home Page, and then click the **OK** button to close the Create Hyperlink dialog box. Notice that the hotspot is indicated by the circle on the image.

TROUBLE? If your Web uses the default.htm file rather than the index.htm file, select the default.htm file and continue with Step 6.

TROUBLE? If your hotspot appears somewhere other than on top of the orange, press the Delete key to remove it, and then repeat Steps 2 through 5.

6. Click the **Save** button 🖫 on the Standard toolbar to save your changes.

You successfully created the hotspot and specified its hyperlink to the Home Page in the Sunny Morning Web. Now, visitors to the Web can click either the orange in the logo or Home in the navigation bar to link to the Home Page.

Highlighting Hotspots

After creating the image hotspots, you should review their location before you make any additions or modifications to the Web page. Depending on the image's colors and features, hotspots might be difficult to see on top of the image. By highlighting hotspots, you can see their location more clearly and confirm their placement.

REFERENCE
window

HIGHLIGHTING HOTSPOTS

- Click the image where the hotspots are located.
- Click the Highlight Hotspots button on the Image toolbar.
- Click anywhere on the page, except on the image, to turn off the hotspot display.

To complete the hotspot creation, you check the location of the hotspot on the logo image to verify its placement.

To highlight an image's hotspots:

1. Make sure that the image is still selected, and then click the **Highlight Hotspots** button 🔲 on the Image toolbar to view the currently defined hotspots for the logo image. See Figure 3-25.

Figure 3-25 ◀
Web page logo
image with
hotspots

location of hotspot
on image

selected image
handles

Highlight Hotspots
button selected

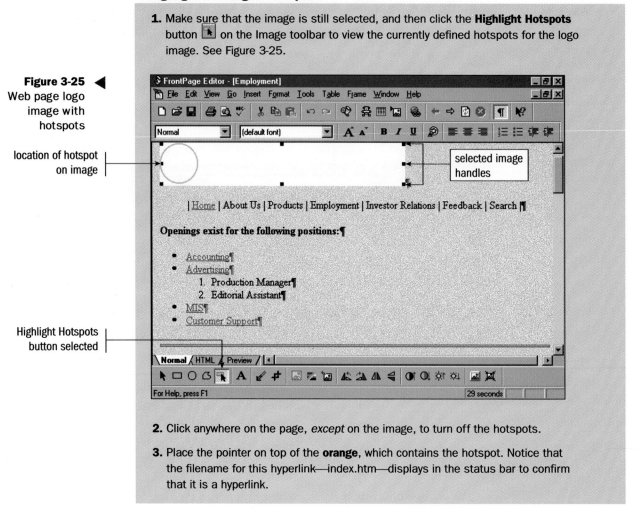

2. Click anywhere on the page, *except* on the image, to turn off the hotspots.

3. Place the pointer on top of the **orange**, which contains the hotspot. Notice that the filename for this hyperlink—index.htm—displays in the status bar to confirm that it is a hyperlink.

Now, you need to test that the hotspot hyperlink works by viewing the Employment Web page in your browser.

To test a hotspot hyperlink using Internet Explorer:

1. Click the **Preview in Browser** button 🔲 on the Standard toolbar to switch to Internet Explorer. The Employment page displays in Internet Explorer.

2. If necessary, click the **Refresh** button 🔲 on the Internet Explorer toolbar to display the revised Web page. The Employment Opportunities logo appears with its transparent background.

3. Place the pointer on top of the **orange** in the logo. The pointer changes to 🖑 and the filename appears in the status bar, both of which indicate that the orange image is a hyperlink. See Figure 3-26.

Figure 3-26 ◀
Testing a
hotspot in
Internet
Explorer

pointer indicates area
of image is a
hyperlink hotspot

partial description of
hyperlink

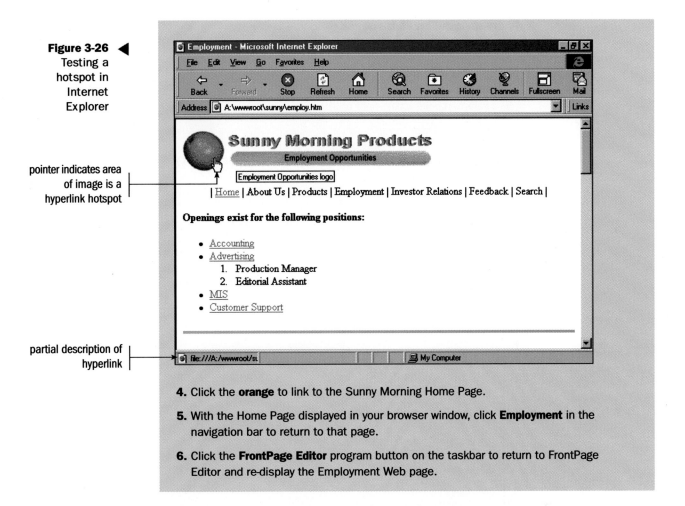

4. Click the **orange** to link to the Sunny Morning Home Page.

5. With the Home Page displayed in your browser window, click **Employment** in the navigation bar to return to that page.

6. Click the **FrontPage Editor** program button on the taskbar to return to FrontPage Editor and re-display the Employment Web page.

The hotspot on the Employment Opportunities logo provides visitors with another way of linking to the Home Page. Now, you need to establish a way for users to get in touch with Sunny Morning Products if they are interested in any of the listed job openings.

Creating an E-Mail Link

A Web page can contain an e-mail link, which is called a mailto. A **mailto** is a special hyperlink that contains an e-mail address. When it is selected, it provides a pre-addressed e-mail form in which you can type your message and send it directly to the addressee. When you type an e-mail address in FrontPage Editor, it is recognized automatically. The mailto parameter that is processed by the Web browser is then created without the need for additional specifications.

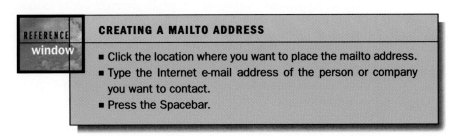

REFERENCE
window

CREATING A MAILTO ADDRESS

■ Click the location where you want to place the mailto address.
■ Type the Internet e-mail address of the person or company you want to contact.
■ Press the Spacebar.

Amanda wants her e-mail address included on the Employment Web page so potential applicants can send their resumes to her.

To create a mailto address:

1. Press **Ctrl + End** to move to the bottom of the Employment Web page. The "via fax" and "via e-mail" headings are now visible.

2. Click anywhere on the **via e-mail** text, and then press the **End** key to place the insertion point to the right of this text.

3. Press the **Enter** key to insert a new paragraph for the mailto address, and then click the **Increase Indent** button [icon] on the Format toolbar to indent this paragraph. Notice that the bold formatting is currently activated because it is carried over from the previous paragraph.

4. Click the **Bold** button [icon] on the Format toolbar to deactivate this formatting.

5. Type **amanda.bay@admin.sunnymorning.com**, and then press the **Spacebar**. FrontPage automatically recognizes the e-mail address as a mailto when a space is inserted after an e-mail address.

6. Position the pointer on **amanda.bay@admin.sunnymorning.com**.

The description of this mailto hyperlink appears in the status bar to indicate that this is a mailto address. See Figure 3-27.

Figure 3-27 ◀
Mailto address
added to
Employment
Web page

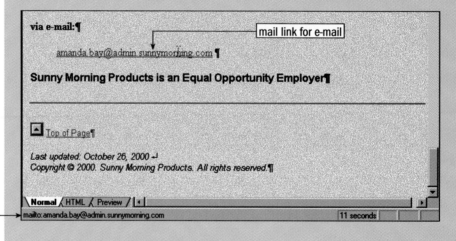

description confirms
mailto address

7. Click the **Save** button [icon] on the Standard toolbar to save these changes.

Amanda's e-mail address is included on the Employment Web page. Now, you need to test this feature.

To test a mailto link using Internet Explorer:

1. Click the **Preview in Browser** button [icon] on the Standard toolbar to switch to Internet Explorer. The Employment Web page displays in Internet Explorer.

2. If necessary, click the **Refresh** button on the Internet Explorer [icon] to view the revised page.

3. Press **Ctrl + End** to move to the bottom of the page and display the mailto address.

4. Click anywhere on the **amanda.bay@admin.sunnymorning.com** mailto address to open the Microsoft Outlook Express program window. See Figure 3-28.

TROUBLE? If your computer uses a different e-mail program than Microsoft Outlook Express (the default mail program for Internet Explorer 4.0), then your e-mail window will be different.

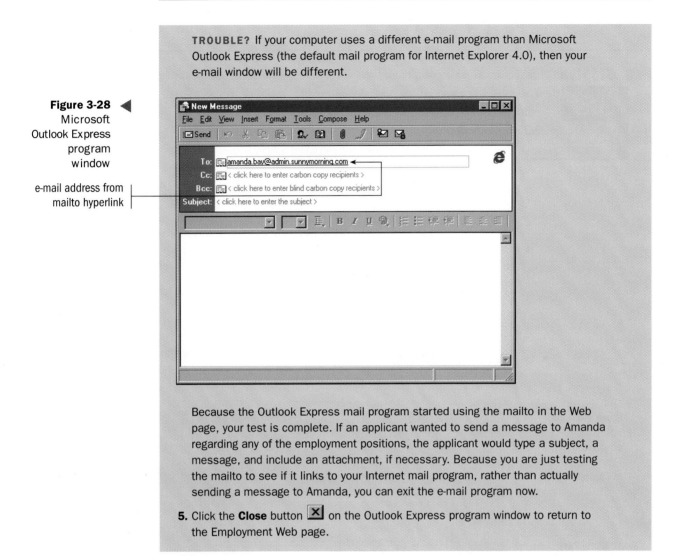

Figure 3-28 ◀
Microsoft
Outlook Express
program
window

e-mail address from
mailto hyperlink

Because the Outlook Express mail program started using the mailto in the Web page, your test is complete. If an applicant wanted to send a message to Amanda regarding any of the employment positions, the applicant would type a subject, a message, and include an attachment, if necessary. Because you are just testing the mailto to see if it links to your Internet mail program, rather than actually sending a message to Amanda, you can exit the e-mail program now.

5. Click the **Close** button ☒ on the Outlook Express program window to return to the Employment Web page.

Quick Check

1 A bookmark identifies a named _____ in a Web page so you can link to it from any other point in the same document or another document.

2 If a bookmark is not associated with a text selection, then a(n) _____ appears in FrontPage Editor to specify the occurrence of the bookmark.

3 Where do you test the hyperlinks within and between Web pages?

4 Which dialog box is used to convert an image from JPEG to GIF format?

5 Which image format allows you to make a single color transparent so the background of a Web page shows through?

6 A(n) _____ is an area of an image that you can click to activate a hyperlink.

7 How do you include an e-mail address in a Web page?

From your test of the Employment Web page, a prospective employee will be able to examine the position descriptions and then access an Internet mail program to send a message to Amanda.

SESSION

3.3

In this session you will view the hyperlinks of a Web site and learn how to use the Tasks list to manage Web page development. You will create a Tasks list, add and complete tasks, and reassign and delete finished tasks. In addition, you will review the HTML code that implements the features of the Employment Web page.

Viewing Hyperlinks

So far, you have made a number of changes and additions to the Sunny Morning Web site. You inserted a new page in the Web and created several links between Web pages. Besides testing the individual hyperlinks using Internet Explorer, you can view these links using the FrontPage Explorer Hyperlinks view, which gives you an overall look at your Web to help ensure that no components are missing.

To view hyperlinks between Web pages:

1. Click the **FrontPage Explorer** program button on the taskbar to switch to this program. The Employment page icon displays in Hyperlinks view in the Explorer window with hyperlinks to and from the Home Page and to the mailto address. See Figure 3-29.

Figure 3-29 ◀
Employment
Web page in
FrontPage
Explorer

link to Home Page

link from Home Page

hyperlink to
mailto address

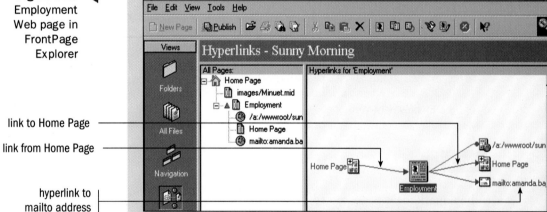

TROUBLE? If Folders view or another view displays, click the Hyperlinks button 🖼 on the Views bar to change to Hyperlinks view.

2. Click **Home Page** at the top of the left pane to display the hyperlinks for that page. See Figure 3-30. Notice that there are links to and from the Employment Web page, as shown in Hyperlinks view. This confirms that you have created the hyperlinks for navigating between these two pages.

Figure 3-30 ◀
Home Page in
FrontPage
Explorer

link to Employment
Web page

link from Employment
Web page

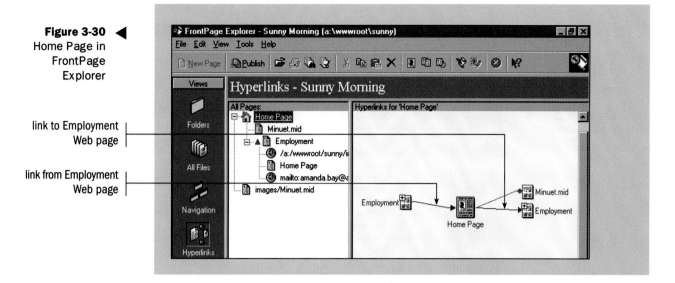

Two of the links in Figure 3-30 end with an arrow, whereas the third link ends with a bullet. An arrow indicates a link you can access, such as another Web page, and a bullet indicates that the item to the right is included as part of the item to the left. For example, if a Web page includes image files or other properties, they display as bulleted links in Hyperlinks view. Recall from Tutorial 1 that an icon with a plus or minus sign in its upper-right corner indicates that you can expand or collapse the hyperlinks to that item.

The two links you created from the Employment Web page to the Home Page—one from Home in the navigation bar and the other as a hotspot from the logo image—are repeated hyperlinks. You can display these types of repeated hyperlinks in Hyperlinks view to confirm each of the links between Web pages. You also can specifically display the links to image files inserted in your Web page to confirm that the page uses the intended files. Amanda wants you to confirm all the hyperlinks you created to make sure they are the ones you want and that nothing has been missed.

To display repeated and image hyperlinks:

1. Click **Employment** in the left pane to select this page as the center focus page in the right pane.

2. Click the **Repeated Hyperlinks** button 🔳 on the toolbar to display the repeated hyperlinks for this page. Notice that two hyperlinks appear from the Employment Web page to the Home Page—one for the navigation bar and the other for the hotspot—confirming these links.

   TROUBLE? If the Repeated Hyperlinks button does not appear depressed on the toolbar, then it was already selected before you completed Step 2. Click the Repeated Hyperlinks button to turn on this feature, and then continue with Step 3.

3. Click the **Hyperlinks to Images** button 🔳 on the toolbar to add these hyperlinks to the current Hyperlinks view of the Employment Web page.

   TROUBLE? If the Hyperlinks to Images button does not appear depressed on the toolbar, then it already was selected before you completed Step 3. Click the Hyperlinks to Images button to turn on this feature, and then continue with Step 4.

4. Place the pointer on the top **Home Page icon** (/a:/wwwroot/sunny/index.htm) in the right pane. (It is the one with a bullet instead of an arrow next to it.) An Include Styled message appears in the floating text box to indicate the use of the background and colors properties from the Home Page. See Figure 3-31. Notice that an envelope icon indicates an e-mail hyperlink whereas a painting icon indicates an image file.

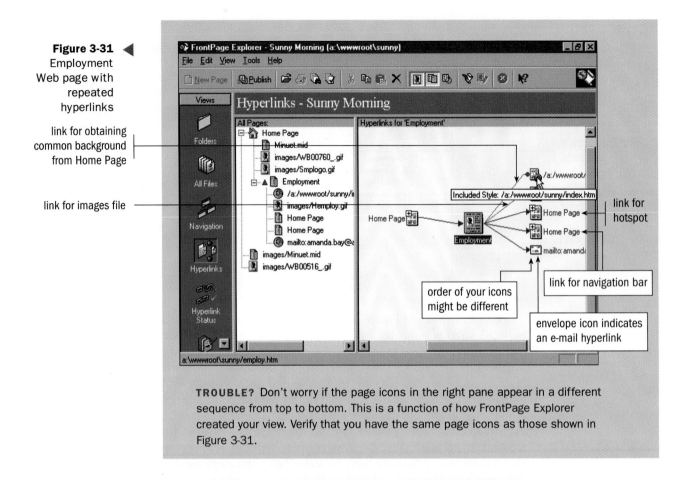

Figure 3-31
Employment
Web page with
repeated
hyperlinks

link for obtaining
common background
from Home Page

link for images file

link for
hotspot

order of your icons
might be different

link for navigation bar

envelope icon indicates
an e-mail hyperlink

TROUBLE? Don't worry if the page icons in the right pane appear in a different sequence from top to bottom. This is a function of how FrontPage Explorer created your view. Verify that you have the same page icons as those shown in Figure 3-31.

Printing a Hyperlinks View

FrontPage Explorer does not have a print command that allows you to print Hyperlinks or Folders views, as it does for Navigation view. This is because these views are designed to be used interactively. At times, however, you might need a printed copy of these views. In this situation, you can copy either view to the Windows Clipboard and then print it using WordPad or another Windows word-processing program.

You need to print a copy of the Employment Web page in Hyperlinks view for your upcoming meeting with Amanda to discuss the progress of your training activities.

To print a Hyperlinks view:

1. With the Employment Web page still displayed in Hyperlinks view, press the **Print Screen** key to copy your current display to the Windows Clipboard.

2. Click the **Start** button, point to **Programs**, point to **Accessories**, and then click **WordPad** to start the WordPad program. A blank WordPad document displays in your window. If necessary, maximize the window.

3. Press **Ctrl + V** to paste a copy of the Windows Clipboard contents at the location of the insertion point in the WordPad document. See Figure 3-32.

Figure 3-32 ◀
WordPad
program
window

information displayed
in your window might
be different

screen capture of
FrontPage Explorer
window

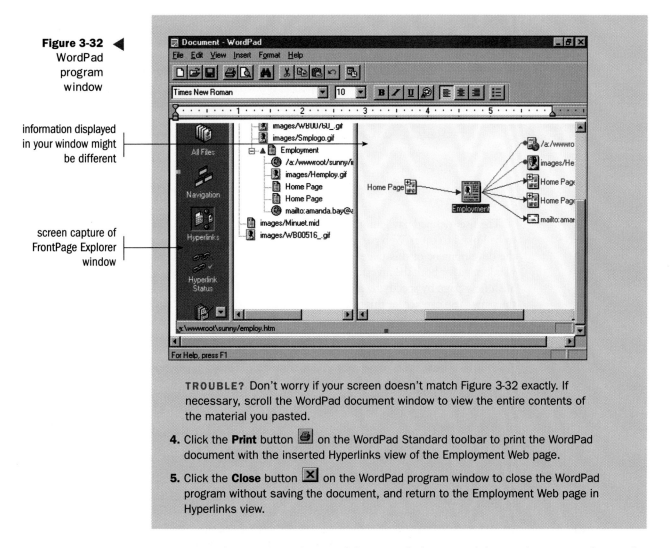

TROUBLE? Don't worry if your screen doesn't match Figure 3-32 exactly. If necessary, scroll the WordPad document window to view the entire contents of the material you pasted.

4. Click the **Print** button on the WordPad Standard toolbar to print the WordPad document with the inserted Hyperlinks view of the Employment Web page.

5. Click the **Close** button on the WordPad program window to close the WordPad program without saving the document, and return to the Employment Web page in Hyperlinks view.

Now you have a printed copy of the Hyperlinks view of the Employment Web page for your meeting with Amanda.

Managing Web Development with a Tasks List

One way to help manage the development of a Web site is to use a **Tasks list,** which is a detailed listing of the necessary activities or items required to complete a Web site. A Tasks list helps you organize and track the tasks to develop a Web site successfully. The Tasks list describes each task, indicates the person assigned to complete it, and specifies its priority. Once you have completed the initial design of your Web site, you can create a Tasks list that describes all of the pages you need to develop. You can add activities to a Tasks list, modify task names, assign developers, include descriptions, and remove a task from the list at any time. When a task is finished, you can mark it as completed and then archive it or delete it from the Tasks list. If the Web page does not already exist, you can use the Create or Edit Hyperlink command in FrontPage Editor to add the task to the Tasks list automatically and link it to the appropriate page or file. When a task is linked to a page in this way, you can open the page in FrontPage Editor from the Tasks list by right-clicking the task and then clicking Do Task on the Shortcut menu. As one of the available views of FrontPage Explorer, a Tasks list is designed to be used interactively. Therefore, if you need a hardcopy of the list, you must print it using the same procedure you used to print a Hyperlinks view.

Adding Tasks to a Tasks List

One of the first activities in using the Tasks list is to add tasks to it. You can do this directly by specifying all the information for the task, or you can have FrontPage add the task to the list as you create hyperlinks.

CREATING A NEW WEB PAGE AND ADDING IT TO A TASKS LIST

- Select the text, image, or hotspot in the open page that will be the hyperlink to the new page.
- Click the Create or Edit Hyperlink button on the Standard toolbar, and then click the Create a page and link to the new page button to open the New dialog box.
- Click the Just add web task check box, click the type of page you want to create, and then click the OK button.
- Enter the Title and URL, and then click the OK button.

The user-defined navigation bar in the Employment page contains several entries that remain to be linked to other Web pages, such as the one for the Investor Relations page. Before adding the development of this page as a task in the Tasks list, Amanda wants you to create a new blank page for both the investor relations and products entries. Keep in mind that when you create a new page by specifying a hyperlink, the selected hyperlink text is suggested as the title for the page. You can accept this title or change it as appropriate for your Web page. Continue with your training by creating these new pages and adding them as tasks to be completed in your Tasks list.

To create a new Web page and add a task to a Tasks list by creating a hyperlink:

1. Click the **FrontPage Editor** program button on the taskbar to switch to this program. The Employment Web page opens in the Editor window.

2. Press **Ctrl + Home** to move to the top of the Employment Web page.

3. Select **Investor Relations** in the navigation bar as the hyperlink.

4. Click the **Create or Edit Hyperlink** button [icon] on the Standard toolbar to open the Create Hyperlink dialog box, and then click the **Create a page and link to the new page** button [icon] to open the New dialog box with a list of available template pages that has the Normal Page selected in the list box. See Figure 3-33. Because a particular template is not currently required, the Normal Page that is suggested is appropriate for this new page.

Figure 3-33 ◀
New dialog box
with available
template pages

selected page
template

click to include
in Tasks list

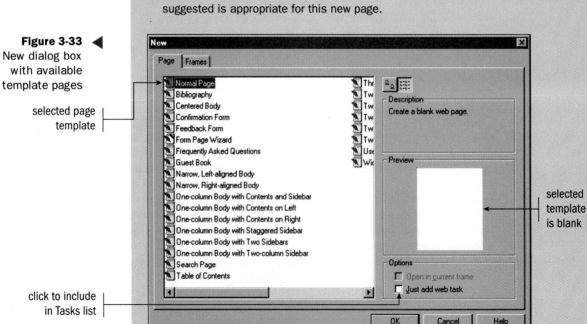

selected
template
is blank

5. Click the **Just add web task** check box to specify this option, and then click the **OK** button. The Save As dialog box opens with a default name for the URL and the Title of the Web page. The suggested URL name appears selected.

6. Press the **Delete** key to remove the suggested URL name, press the **Tab** key to select the suggested name displayed for the Title, and then type **Investor** as the desired page Title. See Figure 3-34. As you type the Title, that value appears in the URL text box as a suggested filename for the page. Any spaces in the Title are replaced by an underscore in the filename.

Figure 3-34 ◀
Save As
dialog box with
user-specified
URL and Title

filename for new page
to add to current Web

title for new page

7. Click the **OK** button to create a new blank Investor page in the Sunny Morning Web and add its completion to the Tasks list.

8. Repeat Steps 3 through 7 for the **Products** entry in the navigation bar and give this page the title of Products. When completed, this new blank page also is added to the Sunny Morning Web (a:\wwwroot\sunny).

Besides using the hyperlink text as the title for the Web page, you can specify a different title when creating a new page. In Amanda's design of the Sunny Morning Web site, the About Us hyperlink is used to open the Company Profile page. Amanda wants you to create the hyperlink for this page using the title "Profile" with a filename of company.htm and include its completion as a task in the Tasks list.

To create a new page and add a new task with a different name:

1. Select **About Us** in the navigation bar.

2. Click the **Create or Edit Hyperlink** button ⬛ on the Standard toolbar to open the Create Hyperlink dialog box, and then click the **Create a page and link to the new page** button ⬜ to open the New dialog box with the Normal Page selected.

3. Click the **Just add web task** check box to specify this option, click the **OK** button to open the Save As dialog box, press the **Delete** key to remove the suggested URL name, press the **Tab** key to select the suggested name displayed for the Title, and then type **Profile** as the desired page Title.

4. Click the **URL** text box, and then type **company** as the filename. You don't need to type the htm file extension because it is included in the filename automatically.

5. Click the **OK** button to create this new page and return to the Employment Web page.

6. Click anywhere on the **About Us** text to deselect it.

7. Click the **Save** button 🖫 on the Standard toolbar to save your changes to the Employment Web page.

Besides adding an activity to the Tasks list as you create a hyperlink or a new page, you can enter a task in the list directly.

REFERENCE window

ADDING A TASK TO A TASKS LIST

- Click the FrontPage Explorer program button on the taskbar to switch to that program.
- Click the Tasks button on the Views bar to display that list.
- Click the New Task button on the Standard toolbar to open the New Task dialog box.
- Enter the information for the task.
- Click the OK button to add the task to the list.

You review the status of the navigation bar on the Employment Web page with Amanda. Two additional pages need to be included in the Web to complete all its entries—the ones for Feedback and Search. However, you don't have time now to create these Web pages so Amanda instructs you to add these tasks to your current Tasks list.

To add a task to a Tasks list:

1. Click the **FrontPage Explorer** program button on the taskbar to switch to that program.

2. Click the **Tasks** button 🗓 on the Views bar to display the FrontPage Tasks view in the right pane.

3. Click the **New Task** button on the Standard toolbar. The New Task dialog box opens.

4. Type **Create Feedback Form** in the Task Name text box, and then press the **Tab** key three times to move to the Description text box.

5. Type **Create a form page that is completed and submitted by a customer.** in the Description text box.

6. Click the **OK** button to finish adding this task to the list.

7. Repeat Steps 3 through 6 to add the second task to the Tasks list based on the following information:

Task Name: **Create Search Page**
Description: **Create a page that performs a search on the Web for a text string match.**

Your Tasks list should match Figure 3-35.

Figure 3-35
Revised Tasks
list for Sunny
Morning Web

priority automatically
selected

list of tasks

your name
appears here

click to select
Tasks view

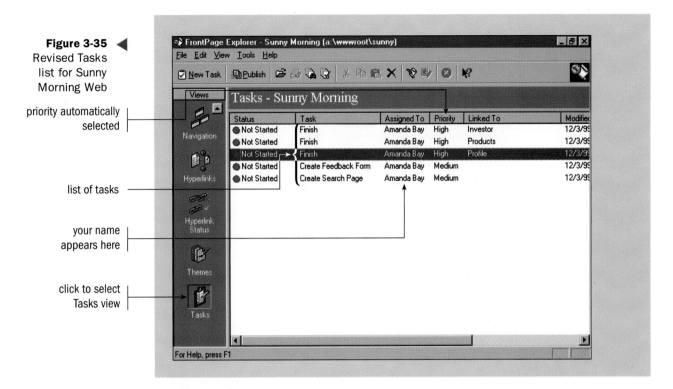

This completes the list of tasks necessary for finishing the development of the Sunny Morning Web site. Now, you organize your Tasks list so that it is easier to reference in managing the remaining development activities for this Web site.

Sorting a Tasks List

When managing your Web site development using a Tasks list, the sort feature is helpful. A sorted list makes it easier to view the tasks that are added to or deleted from the list. You can sort a Tasks list by any of the columns in the list. Each column label or title in the Tasks list is a button that you can click to sort the information in that column, such as sorting the list by task. Before continuing, sort the Tasks list alphabetically by task and view the items' priorities.

To sort a Tasks list:

1. With the current Tasks list displayed in your window, click the **Task** column label button to sort the tasks alphabetically by this field.

    With the list sorted, view the tasks according to priority.

2. Double-click the **Finish** task that is linked to the Profile page to open the Task Details dialog box. See Figure 3-36. This is where you can edit the status of a task as well as adjust the task's description and the person assigned to it. Notice the current description of this task in the Description text box.

Figure 3-36 ◄
Task Details
dialog box

your name
appears here

current description
of this task

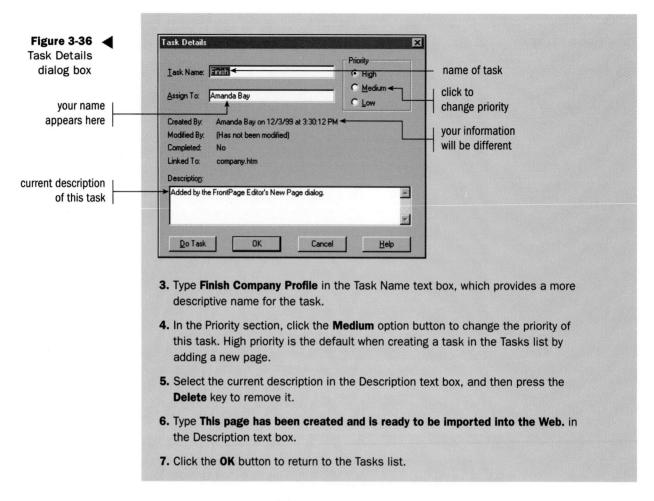

name of task

click to
change priority

your information
will be different

3. Type **Finish Company Profile** in the Task Name text box, which provides a more descriptive name for the task.

4. In the Priority section, click the **Medium** option button to change the priority of this task. High priority is the default when creating a task in the Tasks list by adding a new page.

5. Select the current description in the Description text box, and then press the **Delete** key to remove it.

6. Type **This page has been created and is ready to be imported into the Web.** in the Description text box.

7. Click the **OK** button to return to the Tasks list.

Now that you've finished organizing the Tasks list, you can complete some of its tasks.

Completing a Task

You continue your development of the Sunny Morning Web by tackling the Finish Company Profile page task. In preparation, Amanda created the company.htm page, which opens from the About Us hyperlink. However, if you were collaborating on the development of a Web site, this could be a page that you obtained from a colleague. Because Amanda has created this page for you, you simply import the page into the Web.

To complete a task:

1. Click the **Hyperlinks** button 🖳 on the Views bar to switch to that view. You need to change views because the Import command is not available from the File menu when Tasks view is selected.

2. Click **File** on the menu bar, and then click **Import** to open the Import File to FrontPage Web dialog box.

3. Click the **Add File** button to open the Add File to Import List dialog box, make sure the drive that contains your Student Disk appears in the Look in text box, double-click the **Tutorial.03** folder, click the **company.htm** file, click the **Open** button to return to the Import File to FrontPage dialog box, and then click the **OK** button.

The Confirm Save message box opens, indicating that the file already exists because you created this as a Normal Page when the task was added to the Tasks list. You want to replace this blank page with the completed Company Profile page.

4. Click the **Yes** button. The page is replaced, and you return to FrontPage Explorer.

5. If necessary, click **Profile**, the page's title, in the left pane to display its hyperlinks in the right pane. See Figure 3-37. Notice the broken links to three of the pages. A **broken link** is a hyperlink that is not completely specified or that has been configured incorrectly and references a bookmark or Web page that does not exist or cannot be located.

TROUBLE? If the Hyperlink to Images and Repeated Hyperlinks buttons on the Standard toolbar appear depressed to indicate these features are turned on, you will have more than three broken links. Click both buttons to deactivate those features of Hyperlinks view.

Figure 3-37 ◀
Company Profile
Web page in
FrontPage
Explorer

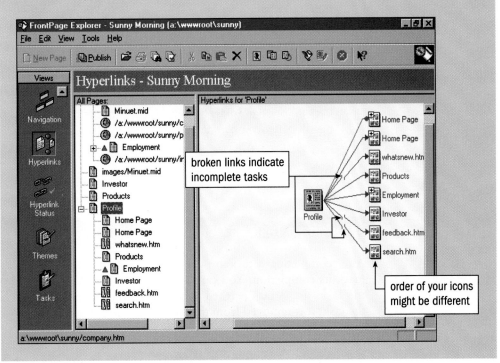

Three broken links in Figure 3-37 indicate uncompleted tasks. The development of two of these pages already has been added to the Tasks list, but a third page now appears as a task to be completed. Whenever you insert an existing page in your Web, it might have links to other pages that you need to consider, as is the case with the Sunny Morning Web. You could add this task to the list in the same manner that you used for the Feedback and Search pages, but you decide to wait until you have talked with Amanda about the page.

Accessing a Web Page from a Tasks List

Once you have added a Web page as a task in the Tasks list, you can use the list to access that page as you work on completing a task. You continue with your training by accessing the Web page for the Finish Company Profile task to review it. There might be some remaining activities to do before you can label the development of this Web page as a completed task.

To access a Web page from a Tasks list:

1. Click the **Tasks** button 📋 on the Views bar to switch to that view, and then right-click the **Finish Company Profile** task to select it and display the Shortcut menu.

2. Click **Do Task** and the Profile page opens in FrontPage Editor. Notice the broken image icon at the top of the Web page. Although this page was included in the Web, you need to include its image as well.

3. Click the **broken image** to select it, right-click it to display the Shortcut menu, and then click **Image Properties** to open that dialog box. The hcompro.gif file information in the Image Source text box indicates the expected location of the file. However, this file is missing from the Sunny Morning Web.

4. Click the **Browse** button to the right of the Image Source text box to open the Image dialog box, and then click the **Select a file on your computer** button 🔍 to open the Select File dialog box.

5. Make sure the drive that contains your Student Disk appears in the Look in text box, double-click the **Tutorial.03** folder, double-click the **Images** folder, click the **hcompro.gif** file, and then click the **OK** button. The Image Properties dialog box reopens with the selected file.

6. Click the **OK** button. The image now appears on the Profile Web page.

7. Click the **Save** button 💾 on the Standard toolbar. A FrontPage Editor dialog box opens and asks if you want to mark the task as completed. Click the **No** button for now. The Save Embedded Files dialog box opens with hcompro.gif listed.

8. Click the **Change Folder** button, click the **images** folder to select it, and then click the **OK** button to return to the Save Embedded Files dialog box.

9. Click the **OK** button to save this GIF file in the images folder of the Sunny Morning Web.

Marking a Task as Completed

After completing a task from your Tasks list, FrontPage gives you the opportunity to mark its completion. You can either mark a task as completed or delete it entirely from the Tasks list. A task marked as completed remains in the Tasks list, whereas if you delete the task, it is removed from the list.

REFERENCE window

MARKING A TASK AS COMPLETED

- Click the Show FrontPage Explorer button on the Standard toolbar to switch to that program, and then click the Tasks button on the Views bar to display the list.
- Right-click the task to select it and display the Shortcut menu, and then click Mark Complete.

Now you are ready to continue with your training by marking the Finish Company Profile task as completed in your Tasks list.

To mark a task as completed:

1. Click the **Show FrontPage Explorer** button 🗗 on the Standard toolbar to switch to that program, and then, if necessary, click the **Tasks** button 🗒 on the Views bar to display the Tasks list.

2. Right-click the **Finish Company Profile** task to select it and display the Shortcut menu, and then click **Mark Complete**. "Completed" appears as the status of the task in the Tasks list.

3. If necessary, click **View** on the menu bar, and then click **Task History** to select this option and display any completed tasks. The Tasks list is updated to reflect the unfinished tasks and the ones marked as completed. See Figure 3-38.

Figure 3-38 ◀
Updated Tasks
list

displays when Task
History is selected

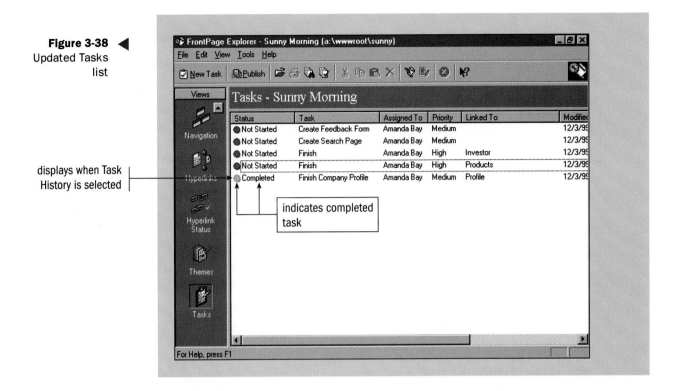

indicates completed
task

Deleting a Task from the Tasks List

A task marked for completion can be removed from the Tasks list by deleting it. Deleting a task is a permanent action. If you delete a task, FrontPage does not give you the option of reestablishing the task in the Tasks list.

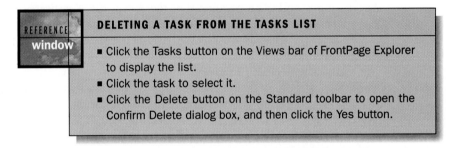

REFERENCE
window

DELETING A TASK FROM THE TASKS LIST

- Click the Tasks button on the Views bar of FrontPage Explorer to display the list.
- Click the task to select it.
- Click the Delete button on the Standard toolbar to open the Confirm Delete dialog box, and then click the Yes button.

Because you have completed the Finish Company Profile task, you no longer want to include it in your Tasks list. Amanda confirms that it is okay for you to remove it from the list.

To delete a completed task from a Tasks list:

1. Make sure the Task History command on the View menu is checked so completed tasks are displayed in the Tasks list.

2. Click the **Finish Company Profile** task to select this completed task.

3. Click the **Delete** button ☒ on the Standard toolbar to open the Confirm Delete dialog box, and then click the **Yes** button to remove it from the Tasks list.

You successfully completed the Finish Company Profile page activity and deleted this task from the Tasks list. Amanda has one more assignment for you.

Reassigning a Task

After adding a task to the Tasks list, you can change any of its details, including reassigning a task. For larger Web sites, several individuals might work on different pages, and thus each task might need assignment to a different person.

So far, the tasks in the Tasks list have been assigned to Amanda, as indicated by her name in the Assigned To column of the Tasks list. Either your name or the name assigned to the computer where the Web is being created will appear in the Assigned To column. Because you will complete the Products Web page in the next tutorial, Amanda wants you to reassign the Finish task that is linked to the Products page to yourself.

To reassign a task:

1. Double-click the **Finish** task that is linked to Products to select it and open the Task Details dialog box.

2. Click in the **Assign To** text box, select the current text, and then type your **first** and **last name**, leaving a space in between names.

3. Click the **OK** button to return to the Tasks list. Notice that your name now appears in the Assigned To column.

Now that you've reassigned this task to yourself, you are finished working with the Tasks list. Before you finish this part of your training, Amanda wants you to view the HTML code for the tasks you completed.

Viewing HTML Code

You enhanced and changed the Employment Web page by including the background from the Home Page, adding bookmarks and internal hyperlinks, creating a hotspot, and including an e-mail link. Each of these features is implemented with different HTML tags. For example, an HREF parameter of the A tag (the A indicates this is an anchor, which implements the hyperlinks) uses a pound sign (#), such as #MIS, to specify an internal page reference, whereas the NAME parameter, such as to_apply, specifies a bookmark location within a Web page. A FrontPage WebBot created the MAP and AREA tags that implement the hotspot of the logo image on the page. FrontPage Editor selected each of these tags and their related parameters as you modified the Employment Web page. Amanda wants you to view specific HTML code for the Employment Web page to gain a better understanding of the code FrontPage produced for you. However, first she asks you check the estimated download time for the page when it is obtained from a Web server to make sure that it downloads quickly.

To view the estimated download time of the Employment Web page:

1. Click the **Show FrontPage Editor** button 🔳 on the Standard toolbar to switch to that program.

2. Click **Window** on the menu bar, and then click **Employment** to open that page in the Editor window.

3. Position the pointer on the word **seconds** displayed at the right side of the status bar. A text box appears indicating this is the estimated download time at 28.8kbs. See Figure 3-39.

Figure 3-39
Estimated
download time
for Employment
Web page

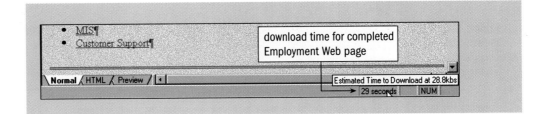

Now that you know the estimated download time for the page, you proceed to view the HTML code for it.

To view HTML code of the Employment page:

1. Click the **HTML** tab to switch to that view and display the HTML codes, click anywhere in the HTML window to deselect any selected code, and then scroll down the page until the BODY tag is at the top of the screen. See Figure 3-40. Notice the specific tags and code associated with tasks, such as including a common background, implementing a hotspot, and creating a bulleted and numbered list.

Figure 3-40
Viewing the
first page of
HTML code

WebBot implements
hotspot image map

href specifies internal
page name

opening tag for
bulleted list

bulleted list item

closing tag for
numbered list

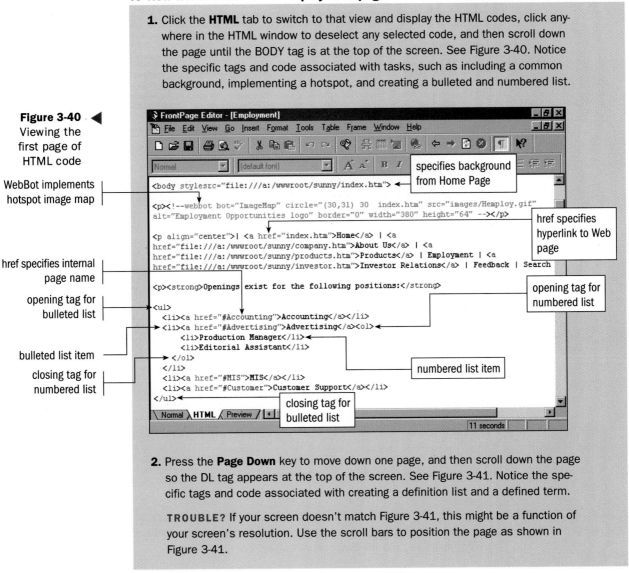

2. Press the **Page Down** key to move down one page, and then scroll down the page so the DL tag appears at the top of the screen. See Figure 3-41. Notice the specific tags and code associated with creating a definition list and a defined term.

   TROUBLE? If your screen doesn't match Figure 3-41, this might be a function of your screen's resolution. Use the scroll bars to position the page as shown in Figure 3-41.

Figure 3-41 ◀
Viewing the
second page of
HTML code

opening tag for
definition list

defined term entry

definition for term

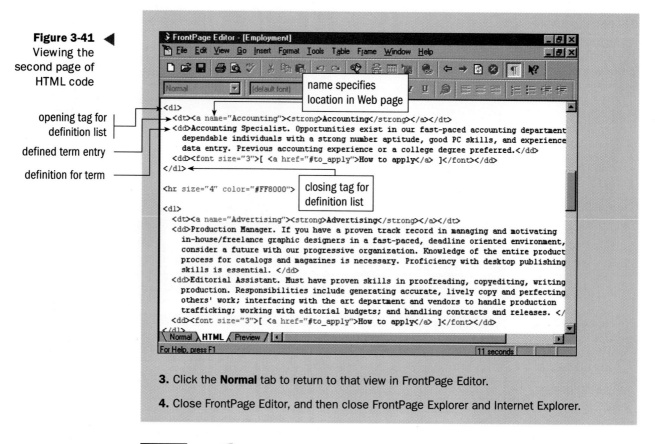

name specifies
location in Web page

closing tag for
definition list

3. Click the **Normal** tab to return to that view in FrontPage Editor.

4. Close FrontPage Editor, and then close FrontPage Explorer and Internet Explorer.

Quick Check

1 A(n) _____ is a record of the details of the tasks necessary for completing a Web site.

2 The _____ check box allows you to add a task to the Tasks list when you create a new page.

3 The Tasks list is sorted whenever you click a(n) _____.

4 A(n) _____ is a hyperlink that is not completely specified and is seen in Hyperlinks view.

5 Which button do you click to begin working on a Web page from the Tasks list?

6 A task that is _____ appears in the Tasks list only when the Task History menu option is checked.

Amanda is pleased with your progress in completing a Web page for employment opportunities at Sunny Morning Products. Under Amanda's guidance, your competence in Web development and maintenance is increasing.

Tutorial Assignments

You must complete some remaining tasks in order to finish the Employment Web page. Some of these tasks you already have practiced, and others will help you gain additional experience in developing Web pages. If necessary, insert your Student Disk into drive A or the appropriate disk drive, start FrontPage Explorer, and then do the following:

1. Access the sunny Web with the revised Employment Web page, and then open that page in FrontPage Editor.

2. Create another position opening on the Employment Web page, where you determine the department name and write the job description. Enter this position information below the description for customer support as a definition list. (*Hint:* Use the same format and organization as for the other job descriptions.)

3. Add the department name for the position you created in Step 2 to the table of contents at the top of the page, and then create the following two hyperlinks: one from this entry to the defined term in the definition list of the job description, and a second one from the definition to the beginning of the job application information at the "to_apply" bookmark.

4. Copy the horizontal rule that is used to separate the MIS and customer support job descriptions and place it after your new job description to separate the description from the job application information.

5. Save your changes, test these changes using Internet Explorer, and then print the page from FrontPage Editor.

6. Create a bookmark named "top" located immediately to the left of the inline image of the logo at the top of the Employment Web page. Do not select any text for the top bookmark.

7. Add the "Top of Page" text in a separate paragraph immediately above the last updated date at the bottom of the Web page, and then create a hyperlink from the "Top of Page" text to the top bookmark you created in Step 6. Format the "Top of Page" text as regular font.

8. Insert the btn_up.gif file as an inline image immediately to the left of the "Top of Page" hyperlink text with a space between the image and the text. (*Hint:* The btn_up.gif file is located in the Tutorial.03\images folder on your Student Disk.) Create a hyperlink from the btn_up.gif image to the top bookmark.

9. Save the revised Employment Web page with its images, and then test it using Internet Explorer.

10. Use FrontPage Editor to print the revised Employment Web page, and then circle the top bookmark and the Top of Page and Up button hyperlinks on your printout.

11. Display and then print the HTML code for the Employment Web page using Notepad or another editor. Circle the HTML code for the new job description and hyperlinks on your printout.

12. Open the Profile Web page (company.htm) in FrontPage Editor. The navigation bar on this page includes the What's New entry. Add a new entry to the Tasks list for finishing the What's New Web page, but do not create the new page. Include a meaningful description of the remaining activities associated with this task.

13. Sort the Tasks list by task. Use WordPad to print the revised Tasks list.

14. Complete the task you added to the Tasks list in Step 12 by importing the What's New Web page (whatsnew.htm) from the Tutorial.03 folder and including it with its logo image (hwhatsne.gif) in the sunny Web. Save your changes.

15. Test the hyperlink from the Profile page to the What's New page, mark the task as complete in the Tasks list, make sure the Task History is on, and then print the list using WordPad. Write a paragraph that describes your test of these hyperlinks.

16. Display the What's New Web page as the center focus page in Hyperlinks view in FrontPage Explorer. Display the repeated hyperlinks, and then print the Hyperlinks view using WordPad. Close WordPad without saving any changes.

17. Create a hyperlink from the Home Page to the Profile page (company.htm) using the "About Us" text in the navigation bar on the Home Page.

18. Use Windows Explorer to find the file sizes of the hemploy.gif and hemploy.jpg files for the logo on the Employment Web page. (*Hint:* The GIF file is in the sunny Web, and the JPG file is in the Tutorial.03 folder.) How many times larger is the JPG file than the GIF file?

19. Close FrontPage Editor, FrontPage Explorer, Internet Explorer, and Windows Explorer.

Case Problems

1. Preparing an Information Page for Royal Hair Care Products The product launch for the Kuick Dry Reliable Solution at Royal Hair Care Products is well underway. Valerie met with Sharon Brock, the Kuick Dry product manager, to discuss the support the company might provide through its Web site. Together, Valerie and Sharon determined that their planned company profile Web page could be used to provide distributors and retailers with information on the product and its promotion. Then Valerie and Nathan, the information systems intern, met with Sharon and her staff to finalize their ideas on the Web page content. They agreed that the page should contain four sections: distribution, promotion, packaging, and legal. Sharon agreed that she would write a draft of the distribution information and provide Nathan with a copy of that file for use with the company profile page. Nathan has started to develop the company profile page, and Valerie wants you to help him complete this task.

If necessary, start FrontPage Explorer, insert your Student Disk in drive A or the appropriate disk drive, and then do the following:

1. Read all the questions for this case problem, and then prepare a planning analysis sheet for the revisions to the Royal Web site.

2. Access the Royal Web. If you did not create this Web in Tutorial 2, create the Web now. (*Hint:* Ask your instructor for the Home Page file that you can import into the Web and for the logo image.)

3. Import the partially completed Company Information (rcompany.htm) page from the Tutorial.03\royal folder into the Web, and then open this page in FrontPage Editor. Review the page and locate the navigation bar, the items listed as a table of contents below the navigation bar, and the four content areas of the page that are separated using horizontal rules.

4. Insert the royal03.jpg file from the Tutorial.03\royal folder as an inline image that appears at the top of the page above the navigation bar and is left-aligned. Then insert the rnews.gif file from the same folder on the same line, but immediately to the right of the royal03.jpg file.

5. Convert the JPG image from Step 4 into a GIF image. Then make the green background of this image transparent.

6. Change the background of this Web page to the same one that you used for the Home Page.

7. Include the text from the distrib.rtf file in the Tutorial.03\royal folder as a definition for Distribution.

8. In each of the other three content sections, format the heading as the defined term and the content paragraphs as their definitions.

9. Format the distribution, promotion, packaging, and legal list of items that make up the table of contents (located immediately below the navigation bar) as a numbered list. Create a bookmark for each of these items where they are described below in the Web page. Then create a hyperlink from each of the numbered list items of the table of contents to its respective bookmark.

10. Include your e-mail address at the bottom of the Web page below the "For additional information contact us:" paragraph. If you don't have an e-mail address, create one or use one your instructor provides.

11. Create the bookmark "Top" as a named reference that is located immediately to the left of the logo inline image at the top of this page. Place the text "Top of Page" in a separate paragraph at the bottom of the Web page. Create a hyperlink from the "Top of Page" text to the "top" bookmark.

12. Insert the btn_up.gif file as an inline image immediately to the left of the "Top of Page" hyperlink text with a space between the image and this text. The btn_up.gif file is located in the Tutorial.03\images folder. Create a hyperlink from the btn_up.gif image to the "top" bookmark.

13. Save the Web page, and place all images for the page in the images folder of the Royal Web. Test all the internal hyperlinks in the browser. If you discover any errors, correct them.

14. Create a hyperlink in the navigation bar from the Company Information page to the Home Page, and then create a link in the navigation bar from the Home Page to the Company Information page.

15. Select News in the navigation bar of the Company Information page. Add a normal page to the Web as the What's New page with the filename of rnews.htm, and then include this as a task to be completed in the Web's Tasks list.

16. Select Feedback in the navigation bar of the Company Information page. Add another normal page to the Web as the Feedback page with the filename of rfeedbak.htm, and include this as a task in the Web's Tasks list.

17. Open the Tasks list, and then change the Finish task for the What's New page to "Import" and add an appropriate description and assign the task to yourself (if necessary) with medium priority. Then change the Finish task for the Feedback page to "Create," change the description to an appropriate one, assign the task to yourself, if necessary, and change to medium priority. Print the Tasks list using Notepad or another editor.

18. Import the What's New page (rnews.htm file) from the Tutorial.03\royal folder into the Royal Web, and replace the current page. Then replace the broken inline image to the left of the Company News logo with the royal03.gif file from the Tutorial.03\royal folder. Save the Web page, and then save the royal03.gif file in the images folder of the Royal Web. Use drag and drop to create the hyperlink from the What's New page to the Home Page. Test these new hyperlinks, and then make any corrections.

19. Mark the task for the What's New page as completed in the Tasks list, but do not delete the task.

20. Add the task of creating the Search page to the Tasks list. Do not add this page to the Web. Print a copy of this revised Tasks list. Save your changes.

21. Display the Company Information page as the focus page in Hyperlinks view in FrontPage Explorer. Display the repeated hyperlinks. Print a copy of Hyperlinks view.

22. Print the Company Information Web page from FrontPage Editor, and then print the HTML code for this page. Circle the HTML code entries for all the hyperlinks and bookmarks.

23. Arrange and clearly identify the printouts and answers for all the case questions.

24. Close any open programs, and save changes to your Web files.

2. Developing the Web Pages for Buffalo Trading Post The recycling business at the Buffalo Trading Post remains strong. Donna and the sales associates have received approximately 50 telephone calls a day from potential customers. As a result, Donna decided to add a page to the Buffalo Web that provides customers with information about the company's recycling process. Donna, Karla, and the sales staff agreed that the page should contain a How It Works section that describes the process of buying and selling and a Frequently Asked Questions (FAQ) section. In addition, a Choose To Re-Use section will describe Buffalo's overall commitment to recycling. Karla began the process of creating this page while Donna wrote the text for the How It Works section. Karla asks you to help her complete the remaining Web development activities.

If necessary, start FrontPage Explorer, insert your Student Disk in drive A or the appropriate disk drive, and then do the following:

1. Read all the questions for this case problem, and then prepare a planning analysis sheet for the revisions to the Buffalo Web site.

2. Access the Buffalo Web. If you did not create this Web in Tutorial 2, create the Web now. (*Hint:* Ask your instructor for the home page file that you can import into the Web, as well as the logo image.)

3. Import the partially completed How (bhow.htm) page in the Tutorial.03\buffalo folder into the Web, and then open this page in FrontPage Editor. Review the page, and then locate the navigation bar, the items listed as a table of contents below the navigation bar, and the three content areas of the page that are separated using horizontal rules.

4. Insert the b_how.jpg file from the Tutorial.03\buffalo folder as an inline image that appears at the top of the page above the navigation bar and is left-aligned.

5. Convert the JPG image from Step 4 into a GIF image.

6. Specify the bwmark.gif file from the Tutorial.03\buffalo folder as the background image. Change the image to a watermark.

7. Import the text from the howworks.rtf file in the Tutorial.03\buffalo folder as a normal paragraph below the How It Works heading that appears between two horizontal rules.

8. In the FAQ area, format each question as a defined term and each answer as the definition for that defined term.

9. Format the How It Works, Frequently Asked Questions, and Choose To Re-Use list that makes up the table of contents located immediately below the navigation bar as a bulleted list.

10. Create a bookmark for each of the table of contents items where they are described below in the Web page, and then create a hyperlink from each of the bulleted list items in the table of contents to its respective bookmark.

11. Include your e-mail address at the bottom of the Web page below the "For additional information please contact us:" paragraph. If you don't have an e-mail address, create one or use one your instructor provides. Change the style of your e-mail address to the Address style.

12. Create the bookmark named "Top" as a named reference located immediately to the left of the "How" inline image at the top of this page. Place the text "Top of Page" in a separate paragraph at the bottom of the Web page. Create a hyperlink from the "Top of Page" text to the "Top" bookmark.

13. Insert an appropriate image from the Clip Art Gallery that users can click to go to the top of the page. Insert the graphic as an inline image immediately to the left of the "Top of Page" hyperlink text with a space between the image and this text. You might use an up arrow or a hand with a finger that points up. (If you cannot locate an appropriate graphic in the Clip Art Gallery, use the btn_up.gif file that is saved in the Tutorial.03\images folder.) (*Hint:* You might have to use the sizing handles to resize the image to an appropriate size after inserting it.) Create a hyperlink from the graphic image to the Top bookmark. Use the Image Properties dialog box to determine the format of the graphic that you inserted. If necessary, convert the image to GIF format.

14. Save the Web page, and save all the images for the page in the images folder of the Buffalo Web. Then test all the internal hyperlinks using the browser. Correct any errors that you discover.

15. Create a hyperlink in the navigation bar from the How page to the Home Page, and then create a link in the navigation bar from the Home Page to the How page.

16. Create a rectangular hotspot that covers the "Buffalo Trading Post" text in the logo image at the top of the How page. Link this hotspot to the Home Page.

17. Save this revised Web page, and then test the hyperlinks between the How page and the Home Page without using the browser or the Preview tab. (*Hint:* Place the pointer on any hyperlink to discover how to test a hyperlink without using the browser.)

18. Select "What" in the navigation bar of the How page. Add a normal page named "What" to the Web with the filename of bwhat.htm, and include this as a task to be completed in the Web's Tasks list.

19. Import the Who page (bwho.htm file) from the Tutorial.03\buffalo folder into the Buffalo Web. Then replace the broken page logo inline image with the b_who.gif file from the Tutorial.03\buffalo folder. Finally, select "Who" in the navigation bar of the How page, and link it to the Who page.

20. Save the Web page, and place the b_who.gif file in the images folder of the Buffalo Web. Create the hyperlinks between the Who page and the Home Page, and then test these new hyperlinks.

21. Mark the task for finishing the Who page as complete in the Tasks list, but do not delete the task.

22. Use FrontPage Editor to add the task of creating the Where page to the Tasks list, but *do not add this page to the Web.* (*Hint:* Use the Edit menu in FrontPage Editor.) Then print the Tasks list.

23. Go to the How page in FrontPage Editor. Notice that the page title is "b_how" in the title bar. Change the page title to "How," and then save your changes. (*Hint:* Use the Page Properties dialog box.)

24. Display the How page as the center focus page in Hyperlinks view in FrontPage Explorer. Display the Repeated hyperlinks. Print a copy of Hyperlinks view.

25. Print the How page from FrontPage Editor, and then print the HTML code for the How page. Circle the HTML code entries for all hyperlinks and bookmarks.

26. Arrange and clearly identify the printouts for all the case questions.

27. Close all open programs.

3. Completing the Employment Page for Pardon My Garden Hiring and retaining the best possible staff is key to the successful growth of Pardon My Garden. Nolan and Shannon met with the corporate human resources director to discuss the content of the planned Employment Opportunities Web page. They want the page to emphasize that Pardon My Garden is a fun place to work and that employees are treated like family. Shannon took notes describing the content of the Employment Opportunities page, which is to include information concerning both management and staff associate positions. By the end of the meeting, Nolan and Shannon clearly understood the page content. The human resources staff wanted more time to complete an introductory narrative for the manager position and indicated they would send this to Shannon as a separate file the next day. Shannon started developing the Employment Opportunities page based on the detailed requirements from the meeting. Nolan wants you to help Shannon complete the development and testing of this Web page.

If necessary, start FrontPage Explorer, insert your Student Disk in drive A or the appropriate disk drive, and then do the following:

1. Read all the questions for this case problem, and prepare a planning analysis sheet for the revisions to the Garden Web site.

2. Access the Garden Web. If you did not create this Web in Tutorial 2, create it now. (*Hint*: Ask your instructor for the home page file that you can import into the Web, as well as the logo image.)

3. Import the partially completed Employment Opportunities (gemploy.htm) page from the Tutorial.03\garden folder into the Web, and then open this page in FrontPage Editor. Review the page, and locate the items listed as a table of contents following "Opportunities exist in these areas:" and the two content areas of the page that are separated using horizontal rules.

4. Insert the garden03.jpg file from the Tutorial.03\garden folder as an inline image that appears at the top of the page and is centered. Then insert the navbar.gif file from the same folder as an inline image immediately below the garden03.jpg file. Center this inline image.

5. Convert the JPG image from Step 4 into a GIF image. Then make the red background of this image transparent. Notice that some "noise" in the form of small dots still appears in the converted image because some pixels are a slightly different shade. Click the Restore button on the Image toolbar to return the image to its original state.

6. Specify the same background for this Web page as that used with the Home Page.

7. Include the text from the manage.rtf file in the Tutorial.03\garden folder as a definition for the Managers job title, and change Managers to a defined item. Then use the Change Style list arrow on the Format toolbar to change the information in the list under the manager definition to a bulleted list.

8. In the staff associates section, format the heading as the defined term and the content paragraph as its definition. Then use the Bulleted List button on the Format toolbar to format the information below the definition paragraph as a bulleted list.

9. Change the format of the bullets in the bulleted lists that you created in Steps 7 and 8 to square bullet characters. (*Hint*: Select the bulleted list, and then use the Bullets and Numbering command on the Format menu.)

10. Format the managers and staff associates items that make up the table of contents (located immediately below the opening paragraph at the top of the page) as a numbered list. Create a bookmark for each of these items where they are described below in the Web page. Then create a hyperlink from each of the numbered list items of the table of contents to its respective bookmark.

11. Include your e-mail address at the bottom of the Web page below the "For additional information contact us:" paragraph. If you don't have an e-mail address, then create one or use one your instructor provides.

12. Create a bookmark named "Top" as a named reference that is located immediately to the left of the logo inline image at the top of this page. Place the text "Top of Page" in a separate paragraph at the bottom of the Web page. Create a hyperlink from the "Top of Page" text to the "top" bookmark.

13. Insert the btn_up.gif file as an inline image immediately to the left of the "Top of Page:" hyperlink text with a space between the image and this text. The btn_up.gif file is located in the Tutorial.03\images folder. Create a hyperlink from the btn_up.gif image to the Top bookmark.

14. Save the Web page, and save all the images for the page in the images folder of the Garden Web. Then test all the internal hyperlinks in the browser. Correct any errors you discover.

15. Use drag and drop to create a hyperlink in the navigation bar image from the Employment Opportunities page to the Home Page. Select the rectangle that contains the word "Home," and make this a hotspot for implementing the link to the Home Page. Then create a link in the navigation bar from the Home Page to the Employment Opportunities page.

16. Replace your text navigation bar in the Home Page with the navbar.gif image file, and create the link from the Home Page to the Employment Opportunities page using the "Jobs" entry as the link's hotspot.

17. Create a hotspot using the text "About Us" in the navigation bar of the Employment Opportunities page. Add a normal page to the Web as the Company Profile page with the filename of gabout.htm, and include this as a task to be completed in the Web's Tasks list.

18. Create a hotspot using the word "Feedback" in the navigation bar of the Employment Opportunities page. Add another normal page to the Web as the Feedback page with the filename of gfeedbak.htm, and include this as a task in the Web's Tasks list.

19. Import the Company Profile page (gabout.htm file) from the Tutorial.03\garden folder into the Garden Web and replace the existing Company Profile page. Then replace the broken inline images with the gabout.gif and navbar.gif files from the Tutorial.03\garden folder. Save the Web page, and save the GIF files in the images folder of the Garden Web. Test these new hyperlinks.

20. Mark the task for the Company Profile page as complete in the Tasks list, but do not delete the task.

21. Add the task of creating the Search page to the Tasks list, but do not add this page to the Web. Print a copy of this revised Tasks list.

22. Display the Company Profile page as the focus page in Hyperlinks view in FrontPage Explorer. Display the repeated hyperlinks. Print a copy of Hyperlinks view.

23. Print the Company Profile Web page from FrontPage Editor, and then print the HTML code for this page. Circle the HTML code entries for all the hyperlinks and bookmarks. What is the download time for this page?

24. Arrange and clearly identify the printouts and answers for all the questions in this case.

25. Close all open programs. Save all of your FrontPage changes.

4. Creating a Deal Page for Replay Music Factory Business has been brisk at the Replay Music Factory. A frequently asked question (FAQ) concerns how the exchange process works when buying, selling, or trading compact discs. Justin and Mary Kay met with their marketing manager to see how they might address this with their Web site. They are convinced that if they expand their Web site to include this information, they will receive fewer phone calls asking for information about the process. They decide to create the "Deal" page to describe their process for recycling used CDs. Justin returns to his office to consider this use of the Web site and is convinced that adding the feature will help delay hiring additional associates to handle phone calls. Mary Kay wants you to assist Justin with this enhancement to their Web.

If necessary, start FrontPage Explorer, insert your Student Disk in drive A or the appropriate disk drive, and then do the following:

1. Read all the questions for this case problem, and prepare a planning analysis sheet for the revisions to the Replay Web site.

2. Design the Deal Web page that describes the process used by Replay in buying, selling, and trading used compact discs. This page should include a table of contents with at least two entries, at least one bulleted list, at least one numbered list, at least two defined terms and their associated definitions, internal hyperlinks from the table of contents to the detailed information for each table of contents entry in the document, an e-mail address, a navigation bar, at least one inline image, and a hyperlink from the bottom of the page to the top of the page. You can use any available reference sources to help you develop your content, including accessing several commercial Web sites.

3. Write at least one paragraph that contains the content you will use in the Deal page. Use Microsoft Word, WordPad, or another word-processing program and create an RTF file with this content. Print this document from the word-processing program, and then save it as deal.rtf in the Tutorial.03\replay folder.

4. Access the Replay Web. If you did not create this Web in Tutorial 2, create the Web and the Home Page, as described in that tutorial.

5. Create a Tasks list that includes all of the tasks that you need to complete for the Replay Web, including the Deal page. Add blank, normal pages to the Web as necessary to create this Tasks list.

6. Sort the tasks in the Tasks list by task name, and then print a copy of the Tasks list.

7. Create the Deal page as described by your design from Step 2, and include it in the Replay Web. Use the background from the Home Page with this page.

8. Import the deal.rtf file from Step 3, and insert its content at the desired location in the Web page.

9. Create a logo for this page as a JPG file. Use any appropriate graphics program. (If you do not have a graphics program available, skip to Step 10.) Save your logo as a JPG file in the Tutorial.03\replay folder.

10. Insert the JPG file from Step 9 as an inline image that appears at the top of the page. If you do not have access to a graphics program, use the deal.jpg file in the Tutorial.03\replay folder.

11. Convert the JPG image from Step 10 into a GIF image. Then convert the image's main background color to be transparent.

12. Save the Web page and save all the images for the page in the images folder of the Replay Web. Then test all the internal hyperlinks in the browser. Correct any errors you discover.

13. Create a hyperlink in the navigation bar from the Deal page to the Home Page, and then create a link in the navigation bar from the Home Page to the Deal page. If the navigation bar in the Home Page does not contain an appropriate entry for the link from the Home Page to the Deal page, then change the Home Page navigation bar as needed.

14. Create a hotspot with a hyperlink from the logo inline image at the top of the Deal page to the Home Page. Save this revised Web page. Then test the hyperlinks between the Deal page and the Home Page using the Normal view of FrontPage Editor. (*Hint:* Use the screen tips to discover how to test the hyperlinks in Normal view.)

15. Mark the task for the Deal page as completed in the Tasks list, but do not delete the task. Print a revised copy of this Tasks list.

16. Display the Deal page as the focus page in Hyperlinks view in FrontPage Explorer. Display the repeated hyperlinks. Print a copy of Hyperlinks view.

17. Print the Deal page from FrontPage Editor, and then print the HTML code for the Deal page. Circle the HTML code entries for all the hyperlinks and bookmarks.

18. Arrange and clearly identify the printouts and answers for all the questions in this case as your documentation for this case.

19. Close all open programs, and save your changes in FrontPage.

Creating Tables and Frames for a Web Site

Completing the Investor Relations and Products Web Pages

OBJECTIVES

In this tutorial you will:

▪ Create a table in a Web page

▪ Modify a table by inserting and deleting rows and columns

▪ Split and merge cells in a table

▪ Enter data in a table

▪ Insert an image in a table

▪ Use FrontPage Help

▪ Create and edit a frame set

▪ Specify target frames in a frame set

CASE

Sunny Morning Products

During the design phase of the Sunny Morning Products Web site, Andrew and Carmen gave detailed requirements to Amanda. Carmen described her vision for the Investor Relations page, whereas Andrew provided requirements for the Products page. For example, Carmen wanted the Investor Relations page to include a summary table of the company's financial performance. Andrew wanted the Products page to include an up-to-date table listing the products available from the Sunshine Country Store. Based on this feedback, Amanda prepared sketches of these Web pages and asked Andrew and Carmen to approve them before starting development.

In this tutorial, you will continue with your Web training course by retracing the activities that Amanda performed to create the Investor Relations and Products pages for the Sunny Morning Products Web site. You will work from Amanda's partially completed Web pages. As you develop each page, you will review Amanda's design notes and documentation to familiarize yourself with the necessary planning activities. Your main activities in completing these Web pages include adding a table to the Investor Relations page and creating a frame set for the Products page. As a management intern in the marketing department, you are especially interested in the Products page because it is used to accept the Sunshine Country Store mail orders.

SESSION

4.1

In this session you will learn how to create a table for a Web page and adjust its formatting by changing the alignment and adding data in the table cells. Also, you will insert and delete rows and columns in a table and insert an image in a table cell. Finally, you will learn about and use FrontPage Help.

Reviewing the Tasks List

Before you begin your next set of training activities, Amanda asks you to review the Tasks list you created in Tutorial 3 that contains the tasks necessary to complete the Sunny Morning Web. After you review the list, Amanda wants you to meet with her to review the details for the Investor Relations Web page that you will work on next. First, you open the Sunny Morning Web (sunny) to review the Tasks list.

To open a disk-based Web:

1. Make sure that your Student Disk is in drive A or the appropriate drive on your computer.

2. Start FrontPage Explorer.

3. Open the Sunny Morning Web (sunny) located in the a:\wwwroot folder.

The Sunny Morning Products Web opens in FrontPage Explorer. Now, you can review the Tasks list.

To review a Tasks list:

1. Click the **Tasks** button 🗒 on the Views toolbar to open the Tasks list.

2. Click the **Task column label** button to sort the revised list. See Figure 4-1.

Figure 4-1 ◄
Current Tasks
list for Sunny
Morning Web

need to finish Investor
and Products pages

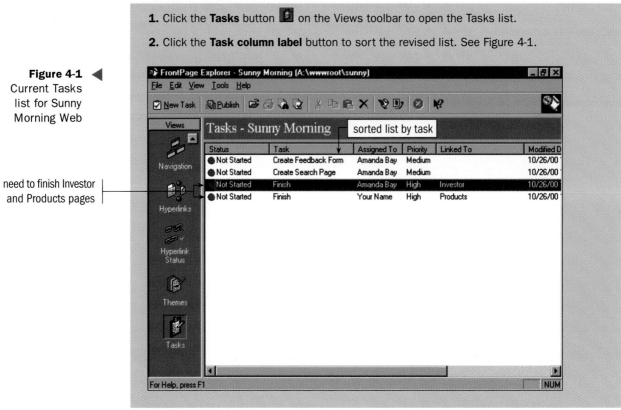

The Investor Relations and Products Web pages must be completed, as noted by the Finish tasks listed in the Tasks list that are linked to the Investor and Product pages. Now that you have confirmed this information, you are finished reviewing the Tasks list.

You meet with Amanda, who asks you to finish the partially completed Investor Relations page.

Replacing a Web Page

After creating a Web page, you might want to replace it later with a different file. Using a replacement file saves time if you have made extensive changes to a Web page. For example, as Amanda developed her training course, she created several partially completed pages for the Sunny Morning Web to decrease the time trainees would have to spend retyping text. You can simply insert these pages as replacement files.

Next, Amanda wants you to replace the current, blank Investor Relations page with the partially completed one that she prepared.

To replace a Web page:

1. Click the **Show FrontPage Editor** button 🔲 on the Standard toolbar to start FrontPage Editor without opening a Web page.

2. Click the **Open** button 🔲 on the Standard toolbar to open the Open dialog box, and then click the **Select a file on your computer** button 🔲 to open the Select File dialog box.

3. Make sure the drive that contains your Student Disk appears in the Look in text box, double-click the **Tutorial.04** folder, and then click the **investor.htm** file.

4. Click the **OK** button to open the Investor Relations page in FrontPage Editor.

5. Click **File** on the menu bar, click **Save As** to open that dialog box, and then click the **OK** button. A FrontPage Editor message box opens to indicate that the file already exists and asks if you want to replace it.

6. Click the **Yes** button. The Save Embedded Files dialog box opens with hinvest.gif in the Name field of the Embedded Files to Save text box. This dialog box specifies the filename and the desired folder that contains the image for the logo.

7. Click **hinvest.gif** to select it, click the **Change Folder** button, click the **images** folder to select it, click the **OK** button to return to the Save Embedded Files dialog box, and then click the **OK** button to save the file. After a few seconds, the Investor Relations Web page reappears.

The partially completed Investor Relations page contains all the desired content, except for a table that summarizes the company's financial performance over the past two years. Next, Amanda wants you to add this table to the current Web page.

Creating Tables

A **table** consists of one or more rows of cells and is used to organize information or arrange data systematically. A **cell** is the smallest component of a table. You can place either text or images in table cells. When creating a table in a Web page, sketch it first instead of trying to create it after inserting it in a Web page. This approach is advisable for two reasons: first, because it usually takes more effort to change a table than to create it correctly initially, and second, because of the manner in which the table description is stored as HTML code, each cell is specified by individual tags. Overall, the task of creating a table using FrontPage Editor is similar to creating a table using a word-processing program. However, the manner in which HTML documents are displayed using a Web browser differs according to the type of computer used.

Recall that HTML documents are organized to be displayed on a variety of computers that have different screen resolutions. In many situations, therefore, the column widths for a table are set as a percentage of the table width rather than as a fixed width. The ability to adjust for varying screen-display widths requires additional settings that you need to specify when creating a table for display in a Web browser; these settings are different from what is used in a word-processing program.

When creating a table, you need to specify the size of the border, the cell padding, the cell spacing, and the table width. A **border** is a line that surrounds a cell or the entire table. **Cell padding** is the distance between the contents of a cell and the inside edge of the cell, measured in pixels. **Cell spacing** is the distance between cells, measured in pixels. Increasing the cell spacing increases the distance between the borders that surround each cell. The **table width** can be specified as a percentage of the width of the screen or as a fixed width in pixels. Specifying the width as a percentage—the most flexible method—is common because it allows easier display of the table on a variety of different computers. Also, you need to specify the number of rows and columns when creating the table. You can add or delete rows or columns after creating the table, but it is better to specify the appropriately sized table initially. For smaller-sized tables, you use the **Insert Table button grid** (a miniature table four rows high by five columns wide) to specify the table's size. If you want your table to be the same size as this grid or smaller, you can click a cell in the lower-right corner of the grid. For larger tables, the Table dialog box allows you to specify any number of rows and columns. For a single-cell table, you can use the Draw Table button on the Table toolbar.

Carmen helped Amanda design the Summary of Financial Performance table that will be included in the Sunny Morning Products Web. Figure 4-2 shows the draft of the table they sketched. You review the sketch with Amanda because you will use it as a basis for completing the Investors Relations Web page. Amanda emphasizes the left, center, and right alignments used for the line items, column headings, and numbers in the table.

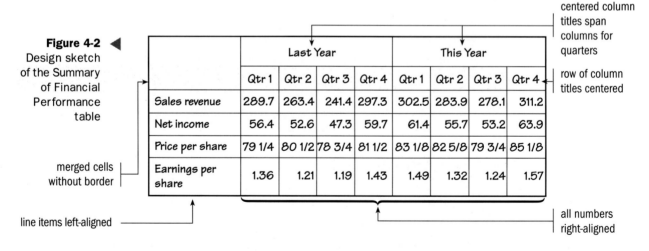

Figure 4-2 ◀
Design sketch of the Summary of Financial Performance table

merged cells without border

line items left-aligned

centered column titles span columns for quarters

row of column titles centered

all numbers right-aligned

	Last Year				This Year			
	Qtr 1	Qtr 2	Qtr 3	Qtr 4	Qtr 1	Qtr 2	Qtr 3	Qtr 4
Sales revenue	289.7	263.4	241.4	297.3	302.5	283.9	278.1	311.2
Net income	56.4	52.6	47.3	59.7	61.4	55.7	53.2	63.9
Price per share	79 1/4	80 1/2	78 3/4	81 1/2	83 1/8	82 5/8	79 3/4	85 1/8
Earnings per share	1.36	1.21	1.19	1.43	1.49	1.32	1.24	1.57

After reviewing the table, Amanda asks you to review the planning analysis sheet that she created when planning the development of this Web page. See Figure 4-3. The planning analysis sheet outlines the design that Amanda wants you to follow throughout your training session as you complete the Investor Relations page.

Planning Analysis Sheet

My goal:

Create an Investor Relations Web page that contains a table of financial

performance information.

What results do I want to see?

An Investor Relations Web page that includes a navigation bar, an

introductory paragraph, and a table of financial performance

information. The table will be centered between the left and right edges

of the browser window. The Web page should share the same

background as the Home Page, and the table should appear on a

separate background for emphasis.

What information do I need?

Financial performance information by quarter for last year and the current

year.

Line items included in the table are sales revenue, net income, price per

share, and earnings per share.

Approved layout sketch of table from Carmen.

Inserting a Table

After you finish designing a table, you are ready to insert it into your Web page. To do this, first you select the desired location.

REFERENCE window	**INSERTING A TABLE**
	■ Click the location where you want the table to appear on your Web page.
	■ Click the Insert Table button on the Standard toolbar to open the Insert Table button grid, and then click a table button in the lower-right corner that indicates the table size.
	or
	■ Click Table on the menu bar, click Insert Table, specify the number of rows and columns, and then click the OK button.

When Amanda prepared the Investor Relations page for your training course, she inserted a note on the page indicating the preferred location for the table. With the Investor Relations page now included in the Sunny Morning Web, you are ready to insert the Summary of Financial Performance table.

To insert a table:

1. With the Investor Relations page still displayed in your window, select the **(financial performance information table goes here)** text, and then press the **Delete** key. This is the desired location of the table.

2. Click the **Insert Table** button 🖼 on the Standard toolbar to open the Insert Table button grid. Notice that this is the same Insert Table button grid that Microsoft Word uses. Click the cell in the lower-right corner of the grid, and then hold down the mouse button while you drag the grid down and to the right to expand it to a size of 5 rows by 9 columns. See Figure 4-4.

Figure 4-4 ◀
Insert Table
button grid

table grid used to
specify table size

table will be inserted
at location of
insertion point

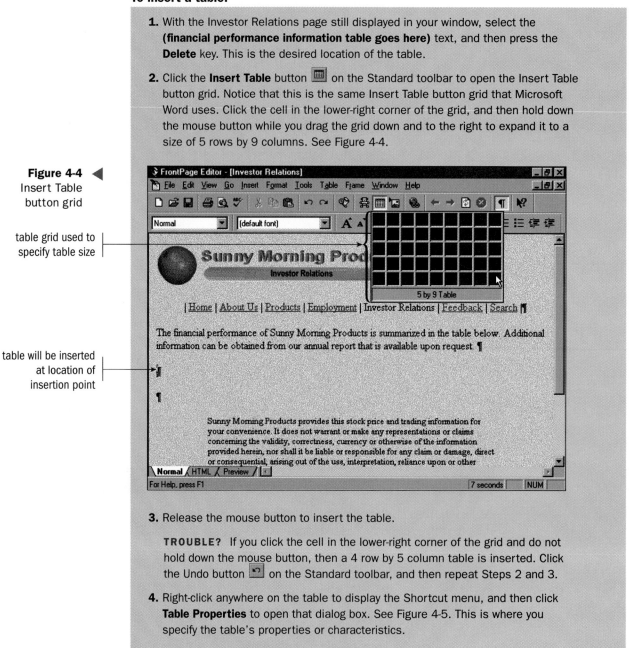

3. Release the mouse button to insert the table.

TROUBLE? If you click the cell in the lower-right corner of the grid and do not hold down the mouse button, then a 4 row by 5 column table is inserted. Click the Undo button 🔙 on the Standard toolbar, and then repeat Steps 2 and 3.

4. Right-click anywhere on the table to display the Shortcut menu, and then click **Table Properties** to open that dialog box. See Figure 4-5. This is where you specify the table's properties or characteristics.

Figure 4-5
Table Properties
dialog box

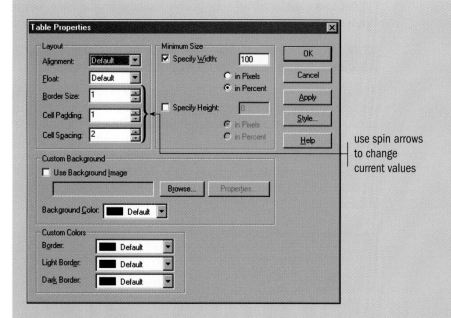

use spin arrows
to change
current values

5. In the Layout section, use the spin arrows to set a Border Size of **2**, a Cell Padding of **4**, and a Cell Spacing of **3** as the desired values for these properties.

6. If necessary, click the **Specify Width** check box in the Minimum Size section to select it, select **100** or the current value in the Specify Width text box and type **95**, and then click the **in Percent** option button to select it.

7. Click the **OK** button. The Insert Table dialog box closes, and the table properties are applied to it.

8. Scroll down the page so you see the entire table. The table appears as an empty grid and is left-aligned on the page. See Figure 4-6.

Figure 4-6
Investor
Relations page
with inserted
table

blank table with
default left alignment

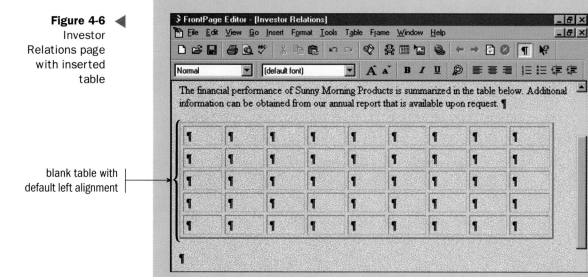

TROUBLE? If the paragraph marks do not appear in your table, click the Show/Hide ¶ button ![¶] on the Standard toolbar to display them.

You inserted the table in the proper location on the page, but the alignment of the table doesn't follow Amanda's design. Now you change the alignment next.

Aligning a Table

The alignment of a table on a Web page is separate from the alignment of the data that occupies a table's cells. A table can have one alignment, whereas all the cells in the table can have a different alignment. Using FrontPage Editor, you select the appropriate alignment button on the Format toolbar in order to left-, center-, or right-align data within each cell. Keep in mind, however, that clicking a specific alignment button on the toolbar aligns the contents of the cell at the location of the insertion point, but it does not align the entire table on the page. You need to change the table's properties to specify a different alignment for the entire table on a Web page.

REFERENCE
window

ALIGNING A TABLE ON A WEB PAGE

- Click anywhere on the table to select it.
- Right-click to display the Shortcut menu.
or
- Click Table on the menu bar.
- Click Table Properties to open that dialog box, click the Alignment list arrow in the Layout section, click the desired alignment, and then click the OK button.

The table you inserted in the Investor Relations Web page is left-aligned because this is the default alignment. Amanda designed this table to be center-aligned to give it a more balanced appearance when viewed in the browser window. She wants you to center the table between the left and right edges of the page.

To align a table on a Web page:

1. Right-click anywhere on the table to display the Shortcut menu, and then click **Table Properties** to open that dialog box.

2. In the Layout section, click the **Alignment** list arrow, and then click **center** to center-align the table (*not* the data) on the page.

3. Click the **OK** button. The table is centered in the Web page.

Inserting Rows or Columns

After creating a table, you can insert additional rows and columns as needed—either before or after entering data in the table's cells. To insert a row or column, first you must select the desired location for the new row or column.

REFERENCE window

INSERTING ROWS OR COLUMNS

- Click in the left border of the table of the desired row or the top border of the desired column to select it, and then click the Insert Rows button or the Insert Columns button, respectively, on the Table toolbar to insert a row above the selected row or a column to the left of the selected column.

or

- Click any cell adjacent to the location where you want to insert rows or columns.
- Click Table on the menu bar, and then click Insert Rows or Columns to open that dialog box.
- Click the Rows or Columns option button, and then use the Number of Rows or Number of Columns spin arrows to specify the number of rows or columns you want to insert.
- Click the Above selection, Below selection, Left of selection, or Right of selection option button to specify the relative location where you want to insert the rows or columns.
- Click the OK button.

After approving the table's initial design, Carmen wants to include another line item for dividends-per-share data. Amanda asks you to accommodate this last-minute change by inserting a row in the table below the current third row for the dividend information. First, you will display the Table toolbar, and then you will insert the desired row using that toolbar.

To display the Table toolbar:

1. Click **View** on the menu bar to display this menu.

2. Click **Table Toolbar** to display this toolbar.

   TROUBLE? If a check mark appeared for the Table Toolbar, then it was already selected and displayed. When you clicked it, you hid the toolbar; repeat Steps 1 and 2 to display it again.

With the Table toolbar displayed, you can insert the row.

To insert a row in a table:

1. Move the pointer to the left border of the third row in the table so it changes to ➡, and then click the left border to select this row as the location where you insert the new row.

2. Click the **Insert Rows** button ⬚ on the Table toolbar. A row is inserted above the selected row. See Figure 4-7.

Figure 4-7 ◀
Inserted row

Table toolbar (yours
might look different)

new row inserted
above selected row 3

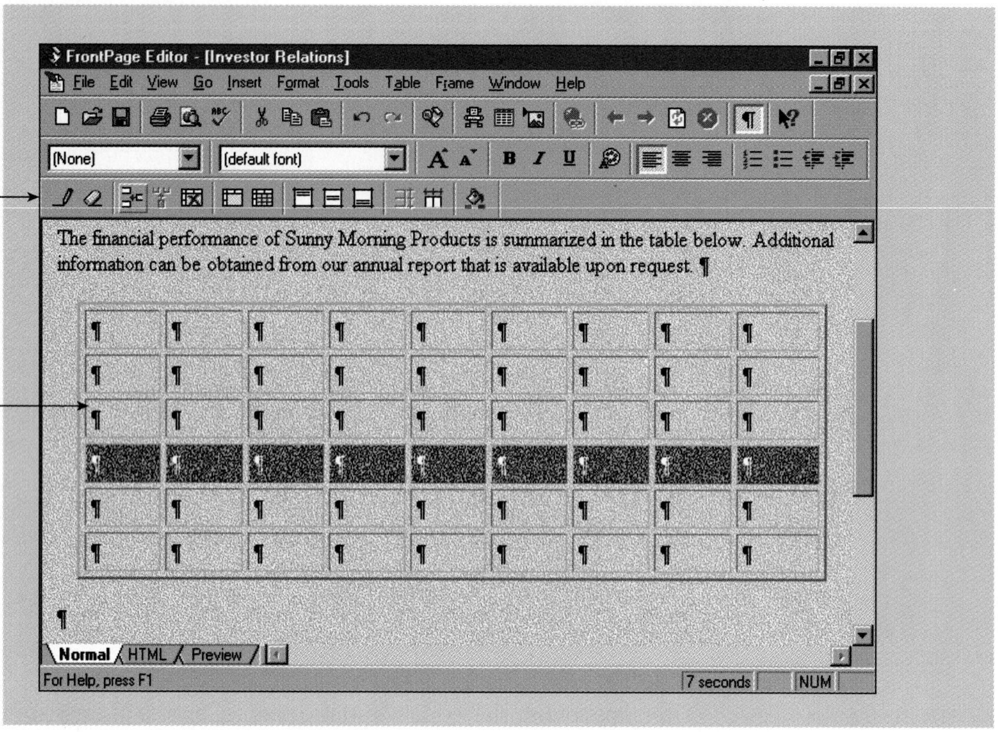

After inserting rows or columns in a table, you can change the cells in many ways, or you can delete them. Before you can make any changes, however, you need to select the cells. You continue developing the Summary of Financial Performance table by selecting, and then subsequently deleting, cells in the table.

Selecting and Deleting Rows or Columns

Often, you might need to delete cells as you finish developing a table to remove an unwanted area. However, you must select cells before you can change any of their properties. The process of deleting rows or columns is straightforward. First, you select the table rows or columns that you want to eliminate. FrontPage Editor provides several methods for selecting rows and columns. You can click the left border of a row or the top border of a column to select an entire row or column. If you have more than one row or column to select, hold down the Ctrl key while you select the other rows and columns. Another method of selection is to click and drag the pointer over a contiguous group of cells that reside in several rows and columns. These selection methods are similar to those you use when selecting table cells in a word-processing program. After selecting a series of cells in one or more rows or columns, you can either delete a cell or deselect it. If, after you have selected one or more cells, you decide you don't want them included, you can **deselect** those cells to undo your current selection. After selecting the rows or columns to delete, press the Delete key or click the Cut button on the Standard toolbar to eliminate them.

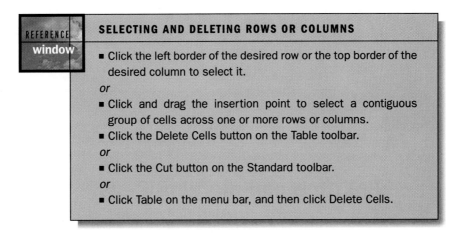

REFERENCE window

SELECTING AND DELETING ROWS OR COLUMNS

- Click the left border of the desired row or the top border of the desired column to select it.

or

- Click and drag the insertion point to select a contiguous group of cells across one or more rows or columns.
- Click the Delete Cells button on the Table toolbar.

or

- Click the Cut button on the Standard toolbar.

or

- Click Table on the menu bar, and then click Delete Cells.

Amanda wants you to delete the row that you just added to the table because Carmen reconsidered and decided she didn't want to include the dividends-per-share information after all. You delete the new row.

To select and delete a row from a table:

1. Click ➡ on the **left border** of the third row in the table to select the row. See Figure 4-8.

Figure 4-8 ◀
Table with
selected row

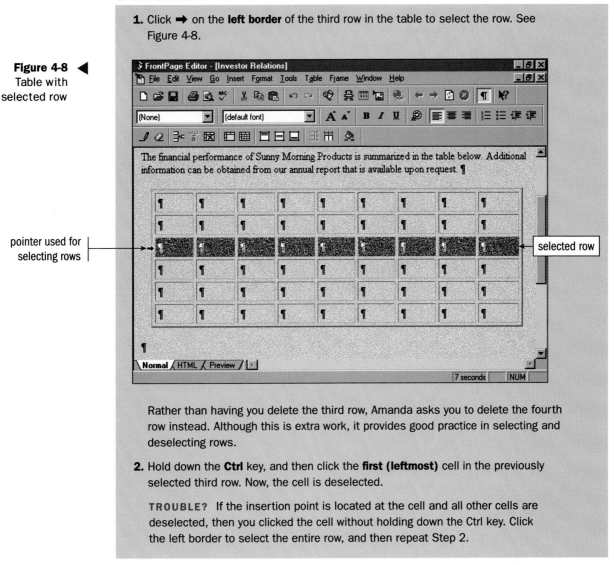

pointer used for
selecting rows

selected row

Rather than having you delete the third row, Amanda asks you to delete the fourth row instead. Although this is extra work, it provides good practice in selecting and deselecting rows.

2. Hold down the **Ctrl** key, and then click the **first (leftmost)** cell in the previously selected third row. Now, the cell is deselected.

TROUBLE? If the insertion point is located at the cell and all other cells are deselected, then you clicked the cell without holding down the Ctrl key. Click the left border to select the entire row, and then repeat Step 2.

3. Click any cell in the table to deselect the entire selection.

4. Click the **fourth row border** to select the entire fourth row.

5. Click the **Delete Cells** button on the Table toolbar. Now, the entire fourth row is removed from the table.

You continue completing the Investors Relations page by creating column headings for the Summary of Financial Performance table.

Splitting and Merging Cells

There are many ways to arrange the information in a table. One popular method is to include column headings to identify the data displayed in each column. You can arrange the cells of a row or column in a custom layout by splitting and merging cells. **Splitting cells** is the process of dividing a single cell into two or more rows or columns, whereas **merging cells** is the process of combining two or more cells in a row or column to form a single cell. This powerful HTML feature gives users flexibility in organizing Web page content and is one reason tables are used so extensively.

Splitting Cells

For the Summary of Financial Performance table, Amanda wants you to split the cells in the eight columns that will contain the column headings for each quarter. You want to leave the first cell in column one as a blank single cell because you will insert an image into this cell later.

<table>
<tr><td>REFERENCE
window</td><td>**SPLITTING CELLS**

■ Select the cells to split.
■ Click the Split Cells button on the Table toolbar.
or
■ Click Table on the menu bar, and then click Split Cells to open that dialog box.
■ Click the Split into Columns or Split into Rows option button.
■ Specify the Number of Columns or Rows, and then click the OK button.</td></tr>
</table>

Now, you split the cells that will contain the column headings for the table.

To split cells:

1. Click the **left border** of the first row in the table to select it, and then hold down the **Ctrl** key and click the cell in **row 1, column 1** to deselect it so this cell will not be split.

2. Click the **Split Cells** button 🔳 on the Table toolbar to open the Split Cells dialog box. See Figure 4-9.

Figure 4-9
Split Cells
dialog box

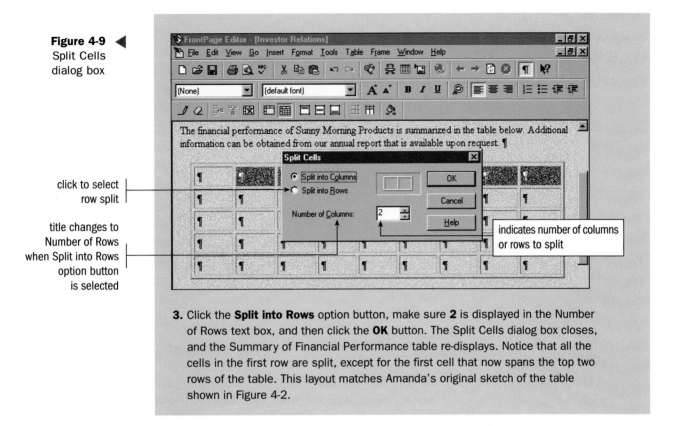

click to select
row split

title changes to
Number of Rows
when Split into Rows
option button
is selected

3. Click the **Split into Rows** option button, make sure **2** is displayed in the Number
of Rows text box, and then click the **OK** button. The Split Cells dialog box closes,
and the Summary of Financial Performance table re-displays. Notice that all the
cells in the first row are split, except for the first cell that now spans the top two
rows of the table. This layout matches Amanda's original sketch of the table
shown in Figure 4-2.

Now that you have split the cells, you are ready to create the cells that will contain the
column headings to identify the years in the table.

Merging Cells

The cells containing the year headings will appear at the top of the columns that contain
the information for their respective four quarters. Unlike some spreadsheet programs,
HTML does not provide tags to display text across several columns. Instead, you need to
merge the cells that you want to contain text or an image spanning multiple rows or
columns. To create the headings for each year, you need to merge the four cells currently
in the first row into a single cell.

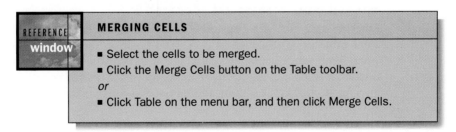

REFERENCE
window

MERGING CELLS

■ Select the cells to be merged.
■ Click the Merge Cells button on the Table toolbar.
or
■ Click Table on the menu bar, and then click Merge Cells.

Amanda next asks you to merge the cells for the year headings.

To merge cells:

1. Click the cell in **row 1**, **column 2**, hold down the mouse button while dragging the
insertion point to the cell in column 5 to select the cells in columns 2 through 5,
and then release the mouse button to select the cells. See Figure 4-10.

Figure 4-10 ◄
Table with
selected cells

selected cells to
merge into one cell

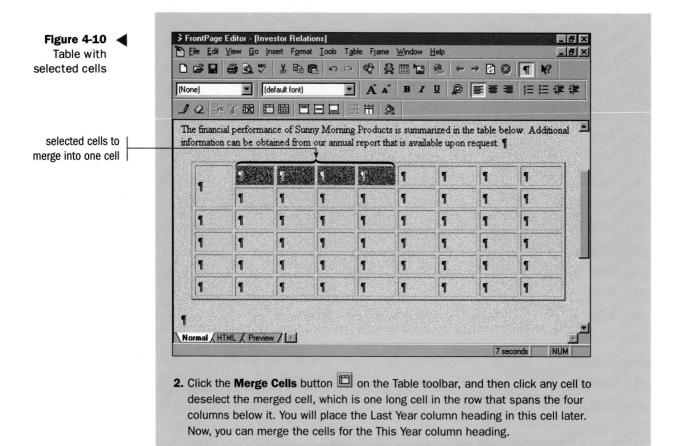

2. Click the **Merge Cells** button ⊞ on the Table toolbar, and then click any cell to deselect the merged cell, which is one long cell in the row that spans the four columns below it. You will place the Last Year column heading in this cell later. Now, you can merge the cells for the This Year column heading.

3. Click the cell in **row 1, column 6**, hold down the mouse button while dragging the insertion point to the cell in column 9 to select the cells in columns 6 through 9, and then release the mouse button.

4. Click the **Merge Cells** button ⊞ on the Table toolbar, and then click any cell to deselect the merged cell. The cell in row 1 now spans the four columns below it.

The table organization is complete: rows have been split and cells merged to match Amanda's table design. Now, you can enter the data into the table.

Entering Data in a Table

Entering data in a Web page table is similar to entering data in a word-processing document table or in spreadsheet cells. You position the insertion point in the desired cell where you want to enter the data, and then type the data. You can select a cell by either clicking it or by moving the insertion point to the desired cell using the appropriate arrow keys or the Tab key. Begin by adding the text for the column headings.

To enter data in a table:

1. Click the cell in **row 1, column 2**, and then type **Last Year**.

   TROUBLE? If you are unsure of the exact location where you are placing the column heading in the table, refer back to Figure 4-2 to confirm the proper organization of the table.

2. Press the **Tab** key to move to the next column, and then type **This Year**.

3. Enter the data shown in Figure 4-11 to complete the table. Make sure to press the Tab key after each typing entry to move the insertion point to the next cell or row. Do not press the Tab key after typing the data in the last cell in the table or you will create a new row. The automatic line wrap feature expands the cells containing the row headings (Sales revenue, Net income, Price per share, and Earnings per share) so that all the text fits in one cell. Your completed table should match Figure 4-11.

Figure 4-11 ◄
Completed
table with
data entered

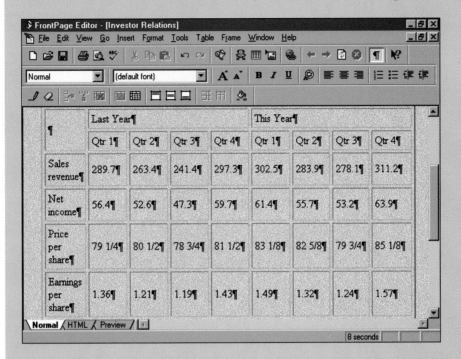

TROUBLE? Don't worry if the line items in column 1 don't wrap to a second line automatically. Line wrapping is a function of the display resolution of your screen. Accept these entries, and continue with Step 4.

4. Click the **Save** button 🖫 on the Standard toolbar.

Notice in Figure 4-11 that all the data in the table are left-aligned because this is the default when creating a table using FrontPage. Now, you need to adjust the alignment of the data to match the requirements in Amanda's sketch.

Aligning Cell Contents

In addition to the horizontal alignment of left, center, and right, you can select a vertical alignment of top, middle, or bottom. Middle is the normal default for the vertical alignment; this is the current alignment for the data in the table shown in Figure 4-11.

You align cell contents by selecting the desired cells and then specifying the desired alignment. One way to align cells is to use the alignment buttons on the Format toolbar, which is what Amanda wants you to use when adjusting the alignment of the table. Now, you center the column headings in the Summary of Financial Performance table to match Amanda's design.

To center-align column headings in a table:

1. Select **rows 1** and **2** at the top of the table containing the year and quarter column headings.

2. Click the **Center** button 🖫 on the Format toolbar to center the column titles.

3. Right-click the selected cells to display the Shortcut menu, and then click **Cell Properties** to open that dialog box. See Figure 4-12.

Figure 4-12 ◀
Cell Properties
dialog box

click to display
list of vertical
alignment options

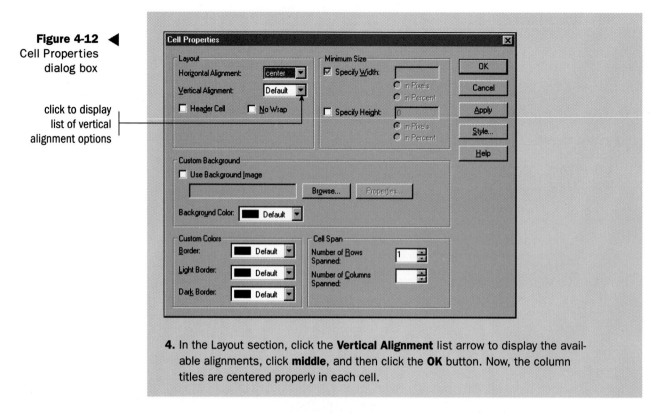

4. In the Layout section, click the **Vertical Alignment** list arrow to display the available alignments, click **middle**, and then click the **OK** button. Now, the column titles are centered properly in each cell.

There is more than one possible method for changing the alignment of cells in a table that contain numeric data. For example, you can select the appropriate rows and change the alignment using the alignment buttons on the Format toolbar. You also can select only the numeric data in each row using the click-and-drag selection method, and then change the alignment using the Cell Properties dialog box. As long as you end up with all the cells aligned appropriately, you should choose the method that works best for you.

With the column titles centered, Amanda wants you to change the alignment of the numeric data in the table so it is right-aligned.

To right-align numeric data in a table:

1. Select all the cells that contain numeric data in rows 3 through 6 and columns 2 through 9.

2. Click the **Align Right** button ▤ on the Format toolbar to right-align the cells.

3. Right-click the selected cells to display the Shortcut menu, and then click **Cell Properties** to open that dialog box. In the Layout section, click the **Vertical Alignment** list arrow, click **middle**, and then click the **OK** button. The data are centered vertically and right-aligned in each of the selected cells in the table.

4. Click the **Save** button ▤ on the Standard toolbar.

If you need to change the size of a cell in your table, you can click and drag the edge of the cell to change the cell's width or height. Keep in mind that if you develop a table that will be displayed on a screen with super VGA (SVGA) resolution, the table's format might appear differently than if it is displayed on a normal VGA screen. This problem is unique to creating a Web page table versus using a general word-processing program. If you want your table to appear the same under several different display-screen resolutions, develop it for VGA resolution and test it under other resolutions. One way to warn users that the page might appear differently is to indicate on the Web's home page that the resolution that works best with the Web page is VGA or SVGA. For example, you might include the message "Best viewed in SVGA."

Inserting an Image

You can insert an image into any table cell. If the image is larger than the current cell, then the size of the cell is adjusted automatically to accommodate the image. You follow the same process for inserting an image in a cell as when inserting an inline image anywhere else on a Web page. The only difference is that you select a cell as the location for the incoming image instead of selecting a line on the Web page. Amanda already created a special GIF logo file that she wants you to include as an image in the first cell of the Summary of Financial Performance table.

To insert an image in a cell in table:

1. Click the **first (empty) cell** in the upper-left corner of the table to select it as the desired location for the image.

2. Click the **Insert Image** button on the Standard toolbar to open the Image dialog box, and then click the **Select a file on your computer** button to open the Select File dialog box.

3. Make sure the drive that contains your Student Disk appears in the Look in text box, double-click the **Tutorial.04** folder, and then double-click the **Images** folder.

4. Click the **finperf.gif** file to select it, and then click the **OK** button. The GIF image appears in the first cell in the table. Notice that the cell size adjusts automatically to accommodate the image. See Figure 4-13.

Figure 4-13 ◀
Revised
Summary of
Financial
Performance
table

logo image
inserted into cell

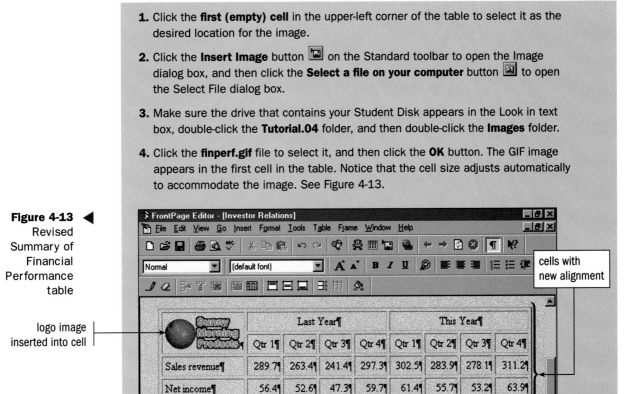

Now that the image has been inserted in the table, Amanda wants you to add a table caption.

Adding a Table Caption

A **table caption** is a title that appears either above or below a table. The table caption can contain one or more lines of text. Although the table caption appears on the same background as that specified for the table, the caption resides outside of the table's border when viewed in the browser. After adding a table caption, you can relocate it by selecting Caption Properties from the Table menu or the Shortcut menu.

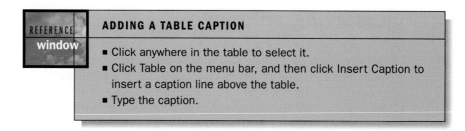

ADDING A TABLE CAPTION

- Click anywhere in the table to select it.
- Click Table on the menu bar, and then click Insert Caption to insert a caption line above the table.
- Type the caption.

Amanda wants you to continue your training by adding a caption that identifies the subject of the table at the top of the Summary of Financial Performance table.

To add a table caption:

1. Click anywhere in the table to select it.

2. Click **Table** on the menu bar, and then click **Insert Caption** to insert a line immediately above the table, which is where you want to place the caption.

3. Type **Summary of Financial Performance**.

4. Select the **Summary of Financial Performance** text you just entered, and then click the **Bold** button **B** on the Format toolbar to apply boldface to the caption.

5. Click anywhere on the Summary of Financial Performance text to deselect it and see the boldface.

After adding a caption to a table, you can change its properties. For example, you might have a multiple-line caption that requires inserting more lines in the caption, or you might want to place one or more blank lines between the caption and the first table row. You can press Shift + Enter to insert one or more lines in your caption. Another way to change an existing caption's properties is to use the settings in the Caption Properties dialog box.

Next, Amanda wants you to move the caption to the bottom of the table to see if this looks better.

To change caption properties:

1. Right-click the **Summary of Financial Performance** caption to display the Shortcut menu, and then click **Caption Properties** to open that dialog box. See Figure 4-14.

Figure 4-14 ◀
Caption
Properties
dialog box

caption added
to table

click to move caption
to bottom of table

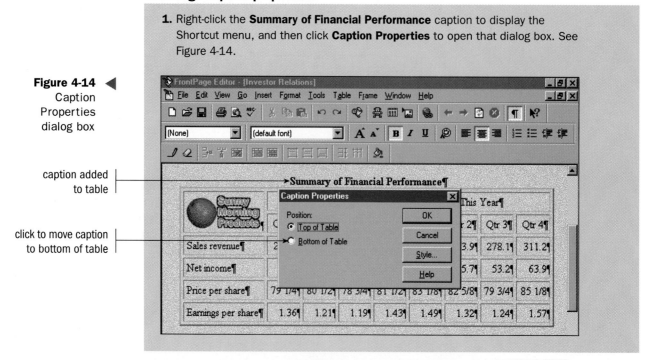

2. In the Position section, click the **Bottom of Table** option button as the location for the caption, and then click the **OK** button. Now, the caption appears at the bottom of the table.

Because you prefer the caption at the top of the table, you undo this action.

3. Click the **Undo** button on the Standard toolbar. The caption moves back to the top of the table.

4. Click the **Save** button 🖫 on the Standard toolbar. The Save Embedded Files dialog box opens with the finperf.gif file in the Embedded Files to Save text box.

5. If **images/** appears as the selected folder of the finperf.gif file, then click the **OK** button. Otherwise, click **finperf.gif** to select that file, click the **Change Folder** button, click the **images** folder to select it, click the **OK** button to display "images/" in the Folder field, and then click the **OK** button to save the file in the images folder.

You and Amanda agree that placing the caption at the top of the table makes more sense for this Web page. The caption of the table appears immediately when the Investor Relations page appears so the user doesn't have to scroll down the page to see the table subject.

You are almost finished completing the table. However, Amanda has some additional table properties that she wants you to adjust to enhance the table's appearance.

Setting Table Properties

You can use FrontPage Editor to set or revise many table properties. In addition to the layout and width properties that you set using the Insert Table dialog box, you also can set the properties for a custom background and border colors. You can set the background to a color, or you can use an image that is different than the current background image for the Web page. When you change a table's background color, you can either select from a list of common colors or open the Color dialog box and choose from a wide color spectrum.

REFERENCE window

SETTING TABLE PROPERTIES

- Click anywhere on the table to select it, and then click Table on the menu bar.

or

- Right-click anywhere on the table to select it and display the Shortcut menu.
- Click Table Properties to open that dialog box.
- Change the desired properties.
- Click the OK button.

Amanda wants you to change the current background color and the border color of the table to white and black, respectively. She thinks this will make the table more attractive to visitors of the Investors Relations Web page.

To set table properties:

1. Right-click anywhere on the table to display the Shortcut menu, and then click **Table Properties** to open that dialog box.

2. In the Custom Background section, click the **Background Color** list arrow to display a list of available colors, and then click **White**.

3. In the Custom Colors section, click the **Border** list arrow to display a list of available colors, and then click **Custom**. The Color dialog box opens.

4. In the Basic colors section, click **Black** (first column, sixth row), click the **OK** button, and then click the **OK** button again. The Summary of Financial Performance table and the image display with a white background. See Figure 4-15.

Figure 4-15
Summary of
Financial
Performance
table

logo appears with
same background
as table

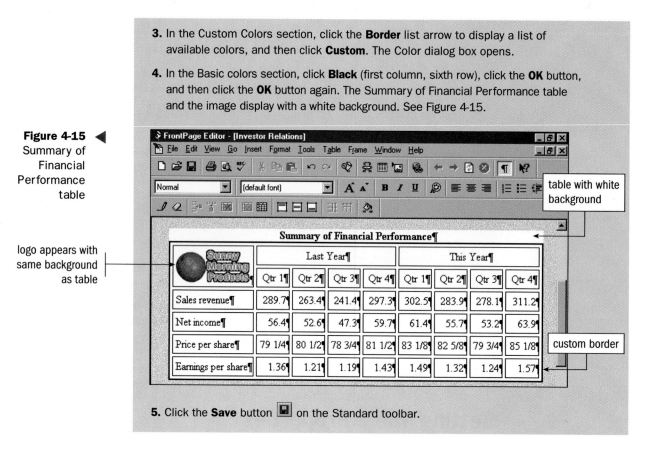

5. Click the **Save** button 🖫 on the Standard toolbar.

Now that you've completed these latest table property changes, you are finished creating the table. However, your task is not complete until you test the appearance of the table in the Web browser.

Testing a Table Using Internet Explorer

Like other Web pages, you need to test the Investor Relations page in your browser to make sure the table you created appears exactly as specified. In this case, testing is especially important because the table is set up to occupy a percentage of the page's width.

To test a table using Internet Explorer:

1. Click the **Preview** tab to display the Investor Relations page with the table in that window.

   This looks acceptable, but now you want to test it with the browser.

2. Click the **Preview in Browser** button 🔍 on the Standard toolbar. The Investor Relations page displays in the Internet Explorer window. If necessary, maximize the window.

3. Review the table appearance. Make sure the data displays as desired and the caption, background, and image all match your specifications.

4. Click the **FrontPage Editor** program button on the taskbar to return to that program, and then click the **Normal** tab to display the page in that document view.

While creating this table, you learned about many HTML table features. However, you can use many other features with tables that are too numerous to list here. When you need more detailed information about other table features, or other features related to FrontPage in general, you can use FrontPage Help.

Using FrontPage Help

FrontPage provides an extensive Help system that is useful if you don't know how to perform a task or forget how to complete a particular task. The FrontPage Help system provides the same options as the Help system in other Windows programs—Help Contents, Help Index, and the Find features. Because there are more options for creating tables that are beyond the scope of these tutorials, you might want to use FrontPage Help as you create and edit future tables.

Amanda wants you to use Help to find out some information on nesting tables. A **nested table** is a table within a table. Although she hasn't included a nested table in the design of the Investor Relations Web page, Amanda thinks you might find this feature useful when designing more complex Web page tables in the future.

To use FrontPage Help:

1. Click **Help** on the menu bar, click **Microsoft FrontPage Help** to open the Help Topics: Microsoft FrontPage Help dialog box, and then, if necessary, click the **Index** tab to display the index.

2. Type **tables, nest** in the Type the first few letters text box. The index list moves to the entry "nesting tables," which now appears selected in the list.

3. Click the **Display** button to open the FrontPage Help dialog box with a description for completing this task. See Figure 4-16.

Figure 4-16 ◄
Nested tables information in FrontPage Help dialog box

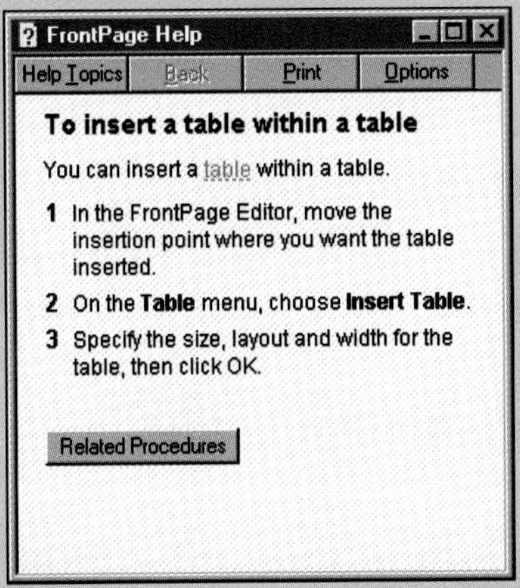

4. Read the information about nesting tables, and then click the **Close** button ⊠ for the FrontPage Help dialog box to exit FrontPage Help and return to FrontPage Editor.

Based on the information you found about nested tables using the FrontPage Help system, you have a general idea how to perform this task. Recall that many Web pages use tables extensively. You might want to consider using nested tables when you design other Web pages in the future.

Alternatives for Creating Tables

There are several alternatives for creating tables using a program other than FrontPage. For example, you can use your word-processing program to create a table and then save it as an RTF (Rich Text Format) file. When you import an RTF file into your Web page, FrontPage Editor recognizes the table and translates it into HTML code. Another option is to create a table using either your word-processing or spreadsheet program, select the table, copy it to the Windows Clipboard, and then paste it into your Web page in FrontPage Editor. The HTML code that is created for a table that was created by another program is the same as if you created the table using FrontPage.

Viewing HTML Tags for a Table

A table, such as the Summary of Financial Performance table you created for the Investor Relations page, makes extensive use of HTML tags. Each cell in the table and its contents are specified individually. For example, the <TABLE> and </TABLE> tags specify the beginning and end of the table. The <TR> and </TR> tags indicate the beginning and end of one row in the table, whereas the <TD> and </TD> tags reflect the beginning and end of the content of each cell. Usually, FrontPage Editor generates a separate line for the definition of the contents of each cell. The <DIV> and <CENTER> tags cause the table to be center-aligned on the page.

In order to gain a better understanding of the HTML tags associated with the Investor Relations table, Amanda wants you to view the HTML code for the Investor Relations page.

To view the HTML code for a table:

1. Click the **HTML** tab to switch to that document view, and then scroll up until the <DIV> tag is at the top of the window. See Figure 4-17.

Figure 4-17 ◄
Viewing HTML code for the Summary of Financial Performance table

specifies table alignment

beginning of table description

specifies first row

specifies second row

each line specifies one row

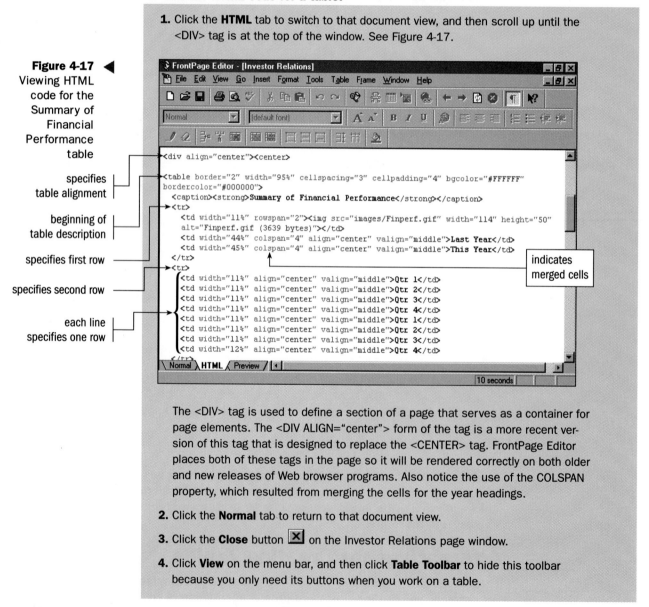

The <DIV> tag is used to define a section of a page that serves as a container for page elements. The <DIV ALIGN="center"> form of the tag is a more recent version of this tag that is designed to replace the <CENTER> tag. FrontPage Editor places both of these tags in the page so it will be rendered correctly on both older and new releases of Web browser programs. Also notice the use of the COLSPAN property, which resulted from merging the cells for the year headings.

2. Click the **Normal** tab to return to that document view.

3. Click the **Close** button ☒ on the Investor Relations page window.

4. Click **View** on the menu bar, and then click **Table Toolbar** to hide this toolbar because you only need its buttons when you work on a table.

Quick Check

1. What is the smallest component of a table?

2. _____ is the distance between the contents of a cell and the inside edge of the cell.

3. True or False: Cell spacing is the distance between cells, measured in pixels.

4. What is the maximum table size that can be specified using the Insert Table button grid?

5. True or False: The Center alignment button on the Format toolbar can be used to center-align an entire table on a Web page.

6. Name two ways to select an entire row in a table.

7. _____ a cell divides it into two or more rows or columns.

Amanda is happy with your progress on the Sunny Morning Products Web site. Your next assignment will be to create a frame set in which to display the navigation bar, table of contents, and individual Web pages.

SESSION 4.2

In this session you will learn how to create and edit a frame set using template frame sets that accompany FrontPage. You will specify target frames for pages displayed in a frame set and learn how to use predefined frame names.

Understanding Frames

You use frames to divide a browser window into two or more windows, each of which contains a separate, scrollable page. A group of frames that define a window is called a **frame set**. You use a frame set when you want the contents of one frame in the browser window to remain unchanged while the contents of other frames change. For example, one frame can display a set of hyperlinks (such as a table of contents), while a second frame can display the target pages of the hyperlinks (the main frame). Recall from Tutorial 1 that the Products Web page (products.htm) was organized as a frame set consisting of three frames: the banner frame with the navigation bar, the contents frame with the table of contents, and the main frame displaying each of the selected pages from the contents frame. By clicking a hyperlink in the first frame, you were able to see the contents of the second frame change accordingly. Figure 4-18 shows how you can select different pages in the contents frame for display in the main frame. As each page is opened, it replaces the previous page in the main frame.

Figure 4-18 ◀
Frame
set action

contents frame ─────▶

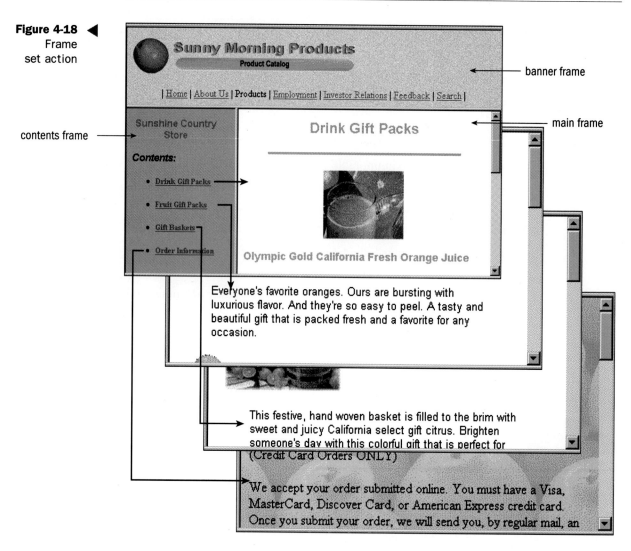

Because the frame set is a Web page, the browser loads a frame set when a user selects a hyperlink to it. The browser first loads the frame set and then loads the target page specified by the source URL for each frame in the frame set. A frame set is specified by a special Web page that defines each window's size and location. Each frame in a frame set has an identifying name, such as main or banner. Also, each frame is assigned a source URL, which is a hyperlink to a separate Web page that displays initially when you load the frame set into the browser window.

Creating a Frame Set

You create a frame set using a template. A **template** is a predesigned format for a Web page that saves time and effort when designing a Web page from scratch. Using a template, you simply enter the specific information you want included in your page and the page is created from this predesigned model. A **frame template** is a predefined format for a frame set in which you select an arrangement that defines the columns for a specific frame set. When you create a frame set with a frame template, FrontPage assigns each frame a default name and source URL. You can resize any of the frames in the frame set after you create them. When you create and edit a frame set, you view the layout of the frame set in FrontPage Editor using a WYSIWYG view. The frame set displays in the Editor window with the initial or default pages that display when the frame first opens in the browser.

In Amanda's design of the Sunny Morning Web, the Products Web page is organized as a frame set. Figure 4-19 shows the portion of Amanda's sketch devoted to the organization of the Products frame set. Specifically, Products is the frame set page, Banner is the page with the navigation bar, contents is the table of contents page, and each of the other pages are those displayed in the main frame of the frame set.

Figure 4-19 ◄
Sketch of
Products
frame set

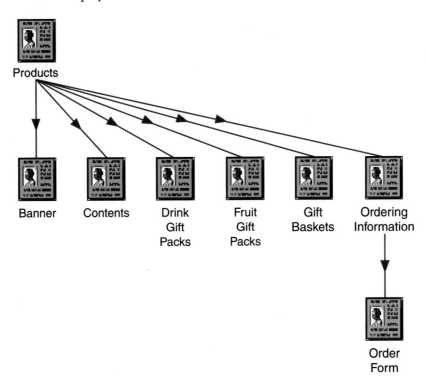

Next, Amanda wants you to create the frame set for the Products page and to modify the banner and content pages. Amanda already created some of the pages shown in the sketch in Figure 4-19 and saved them in the Tutorial.04 folder with their respective images stored in the Tutorial.04\images folder. Amanda also gives you a list of the filenames for each of the pages depicted in the sketch of the Products frame set. Figure 4-20 shows the list of these files.

Figure 4-20 ◄
Files for
Products
frame set

Page Name	Filename
banner	banner.htm
contents	contents.htm
drink gift packs	drink.htm
fruit gift packs	fruit.htm
gift baskets	basket.htm
ordering information	ordrinfo.htm
order form	ordrform.htm

Finally, Amanda asks you to review the planning analysis sheet for the Products frame set so you understand the activities that must be completed before you create your frame set. See Figure 4-21. Amanda prepared this document when she created the Sunny Morning Products Web.

Figure 4-21
Amanda's
planning
analysis sheet
for the
Products
frame set

Planning Analysis Sheet

My goal:

Create a frame set for displaying product information. The page should

display the navigation bar, a table of contents, and individual product

pages.

What results do I want to see?

A Products Web page organized as three frames. The frame set will

include a banner frame for the navigation bar, a contents frame for the

table of contents, and a main frame to display each of the product

information pages.

Selecting each hyperlink in the table of contents frame displays the

selected page in the main frame.

Selecting a hyperlink in the banner frame removes the frame set and

displays the selected page.

What information do I need?

Page for banner frame

Page for contents frame

Pages for main frame—one for each hyperlink in table of contents frame

Images for banner page and each page displayed in main frame

REFERENCE
window

CREATING A FRAME SET

■ Click File on the menu bar, click New to open the New dialog
box, and then click the Frames tab to display the list of available
templates.
■ Click the desired layout from the list of templates, and then
click the OK button.

The plan you reviewed with Amanda uses the "Banner and Contents" layout selection from
the FrontPage template frame set. This frame set has a banner at the top, a contents frame, and
a main frame. Amanda wants you to create this frame set as the next activity in your training.

To create a frame set:

1. If necessary, click the **FrontPage Editor** program button on the taskbar to make
this the active program.

   TROUBLE? If the Sunny Morning Web (sunny) is not open in FrontPage Explorer,
open it and repeat Step 1.

TROUBLE? If the Table Toolbar appears, click View on the menu bar, and then click Table Toolbar to hide it.

2. Click **File** on the menu bar, click **New** to open the New dialog box, and then click the **Frames** tab to display the list of available frame layouts, which is where you select one of the predefined template layouts.

3. Click **Banner and Contents** to select that layout. Its description and a preview of the frame set arrangement appears to assist you. See Figure 4-22.

Figure 4-22 ◄
New dialog box

select desired
frame from list
of available templates

description of
frame layout

sample
arrangement
of layout

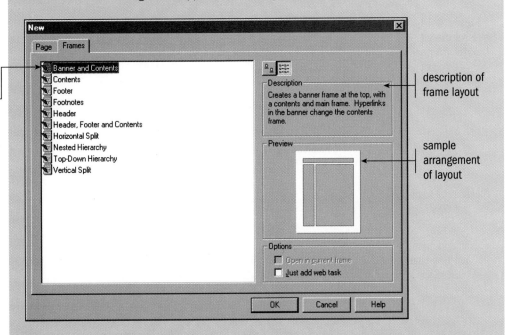

4. Click the **OK** button to create the frame set and open it in FrontPage Editor. See Figure 4-23.

Figure 4-23 ◄
New frame set
displayed in
FrontPage
Editor

click to include
existing page
in each frame

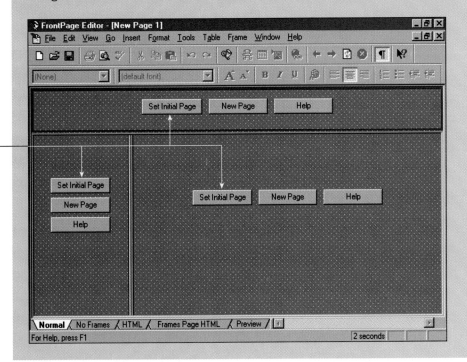

5. Click **File** on the menu bar, and then click **Save As** to open that dialog box with the URL selected.

6. Press the **Delete** key to remove the highlighted URL value, press the **Tab** key to move the insertion point to the Title text box with the current value automatically selected, and type **Products** in the Title text box. Then **products.htm** appears automatically in the URL text box to specify the desired name for the frame set. See Figure 4-24.

Figure 4-24 ◀
Save As dialog
box for frame
set

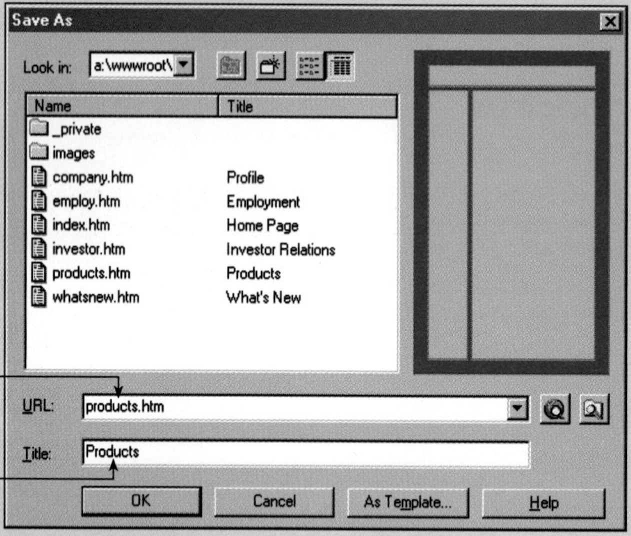

filename for frame
set Web page

title for frame
set Web page

7. Click the **OK** button to open the FrontPage Editor message box indicating a file by this name already exists. Click the **Yes** button to replace the file—the existing file is a blank page that you created when you added this page to the Tasks list in Tutorial 3.

Now that you have created and opened the frame set in FrontPage Editor, your next activity is to include the pages that Amanda created for the Products frame set. Keep in mind that when you create a Web on your own, you will need to create each of these pages yourself. Also, once you've created the pages that make up a frame set, you need to save your changes before you open the frame set in the browser window because the browser opens the saved files from the Web.

Importing Web Pages for a Frame Set

You import the pages for a frame set in the same manner as for other Web pages into an existing Web—either one at a time or all at once. Amanda wants you to import the pages that she created for the frame set. When you do this, you will place the pages in the Sunny Morning Web so they are available for use with the Products frame set. You begin by selecting the banner file as the first page to import for use with the Products frame set.

To import pages for a frame set:

1. Click the **FrontPage Explorer** program button on the taskbar to switch to that program.

2. Click **File** on the menu bar, and then click **Import** to open the Import File to FrontPage Web dialog box.

3. Click the **Add File** button to open the Add File to Import List dialog box, make sure the drive that contains your Student Disk appears in the Look in text box, double-click the **Tutorial.04** folder, and then click the **banner.htm** file.

Rather than importing the rest of the files from the list one at a time, you select the remainder of the files to import all seven files as a single action.

4. Hold down the **Ctrl** key, and click the following files: **basket.htm**, **contents.htm**, **drink.htm**, **fruit.htm**, and **ordrform.htm**, **ordrinfo.htm**, and then release the Ctrl key.

5. Click the **Open** button to return to the Import File to FrontPage Web dialog box. The seven files you selected in Steps 3 and 4 appear in the list box.

6. Click the **OK** button to import the files. It will take a few minutes to add these pages to the Web.

The pages for use with the Products frame set now are imported into the Sunny Morning Web, so they are available with the frame set.

Setting Initial Pages for Frames

The frame set displays originally with three buttons—Set Initial Page, New Page, and Help—in each of the frames in the frame set. These buttons remind you of the actions you can take when specifying or creating the page that is displayed when the frame's page appears initially in a user's browser. You click the Set Initial Page button to specify an existing page that you want to use with the frame set. Click the New Page button if you want to open a new blank page and enter its content. Clicking the Help button opens the Getting Started with Frames description in the Help window. Creating a new page for use within any of the frames in the frame sets is the same as creating any other Web page in FrontPage Editor. Clicking the Set Initial Page button lets you select a Web page that already is part of the existing Web or obtain it from another location. Because you already imported the Web pages for use with the frame set, they now exist in the Sunny Morning Web, which is the easiest method to specify their use with frame set.

Amanda wants you to continue developing the frame set for Sunny Morning Products by specifying the initial pages for each of the three frame in the Products frame set.

To set the initial pages for a frame set:

1. Click the **FrontPage Editor** program button on the taskbar to switch back to that program.

2. Click the **Set Initial Page** button in the banner frame to open the Create Hyperlink dialog box.

3. Double-click **banner.htm** as the name of the desired Web page to display in this frame. The page displays without the image—you'll take care of this problem later.

   TROUBLE? If you accidentally select the wrong page, click the frame, click Frame on the menu bar, click Set Initial Page, and then repeat Step 3.

4. Repeat Steps 2 and 3 to select the contents.htm page to display in the contents frame on the left side of the frame set.

5. Repeat Steps 2 and 3 to select the drink.htm page to display in the main frame of the right side of the frame set. Again, the image is missing.

6. Click the frame border at the bottom of the banner frame, and drag it down about one-half inch until the user-defined navigation bar appears. Then click the frame border between the contents and main frames and drag it to the right about one-half inch until each of the hyperlink choices appears on a single line. See Figure 4-25. This lets the user view the navigation bar in the banner frame without having to scroll to see the choices, which reduces the amount of scrolling in the contents frame.

Figure 4-25
Initial pages
displayed in
frame set

initial page displays
in each frame

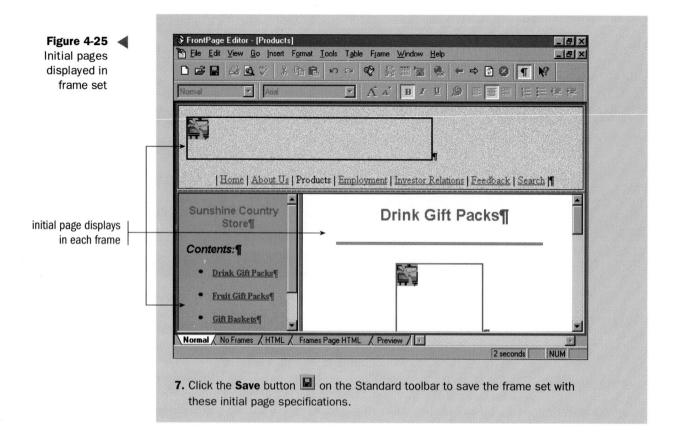

7. Click the **Save** button on the Standard toolbar to save the frame set with these initial page specifications.

Specifying the Target Frame

A **target frame** is the designated frame or window in a frame set where a hyperlink page opens. For example, the target frame for the drink.htm page in the sunny Web is the main frame of the Products frame set. When Amanda created the contents.htm page, she specified all the hyperlinks, including their target frame, *except* for the Order Information page link. Next, Amanda wants you to modify the Contents page so it includes the hyperlink to the Order Information page.

To specify the target frame:

1. In the contents frame, scroll down until you see Order Information, select **Order Information** as the text for the hyperlink, and then click the **Create or Edit Hyperlink** button on the Standard toolbar to open the Create Hyperlink dialog box.

2. Scroll down the list of open files until you see ordrinfo.htm, and then click **ordrinfo.htm** to select the Order Information page.

3. Look at the Target Frame text box and verify that **Page Default (main)** is specified as the frame where you want the Order Information page to display. Your completed Create Hyperlink dialog box should match Figure 4-26.

Figure 4-26 ◀
Create
Hyperlink
dialog box

indicates name of
Web page to display

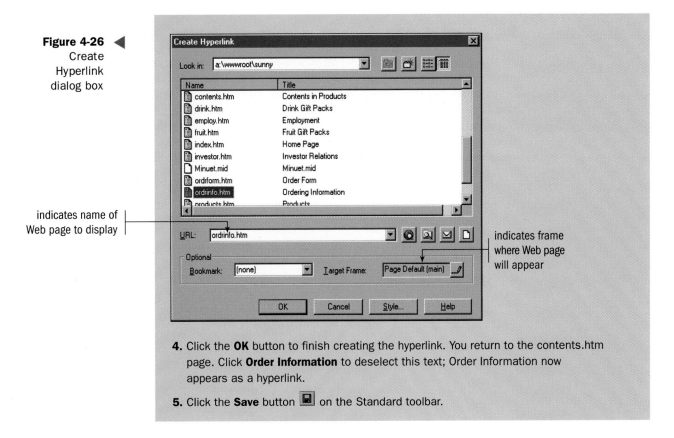

indicates frame
where Web page
will appear

4. Click the **OK** button to finish creating the hyperlink. You return to the contents.htm page. Click **Order Information** to deselect this text; Order Information now appears as a hyperlink.

5. Click the **Save** button on the Standard toolbar.

As you can see in Figure 4-26, unless you enter a different specification, each of the hyperlinks in the contents frame automatically displays the selected page in the main frame of the frame set. If you experience difficulties with the display of pages in your frame set, then you should check the target frame in the Edit Hyperlink dialog box.

Now that you've verified the default pages for the frame set, you are ready to continue your training by opening the frame set in the browser window to review it. Amanda asks you to review the frame set next.

To review a frame set using Internet Explorer:

1. Click the **Preview in Browser** button on the Standard toolbar to open the Products frame set in the browser.

2. Click the **Refresh** button on the Internet Explorer toolbar. Notice that the banner frame is missing an image file.

   TROUBLE? If the navigation bar is not visible in the banner frame, scroll down the banner frame until you see the navigation bar.

3. Click the **Fruit Gift Packs** link in the contents frame to display that page in the main frame. Notice that the page displays without its images.

4. Click the **Drink Gift Packs** link in the contents frame to re-display that page in the main frame.

Now that you have completed importing the HTML Web pages and reviewed the frame set in the Web browser, Amanda wants you to include the images for these pages.

Including Images in Frame Set Pages

As you learned in Tutorial 3, when you import an existing page into a Web, its associated images are not imported automatically. This is the same situation as when you imported other pages into the current Web. The pages associated with the Products frame set contain several image files. As you finish completing the Web pages used with the Products frame set, Amanda wants you to include two of the images that currently are missing from their respective pages. You must include the logo in the Banner page and the drink image included in the Drink Gift Packs page. Later, you will finish including the other images in the Sunny Morning Web.

To include an image in an imported Web page:

1. Click the **FrontPage Editor** program button on the taskbar to switch to that program, and then click anywhere on the Banner frame page to select it as the active page, which is indicated by the line that surrounds the inside of the frame border for the selected page.

   TROUBLE? If the ocean themes textured background from the Home Page (index.htm) does not appear, click Format on the menu bar, click Background, click the Get Background and Colors from Page option button to select it, click the Browse button, scroll down the Name list box, click index.htm, click the OK button, and then click the OK button again. Continue with Step 2.

2. Right-click the **missing image** icon in the upper-left corner of the page to select it and display the Shortcut menu.

3. Click **Image Properties** to open that dialog box. In the Image Source section, click the **Browse** button to open the Image dialog box, and then click the **Select a file on your computer** button 🔍 to open the Select File dialog box.

4. Make sure the drive that contains your Student Disk appears in the Look in text box, double-click the **Tutorial.04** folder, and then double-click the **images** folder to display the list of files.

5. Click the **hproduct.gif** file to select it, and then click the **OK** button. The Image Properties dialog box re-displays with ../../Tutorial.04/Images/Hproduct.gif in the Image Source text box.

6. Click the **OK** button to close the Image Properties dialog box. The Banner page re-displays with the image inserted on the page.

7. Click the **Save** button 💾 on the Standard toolbar to open the Save Embedded Files dialog box, make sure **images/** appears as the Folder in the Embedded Files to Save text box, and then click the **OK** button to save the image. As your Web grows, saving it will require more time, especially when you are saving files to drive A. When you create Web pages on your own, saving will be faster because normally you will save the Web on a hard drive.

   Now that you've inserted the logo on the Banner page, you include the image on the Drink Gift Packs page.

8. Click anywhere on the page in the main frame to select it as the frame with the active page.

9. Repeat Steps 3 through 8 to add the image to the Drink Gift Packs page. Make sure to select the **drink.gif** file from the Tutorial.04 folder, and save it in the images folder of the Web.

Editing a Frame Set

You edit a frame set in FrontPage Editor after opening the frame set's Web page using the same procedures and dialog boxes as when you created the frame set initially. Amanda wants you to verify that the Drink Gift Packs page has been specified as the default target page that displays in the main frame when the frame set first opens. She asks you to check this default now.

To edit the default page display for a frame set:

1. Click anywhere in the **main frame** to select it.

2. Right-click anywhere in the main frame to display the Shortcut menu, and then click **Frame Properties** to open that dialog box. See Figure 4-27.

Figure 4-27 ◀
Frame
Properties
dialog box

frame where
page displays

page to display

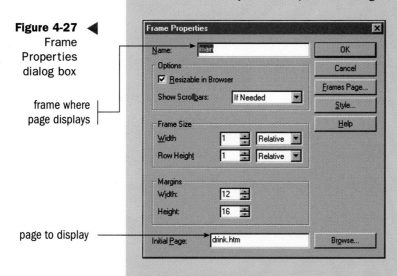

3. Look at the information in the Frame Properties dialog box. Verify that the Name text box displays the value "main" and that the Initial Page text box has the value "drink.htm." These values were set automatically when you placed the initial pages in the frame set. If you needed to revise any of these values, you could. However, for the Products frame set, they are acceptable.

4. Click the **Cancel** button to close the dialog box, and return to the Drink Gift Packs page in the Products frame set.

With this target page verified for the drink.htm page, Amanda wants you to test the frame set by opening it in the browser window.

To test a frame set using Internet Explorer:

1. Click the **Internet Explorer** program button on the taskbar to switch to this program.

2. Click the **Refresh** button 🔄 on the Internet Explorer toolbar to view the frame set and the initial pages.

3. Click the **Home** hyperlink on the navigation bar in the banner frame. The Home Page opens in the Contents window, which indicates that there is a problem with the target frame for this page. See Figure 4-28.

Figure 4-28 ◄
Products frame
set after
clicking Home
hyperlink

Home hyperlink
selected in
Banner frame

Home Page appears
in Contents frame

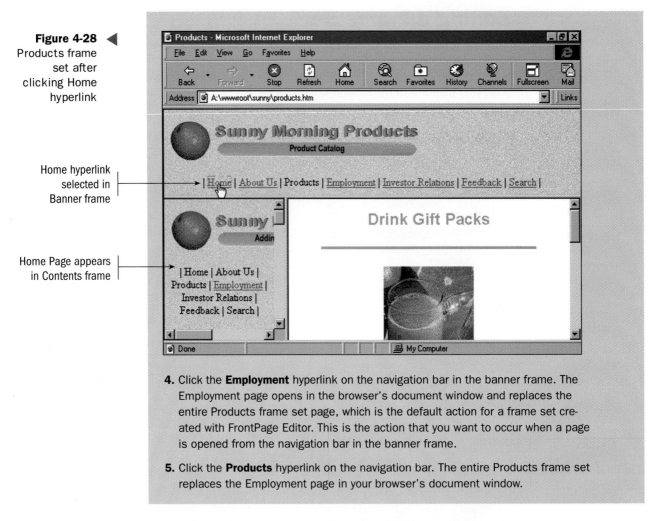

4. Click the **Employment** hyperlink on the navigation bar in the banner frame. The Employment page opens in the browser's document window and replaces the entire Products frame set page, which is the default action for a frame set created with FrontPage Editor. This is the action that you want to occur when a page is opened from the navigation bar in the banner frame.

5. Click the **Products** hyperlink on the navigation bar. The entire Products frame set replaces the Employment page in your browser's document window.

The Home Page did not completely replace the Products frame set page. Instead, it opened in the contents frame. You need to change the target frame for the Home Page by modifying its hyperlink in the navigation bar on the Banner page so the frame set disappears before the Home Page opens. In other words, the target of the hyperlink should open in the browser window without any frame set, which is achieved by using predefined target frame names.

Using Predefined Frame Names

Along with the names assigned to each frame when you create a frame set, there are four predefined frames that have significant meaning to the browsers used to view them. A **predefined frame name** is a value for the target property in an <A> tag that specifies a target frame for a Web browser. A target frame specifies a frame in which pages referenced by hyperlinks are displayed. Figure 4-29 describes the four predefined names that are used to specify target frames. To replace an entire frame set with a different page, you must use the special target frame name of _top, where _top is the predefined frame name that implements the page-replacement action.

Figure 4-29 ◀
Predefined
frame names

Predefined Frame Name	Description
_blank	Specifies that the target of a hyperlink should be loaded into a new window.
_self	Specifies that the target of a hyperlink should be loaded into the same frame as the page containing the hyperlink.
_parent	Specifies that the target of the hyperlink should be loaded into the parent of the current frame. (This is an advanced feature.)
_top	Specifies that the browser should remove all loaded frame sets before displaying the target of a hyperlink, so the target of the hyperlink is displayed in the full window of the browser.

When you set the default target frame, any hyperlinks on the page that do not have target frames directly associated with them will be assigned to their default target frame. For example, for the Banner page in the sunny Web, the target is the contents frame, and for the contents frame, it is the main frame.

When Amanda created the navigation bar in the frbanner.htm page, she specified the _top target frame for every hyperlink, *except* for the Home hyperlink. This is why the Home Page opened in the contents frame during testing, whereas the Employment page replaced the entire frame set correctly. When you create your own page for use in the banner frame, you will need to specify the desired target frame for each hyperlink. Continue your training by specifying the _top predefined name for the target frame of the Home hyperlink.

To use a predefined frame name:

1. Click the **FrontPage Editor** program button on the taskbar to switch to this program.

2. Click anywhere in the banner frame to select that Web page as indicated by the outline surrounding the page in the frame set.

3. Click the **Home** hyperlink in the navigation bar to select it, and then click the **Create or Edit Hyperlink** button 🖳 on the Standard toolbar to open the Edit Hyperlink dialog box. The index.htm filename, which represents the Home Page, appears selected in the URL text box, and "Page Default (content)s" appears in the Target Frame text box.

4. Click the **Change Target Frame** button 🗹 next to the Target Frame text box to open the Target Frame dialog box, and then click **Whole Page** in the Common Targets section to specify _top as the predefined frame name. See Figure 4-30.

Figure 4-30 ◀
Target Frame
dialog box

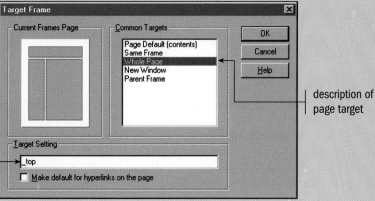

predefined name
for target

> **5.** Click the **OK** button to return to the Edit Hyperlink dialog box.
>
> **6.** Click the **OK** button to finish specifying the revised hyperlink and return to the Banner page in the Products frame set.
>
> **7.** Click the **Save** button 🖫 on the Standard toolbar.

Now, you have specified the target frame name successfully. You will need to use this procedure only when the desired target frame is not selected automatically when you create your frame set. If you change the target frame, then you should use Internet Explorer to test your newly selected predefined target setting.

Amanda reminds you of an important consideration when creating banner pages for other frame sets in the future. That is, you need to make sure the _top predefined frame target setting is specified for each of the entries in your navigation bar so the selected page will replace the entire frame set.

Adding a New Frame to an Existing Frame Set

After you create a frame set, you can revise it by dividing an existing frame, which allows you to include new frames where you can place additional information. Also, if you create a frame set and then find that you need a different frame set arrangement, you can change the frame set instead of re-creating it. To divide one existing frame into two frames within the same frame set, you hold down the Ctrl key while you drag the border of the existing frame that you want to divide to create a new frame. After the new frame is added to the existing frame set, you specify the page displayed in the frame in the same manner as you did for the other frames in the frame set.

Amanda wants to see what the frame set would look like if you add a sales slogan in a separate frame below the main frame that displays each of the content pages. She asks you to split the current main frame into two frames.

To add a new frame to an existing frame set:

> **1.** Hold down the **Ctrl** key and then click the bottom border of the main frame that displays the Drink Gift Packs page. The pointer changes to the Resize pointer ↕.
>
> **2.** While still holding down the **Ctrl** key, drag the bottom frame border up about an inch, and then release the mouse button and the Ctrl key. A new frame is created with the Set Initial Page, New Page, and Help buttons.
>
> As you look as the result, it appears that this change makes the main frame too small for this frame set, so you talk to Amanda and decide to leave the main frame undivided.
>
> **3.** Click the **Undo** button 🖮 on the Standard toolbar to restore the main frame to its original size.
>
> **4.** Click the **Save** button 🖫 on the Standard toolbar.

FrontPage allows you to subdivide existing frames within an existing frame set easily and quickly to provide the best presentation for your Web pages. However, you need to exercise care so that you do not make a frame too small to be useful. Now, the Products frame set and its accompanying Web pages are complete, except that you still have to include the additional image files for use with the remaining Web pages. Because Amanda is confident in your ability to create and modify a frame set, she decides to let you include the images later.

Viewing HTML Tags for Frame Sets

Recall that a frame set is a separate Web page that describes the layout and initial pages that are displayed when the frame set opens. A series of specific HTML tags describe the frame set. For example, each frame in the frame set is specified by FRAMESET tags that indicate the beginning and end of the frame-set specification. Within the FRAME tag, the SRC property indicates the filename for the displayed page, whereas the NAME property identifies the name of the frame in the frame set where that page is displayed. The ROWS and COLUMNS properties of the FRAMESET tag indicate the layout of the frames as a percent of the size of the page.

Amanda wants you to view the HTML tags for the frame set next.

To view the HTML code for a frame set:

1. With the Products page displayed in FrontPage Editor, click the **Frames Page HTML** tab to display the HTML code for the Products page frame. See Figure 4-31.

Figure 4-31 ◀
Viewing HTML
code for the
Products page
frame set

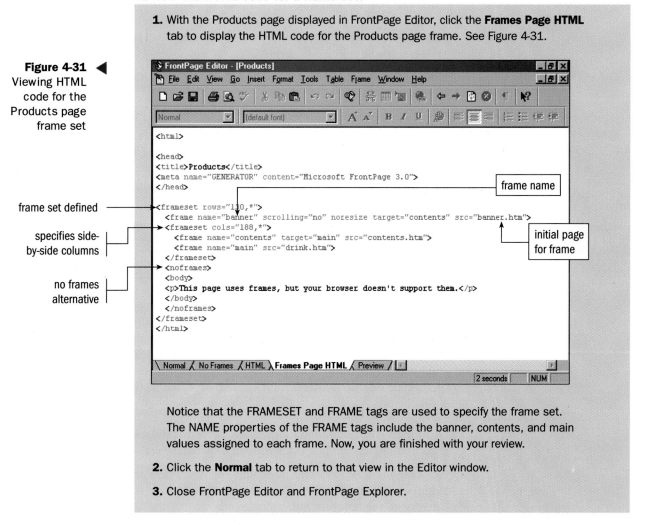

Notice that the FRAMESET and FRAME tags are used to specify the frame set. The NAME properties of the FRAME tags include the banner, contents, and main values assigned to each frame. Now, you are finished with your review.

2. Click the **Normal** tab to return to that view in the Editor window.

3. Close FrontPage Editor and FrontPage Explorer.

FrontPage automatically inserted the NOFRAMES tags in case the page is opened using a browser that does not support frames. Because this doesn't affect Internet Explorer, Amanda advises you to leave this option in the Web page.

Quick Check

1 A group of frames that define a window is called a(n) _____.

2 A(n) _____ is a predefined format that is used to design a Web page so a user doesn't have to start from scratch.

3 True or False: When a frame set is displayed in your Web browser window, the hyperlink page is opened in the target frame.

4 To change a frame set, you access the frame set Web page by opening it in the _____ program.

5 To change the default page displayed in a frame created with a frame template, you _____ the frame set.

6 Which predefined frame name causes the browser to remove all loaded frame sets before displaying the target of a selected hyperlink?

7 True or False: A WYSIWYG view of a frame set is available only by using a special command in FrontPage Editor.

With the Investor Relations and Products pages complete, you review your progress with Amanda. The Summary of Financial Performance table adds key information to the Investor Relations page in an organized and attractive format, whereas the Products frame set allows customers to examine the different categories of products available from the Sunshine Country Store easily.

Tutorial Assignments

During lunch with a couple of interns who are just starting Amanda's training course, the topic of your progress comes up. You explain that you just finished creating and inserting a table and creating a frame set for one of the company's Web pages. Also, you mention that you are particularly pleased with your new expertise in creating the Products frame set because of your interest in using the WWW for future marketing tasks. Because you plan to practice creating tables and frame sets for Web pages after lunch, you invite your colleagues to join you in practicing these skills. If necessary, insert your Student Disk in drive A or the appropriate disk drive, start FrontPage Explorer, and then do the following:

1. Open the Sunny Morning Web (sunny) in FrontPage Explorer.

2. Open the Tasks list, and mark the Finish Investor Relations and Finish Products tasks as completed. Then use WordPad to print the revised Tasks list.

3. Open the Investor Relations page, and add a new row to the bottom of the Summary of Financial Performance table. Then merge the cells from the nine columns of the new row into a single cell.

4. Using the cell you created in Step 3, add a centered footnote with the text "Note: All amounts in millions except per share amounts, which are in dollars." to the Summary of Financial Performance table. Decrease the size of the font by one size from the default size, and then change the color of this footnote message to red.

5. Add the table of stock trading information shown in Figure 4-32 immediately below the Summary of Financial Performance table in the Web page. Use one blank line to separate the two tables, and use the same settings for the new table as the Summary of Financial Performance table. (*Hint:* Use the Table Properties and Cell Properties dialog boxes to check the format of the Summary of Financial Performance table, if necessary.) Your completed table should match Figure 4-32.

Figure 4-32 ◀

Sunny Morning Products (SMP) New York Stock Exchange (NYSE)			
Last Traded at	**85 1/8**	Date/Time	Oct 26 4:02:03
$ Change	2 1/8	% Change	2.59
Volume (000)	84.7	# of Trades	104
Open	82 1/2	Previous Close	81 7/8
Day Low	82 1/4	Day High	83 1/4
52 Week Low	73 1/4	52 Week High	87 1/4

6. Add the caption "Stock Trading Information" to the top of the table. Test the completed page using Internet Explorer, and then print it.

7. Use a word-processing or spreadsheet program to create a third table of information that you will add to the Investor Relations page. Your table should have a minimum of four rows and four columns. Determine the information to include, and design the table appropriately. If you use a word-processing program, make sure to create a table in that program using its Table commands. Save the file as "table" in the Tutorial.04 folder on your Student Disk with the default file extension.

8. Copy the table you created in Step 7 to the Windows Clipboard, and then paste it into the Investor Relations page. Add an appropriate caption to the top of the table. Change the background color and border colors to match the style of the other tables that appear on this page.

9. View the HTML code for the table that you created in Step 7 to verify that the translation was completed correctly. Display the completed page in your browser window, and then print it.

10. Design and create a new Web page named "Clothing" for Sunny Morning Products to reflect the company's new product line of T-shirts, sweatshirts, and tote bags. Write the content of the page based on the writing style and content of other pages in the sunny Web. Revise the Contents page of the Products frame set to include a hyperlink to this new page so it opens in the main frame to add a page to this frame set.

11. Test the changes from Step 10 using Internet Explorer, and then print a copy of the revised Contents page and the new Clothing page.

12. Revise the frame set's banner page by creating a table that contains each of the navigation entries. (*Hint:* Rather than using the vertical bar to separate navigation choices, display them in a table with a single row.) Use the Help system to learn more about the Convert Text to Table command on the Table menu to revise the navigation bar. Separate each of the entries using borders around each cell. Test the revised frame set banner page in the browser window, and then print a copy of this revised page.

13. Review each of the pages that have the main frame as their target, and include the appropriate images in each of these files. Specify the orngback.jpg file as the background for the Ordering Information (ordrinfo.htm) page. (*Hint:* All of the image files are located in the Tutorial.04\images folder on your Student Disk.)

14. Print each of the pages from Step 13 using either Internet Explorer or FrontPage Editor to show the inclusion of the images in these Web pages.

15. Close any open programs, and save changes to your Web files.

Case Problems

1. Building an Investors Page for Royal Hair Care Products The Kuick Dry Reliable Solution has enhanced the profitability of Royal Hair Care Products' operations. Valerie met with the company's senior managers to present an update on her Web site development. The management team asked Valerie to expand the Web site to include information that the company's investors might need, such as information on both Royal's financial performance and current stock market activities. Afterward, Valerie revised her design to include this additional Web page and collected the necessary information. She had Nathan create a Web page of the stock market performance information and sketched a table of the financial performance information. Valerie asks you to help Nathan complete developing this additional Web site information.

If necessary, start FrontPage Explorer, insert your Student Disk in drive A or the appropriate disk drive, and then do the following:

1. Read all the questions for this case problem, and prepare a planning analysis sheet for the changes to the Royal Web site.

2. Open the Royal Web. If you did not create this Web in Tutorial 2 and change it in Tutorial 3, then create this Web and see your instructor.

3. Create a frame set using the Banner and Contents frame template layout to implement the investors' information with a separate page for each of the financial performance and stock performance information.

4. Create the financial performance information page, and include the table shown in Figure 4-33. The page should include a heading that identifies the information contained on the page. Specify a color for the table's background, and then choose an appropriate border, light border, and dark border. Save this file as rfininfo.htm in the Royal Web.

Figure 4-33 ◀

	Current Year			
	Qtr 1	Qtr 2	Qtr 3	Qtr 4
Sales revenue	421.3	474.2	508.1	480.3
Net income	14.0	14.1	14.5	14.2
Price per share	34.250	33.625	36.125	32.250
Earnings per share	2.20	2.19	2.30	2.01
Note: All amounts in thousands except per share amounts, which are in dollars.				

5. Import the rstock.htm file into the Web. This file, which contains the stock performance information, is located in the Tutorial.04\royal folder on your Student Disk. This is one of the files used in the main frame of the frame set.

6. Create a page for the banner frame that contains a user-defined navigation bar. This navigation bar should include all the navigation choices that are available on the Home Page. Create a table that contains each of the navigation choices, and enter the text for each hyperlink in a separate cell. Use an appropriate target for these hyperlinks so the selected page replaces the entire frame set in the browser window. Include a border in this table to provide a visual cue that separates the navigation choices.

7. Create a table of contents (TOC) page that opens in the contents frame. Design this as a bulleted list for the two pages that are displayed in the main frame. The TOC should include hyperlinks for each of the respective pages to open in the main frame.

8. Edit the frame set so the rfininfo.htm page is the default page that opens in the main frame when the frame set is opened.

9. Create a hyperlink from the Home Page to the Investors page. Modify the navigation bar on the Home Page to include a choice for the Investors page.

10. Test the frame set to make sure each of the hyperlinks results in the appropriate action. If you encounter any problems during your test, note and then correct them.

11. Print the HTML code for the frame set. Circle the FRAME tags that include the name of the default page that is displayed in a frame together with the name of the frame in which it is displayed.

12. Print a copy of the Banner page, the Contents page, and each of the investor information pages using Internet Explorer or FrontPage Editor.

13. Display the Investors page as the center focus in FrontPage Explorer using Hyperlinks view, and then print the Hyperlinks view.

14. Arrange and clearly identify the printouts and answers for all the questions in this case.

15. Close any open programs, and save changes to your Web files.

2. Creating a What Page for Buffalo Trading Post Retail-clothing customers usually want to know which items are the current best-sellers. At Buffalo Trading Post, Donna and Karla decided that a list of the current top 10 hot items would be a great addition to their Web site. As you discuss this concept with a sales associate, you conclude that there are three main areas of interest: women's clothing, children's clothing, and accessories. Karla asks you to help her create this "what" page for Buffalo's Web site.

If necessary, start FrontPage Explorer, insert your Student Disk in drive A or the appropriate disk drive, and then do the following:

1. Read all the questions for this case problem, and prepare a planning analysis sheet for the changes to the Buffalo Web site.

2. Open the Buffalo Web. If you did not create this Web in Tutorial 2 and change it in Tutorial 3, then create this Web and see your instructor.

3. Donna wants you to use a frame set to implement the top 10 list of hot items by category with a separate Web page for each of the following categories: women's clothing, children's clothing, and accessories. Create this frame using the Banner and Contents frame template layout. The frame set should replace the Bwhat.htm file with the blank page, which you created with the Tasks list in Tutorial 3.

4. Design a table for use as the navigation bar in the banner frame of the frame set. This table design should include a cell for each navigation choice with an image for each of the Home, Who, How, Where, and Contact pages.

5. Create the table you designed in Step 4 as the banner page for the frame set. Use the same color for the table's background, border, light border, and dark border. Use the b_what.gif image as the logo on this page, and use the nb_home.gif, nb_who.gif, nb_how.gif, nb_where.gif, and nb_conta.gif files for the inline images in the table. (*Hint:* These files are located in the Tutorial.04\buffalo folder on your Student Disk.) Include the hyperlinks for each navigation choice. Use an appropriate target for each of these hyperlinks so those pages will replace the entire frame set in the browser window.

6. Create a table of contents (TOC) page that opens in the contents frame. Design this as a bulleted list of the hot item pages for each of the three categories. The TOC should include hyperlinks for each of the respective pages to open in the main frame.

7. Design a table for the hot items list for each category. Each table should include the name of the item, a brief description, and a current price range.

8. Create a separate Web page for each of the tables you designed in Step 7. Use the cell width in percent option to adjust the width of the cells, if necessary.

9. Create a hyperlink from the Home Page to the What page.

10. Test the frame set using Internet Explorer and make sure that each of the hyperlinks results in the appropriate action. If you encounter any problems during your test, note and then correct them.

11. Print the HTML code for the frame set. Circle the FRAME tags that include the name of the default page that is displayed in a frame together with the name of the frame in which it is displayed.

12. Print a copy of the Banner page, the Contents page, and each of the three top 10 list of hot items pages using Internet Explorer or FrontPage Editor.

13. Display the What page as the center focus in FrontPage Explorer using Hyperlinks view, and then print the Hyperlinks view.

14. Arrange and clearly identify the printouts and answers for all the questions in this case.

15. Close any open programs, and save changes to your Web files.

3. Developing the Menu Pages for Pardon My Garden Nolan and Shannon, members of the Web site development team at Pardon My Garden, just returned from a meeting with Samantha Wyman in the marketing department. Samantha described how she wants Nolan to implement the restaurant menu Web pages so that Pardon My Garden can remain competitive in the casual, full-service restaurant industry. Her goal is for customers to be able to view the menu from their home or office before coming to the restaurant. There will be four separate pages—one each for appetizers, sandwiches, entrees, and desserts. Nolan wants to use a table to arrange the entries for each menu and make it easier for customers to read. He asks you to help Shannon develop these Web pages.

If necessary, start FrontPage Explorer, insert your Student Disk in drive A or the appropriate disk drive, and then do the following:

1. Read all the questions for this case problem, and prepare a planning analysis sheet for this enhancement to the Garden Web site.

2. Use the Contents frame template layout to implement the menu as a frame set. Sketch the menu frame set that you will use to implement this design.

3. Prepare a design sketch of each of the tables that you will use in each of the four pages for the menu categories. Include a minimum of three menu items of your choice on each menu. Each should list a name in boldface, a short description, and a price.

4. Open the Garden Web in FrontPage Explorer. If you did not create this Web in Tutorial 2, create the Web and see your instructor for the Home Page file that you can import into the Web; also include the image for the logo in this page. If your instructor provides you with any additional pages for the Web, then import them as well.

5. Create the four Web pages according to the design you prepared in Step 3. The titles of these Web pages should be Appetizers, Sandwiches, Entrees, and Desserts. The filename for each page should be the default name of the first eight characters of the page's title.

6. Insert either the GARDEN01.GIF or GARDEN02.GIF image from the Tutorial.02\Garden folder as an inline image for the logo at the top of each of these pages.

7. Create the Contents frame set.

8. Print a copy of the frame set page you created in Step 7, and then view the HTML source code for the frame set.

9. Create a Contents Web page with a navigation bar that includes a list of the four menu categories and an entry to return to the Home Page. The Contents page should include hyperlinks to each of the menu pages with the main frame as the target for the four menu category pages and an appropriate target for the Home Page so that it replaces the entire frame set in the browser window.

10. Edit the frame set so the Appetizers page is displayed as the initial page when the Menu frame set opens in the browser window.

11. Create a hyperlink from the Home Page to the Menu page, and then test each of the hyperlinks in the frame set. If you encounter any problems during your test, note and then correct them.

12. Print the HTML code for the frame set. Circle the FRAME tags that include the name of the initial page that is displayed in a frame together with the name of the frame in which it is displayed.

13. Print a copy of the Contents page and each of the four menu item pages using Internet Explorer or FrontPage Editor.

14. Display the Menu page as the center focus in FrontPage Explorer using Hyperlinks view, and then print the Hyperlinks view.

15. Arrange and clearly identify the printouts and answers for all the questions in this case.

16. Close any open programs, and save changes to your Web files.

4. Preparing a Specials Page for Replay Music Factory Mary Kay is pleased with your progress in assisting Justin in the development of the Replay Music Factory Web site. During a recent management meeting, Mary Kay presented the Replay Web and received feedback on its content. Bob Gustafson, a senior marketing manager, suggested including a Specials page in the Web that would contain a list of the CDs for which Replay wants to provide additional exposure. Bob described how he wanted to use the Specials page to promote several different categories of music and how it was important to present specials to users by category. Mary Kay gave Bob an overview of how frame sets work. Bob believes this feature would provide the interaction with the Web page that he would like for Replay's customers. Bob approved a design using a frame set in which the Contents page would display the selection of music types, while the Main page displayed the available specials for that music type. Furthermore, Bob wants the specials for each music type arranged as a table so the information describing each special is easy to read. Mary Kay asks you to assist Justin with this Web revision.

If necessary, start FrontPage Explorer, insert your Student Disk in drive A or the appropriate disk drive, and then do the following:

1. Read all the questions for this case problem, and prepare a planning analysis sheet for this enhancement to the Replay Web site.

2. Select a template frame set for implementing this page. Notice the names of the frames in the template. Your selected template must include at least one frame for the table of contents with each of the types of music and one frame to display the individual page with the details of each type of music.

3. Sketch the Specials frame set that you will use.

4. Prepare a design sketch of each of the tables that you will use in each of the music type pages. Include a minimum of three different music types of your choice. Each special music offering should include information that indicates the artist, title, identification number, and current price.

5. Open the Replay Web in FrontPage Explorer. If you did not create this Web in Tutorial 2, create the Web and see your instructor for any pages that might be available.

6. Create the frame set that you designed in Steps 2 through 4.

7. Print the HTML code for this frame set.

8. Create all the Web pages for your design using real or fictitious data. (*Hint:* Recall that you need at least one page for each of the frames in your frame set.) The user should be able to return to the Home Page from a hyperlink displayed in one of the frames.

9. Using the Contents page, specify the hyperlinks for displaying each of the pages for the type of music in a main frame.

10. Using either the Contents page or a page displayed in another frame, specify that the hyperlinks for all the other pages that are opened from this frame set. For any page that is not part of the frame set, that page should replace the entire frame set in the browser window when the page opens.

11. Display one of the music type pages as the initial page in the main frame when the frame set opens in the browser window.

12. Test the frame set to make sure each of the hyperlinks results in the appropriate action. If you discover any problems during your test, note and correct them.

13. Print the HTML for the frame set, and then print a copy of each page used with the frame set using Internet Explorer or FrontPage Editor. (*Hint:* Do not print the HTML code for the individual pages.)

14. Display the Specials page as the center focus in FrontPage Explorer using Hyperlinks view, and then print the Hyperlinks view.

15. Arrange and clearly identify the printouts and answers for all the questions in this case.

16. Close any open programs, and save changes to your Web files.

Creating Shared Borders and Applying Web Themes

Changing the Navigation Structure and Applying a Theme to the New Recipes Web

OBJECTIVES

In this tutorial you will:

▨ Change image properties

▨ Create a hover button

▨ Add page transitions and animations

▨ Create a Web site with shared borders and navigation bars generated by FrontPage

▨ Create and change the navigation structure of a Web site

▨ Apply a theme to a Web site and a Web page

▨ Change a Web site theme

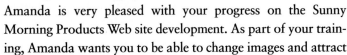

Sunny Morning Products

CASE Amanda is very pleased with your progress on the Sunny Morning Products Web site development. As part of your training, Amanda wants you to be able to change images and attract the user's attention so that navigation through the Web site is easy. There are many ways to make a Web site interesting and fun to use, including adding hover buttons, page transitions, and animations. With FrontPage, it is easy to apply these effects.

Andrew and Carmen sent Amanda an e-mail message to remind her that they want to include Web pages in the Sunny Morning Products Web that feature recipes using Sunny Morning products. After much discussion, the team decides to create a new FrontPage Web and link it to the existing Sunny Morning Products (sunny) Web to give the team more control over the site's appearance. FrontPage lets you apply a common, cohesive theme to a Web site. Amanda wants you to change the navigation structure of the Web and then apply a theme to the site to accomplish this request. The creation of the second Web will let you apply the theme quickly and easily without letting users realize that they are viewing two different Webs.

In this session you will learn how to create a thumbnail image and to edit the appearance of images. You will place text over an image, create a hover button, and apply animated effects for page transitions.

Using Advanced Image Properties

In prior tutorials, you have included inline images in a Web page, changed a color to transparent, and created a hotspot. FrontPage Editor lets you alter an image's appearance in several ways: by creating a thumbnail image, washing out an image, and adding a beveled edge to an image. You also can add dynamic effects to images, such as changing the appearance of an image when the user places the pointer on it or when a page initially appears in the Web browser. Amanda wants you to enhance the appearance of the Sunny Morning Web by using several of these advanced features.

Creating a Thumbnail Image

A **thumbnail** is a small version of an image on a page that contains a hyperlink to a full-sized version of the same image. By putting a thumbnail image on a page, you reduce the amount of information to download over the Internet before a user can view the complete page in the Web browser. Users who want to view the full-sized image linked to a thumbnail can click the thumbnail. The link might be to a GIF file or to an HTML file that contains the complete GIF file. With the GIF file, only the image file is displayed and the browser's Back button is used to return to the previous Web page. With an HTML file, you can add other hyperlinks to the page with the full-sized image to provide better control over the user options to access another Web page. You can create thumbnail images quickly using the Auto Thumbnail command on the Tools menu. FrontPage creates the thumbnail image, inserts it in place of the full-sized image, and then creates a hyperlink to the full-sized image from the thumbnail image.

At one of their weekly meetings, Andrew and Amanda mentioned that many customers call the Sunshine Country Store to find its location. Amanda suggested adding a thumbnail image of the map to the Sunny Morning Web that would help customers locate the store. The thumbnail image could be linked to the full-sized image, so the full image would not overwhelm the Home Page. Amanda asks you to review the planning analysis sheet she prepared before starting the new task. See Figure 5-1.

Figure 5-1
Amanda's
planning
analysis sheet
for the
Map page

Planning Analysis Sheet

My goal:

Create a map page that shows the location of the Sunshine Country Store
and uses special effects to increase interest in the page's display.

What results do I want to see?

A Map Web page that includes an image with the location map, a hover
button to return to the Home Page, and special effects for displaying the
page and the heading for the page. The Map page opens after the user
clicks a thumbnail of the map image on the Home Page.

What information do I need?

The map image that shows the location of the Sunshine Country Store.
The Map Web page for displaying the map and the navigation options.

Amanda created the full-sized image file that you will use to create the thumbnail.

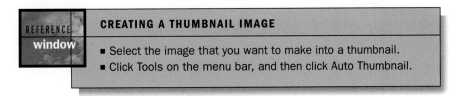

REFERENCE
window

CREATING A THUMBNAIL IMAGE

- Select the image that you want to make into a thumbnail.
- Click Tools on the menu bar, and then click Auto Thumbnail.

As you continue your training, Amanda wants you to create the thumbnail image with
a link to the full-sized image. She prepared a full-sized image file that is available for creating the thumbnail image.

To create a thumbnail image:

1. Make sure that your Student Disk is in drive A or the appropriate drive on your computer, and then start FrontPage Explorer.

2. Open the Sunny Morning Web (sunny) from your Student Disk, and if necessary change to Folders view.

3. Scroll down the Name list until you see the Home Page, and then double-click **index.htm** to open the page in FrontPage Editor.

4. Scroll to the bottom of the Home Page, click anywhere in the last line of text in the paragraph immediately above the marquee, press the **End** key to position the insertion point at the end of that line of text, press the **Enter** key to insert a new paragraph to place the image, and then click the **Center** button ≡ on the Format toolbar to center this paragraph.

   Now, you are ready to import the map image that shows the Country Store's location.

5. Click the **Insert Image** button 🖾 on the Standard toolbar, click the **Select a file on your computer** button 🔍 to open the Select File dialog box, make sure the drive that contains your Student Disk appears in the Look in text box, double-click the **Tutorial.05** folder to open it, double-click the **Images** folder to open it, and then double-click the **map.gif** filename to open this as an inline image on the Home Page.

6. If necessary, scroll down until you see the entire map, and then click the map image to select it and display the Image toolbar.

7. Click **Tools** on the menu bar, and then click **Auto Thumbnail** to create the thumbnail image. See Figure 5-2.

Figure 5-2 ◀
Home Page
with thumbnail
map image

thumbnail
image centered
above marquee

Image toolbar
contains special
effects buttons

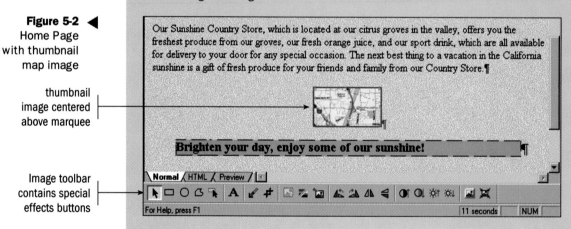

The thumbnail image replaced the full-sized image on the Home Page. Later, when you save the Home Page, this smaller image is saved to your Web. Before you save the image, Amanda wants you to experiment with some other changes you can make to images in FrontPage Editor.

Changing Image Characteristics

With FrontPage Editor, you can change many image characteristics. Editor lets you make several enhancements to the image as you determine the most appropriate appearance. For example, you can convert an image to black and white, rotate an image, change the contrast of an image, change the level of brightness, add a bevel edge to the image's frame, and washout an image. When you **washout** an image, you reduce the brightness and contrast to create a faded appearance.

REFERENCE window

CHANGING IMAGE CHARACTERISTICS

- Click the image to select it.
- Click the button for the desired image characteristic on the Image toolbar.

Amanda wants you to make several changes to the thumbnail image for locating the Sunshine Country Store. Although she asks you to make these changes to the thumbnail, be aware that they can be made to full-sized images as well.

To change image characteristics:

1. Click the **Black and White** button ⬜ on the Image toolbar to apply that effect. Look at the image, and then click ⬜ again to return to the full-color map.

2. Click the **Reverse** button ⬜ on the Image toolbar to flip the image from left to right. Look at the image, and then click ⬜ again to return the image to its original orientation.

3. Click the **Rotate Left** button ⬜ on the Image toolbar to apply that effect. Observe the orientation of the image on the page, and then click the **Rotate Right** button ⬜ to return the thumbnail image to its original orientation.

4. Click the **Washout** button ⬜ on the Image toolbar to create that effect on the image.

5. Click the **Restore** button ⬜ on the Image toolbar to reverse the washout effect and restore the image to its original size. You can click the Restore button to remove all image effects.

6. Click the **Undo** button ⬜ on the Standard toolbar to return to the thumbnail map image with the washout effect.

   Amanda feels that the washout effect provides the best appearance for the thumbnail image, so she wants you to use it.

7. Click the **Bevel** button ⬜ on the Image toolbar to apply that effect to the thumbnail image. You can apply several effects to the same image, or you can apply any one of these effects individually.

8. Click the **Save** button ⬜ on the Standard toolbar to open the Save Embedded Files dialog box for saving these new images with the revised Home Page. A suggested filename of Map_small.gif appears in the Name field and images/ appears in the Folder field. FrontPage automatically generates the name for the thumbnail file by appending "_small" to the filename.

9. Make sure that the settings described in Step 8 are correct, and change them if necessary. Then click the **OK** button to accept the suggested name and folder and to save the files to the Sunny Morning Web.

You added several effects to the thumbnail image. However, Amanda wants you to add text over the image to indicate that the thumbnail is a hyperlink.

Adding Text Over an Image

FrontPage Editor lets you add text to a GIF image that appears on top of the image. When creating images that are used as hyperlinks, this text is useful to indicate the action of the hyperlink and is more convenient than placing the text adjacent to an inline image. You place text over an image by selecting the image and then using the Text button on the Image toolbar to create the text.

REFERENCE window

ADDING TEXT OVER AN IMAGE

- Click the image to select it.
- Click the Text button on the Image toolbar to open a text box on top of the selected image.
- Type the desired text. Press the Enter key to start a new line.
- Click anywhere on the Web page to finish entering the text.

As you continue enhancing the Home Page, Amanda wants you to place text on the thumbnail image for locating the Sunshine Country Store.

To add text to an image:

1. If necessary, click the **thumbnail image** to select it and display the Image toolbar.

2. Click the **Text** button **A** on the Image toolbar to open a text box on top of the image.

3. Type **Country**, press the **Enter** key to start a new line, type **Store**, press the **Enter** key to insert another new line, and then type **Locator** as the text for this label on the image.

   Next, you will change the color and font of the text on the image.

4. Select the **Country Store Locator** text, click the **Text Color** button on the Format toolbar to open the Color dialog box, click the **orange** box (fourth row, second column), and then click the **OK** button.

5. Click the **Save** button on the Standard toolbar to save the image with this change.

   TROUBLE? If the Save Embedded Files dialog box opens, click the OK button to accept the suggested name and folder values.

You created the thumbnail image, changed several of its characteristics, and added text over it. Now, Amanda wants you to test the thumbnail image to make sure the hyperlink works correctly by displaying the full-sized image.

To test the thumbnail image:

1. Click the **Preview in Browser** button on the Standard toolbar to open the Home Page in the browser, and then scroll to the bottom of the page so you see the thumbnail image.

2. Click the **thumbnail image** to open the map.gif file as a separate page in the browser window. Notice that this is only the GIF image, and not an HTML page. Also, when only the image is open, there are no navigation buttons because an HTML page is required for including any links to other pages.

3. Click the **Back** button on the Internet Explorer toolbar to return to the Home Page, and then press the **Esc** key to stop the music.

In order to provide navigation options to a user, you need to include the full-sized image on a Web page. That way, you can add hyperlinks for the user, rather than relying on the browser's Back button. Amanda wants you to include this capability for the map to the Sunshine Country Store in the Sunny Morning Web. She already created a Map Web page for you to use to implement this feature. You just need to import that page and set up the hyperlinks.

To import the Web page for the full-size image:

1. Click the **FrontPage Explorer** program button on the taskbar to return to that program.

2. Click **File** on the menu bar, and then click **Import** to open the Import File to FrontPage Web dialog box.

3. Click the **Add File** button to open the Add File to Import List dialog box, make sure the drive that contains your Student Disk appears in the Look in text box, double-click the **Tutorial.05** folder, and then click the **map.htm** file.

4. Click the **Open** button to return to the Import File to FrontPage Web dialog box, and then click the **OK** button to import the file.

With the Web page for the map imported into the Sunny Morning Web, you are ready to add the navigation links. First, you'll add the link from the Home Page to the Map page. Then you'll create the link from the Map page back to the Home Page.

To add the hyperlink to the thumbnail image:

1. Double-click **index.htm** to return to the Home Page in FrontPage Editor.

2. Click the **thumbnail image** to select it, and then click the **Create or Edit Hyperlink** button 🖼 on the Standard toolbar to open the Edit Hyperlink dialog box.

3. Scroll down the Title list until you see Sunshine Country Store Map, and then double-click **map.htm** to specify that file for the link.

4. Click the **Save** button 💾 on the Standard toolbar.

With this revision to the hyperlink to the Map page, you need to test your changes to make sure that they work correctly.

To test the hyperlink from the thumbnail image:

1. Click the **Preview** tab to open that document window in FrontPage Editor.

2. Scroll down the Home Page until you see the thumbnail image, and then click the **Country Store Locator image** to open that page in the Preview window.

   TROUBLE? If the Country Store Locator image looks different than it did in Normal view, don't worry—it will display correctly in the browser.

3. Scroll down the Map page and notice the map image is missing and this page does not contain a navigation link back to the Home Page. You still need to add that link.

4. Click the **Normal** tab to return to the Home Page in Normal view.

You successfully created the link from the Home Page to the Map page. Now, you need to complete the link in the other direction from the Map page back to the Home Page. One way to do this is to use a hover button.

Creating a Hover Button

A **hover button** is a button containing special effects that is used as a hyperlink. You can set an effect from a list of available effects, or you can use the custom option and use images with a change to a different image on mouse over. **Mouse over,** or mouse fly over, refers to the act of moving the mouse pointer over the top of a hover button or another object. When you move the pointer over a hyperlink, the pointer changes to the hand pointer 👆. When you move the pointer over a hover button, the appearance of the button changes, depending on the specified mouse over effect.

Amanda wants you to create a hover button that changes on mouse over and is used to return to the Home Page after the user is finished looking at the map. First, you need to include the map image on the Map page. Then you will create the hover button. Although you used the map image on the Home Page, the thumbnail of this was saved to the images folder and not to the map.gif file itself. First, Amanda asks you to include the full-sized image on the Map page. Then you can create the hover button with the hyperlink back to the Home Page.

To include the map image on the Home Page:

1. Click the **FrontPage Explorer** program button on the taskbar to switch to that program, and then double-click **map.htm** to open that page in FrontPage Editor.

   Notice that the image is missing from the Map page. Although you used this image with the thumbnail, it was not added to the Web images folder.

2. Right-click the **broken image** at the location for the map, click **Image Properties** on the Shortcut menu to open that dialog box, click the **Browse** button in the Image Source section, click the **Select a file on your computer** button 🔍 to open the Select File dialog box, make sure the drive that contains your Student Disk appears in the Look in text box, double-click the **Tutorial.05** folder to open it, double-click the **Images** folder to open it, double-click the **map.gif** filename to return to the Image Properties dialog box, type **Sunshine Country Store Map** in the Text text box in the Alternative Representations section, and then click the **OK** button to open this image.

3. Click the **Save** button 💾 on the Standard toolbar to open the Save Embedded Files dialog box. Click the **OK** button to accept the suggested name and folder values and save the file.

The map is included in the images folder and appears on the Map page. Now, you are ready to use a hover button to create the link back to the Home Page.

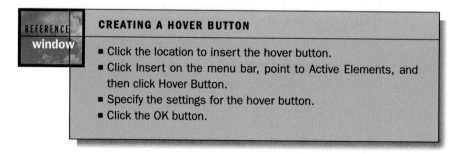

REFERENCE
window

CREATING A HOVER BUTTON

- Click the location to insert the hover button.
- Click Insert on the menu bar, point to Active Elements, and then click Hover Button.
- Specify the settings for the hover button.
- Click the OK button.

With the map image included in this page and saved to the images folder, your next step is to create the hover button.

To create a hover button:

1. Scroll to the bottom of the page, and notice the empty table that contains two cells below the map.

2. Click the left cell of the table to select it. This cell is the desired location for the hover button.

3. Click **Insert** on the menu bar, point to **Active Elements**, and then click **Hover Button** to open the Hover Button dialog box with the value in the Button text text box selected. See Figure 5-3.

Figure 5-3 ◀
Hover Button
dialog box

type text here
for button

default hover button
inserted on page

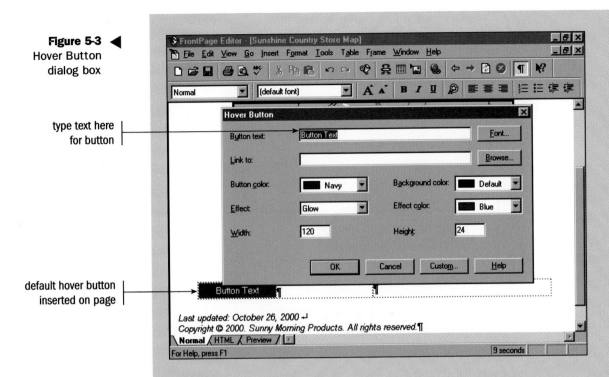

4. Type **Return to Home Page** as the Button text, and then click the **Font** button to open the Font dialog box. See Figure 5-4.

Figure 5-4 ◀
Font
dialog box

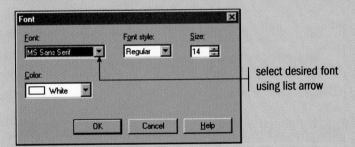

select desired font
using list arrow

5. Click the **Font** list arrow, and then click **Arial**; click the **Font style** list arrow, and then click **Bold**; click the **Size** spin arrow and change the size to **18**; click the **Color** list arrow and hold down the mouse button and point to **Yellow;** and then release the mouse button to select that color.

6. Click the **OK** button to close the Font dialog box and return to the Hover Button dialog box.

7. Click the **Browse** button to open the Select Hover Button Hyperlink dialog box, make sure that a:\wwwroot\sunny appears in the Look in list box, scroll the Name list to display the Home Page selection in that list, and then double-click **index.htm** to select the Home Page and return to the Hover Button dialog box.

8. Click the **Button color** list arrow, hold down the mouse button and point to **Green**, and then release the mouse button to select that color.

9. Click the **Effect** list arrow, and then click **Glow** to select that effect.

10. Click the **Effect color** list arrow, hold down the mouse button and point to **Custom**, and then release the mouse button to open the Color dialog box. Click the **orange** box (fourth row, second column) to select this color, and then click the **OK** button to close the Color dialog box. Look at the other available selections in this dialog box, which all are acceptable settings.

11. Click the **OK** button to finish specifying the parameters for the hover button. The button appears in the table, but some of the text is not visible.

The default size of the hover button is too small for the text displayed on the button. You can resize the button so all the text displays by selecting the button and dragging one of its corners until it is the desired size. Amanda asks you to increase the size of the hover button.

To resize a hover button:

1. Click anywhere on the hover button to select it.

2. Click and drag any one of the four corners to increase the size of the hover button so all of the text appears. See Figure 5-5.

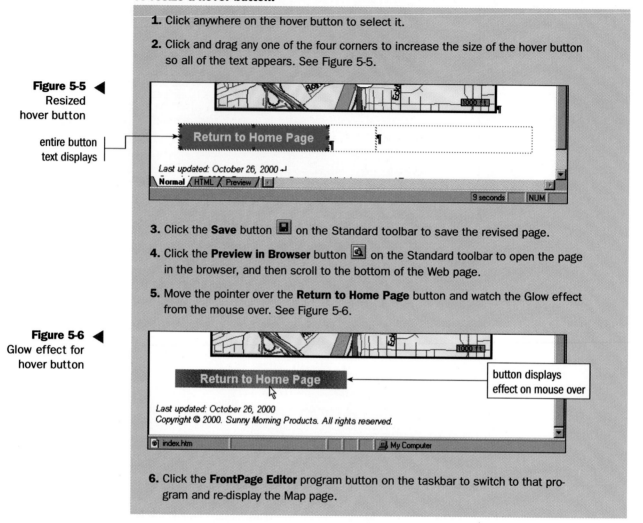

Figure 5-5 ◄
Resized
hover button

entire button
text displays

3. Click the **Save** button 🖫 on the Standard toolbar to save the revised page.

4. Click the **Preview in Browser** button 🔍 on the Standard toolbar to open the page in the browser, and then scroll to the bottom of the Web page.

5. Move the pointer over the **Return to Home Page** button and watch the Glow effect from the mouse over. See Figure 5-6.

Figure 5-6 ◄
Glow effect for
hover button

button displays
effect on mouse over

6. Click the **FrontPage Editor** program button on the taskbar to switch to that program and re-display the Map page.

The hover button provides a more visually appealing method for creating a hyperlink for users. The hover button effect helps draw the user's attention to the button for selecting the hyperlink.

Changing Component Properties

A hover button is implemented using a Java applet that is one of several advanced components built into FrontPage. A **Java applet** is a short program written in the Java programming language that is attached to a Web page and executed by the user's Web browser. Java applets provide dynamic features on a Web page, including the hover button's animation effect. After you create a hover button or other advanced component, you can modify its action or appearance by changing its properties. Amanda wants to change the properties of the hover button by revising the button's background color.

To change a FrontPage component property:

1. Right-click the **Return to Home Page** hover button to display the Shortcut menu, and then click **Java Applet Properties** to open the Hover Button dialog box.

2. Click the **Button color** list arrow and hold down the mouse button while you point to **Maroon**, and then release the mouse button to select that color.

3. Click the **OK** button to close the dialog box, and then click the **Save** button 🖫 on the Standard toolbar to save this change to the Web page.

4. Click the **Preview** tab, scroll to the bottom of the page, and then move the pointer over the hover button. The orange glow now appears with the maroon background.

Amanda feels that this color combination is more appealing. Now, she wants you to test the action of the hover button in the browser.

To test the hover button:

1. Click **Window** on the menu bar, and then click **Home Page** to switch to that page in FrontPage Editor.

2. Click the **Preview in Browser** button 🖳 on the Standard toolbar to open the page in the browser. If necessary, click the **Yes** button to save your changes first.

3. Scroll down the page until you see the Country Store Locator button, and then click the **Country Store Locator** button to display the map Web page.

4. Scroll to the bottom of the Web page, move the pointer over the **Return to Home Page** hover button and observe the orange glow, and then click the **Return to Home Page** button. Press the **Esc** key to stop the music, if necessary.

The hover button provides the desired effect of increased attention when the pointer moves over the button. As you do with other Web page features, you should apply these effects carefully to avoid overwhelming users.

Using Dynamic HTML

Dynamic HTML gives you the ability to control the display of elements on a Web page. When a dynamic HTML command is applied to text or graphics, Microsoft Internet Explorer 4.0 (and other Web browsers that support this feature) will animate the text or graphics or apply other effects that you specify. Because dynamic HTML does not require fetching information from the Web server, it is very efficient and presents the user with a lively, interesting page without requiring time-consuming network activity. Page transitions and animations are two methods of making a Web page more interesting. You will apply each of these features to enhance the Map page when it opens in the browser.

Adding Page Transitions

A **page transition** is an animated effect that can occur when a user opens a page in the browser or leaves the page by opening another page. Transition effects can be limited to occur only when a user enters or leaves the page.

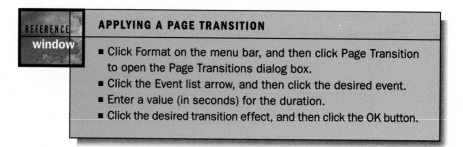

REFERENCE window

APPLYING A PAGE TRANSITION

- Click Format on the menu bar, and then click Page Transition to open the Page Transitions dialog box.
- Click the Event list arrow, and then click the desired event.
- Enter a value (in seconds) for the duration.
- Click the desired transition effect, and then click the OK button.

As you continue with your training, Amanda wants you to apply the Vertical blinds transition effect to the Map page.

To add a page transition:

1. Click the **FrontPage Editor** program button on the taskbar to switch to that program, click **Window** on the menu bar, click **Sunshine Country Store Map** to select that page, and then click the **Normal** tab to return to that view in Editor.

2. Click **Format** on the menu bar, and then click **Page Transition** to open the Page Transitions dialog box. See Figure 5-7.

Figure 5-7 ◀
Page Transitions dialog box

specify when effect displays

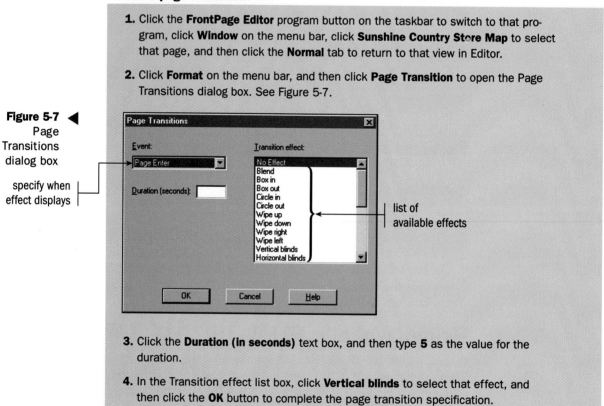

list of available effects

3. Click the **Duration (in seconds)** text box, and then type **5** as the value for the duration.

4. In the Transition effect list box, click **Vertical blinds** to select that effect, and then click the **OK** button to complete the page transition specification.

Besides the animation of the initial display of the Web page, you also can control the manner in which individual objects appear on the Web page. An animation effect can be applied to either text or an image on a Web page. By using different animation effects, you can display several different objects on the page.

Using Animation

You can apply dynamic animation to selected page elements. **Animation** is an effect that causes an element to "fly" into view from a corner or side of the page or the element to appear on the page in some other eye-catching way, such as spiraling into view. Animation can be applied to either text or images.

ADDING ANIMATION TO TEXT OR AN IMAGE

- Select the text or image that you want to animate.
- Click Format on the menu bar, and then point to Animation to display a list of available animations.
- Click the desired animation effect.

Amanda wants you to apply animation to the heading text above the Country Store map for additional emphasis.

To add text animation:

1. Scroll to the top of the page, and then select the text **Visit our Sunshine Country Store** that is located above the map image.

2. Click **Format** on the menu bar, point to **Animation** to display a menu of available effects, and then click **Drop In By Word** to select that animation effect.

3. Click the **Save** button 🖫 on the Standard toolbar to save the file with these effects.

The page transition and animation effects occur when the page opens in the browser. Amanda wants to open the Map page from the Home Page so you can see the full effect in the browser. Recall that these effects only work in Internet Explorer 4.0 or later versions. If a browser is not capable of handling these effects, then the browser ignores them and opens the page. To make sure these effects work correctly, Amanda asks you to test the page transition and text animation that you created for the Map page.

To test the page transition and text animation:

1. Click **Window** on the menu bar, and then click **Home Page** to switch to that page in the Editor window because that is the page from which you want to open the Map page with its effects.

2. Click the **Preview in Browser** button 🔳 on the Standard toolbar to open the Home Page in the browser, and then scroll down the page until you see the thumbnail image.

3. Click the **Country Store Locator** thumbnail image, and observe the Vertical blinds page transition and the Drop In By Word animation. Keep in mind that a user must have Internet Explorer 4.0 or higher in order to see these special effects.

You successfully included several animation effects with the Map page. These effects should help draw the user's interest to the page content.

Viewing HTML Code for a Java Applet

Java applets are used for several animation effects on the Map page. The hover button, page transition, and text animation were implemented with Java scripts created by FrontPage Editor when you added these dynamic HTML features to the Map page. These effects are implemented with the APPLET and SCRIPT tags. An **applet** makes use of a series of parameters that specify an object's behavior. A **script** is code that is included in the Web page and executed by the Web browser. Amanda asks you to examine the HTML code for the hover button that is implemented using an APPLET tag.

To view the HTML for a Java applet:

1. Click the **FrontPage Editor** program button on the taskbar, and then click the **HTML** tab to switch to that view.

2. Press **Ctrl** + **End** to view the code at the bottom of the page. See Figure 5-8. Notice the parameters for the text value and the effect value.

Figure 5-8
Map page
HTML code

specifies Java applet

specifies
button effect

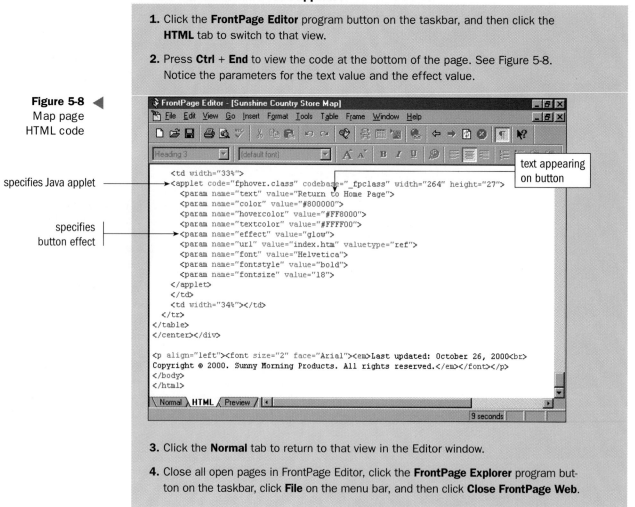

3. Click the **Normal** tab to return to that view in the Editor window.

4. Close all open pages in FrontPage Editor, click the **FrontPage Explorer** program button on the taskbar, click **File** on the menu bar, and then click **Close FrontPage Web**.

FrontPage inserted the code in Figure 5-8 based on the values you specified for the hover button. This allowed you to implement that complex component in a simple manner.

Quick Check

1. A small version of an image on a Web page that contains a hyperlink to a full-sized version of the same image is called a(n) ——————.

2. List three effects that you can apply to an image using the Image toolbar.

3. True or False: Text can be placed only next to an inline image on a Web page.

4. When you move the mouse pointer over a hover button, this is called ——————.

5. True or False: You implement a hover button on a Web page using a Java applet.

6. An animated effect that can occur when a user opens or closes a Web page in the browser is called a(n) ——————.

7. True or False: Animation is an effect that causes an element to "fly" into view from a corner or side of the page in an eye-catching way.

Amanda likes the map image and feels that the hover button will make it easy for users to navigate the Web site.

In this session you will learn how to create shared borders and navigation bars from Navigation view. You will revise shared borders and navigation bars and apply themes to an entire Web and to an individual Web page.

Using Shared Borders and Navigation Bars

Shared borders, navigation bars, and themes are advanced features that allow you to create Web pages that have a common appearance across your Web site. These features provide a consistent manner or standardized way of displaying information on Web pages.

Shared borders are a useful way to present recurring information in a consistent manner across a number of Web pages or the entire Web. Using FrontPage Explorer, you can specify that one or more shared borders be included on all pages that are part of the FrontPage Web's navigational structure that is displayed in the Navigation pane, or the top pane of Navigation view. You also can add or change shared borders for individual Web pages using FrontPage Editor. Shared borders can be used to create navigation bars automatically that help users navigate your Web site. These navigation bars are created in a standard way from the navigation structure. If you like this standard and it meets your requirements, it is very easy to create the navigation bars. If you prefer or require a different arrangement, then you need to create a user-defined navigation bar as you learned in Tutorial 3.

Shared borders typically are used on every page in a FrontPage Web. FrontPage maintains a single set of borders—top, bottom, left, and right—for the entire FrontPage Web. When you edit the contents of a shared border, the changes apply to all pages in the current FrontPage Web that uses the shared borders. For example, adding a company name or logo to a shared border will cause all other pages in that Web to display the same name or logo in the same location in the shared border. However, *you cannot insert a shared border on a frames page.*

You edit the contents of shared borders in FrontPage Editor. An outline surrounds a border in FrontPage Editor to indicate that it is an active element that you can revise.

You edit the contents of a shared border in FrontPage Editor by selecting that region of the page and editing it in the same manner as you revise any other part of the page. When you save the page, all edits to shared borders are saved in the same process as the page is saved. Each shared border is used throughout a FrontPage Web. When you edit a border, you are changing its appearance on every page that includes the border. For example, if you add your e-mail address to the Bottom shared border on one page, all other pages that include the Bottom border will display your e-mail address.

To navigate through a Web site, users follow hyperlinks, as you learned in Tutorial 3. FrontPage provides you with a means for creating and managing hyperlinks in a standard way using navigation bars, which are page regions that provide access to other pages in your Web using text or graphical hyperlinks. Navigation bars can be added automatically when you create a new FrontPage Web in Navigation view of FrontPage Explorer. You also can insert standard FrontPage navigation bars on individual pages using FrontPage Editor. Typically, the FrontPage standard navigation bars are placed inside a shared border, which then displays similar navigation bars on every page in the FrontPage Web that includes the shared border. If you change the FrontPage Web's structure in Navigation view, FrontPage will update the hyperlinks on the navigation bar automatically.

The navigation structure of a FrontPage Web links the most important pages in your FrontPage Web. The new structure is displayed in Navigation view of FrontPage Explorer as a diagram, similar to an organization chart. The Home Page is at the top, its "child" pages or immediate successors appear at the next level, the children of those pages appear at the next level, and so on. You design and create the structure of a FrontPage Web in Navigation view. To navigate the structure of a FrontPage Web, users follow hyperlinks from one page to another. FrontPage manages these hyperlinks for you with navigation bars that it automatically creates from the structure.

After reviewing the Sunny Morning Web, Amanda and Andrew decided that although they could apply advanced features to that Web, a new Web for the Sunshine Country Store would be better for applying these features. Andrew suggested that you create a Web to include a number of recipes that could be prepared using products available from the Sunshine Country Store. Amanda believes that this a good way to introduce you to creating multiple FrontPage Webs for a Web site. The Webs could remain separate, or they could be linked. By creating a separate Web for the recipes, you would have a smaller, more manageable Web than if a number of additional pages were added to the current Sunny Morning Web. Amanda's planning analysis sheet for the new Recipes Web is shown in Figure 5-9.

Figure 5-9 ◄
Amanda's
planning
analysis sheet
for the
Recipes Web

Planning Analysis Sheet

My goal:

Create a Recipes Web that includes popular recipes using Sunny Morning Products items. The Web will include shared borders with navigation bars created by FrontPage and will use a theme to make the Web more interesting visually.

What results do I want to see?

A Web with a home page that includes an introduction and lists the available recipes.

Navigation bars for each Web page that are updated by FrontPage automatically as new recipes are added to the Web and are shared across the Web pages.

A Web page for each recipe.

A navigation structure that indicates the relationships among the Web pages.

A theme that increases the visual interest of the Web; a different theme will be used for the home page.

What information do I need?

Home Page for Web.

Web page for each of the recipes.

Amanda asks you to create a new Recipes Web for use by the Sunshine Country Store.

To create a new Web:

1. Click the **FrontPage Explorer** program button on the taskbar to switch to that program.

2. Click **File** on the menu bar, point to **New**, and then click **FrontPage Web** to open the New FrontPage Web dialog box.

3. Click the **One Page Web** option button, select the value in the Choose a title for your FrontPage web text box, and then type **Recipes**.

4. Click the **OK** button to create the Recipes Web. After a few moments, the new Web is created and opens in Navigation view.

A single page is created for the Home Page, and its icon displays in the Navigation pane of Navigation view. Your first task is to rename the Home Page with a more appropriate title.

REFERENCE window

RENAMING A PAGE IN NAVIGATION VIEW

- Right-click the page icon in the Navigation pane to select it and display the Shortcut menu, click Rename, and then type the new title for the Web page.
or
- Click the page icon to select it, click the current title in the page icon, pause while the current title is selected, and then type the new title for the Web page.
- Press the Enter key to finish renaming the page.

Amanda wants you to rename this page for use with the Web.

To rename a page in Navigation view:

1. Right-click the **Home Page** icon in the Navigation pane to display the Shortcut menu, click **Rename**, and then type **Country Recipes**. This changes the title of the Web page, but not the filename, which is still index.htm.

2. Press the **Enter** key to complete renaming the page with the new title displayed in Navigation view. Notice that the title is truncated because it is longer than the space available in the page icon. This is not a problem because the entire page title will appear when it is referenced in a Web page.

You need to add an additional blank first page to this Web with the single Home Page in order to establish the initial structure of the Web. Amanda wants you to continue your training by doing this.

Adding Web Pages and Initial Navigation Bars

Any changes you make to the Web site structure in Navigation view are not applied until you take one of several actions, including switching views in FrontPage Explorer or opening a page in FrontPage Editor.

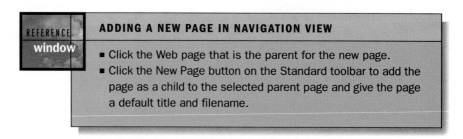

REFERENCE window

ADDING A NEW PAGE IN NAVIGATION VIEW

- Click the Web page that is the parent for the new page.
- Click the New Page button on the Standard toolbar to add the page as a child to the selected parent page and give the page a default title and filename.

Your next activity is to add another page to the Web and open it in FrontPage Editor, which will create the navigation structure.

To add a new page to the Web and specify navigation bars:

1. Click the **New Page** button 🗋 New Page on the Standard toolbar. The FrontPage Explorer message box opens and asks if you want navigation bars placed in the borders of each page.

2. Click the **Yes** button. New Page 1 is added as a page icon in the Navigation pane, which is a child of the Country Recipes page, and shared borders are created for use with this Web.

   Next, rename the new page.

3. Right-click the **New Page 1** page icon to display the Shortcut menu, and then click **Rename**.

4. Type **Cake** as the page's title, and then press the **Enter** key. The name of the file does not appear in the lower pane because the page remains a temporary object in the Web until you open the page in FrontPage Editor or otherwise use this file.

5. Press the **Enter** key. "Saving navigation changes…" displays in the status bar, and then the selected Cake page opens in FrontPage Editor, which creates the file in the Recipes Web. Notice the shared borders at the top and left of the Web page. See Figure 5-10. These are the default shared borders that were created when the new page was added to the Web.

Figure 5-10 ◀
Cake page with
shared borders

Top shared border
with navigation bar

Left shared border
with navigation bar

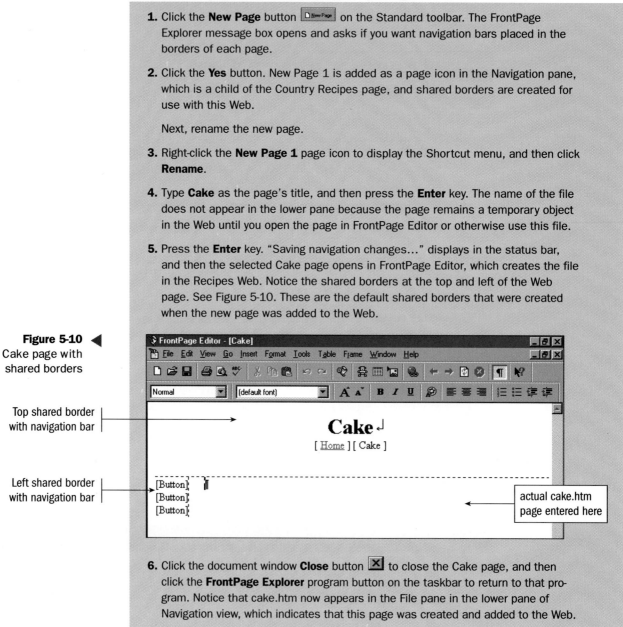

actual cake.htm
page entered here

6. Click the document window **Close** button ☒ to close the Cake page, and then click the **FrontPage Explorer** program button on the taskbar to return to that program. Notice that cake.htm now appears in the File pane in the lower pane of Navigation view, which indicates that this page was created and added to the Web.

Now that you have created the Recipes Web and several Web pages, you are ready to examine values set for the shared borders. This will help increase your understanding of these features in case you need to make changes to them as you develop other Webs.

To review the shared borders and navigation bars for the entire Web:

1. Click **Tools** on the menu bar, and then click **Shared Borders** to open that dialog box. See Figure 5-11. Notice that the Top and Left borders are selected. These borders were created when you added New Page 1 to the Web. These locations are satisfactory for the Recipes Web.

Figure 5-11 ◀
Shared Borders
dialog box

diagram indicates
borders selected

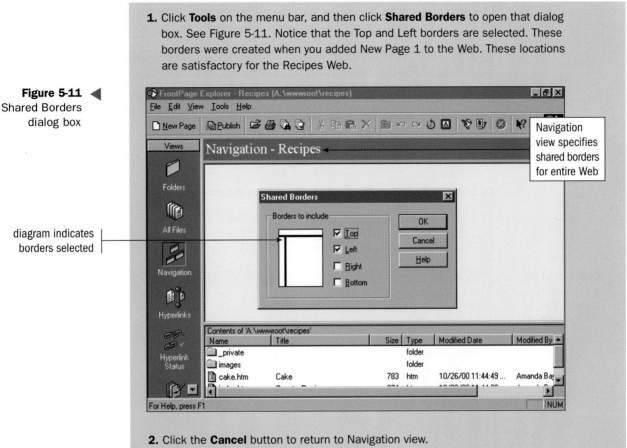

2. Click the **Cancel** button to return to Navigation view.

Amanda already created the other pages for the Recipes Web that she wants you to use in your training. All you need to do is import these pages, and then you can examine the shared borders. She asks you to do that next.

To import the other pages for the Recipes Web:

1. Click **File** on the menu bar, click **Import**, click the **Add File** button, make sure the drive that contains your Student Disk appears in the Look in text box, double-click the **Tutorial.05** folder, double-click the **Recipes** folder, and then press **Ctrl + A** to select all the files.

2. Click the **Open** button to return to the Import File to FrontPage Web dialog box, and then click the **OK** button to import the files.

3. When the Confirm Save dialog box opens, click the **Yes to All** button to replace the existing files in the Web with new ones that contain the completed descriptions and recipes. Although the files have been added to the Web, as indicated by the appearance of their filenames in the lower pane, you still need to add them to the navigation structure diagram in the top pane.

   But first, Amanda wants you to change the Cake page title to Chiffon Cake to more closely match the names used with the other recipe pages. When the page was created in Navigation view, the filename was derived automatically from the page title, which did not provide the desired filename and page title combinations.

4. Right-click the **Cake** page icon to display the Shortcut menu, click **Rename**, type **Chiffon Cake**, and then press the **Enter** key to complete this revision of the page title.

With several pages included in the Recipes Web, you can include these in the navigation structure easily. FrontPage Explorer supports adding newly created pages, imported pages, or existing pages to the navigation structure.

Creating a Navigation Structure

After you import the Web pages into the Web, they are available for use in the navigation structure. You add a file to the navigation structure by dragging its filename from the File pane to the Navigation pane and positioning the page icon so the connector specifies the desired level for the page in the structure. Amanda wants you to create the navigation structure for the pages that you added to the Web as your next training activity.

To add existing Web files to the navigation diagram:

1. Click **pie.htm** in the File (lower) pane and drag it to the Navigation (top) pane so it is at the same level as the Chiffon Cake page icon that is indicated by the outlined page icon and connector. See Figure 5-12.

Figure 5-12 ◀
Specifying the
level of the
Web page

page selected
to add to
navigation structure

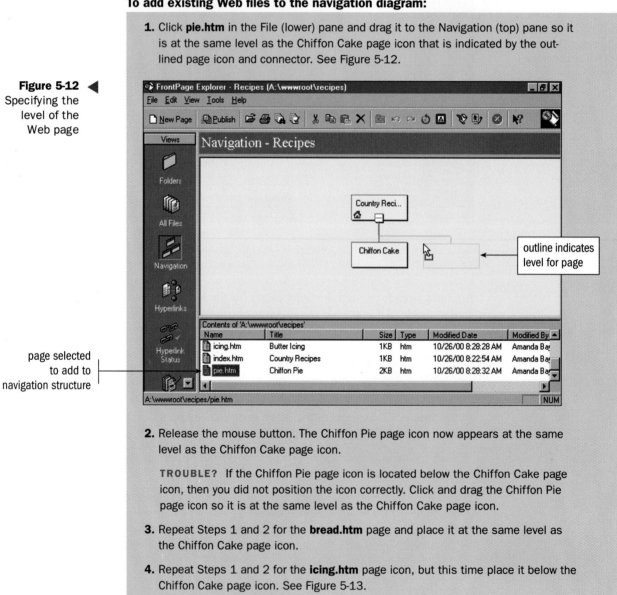

2. Release the mouse button. The Chiffon Pie page icon now appears at the same level as the Chiffon Cake page icon.

   TROUBLE? If the Chiffon Pie page icon is located below the Chiffon Cake page icon, then you did not position the icon correctly. Click and drag the Chiffon Pie page icon so it is at the same level as the Chiffon Cake page icon.

3. Repeat Steps 1 and 2 for the **bread.htm** page and place it at the same level as the Chiffon Cake page icon.

4. Repeat Steps 1 and 2 for the **icing.htm** page icon, but this time place it below the Chiffon Cake page icon. See Figure 5-13.

Figure 5-13 ◄
Navigation
diagram

child level from
Chiffon Cake

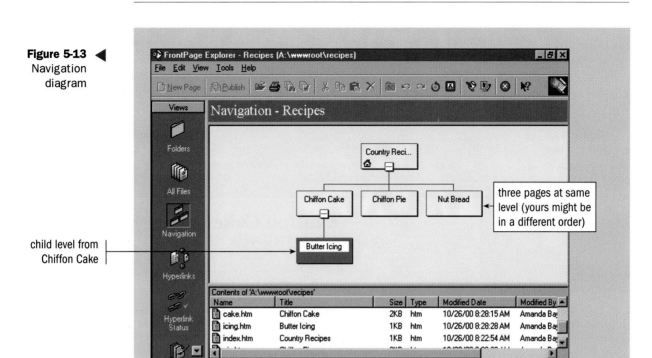

With the navigation structure created in FrontPage Explorer, you can examine the application of the built-in navigation bars in FrontPage Editor. Amanda asks you to do this next.

To review the shared borders:

1. Double-click the **Country Recipes** page icon to open that page in FrontPage Editor. See Figure 5-14. Look at the shared border at the top and left of the page. While page titles appear for the navigation bar in the Left border, the word "[Button]" serves as a placeholder for the navigation bar in the Top border, which indicates that the specified navigation bar does not contain any entries for this border. The navigation bar in the Top border will contain the Home Page and the other pages that are at the same level in the navigation structure. If the structure changes in Navigation view and additional pages were available, then they would appear automatically in the border.

Figure 5-14 ◄
Country
Recipes Home
Page in
FrontPage
Editor

Top shared border

child pages
at same level
(yours might be in
a different order)

Left shared border

2. Click the **FrontPage Explorer** program button on the taskbar to return to that program, and then double-click the **Chiffon Cake** page icon to open it in FrontPage Editor. See Figure 5-15. Notice the entry in the Left border for the child pages to the Chiffon Cake page. When a child page exists, its title appears automatically because this is the current default specification for the navigation bar.

Figure 5-15 ◀
Chiffon Cake
page in
FrontPage
Editor

no hyperlink
for active page

child page to
active page

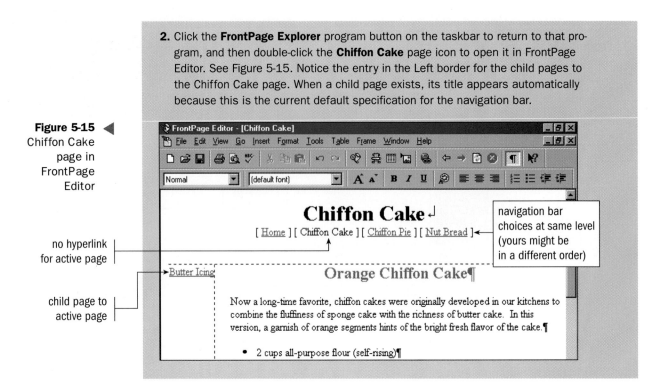

navigation bar
choices at same level
(yours might be
in a different order)

You successfully confirmed the built-in navigation bars created by FrontPage Explorer from Navigation view. Amanda asks you to test these to observe their actions in the Web browser.

To test the shared borders and navigation bars in a browser:

1. Click the **Preview in Browser** button 🖼 on the Standard toolbar to open the Chiffon Cake page in the browser. Notice the display of both the Top and Left borders with their navigation bars.

2. Click the **Butter Icing** link to open that page. Notice the Left border does not appear because this page has no child pages and the only content of the Left border is the navigation bar. The Top navigation bar contains only the Home and Up links because there are no other pages at the same level.

3. Click the **Home** link to open that page. The navigation bar does not display in the Top shared border. See Figure 5-16. Because this is the Home Page for the Web, there are no other pages at the same level or at a higher level. Again, when no items are defined by the navigation structure, then the built-in navigation bar does not appear.

Figure 5-16 ◀
Country
Recipes Home
Page in browser

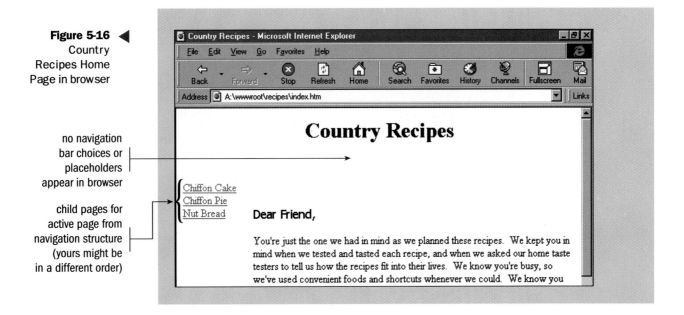

no navigation
bar choices or
placeholders
appear in browser

child pages for
active page from
navigation structure
(yours might be
in a different order)

The FrontPage Explorer navigation structure provides a convenient way to create navigation bars and shared borders. Amanda wants you to make some changes to the content of the Top shared border.

Editing a Shared Border

After you create the shared borders, you can modify them using FrontPage Editor. The shared borders for a Web page are displayed with that page in FrontPage Editor. You select the border that you want to change by clicking anywhere within that border, which is indicated by an outline around the border area. Then you make changes to the content of the shared border in the same manner that you would revise a regular Web page using FrontPage Editor. However, keep in mind that any change you make to a shared border will appear on all other Web pages that use that border. As you make changes, make sure that they are appropriate for the other pages in your Web that share them.

As you continue your training, Amanda wants you to add a horizontal line near the bottom of the top shared border. This will provide a visual queue that separates the common shared border content from the content of the other Web pages.

To edit a shared border:

1. Click the **FrontPage Editor** program button on the taskbar to return to that program.

2. Click anywhere in the Top shared border to select it. An outline around the border area indicates that it is selected.

3. Click the navigation bar in the Top border to select it. Notice that the pointer changes to the WebBot pointer 🖱 when it is positioned on the navigation bar. Press the **down** arrow key to position the pointer at the bottom line in this border, and then press the **Delete** key to remove this unwanted paragraph.

4. Click **Insert** on the menu bar, and then click **Horizontal Line**. A horizontal line appears in the shared border.

5. Click the **Save** button 🖫 on the Standard toolbar to save the changes to the Top shared border. If you made any other changes to the Chiffon Cake page, they also are saved during the same update processing.

6. Click **Window** on the menu bar, and then click **Country Recipes** to switch to that open page in FrontPage Editor. The change to the shared border does not appear with this page.

7. Click the **Refresh** button 🗋 on the Standard toolbar to re-display the Top shared border with the horizontal rule. It was necessary to refresh the page to display the changes to the shared border.

Changes to any of the other shared borders are made in the same manner. However, the default navigation bars could provide better choices for the user. Amanda asks you to review the navigation bars to see if they might be improved.

Revising Navigation Bars

One of the potential problems with the current navigation bar is that if there are a lot of recipes, then a horizontal listing would make it difficult to display all of them. In that situation, you might want to revise the navigation bar in the Top shared border and include its current links in the Left border. When rearranging the navigation bars, you need to remember that you do not display a border that is unique for an individual Web page. Any change you make will apply to all pages that use the shared borders. Amanda asks you to revise the links displayed in the navigation bar so the list of available recipes displays in the Left shared border on the page for each individual recipe. You do this by changing the navigation bar properties.

To change a navigation bar:

1. Click anywhere on the navigation bar in the Top shared border to select it. The pointer changes to the WebBot pointer 🖑 when the pointer is over the navigation bar.

2. Right-click the navigation bar, and then click **FrontPage Component Properties** to open the Navigation Bar Properties dialog box. See Figure 5-17. Notice in the Hyperlinks to include section that most of the choices are option buttons, so only one arrangement can be selected. This is the standard set of alternatives that are available when using the FrontPage navigation bars.

Figure 5-17 ◀
Navigation Bar
Properties
dialog box

diagram indicates
pages included in
navigation bar

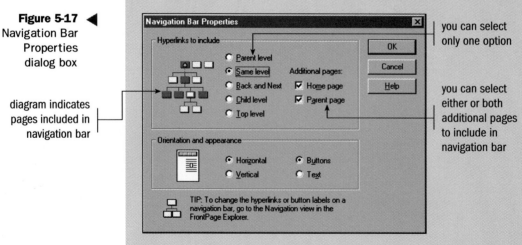

3. Click the **Back and Next** option button to select that option. The Home page and Parent page check boxes should be selected. Notice the change in the diagram indicating these changes in the hyperlinks included in the navigation bar.

4. Click the **OK** button to complete the change to the navigation bar, and then click anywhere below the shared border to deselect the navigation bar.

5. Click **Window** on the menu bar, and then click **Chiffon Cake** to select that page. Notice that Home and Next are the only two links for this page.

6. Click the navigation bar in the Left shared border to select it, right-click the navigation bar to display the Shortcut menu, and then click **FrontPage Component Properties** to open the Navigation Bar Properties dialog box.

7. Click the **Same level** option button to select that option. If necessary, click the **Home page** check box and click the **Parent page** check box so both of the additional pages are deselected.

8. Click the **OK** button, and then click the **Save** button 🔲 on the Standard toolbar to complete the changes to the navigation bars in the shared borders as the page is saved.

   TROUBLE? If the Server Busy warning message box opens, click the Retry button. This is not a problem—it opens because you are using a disk-based Web.

These changes to the shared borders will appear in every page in the Web that uses the shared borders option. Now look at the Country Recipes Home Page. Although the individual recipe pages look better, there are no links displayed to the child-level recipe pages. A user accessing this Home Page for the Web would be unable to open any of the other Web pages easily.

Turning Off Shared Borders for a Single Page

If the content of a shared border is not appropriate for a single Web page, then you can turn off the display of any of the shared borders for that single Web page. For the home page, the FrontPage navigation bars contain only placeholders that indicate there are no entries for these navigation bars. Rather than displaying the placeholders on the home page, you can turn off their display so the borders do not appear at all. You can turn off any one or all of the shared borders for any page in the Web.

REFERENCE window

TURNING OFF SHARED BORDERS FOR AN INDIVIDUAL PAGE

- Open the page in FrontPage Editor.
- Click Tools on the menu bar, and then click Shared Borders to open that dialog box.
- Click the Set for this page only option button.
- Click the Top, Left, Right, and Bottom check boxes, as necessary, to turn off the appropriate borders.
- Click the OK button.

Because the shared borders no longer contain any navigation bar entries, Amanda wants you to turn off their display for the Home Page.

To turn off shared borders for an individual page:

1. Click **Window** on the menu bar, and then click **Country Recipes** to switch to that page. Click the **Refresh** button 🔄 on the Standard toolbar to update the display. The "[Button]" placeholders appear in both navigation bars to indicate that these navigation bars are not necessary. Rather than leaving these navigation bars, you can remove all the shared borders from this page.

2. Click **Tools** on the menu bar, and then click **Shared Borders** to open the Page Borders dialog box. See Figure 5-18.

Figure 5-18 ◀
Page Borders
dialog box

options to select Web
default or active page

diagram indicates
shared borders for
active page

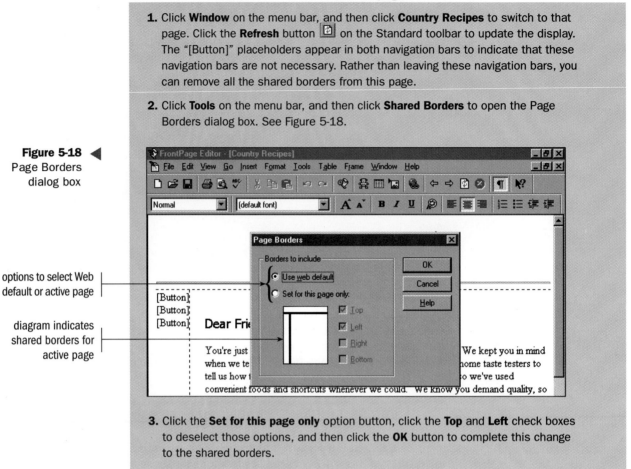

3. Click the **Set for this page only** option button, click the **Top** and **Left** check boxes to deselect those options, and then click the **OK** button to complete this change to the shared borders.

Without any shared borders, there is no navigation bar for the Country Recipes Home Page. You could create a user-defined navigation bar, or you could use a built-in navigation bar that is placed directly on an individual Web page itself.

Adding a FrontPage Navigation Bar to a Web Page

You can add a FrontPage navigation bar to any Web page. Navigation bars are not limited for use only in shared borders. Amanda wants you to include a navigation bar on the Country Recipes Home Page that is a table of contents for the recipes included in the Web. One reason for doing this is that she wants a different arrangement of hyperlinks for the table of contents than those available in the shared borders. This could be done manually, but it would require more work to maintain than using a FrontPage navigation bar that is generated automatically from the pages in the Web. This navigation bar must be separate from those for the shared borders.

To add a FrontPage navigation bar to a Web page:

1. Press **Ctrl** + **End** to move to the bottom of the Web page where the table of contents will appear.

2. Click **Insert** on the menu bar, and then click **Navigation Bar** to open the Navigation Bar Properties dialog box.

3. Click the **Child level** option button to select that option. If necessary, click the **Home page** and **Parent page** check boxes to deselect these options.

4. In the Orientation and appearance section, click the **Vertical** option button to select that option, click the **Buttons** option button to select that option, and then click the **OK** button to finish specifying the navigation bar.

5. Click the **Save** button 🖫 on the Standard toolbar to save your changes.

A FrontPage navigation bar is added to the Country Recipes Home Page. When any pages are added to the navigation structure, the entries in this navigation bar are updated automatically by FrontPage. However, without the shared borders displayed with this page, the page needs a heading or banner to identify its content.

Creating a Page Banner

A **banner** is an image, usually displayed at the top of each page in a Web site, that contains text and design elements. The Page Banner Properties dialog box is used to insert or edit a page banner on the active page in FrontPage Editor. When the page banner is not used with either a theme or shared borders, the page banner inserts only the page title as text with no visual images. The page must be included in the navigation structure before you can include the page banner generated by FrontPage in a Web page.

REFERENCE
window

CREATING A PAGE BANNER

- Click the location where you want the banner to appear on the Web page.
- Click the Insert FrontPage Component button on the Standard toolbar to display that dialog box, and then click Page Banner to select that component.
- Click the OK button to open the Page Banner Properties dialog box, and then click the OK button to insert the page banner on the page.

You can create a page banner manually, or you can have FrontPage generate a page banner using the page's title from the navigation structure. Now, Amanda wants you to create a page banner generated by FrontPage.

To add a page banner generated by FrontPage to a Web page:

1. Press **Ctrl** + **Home** to position the insertion point at the top of the page.

2. Click the **Insert FrontPage Component** button 🏛 on the Standard toolbar to open the Insert FrontPage Component dialog box. See Figure 5-19.

Figure 5-19 ◀
Insert
FrontPage
Component
dialog box

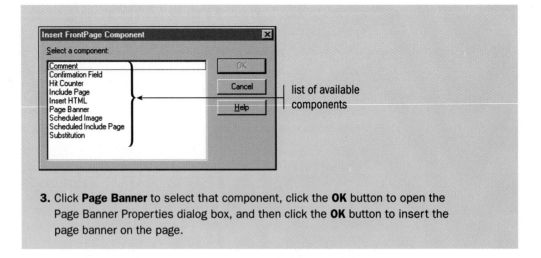

list of available
components

3. Click **Page Banner** to select that component, click the **OK** button to open the
Page Banner Properties dialog box, and then click the **OK** button to insert the
page banner on the page.

The page banner helps identify the page for the user. If the page title is revised in the
future, then the banner will be updated automatically to reflect that change.

Deleting a Page from the Navigation Structure

An existing page in the navigation structure can be deleted from the structure. When you
delete the page, you have the option of removing only the page from the structure or of
deleting it from the entire Web. If you remove only the page from the structure, then it is
removed from any of the navigation bars generated by FrontPage.

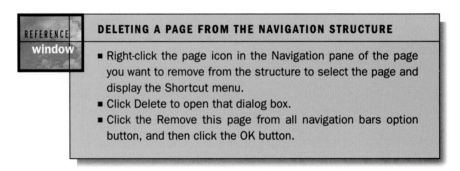

REFERENCE
window

DELETING A PAGE FROM THE NAVIGATION STRUCTURE

■ Right-click the page icon in the Navigation pane of the page
   you want to remove from the structure to select the page and
   display the Shortcut menu.
■ Click Delete to open that dialog box.
■ Click the Remove this page from all navigation bars option
   button, and then click the OK button.

Amanda wants you to delete the Nut Bread page from the navigation structure, but not
from the Web.

To delete a page from the navigation structure:

1. Click the **FrontPage Explorer** program button on the taskbar to switch to that program and return to Navigation view.

2. Right-click the **Nut Bread** page icon to display the Shortcut menu, and then click
   Delete to open the Delete Page dialog box with the two options of removing the
   page from the navigation bars or deleting it from the current Web.

3. Click the **Remove this page from all navigation bars** option button to select that
   option, and then click the **OK** button to remove the page icon from the navigation
   structure.

   Amanda decides that she prefers to keep this page for use with the Country
   Recipes Web, so you need to reverse this change.

4. Click the **Undo** button 🔙 on the Standard toolbar to return the Nut Bread page
   icon to the navigation structure so it is included in the navigation bars.

You have completed the navigation bars for the Recipes Web using the built-in FrontPage navigation bar component. These navigation bars display choices in a standard way, and their content was selected for the best arrangement for this Web. However, the visual impact of this Web could be enhanced by applying a background and using graphics.

Applying a Theme to a Web

Themes are a collection of design elements—bullets, backgrounds, table borders, fonts, and graphics—that you can apply to an entire FrontPage Web or to a single page. A Web with a theme applied to it has a consistent, professional appearance. Everything on the page—from its bullets to its background pattern—is predesigned to fit together. When you insert new bullets, horizontal lines, banners, navigation bars, and other graphical elements on a page that has a theme applied to it, they match the theme. Also, if a theme has been applied to a FrontPage Web, any new pages that you create will use the same theme automatically. FrontPage comes with over 50 built-in themes in a range of styles from conservative to flashy. You also can change the theme for an individual page in FrontPage Editor. Theme options allow you to select a bright set of colors, an active set of banners, buttons, and bullets, and a textured page background. The options are available for both the entire Web and for an individual page.

REFERENCE window	**APPLYING A THEME TO THE ENTIRE WEB**
	■ Open the Web to which you will apply the theme in FrontPage Explorer. ■ Click the Themes button on the Views bar to display a list of available themes. ■ Click the Use Selected Theme option button, and scroll the list of available themes to the one you want. ■ Click the theme name to select it and display a sample page in the Theme Preview box. ■ Click the Apply button, and then click the Yes button to apply the theme to the current Web.

As you continue your training, Amanda wants you to apply a theme to the Recipes Web. You will select a theme that compliments the Web's content.

To apply a theme to the entire Web:

1. Verify that FrontPage Explorer is your active program, and then click the **Themes** button 🄫 on the Views bar to display that view with a list of available themes.

2. Click the **Use Selected Theme** option button to activate this option. Scroll down the list of available themes until you see Citrus Punch, and then click **Citrus Punch** to display an example in the Theme Preview box. See Figure 5-20. Notice the default selections of Active Graphics and Background Image. These are acceptable features.

Figure 5-20 ◄
Theme preview
for Citrus Punch

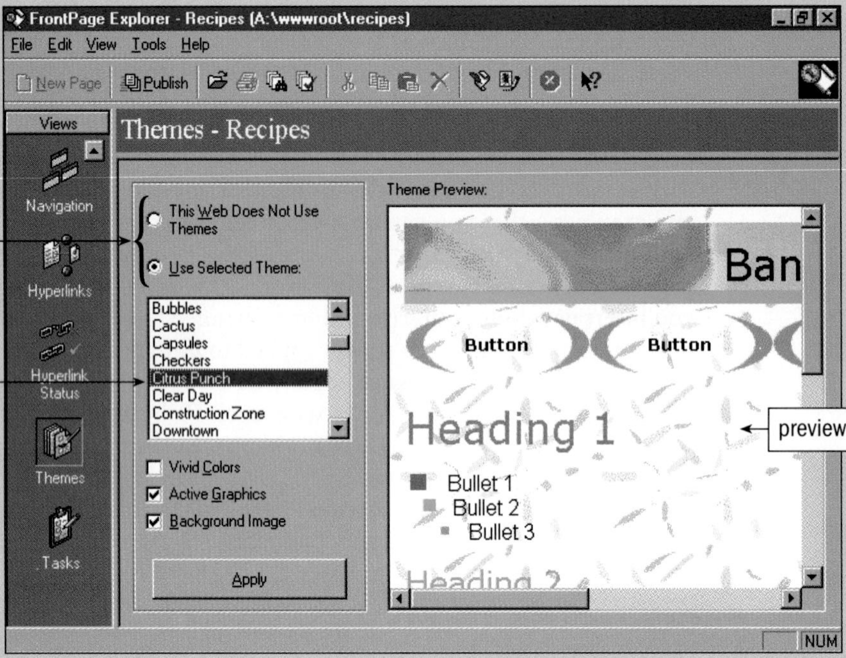

options to select
use of theme

select from list of
available themes

preview of theme

3. Click the **Apply** button. A FrontPage Explorer warning message box opens to indicate that this action will replace some of the existing formatting information permanently.

4. Click the **Yes** button to apply the theme to the Recipes Web. It will take several minutes for FrontPage to add these changes to all the pages in the current Web, including the pages that define the borders. Several messages are displayed in the status bar while this action is being performed—uploading, applying theme, and loading web.

5. After the theme has been applied, click the **Navigation** button 🖿 on the Views bar to switch to that view, and then double-click the **Country Recipes** page icon to open that page in FrontPage Editor. See Figure 5-21.

Figure 5-21 ◄
Country
Recipes
Home Page
with Citrus
Punch theme

banner for theme
displays page title

theme background
applied

6. Click the **Save** button 🖫 on the Standard toolbar to save your changes, click the **Preview in Browser** button 🔍 on the Standard toolbar to open the page in the browser, and then scroll down the page to display the buttons for the Table of Contents.

7. Click the **Chiffon Cake** button to open that Web page. See Figure 5-22. Notice that the navigation bars have been changed to include the default setting for the theme, rather than those specified previously when you changed them to meet the requirements for the Recipes Web. As a result, if you have existing FrontPage navigation bars in shared borders, you might need to respecify them after you apply a theme to an existing Web. Also notice the changes to the horizontal line and bullets used with this theme.

Figure 5-22 ◀
Chiffon Cake
page with
revised
navigation bar

Top shared border
includes banner,
navigation buttons,
and horizontal line

Left shared border
includes navigation
button text

bullet from
selected theme

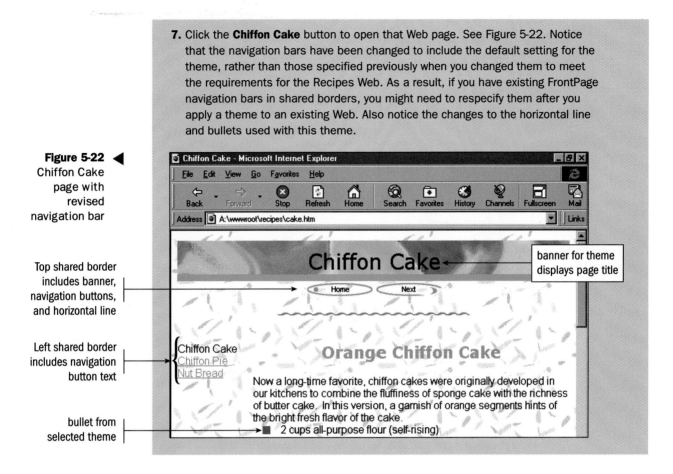

banner for theme
displays page title

The Citrus Punch theme has added considerable visual stimulation to the Recipes Web. You review this choice with Amanda, and she informs you that Andrew would like a somewhat more conservative look for this Web. She asks you to apply a different theme to the Web.

Changing a Theme for the Entire Web

After applying a theme to a Web, you can change the appearance of the Web by changing the theme. FrontPage automatically makes all the changes to convert the Web from one theme to the other. Amanda asks you to apply the Nature theme to the Web as your next training activity.

To change a theme across an entire Web:

1. Click the **FrontPage Explorer** program button on the taskbar to switch to that program, and then click the **Themes** button 🖼 on the Views bar to return to that view.

2. Scroll down the list of available themes until you see Nature, and then click **Nature** to select it and display its preview.

3. Click the **Vivid Colors** check box to select that option. Notice that the color of the Heading 1 and the body text changes.

4. Click the **Apply** button and wait while FrontPage performs the actions for this change. Several actions are performed, and a message describing the action is displayed in the status bar while they are performed—uploading, processing web updates, applying theme, and loading web. While you wait for this change to be made to the Web's theme, keep in mind the amount of time it takes for this action (and this Web has only five pages). The time increases significantly for a larger Web, so you should choose your theme carefully.

5. Click the **Navigation** button ▨ on the Views bar to switch to that view, and then double-click the **Country Recipes** page icon to open the revised page in FrontPage Editor. See Figure 5-23.

Figure 5-23 ◀
Country
Recipes Home
Page with
Nature theme

background changes
for selected theme

font color changes
for selected theme

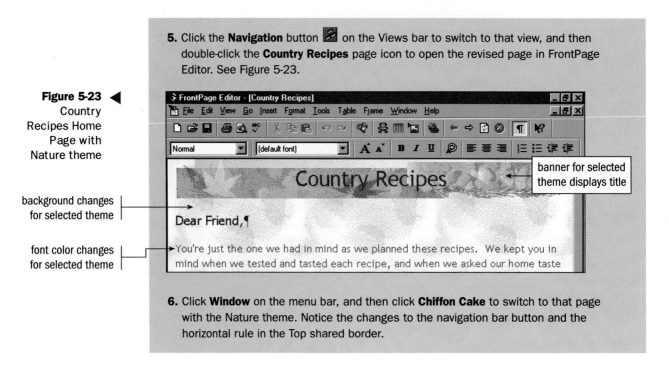

6. Click **Window** on the menu bar, and then click **Chiffon Cake** to switch to that page with the Nature theme. Notice the changes to the navigation bar button and the horizontal rule in the Top shared border.

The theme is revised across the entire Recipes Web. Amanda feels that Andrew also will prefer this appearance.

Applying a Theme to a Single Page

FrontPage allows you to apply a theme to an individual page, as well as to an entire Web site. For example, you can use one theme for most of the Web and a separate theme for selected pages. Because a theme automatically generates a number of additional pages that are included in your Web, you should limit the number of different themes that you use.

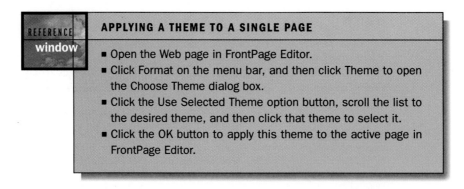

REFERENCE
window

APPLYING A THEME TO A SINGLE PAGE

- Open the Web page in FrontPage Editor.
- Click Format on the menu bar, and then click Theme to open the Choose Theme dialog box.
- Click the Use Selected Theme option button, scroll the list to the desired theme, and then click that theme to select it.
- Click the OK button to apply this theme to the active page in FrontPage Editor.

After viewing the revised theme, Andrew now prefers the Citrus Punch theme for the Home Page. Amanda asks you to apply the Citrus Punch theme to only the Country Recipes Home Page.

To change the theme for an individual Web page:

1. Click **Window** on the menu bar, and then click **Country Recipes** to switch to that page.

2. Click **Format** on the menu bar, and then click **Theme** to open the Choose Theme dialog box. See Figure 5-24.

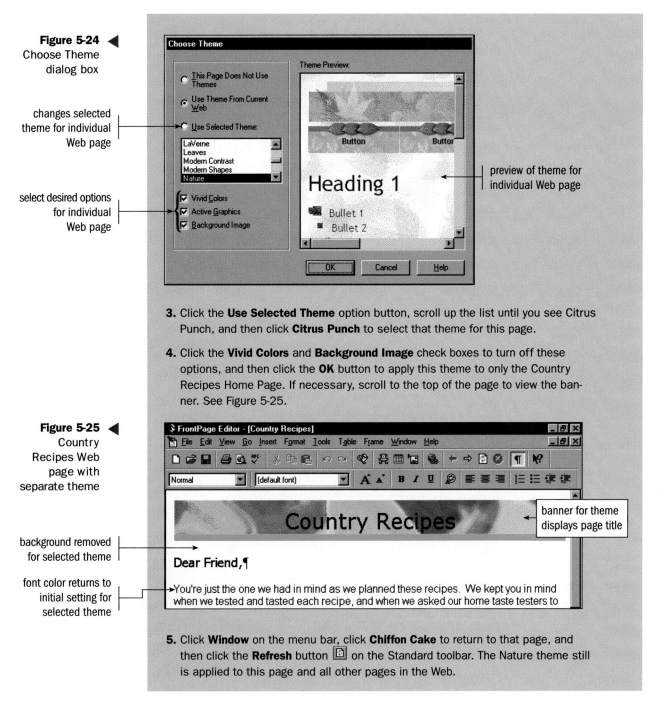

Figure 5-24 ◀
Choose Theme
dialog box

changes selected
theme for individual
Web page

select desired options
for individual
Web page

preview of theme for
individual Web page

3. Click the **Use Selected Theme** option button, scroll up the list until you see Citrus Punch, and then click **Citrus Punch** to select that theme for this page.

4. Click the **Vivid Colors** and **Background Image** check boxes to turn off these options, and then click the **OK** button to apply this theme to only the Country Recipes Home Page. If necessary, scroll to the top of the page to view the banner. See Figure 5-25.

Figure 5-25 ◀
Country
Recipes Web
page with
separate theme

banner for theme
displays page title

background removed
for selected theme

font color returns to
initial setting for
selected theme

5. Click **Window** on the menu bar, click **Chiffon Cake** to return to that page, and then click the **Refresh** button on the Standard toolbar. The Nature theme still is applied to this page and all other pages in the Web.

The application of a theme to the Recipes Web provided a convenient method of enhancing the visual impact of this Web, including the appearance of the shared borders and navigation bars.

Viewing HTML for Shared Borders and Themes

Most of the HTML code for shared borders, navigation bars, and themes is hidden from view by FrontPage in special folders and files that FrontPage automatically creates. The _borders and _themes folders are the primary folders where the various image and HTML files are stored. FrontPage does not allow you to see these folders using FrontPage Explorer. However, you can see these folders and the files they contain using Windows Explorer. Shared borders and themes are implemented in FrontPage using META tags, as described in Tutorial 2. These META tags are created automatically by FrontPage and inserted in each page that belongs to the Web. Then, using these META tags, FrontPage displays the desired arrangement of borders and themes. For the Recipes Web, FrontPage created the Top and Left HTML pages in the _borders folder. For the FrontPage components included in a Web page, such as the banner and navigation bar components of the Country Recipes Home Page, WebBots are used to specify these components within an individual page. WebBots are included inside of a comment tag of <!-- ... --> so that if the browser used to view the page cannot process a WebBot, then the WebBot is ignored. In order to help you understand the part of the processing that is done by FrontPage when you use these features, Amanda wants you to view the META tags and WebBots included in the Country Recipes page.

To view the HTML code for themes, shared borders, and navigation bars:

1. Click **Window** on the menu bar, click **Country Recipes** to switch to that page, click the **HTML** tab to display that view in the Editor window, and then click anywhere to deselect any selected text. See Figure 5-26.

Figure 5-26 ◀
Viewing the
first page of
HTML code

META tags
for shared borders
and Web theme

WebBot for built-in
navigation bar

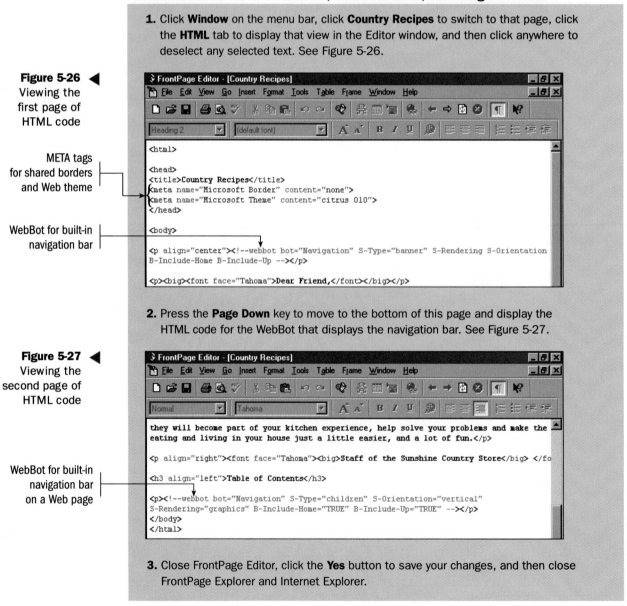

2. Press the **Page Down** key to move to the bottom of this page and display the HTML code for the WebBot that displays the navigation bar. See Figure 5-27.

Figure 5-27 ◀
Viewing the
second page of
HTML code

WebBot for built-in
navigation bar
on a Web page

3. Close FrontPage Editor, click the **Yes** button to save your changes, and then close FrontPage Explorer and Internet Explorer.

Quick Check

1. A useful way to present recurring information consistently across a number of Web pages or the entire Web site is implemented using a(n) _____.

2. True or False: If you change a Web's structure in the Navigation pane, the hyperlinks in built-in FrontPage navigation bars will be updated automatically.

3. True or False: A FrontPage built-in navigation bar that is created from Navigation view can be used only in a shared border.

4. True or False: A single FrontPage built-in navigation bar can contain hyperlinks to both child-level pages and pages at the same level.

5. A(n) _____ is a collection of design elements that you can apply to an entire FrontPage Web to give it a consistent, professional appearance.

6. True or False: When a theme is applied to a Web, any modified navigation bars from Navigation view are not changed to the theme's default.

7. You can apply an individual theme to a Web page using FrontPage _____.

Amanda is satisfied with your progress in developing Web pages for the Sunny Morning Web and with the creation of the Recipes Web and its shared borders, FrontPage navigation bars, and themes. By completing these training activities, you are increasing your proficiency in developing and maintaining Webs.

Tutorial Assignments

Amanda is pleased with your progress on the new Recipes Web. She asks you to make some additional changes to the site to improve its functionality. You also will create two new recipe pages as placeholders in the Web until you receive the recipe text from the kitchen. First, you will make some changes to the Sunny Morning Products Web to finish some remaining tasks. If necessary, insert your Student Disk in drive A or the appropriate disk drive, start FrontPage Explorer, and then do the following:

1. Open the Sunny Morning Web in FrontPage Explorer.

2. Open the Clothing Web page that you created in Tutorial 4 in FrontPage Editor. Add a hover button to the bottom of the page that links back to the Home Page. Add an appropriate color combination and mouse over effect to your hover button.

3. Insert an appropriate clip art image from the Microsoft Clip Gallery or any other source in an appropriate location on the Clothing Web page. Resize the image to make it larger, and then apply the washout and bevel effects. Save the page, print it, and then test your changes in Internet Explorer.

4. Create a second hover button on the Map page in the right cell of the table below the map image using the text "Go To Recipes Web" that contains a hyperlink to the Country Recipes Home Page in the Recipes Web. Save your changes, print the Map page, and then test your changes in Internet Explorer.

5. Apply a page transition of your choice to the Investor Relations page, and then test this transition.

6. Animate the navigation bar on the Investor Relations page so the words in the navigation bar fly across the screen from the left side.

7. Open the Recipes Web in FrontPage Explorer for Questions 8 through 14.

8. Select a theme of your choice and apply it only to the Butter Icing page. Print the page from FrontPage Editor. Which theme did you select, and why?

9. Use Navigation view to create a new page named punch.htm for a recipe for Citrus Punch (you won't actually enter the recipe). Add this page at the same level as the Chiffon Cake page. The page title is Citrus Punch.

10. Use Navigation view to create a new page named gpfruit.htm for a recipe for Grapefruit Punch (you won't actually enter the recipe). Add this page as a child page to the recipe page you added in Question 9 and apply the same theme to it as you applied to the Butter Icing page. The page title is Grapefruit Punch.

11. Modify the built-in navigation bars in the shared borders. The Top border should contain buttons for the Back and Next pages, the Home page, and the Parent page. The Left border should contain buttons for only the child-level pages. Test these changes to the navigation bars.

12. Add a Bottom shared border to the Web with the text "To order from Sunny Morning Products, click" and then add a hover button at the end of the sentence that includes the text "Sunny Morning Products" and a link to the appropriate page in the sunny Web. Test your changes in Internet Explorer.

13. You decide to wait until grapefruits are in season to add the Grapefruit Punch recipe to the Web. Rather than deleting this page, use the Help system to find out how to hide a Web page, and then hide the Grapefruit Punch Web page in the Recipes Web. (*Hint:* FrontPage hides pages only from *other* users. You will be able to hide the page, but you can still access it from your system. Hiding a page only takes effect on pages opened from the WWW.)

14. Use FrontPage Explorer to print Navigation view, and then use Internet Explorer to print the HTML code for the Grapefruit Punch page. Arrange and clearly identify the printouts and answers for all the questions in the tutorial assignments.

15. Close any open programs, and save changes to your Web files.

Case Problems

1. Changing the Appearance of the Royal Hair Care Products Web Site Valerie is pleased with the financial performance and current stock market activities tables that you added to the Web in Tutorial 4. Now that the Web includes many different pages of information, Valerie asks you to work on the appearance of the Web to ensure that it is visually interesting and easy to use. First, you will change the navigation bar to include hover buttons. Then you will change the appearance of the pages that open in the main frame of the frame set. After you are finished making these changes, Valerie will meet with a selected group of employees who will comment on the Web's content and appearance.

If necessary, start FrontPage Explorer, insert your Student Disk in drive A or the appropriate disk drive, and then do the following:

1. Read all the questions for this case problem, and prepare a planning analysis sheet for the changes to the Royal Web site.

2. Open the Royal Web. If you did not create this Web in Tutorial 2 and change it in Tutorials 3 and 4, then create this Web now and see your instructor.

3. Open the banner and contents frame set page that you created in Tutorial 4.

4. Create a thumbnail of the ROYAL01.GIF image in the Tutorial.02\royal folder, and place it in the cell in the upper-left corner of the Financial Performance Information table that opens in the main frame. Change the image so it has a beveled edge. Then create a hyperlink from the thumbnail image to the Royal Home Page.

5. Change the user-defined navigation bar in the Banner frame to include a hover button for each item in the navigation bar and links to the corresponding pages. Use complimentary effects and colors for each button. Then test your changes in Internet Explorer. Print the Banner page from FrontPage Editor.

6. Add page transitions to every page in the Royal Web. The transitions should occur when the user enters the page.

7. Animate the words in the contents frame. Experiment with the different effects, and then select the one that you like the best.

8. Apply a common theme to the pages that open in the main frame of the frame set page. Print the Financial Performance Information page from FrontPage Editor.

9. Print the HTML code for the Banner page using FrontPage Editor. Circle the code that is used to implement the hover buttons.

10. Arrange and clearly identify the printouts and answers for all the questions in this case.

11. Close any open programs, and save changes to your Web files.

2. Adding Shared Borders and a Theme to the Buffalo Trading Post Web Site Donna and Karla realize that as business at the Buffalo Trading Post continues to grow, more Web pages will be added to the Web site. They are pleased with the appearance of the site so far. Donna wants to make sure that it is easy to update the site when new pages are added, so she asks you to change the existing navigation bars to ones generated by FrontPage so they are updated automatically when changes are made to the site. Also, Karla wants you to add a theme to the pages to present a consistent appearance.

If necessary, start FrontPage Explorer, insert your Student Disk in drive A or the appropriate disk drive, and then do the following:

1. Read all the questions for this case problem, and prepare a planning analysis sheet for the changes to the Buffalo Web site.

2. Open the Buffalo Web. If you did not create this Web in Tutorial 2 and change it in Tutorials 3 and 4, then create this Web and see your instructor.

3. Create a navigation structure for the Web using the existing pages. The Home Page should be on the first level; the What, How, and Who pages should be children of the Home Page; and the Accessories, Women's Clothing, and Children's Clothing pages should be children of the What page. Print a copy of the Navigation view.

4. Use FrontPage Explorer to add Top and Left shared borders to all pages in the Buffalo Web.

5. Change the Top shared border to include links to the previous and next pages, the Home Page, and the parent page.

6. Change the Left shared border to include links to the child-level pages and the Home Page.

7. Turn off all shared borders for the Home Page.

8. Add a FrontPage navigation bar that includes links to child-level pages at the bottom of the Web page. Include links to the Home Page and the parent page.

9. Move the FrontPage navigation bar that you created in Question 8 so it appears above the copyright information. (*Hint:* You can move a FrontPage-generated navigation bar just like any other object.)

10. Use FrontPage Help to find out about adding a comment to a page in FrontPage Editor. Then insert the following comment at the top of the page to remind yourself to add the new company logo to the Web page: "Update the BTP logo when the new one becomes available next week." Test your comment in Internet Explorer to make sure that it works correctly.

11. Apply an appropriate theme to the Web using Themes view in FrontPage Explorer. Which theme did you select, and why?

12. Change the theme's attributes by changing it to use vivid colors.

13. Print the Home Page in FrontPage Editor, and then print the HTML code for the Home Page in FrontPage Editor.

14. Arrange and clearly identify the printouts and answers for all the questions in this case.

15. Close any open programs, and save changes to your Web files.

3. Enhancing the Appearance of the Menu Pages for Pardon My Garden Nolan and Shannon want to make sure that the new menu pages that you added to the Web site in Tutorial 4 are easy and fun to read. Nolan wants customers to feel like they are reading a menu at the Garden, so it is important to include restaurant logos and a professional appearance. Nolan asks you to use FrontPage to add logos and themes to the menu pages so they are interesting and professional-looking.

If necessary, start FrontPage Explorer, insert your Student Disk in drive A or the appropriate disk drive, and then do the following:

1. Read all the questions for this case problem, and prepare a planning analysis sheet for this enhancement to the Garden Web site.

2. Open the Garden Web in FrontPage Explorer. If you did not create this Web in Tutorial 2, create the Web and see your instructor for the Home Page file that you can import into the Web; also include the image for the logo in this page. If your instructor provides you with any additional pages for the Web, then import them as well.

3. Place a thumbnail of either the GARDEN01.GIF or GARDEN02.GIF image from the Tutorial.02\Garden folder as an inline image for the logo at the top of the pages for the Appetizers, Sandwiches, Entrees, and Dessert pages that you created in Tutorial 4.

4. Select and apply the same theme to each of these four Web pages. The theme should not include any shared borders. Which theme did you apply, and why?

5. Revise the Contents Web page with a navigation bar that includes a list of the four menu categories and an entry to return to the Home Page. Create the navigation bar for the four menu categories from a structure in Navigation view. The Contents page will include hyperlinks to each of the menu pages with the main frame as the target for the four menu category pages. Create a separate hyperlink to the Home Page with an appropriate target for the Home Page so that it replaces the entire frame set in the browser window.

6. Create a Specials page that lists the daily restaurant specials. Write the content of this page. Include either the GARDEN01.GIF or GARDEN02.GIF image from the Tutorial.02\Garden folder and place text over the image that identifies this as the Specials page. The page should open from the Home Page. Include a hover button from the Home Page to the Specials page and another hover button from the Specials page back to the Home Page. Select the effect to use with the hover button.

7. Select and apply a theme of your choice to the Specials page.

8. Select and apply a page transition and animation of your choice to the Specials page. Which transition and animation effects did you select, and why? Test these effects in your browser.

9. Create a shared border that is used at the bottom of the Specials page. Write the content of this shared border.

10. Print the Specials page from FrontPage Editor.

11. Open the Contents page. Insert the GARDEN01.GIF image from the Tutorial.02\Garden folder. Make a thumbnail of this image, and then apply the washout effect. Save the page, and rename the thumbnail image as the GARDEN01_WASH.GIF file in the images folder.

12. Delete the thumbnail image from the Contents page. Make the GARDEN01_WASH.GIF image the background for the Contents page. Is the washout thumbnail image repeated as the background for this page? Save the Contents page.

13. View and print the HTML code for the Specials page using Internet Explorer.

14 Arrange and clearly identify the printouts and answers for all the questions in this case.

15. Close any open programs, and save changes to your Web files.

4. Enhancing the Replay Music Factory Web Bob is pleased with the Specials page that you added to the Replay Music Factory Web site. Based on feedback from the marketing department, Bob asks you to add an image to the Specials page and then create hover buttons with hyperlinks to navigate the Web site. Next, Bob wants you to create a navigation structure to make it easier for him to add pages based on current market trends in the industry.

If necessary, start FrontPage Explorer, insert your Student Disk in drive A or the appropriate disk drive, and then do the following:

1. Read all the questions for this case problem, and prepare a planning analysis sheet for this enhancement to the Replay Web site.

2. Open the Replay Web in FrontPage Explorer. If you did not create this Web in Tutorial 2, create the Web and see your instructor for any pages that might be available.

3. Add an image from any source, such as the Microsoft Clip Gallery or your Student Disk, in at least one of the specials Web pages that you created in Tutorial 4. Then apply a common theme to all the pages for the music types, but not to the entire Web.

4. Create a hover button hyperlink from the Home Page to the Specials page. If necessary, modify the navigation bar in the Home Page for this method of opening the Specials page. Then create another hover button on the Contents page that returns the user to the Home Page. Test the hover buttons, and then change the effect used with the hover button on the Home Page. What was your initial effect, and which effect did you use the second time?

5. Create a navigation structure that contains the Home Page and its child pages. Print this navigation structure.

6. Use the navigation structure from Question 5 to create the navigation bar in the Banner page or another page of the Specials frame set. Where you place the navigation bar depends on the frame set you created in Tutorial 4.

7. Test the navigation bar, and then print the page containing the navigation bar and the Navigation view showing the site structure.

8. Print the HTML code for the Home Page.

9. Arrange and clearly identify the printouts and answers for all the questions in this case.

10. Close any open programs, and save changes to your Web files.

Developing Form Applications

Preparing the Search and Feedback Web Pages

OBJECTIVES

In this tutorial you will:

- Create a new Web page from a template
- Use the Search WebBot
- Create a custom user input form
- Add form fields to a form and set their properties
- Set form field validation criteria
- Use a form handler
- Use a personal Web server
- Publish a Web and process forms on the server
- Recalculate and verify hyperlinks
- Set Web access permissions

CASE

Sunny Morning Products

One of Andrew's initial concerns about the Sunny Morning Products Web site concerned how visitors would locate information. He was pleased that Amanda's initial Web site design included a navigation bar to link users directly to various information categories. However, Andrew remained uneasy about the users' abilities to find other information that might not be obvious from the navigation bar. To address this concern, Amanda added a search feature that allows users to search for information. Andrew also wanted to collect information about the users who visited the Sunny Morning Products Web site and provide them with the means to send comments or inquiries directly to the corporate offices. To implement these requirements, Amanda included a feedback form as part of the Feedback Web page. Both the search feature and the feedback form make use of dynamic Web pages that require processing on a Web server.

In this tutorial you continue with Amanda's training course by finishing the development of the Search and Feedback Web pages for the Sunny Morning Products Web site. You will add a search feature and a feedback form to these pages, respectively. To complete these tasks, you will use a template Web page and a partially completed Web page that Amanda prepared. After you develop these pages, you will test them using a Web server before publishing them to a WWW server. As you develop each page, you review Amanda's detailed design notes and documentation.

SESSION

6.1

In this session you will learn how to use a template page to create a Web page. You also will create a custom user input form and add form fields, such as radio buttons, drop-down menus, and one-line and scroll text boxes to the form.

Reviewing the Tasks List

Amanda wants you to review your current Tasks list to confirm that completing the Search and Feedback Web pages still appear in the list. After you review the list, Amanda asks you to meet and discuss the details involved in the next part of your Web training. You begin by opening the Sunny Morning Web.

To open the disk-based Web:

1. Start FrontPage Explorer.

2. Open the Sunny Morning Web (sunny) located in the a:\wwwroot folder on your Student Disk.

With the Web opened in the FrontPage Explorer, you are ready to review your Tasks list.

To review a Tasks list:

1. Click the **Tasks** button 🖾 on the Views bar to open the Tasks list.

2. Click the **Task** column label to sort the current list. See Figure 6-1.

Figure 6-1 ◄
Current Tasks list for Sunny Morning Web

remaining pages to complete

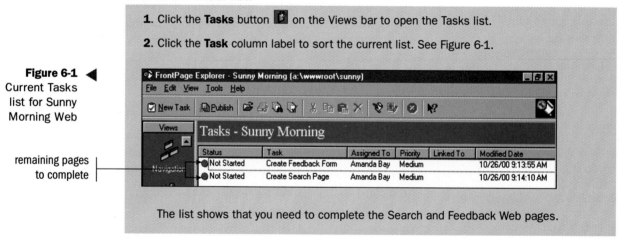

The list shows that you need to complete the Search and Feedback Web pages.

During your meeting with Amanda, she explains how you can use a FrontPage template to create the Search page instead of building it from scratch. Before you create the Search Web page from this template, however, Amanda asks you to review the planning analysis sheet she created to develop this page. See Figure 6-2.

Figure 6-2 ◀
Amanda's
planning
analysis sheet
for the Search
Web page

Planning Analysis Sheet

My goal:

Create a Search page that permits the user to enter a text string that is

processed on the server to obtain a list of pages in the Web that contain the text

string.

What results do I want to see?

A Search Web page that includes the Sunny Morning Products logo, a title, and a

text box for the Search WebBot that executes the search on the server. The Web

page should have the same background as the Home Page.

What information do I need?

Template Web page for a search page.

Image file for logo.

Using a Template to Create a Web Page

A **Web page template** is a predesigned Web page on which you can base your Web page. After creating a page using a template, you can modify it to meet your specific requirements. Figure 6-3 describes several page template types that are available with FrontPage.

Figure 6-3 ◀
Selected
template Web
pages available
with FrontPage

Template Name	Description
Bibliography	A page that makes references to printed or electronic works.
Feedback Form	A page where users submit comments about a Web site, product, or organization.
Frequently Asked Questions	A page that answers common questions about a specific topic.
Search Page	A page where users can search for keywords across all the documents in the active Web.
Table of Contents	A page that links every document in a Web and displays it in an outline format.

REFERENCE window

CREATING A WEB PAGE FROM A TEMPLATE PAGE

- Click File on the menu bar in FrontPage Editor, and then click New to open the New dialog box.
  or
- Press Ctrl + N to open the New dialog box.
- Scroll the template list, and then click the desired template.
- Click the OK button.

Amanda asks you to create and modify the Search Web page next. You can create a new Web page based on the FrontPage Search Page template. You need to add a few items, such as the Sunny Morning Products logo, to modify the template.

To create a Web page using a template:

1. Click the **Show FrontPage Editor** button 📄 on the FrontPage Explorer toolbar to start the program.

2. Click **File** on the menu bar, and then click **New** to open the New dialog box. A list of the current template pages appears on the Page tab.

3. Scroll the template list until you see Search Page, and then click **Search Page** to select it. See Figure 6-4.

Figure 6-4 ◀
New dialog box

your template list
might be different

description of
selected Search
Page template

desired template
page

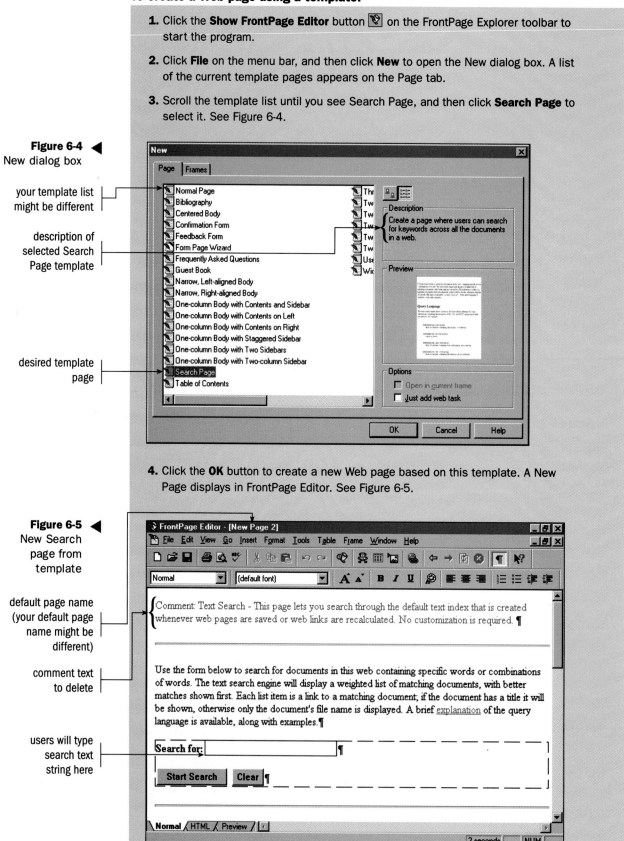

4. Click the **OK** button to create a new Web page based on this template. A New Page displays in FrontPage Editor. See Figure 6-5.

Figure 6-5 ◀
New Search
page from
template

default page name
(your default page
name might be
different)

comment text
to delete

users will type
search text
string here

After creating a Web page from a template, you can customize it. For example, you need to make some minor changes to convert this generic Search Page template page into the specific Search Web page you need. Amanda wants you to remove the comment from the top of the page, include the same background that is used on the Home Page, insert the Sunny Morning Products logo, and change the title of the page from "New Page" to "Search."

To revise a Web page created from a template:

1. Place the pointer on top of the purple **"Comment: Text Search - This page..."** text at the top of the page. The pointer changes to the WebBot pointer 🔧 to identify the location of a WebBot within a Web page. The comment is a WebBot that inserts text that you can see in FrontPage Editor, but not in a Web browser.

2. Right-click anywhere in the **"Comment: Text Search - This page..."** text to select it and display the Shortcut menu, and then click **Cut** to delete this comment.

3. Type **Search** as a heading for the page, click the **Change Style** list arrow on the Format toolbar, and then click **Heading 2**.

   Now you assign the same ocean themes background to the Search page that you used for the Home Page.

4. Right-click anywhere on the page to display the Shortcut menu, click **Page Properties**, click the **Background** tab, click the **Background Image** check box to select it, and then click the **Browse** button to open the Select Background Image dialog box.

5. Double-click the **Images** folder name, scroll the filename list, click **WB00760_.gif** to select the ocean themes background, and then click the **OK** button to return to the Page Properties dialog box.

6. Click the **OK** button to close the Page Properties dialog box. The Search page re-displays with the same ocean themes background as the Home Page.

   Now, you apply the image for the Sunny Morning Products logo to the page.

7. If necessary, press **Ctrl + Home** to move the insertion point to the top of the page, press the **Enter** key to insert a new line, and then click the new paragraph. The insertion point is at the desired location for inserting the image.

8. Click the **Insert Image** button 🖻 on the Standard toolbar, click the **Select a file on your computer** button 🔍 to open the Select File dialog box, click the **Look in** list arrow and select the appropriate drive for your Student Disk, double-click the **Tutorial.06** folder, and then double-click the **Images** folder.

9. Click the **Hsearch.gif** file, and then click the **OK** button to insert the logo image on the page.

10. Click **File** on the menu bar, click **Save As** to open that dialog box, make sure a:\wwwroot\sunny appears in the Look in text box, and then click the **OK** button to accept the suggested title of Search in the Title text box and the suggested filename of search.htm in the URL text box.

    TROUBLE? If a:\wwwroot\sunny does not appear in the Look in text box, click the Look in list arrow, and then click a:\wwwroot\sunny to select it.

11. When the Save Embedded Files dialog box opens, click the **OK** button to save the file in the images folder.

    TROUBLE? If the folder is not set to images/, then click the Change Folder button to open that dialog box, click the images folder, and then click the OK button to return to the Save Embedded Files dialog box. Repeat Step 11.

When you created the Search page from the template, it automatically included the Search WebBot. This is an example of the type of predefined feature that templates can include.

Using the Search WebBot

Amanda wants you to review the Search WebBot properties and to increase the size of the text box for the search text string.

To change the properties of a Search WebBot:

1. If necessary, scroll down the Search page until you see the Search for text box and the Start Search and Clear push buttons, and then place the pointer anywhere within the dashed-line box surrounding these objects. The pointer changes to 🢡 to indicate that this is the location of a WebBot within the Web page. See Figure 6-6.

Figure 6-6 ◀
Search page
with search
objects

dashed line
surrounds WebBot
area

WebBot pointer

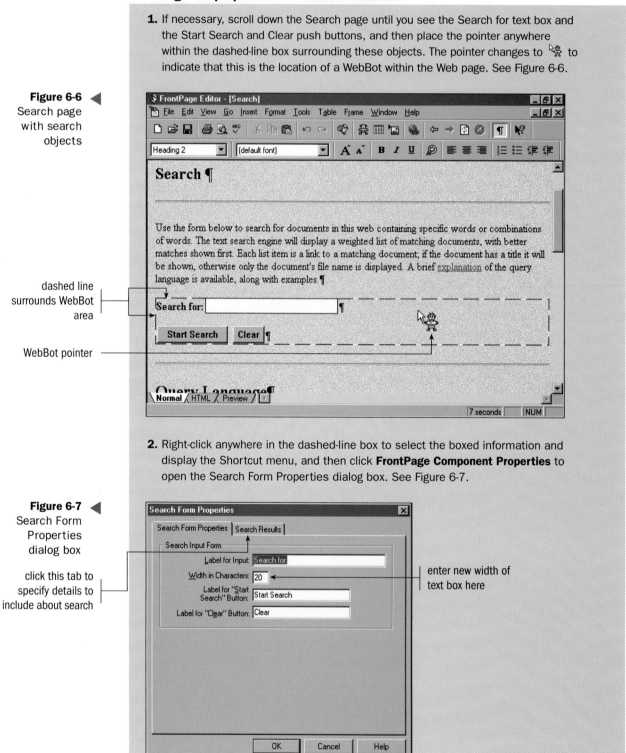

2. Right-click anywhere in the dashed-line box to select the boxed information and display the Shortcut menu, and then click **FrontPage Component Properties** to open the Search Form Properties dialog box. See Figure 6-7.

Figure 6-7 ◀
Search Form
Properties
dialog box

click this tab to
specify details to
include about search

enter new width of
text box here

3. In the Search Input Form section, select the current text in the Width in Characters text box, and then type **24** to increase the size of the Search for text box.

4. Click the **OK** button to return to the Search page, and then click anywhere on the Web page outside of the dashed-line box to deselect the WebBot. Notice that the size of the Search for text box increased to 24 characters.

5. Click the **Save** button 🖫 on the Standard toolbar to save your changes.

With all the properties specified, Amanda asks you to test the Web page.

To test the Search WebBot using Internet Explorer:

1. Click the **Preview in Browser** button 🔍 on the Standard toolbar to open a FrontPage Editor message box that advises you of the need to save or publish the page to preview it correctly, and then click the **OK** button to switch to Internet Explorer. The Search page opens in Internet Explorer. If necessary, maximize the window.

2. If necessary, scroll down the page until you see the Search for text box, click in the Search for text box, and then type **MIS**.

3. Click the **Start Search** push button. A dashed line appears inside the button to indicate that it is selected. Then, the FrontPage Run-Time Component Page opens in the browser to advise you that a Web server is required for the page to function correctly. You will use a Web server to process this request later in this tutorial.

4. Click the **Back** button 🔙 on the Internet Explorer toolbar to return to the Search page, and then click the **Clear** push button to remove the MIS text from the Search for text box. Now the Clear button is selected, as indicated by the dashed line inside that button.

Your test was successful; the Clear push button performed the desired action of removing the previously entered text from the Search for text box. Keep in mind, however, that the search could not be completed because you are using a disk-based Web rather than a server-based Web. A server-based Web is necessary to process the Search WebBot and actually search the Web site. Later in this tutorial, you will place the Sunny Morning Web on a server to perform a search on its pages.

Creating User Input Forms

After preparing a design for a feedback form, you can begin creating your own custom user input forms. A **form** is a set of form fields on a page that enables a user to enter data that is processed on the server. A **form field** is a data-entry field on a page. A user supplies the form field information by typing text directly into the field or by selecting the field. A **name-value pair** is the name of a form field and the value contained in the field when the form is submitted to the server. A **form handler** is a program that resides on a server and is executed when a user submits a form.

You create a form Web page by placing a form field on the page, which inserts the <FORM> tag that identifies the Web page as a form. Then the <FORM> tag is available for use with all the other fields on the form. There are two steps to creating a form field. First, you add the field to the form, and then you set the properties of the field. Although default settings are assigned to field properties, you need to revise them so they have more meaningful values. You can add form fields to a form in any order.

Creating form fields is similar to inserting an inline image on a page because form fields are created inline with other text on the page. Once you insert a form field on the page, FrontPage Editor treats it like a character. For example, if you click to the left of a field and start typing text to label a form field, the field moves right to make room for the text. Pressing the Enter key to the left of a field inserts a new paragraph, which causes the field to appear at the beginning of the new line. You can cut and copy form fields to the Clipboard and paste them into a form. Although a single Web page can contain more than one form through the use of multiple pairs of <FORM> tags, the most common situation is to create a single form on a Web page. This is the approach Amanda used for the Sunny Morning Products Web site.

Before creating a form Web page, you should prepare a planning analysis sheet that describes the form's content. After completing that sheet, draw a sketch that identifies which form fields you want to use and their approximate locations on the Web page. Amanda asks you to review the planning analysis sheet shown in Figure 6-8, as well as the design sketch shown in Figure 6-9, that she completed for the Feedback Web page. This information will serve as a useful reference when you create the custom input form.

Figure 6-8 ◄
Amanda's planning analysis sheet for the Feedback Web page

Planning Analysis Sheet

My goal:

Create a custom Feedback Web page that permits the user to enter comments

and suggestions about the company, its products, or the Web site, including

obtaining contact information from the user.

What results do I want to see?

A Feedback Web page that includes the Sunny Morning Products logo, a title,

and form fields that collect the desired data. The user's data is stored in a results

file on the server that can be used for additional processing. The results file is

sent as an e-mail message to a designated address.

What information do I need?

A sketch of the feedback form that identifies the fields used to collect data from

the user.

Categories for three types of comments: suggestion, praise, and problem.

Categories for three areas addressed by comments: Web site, company, and

product.

Edit criteria for the number of visits, which can be from zero to 100 as an integer

number.

Figure 6-9
Design sketch
of the Feedback
Web page

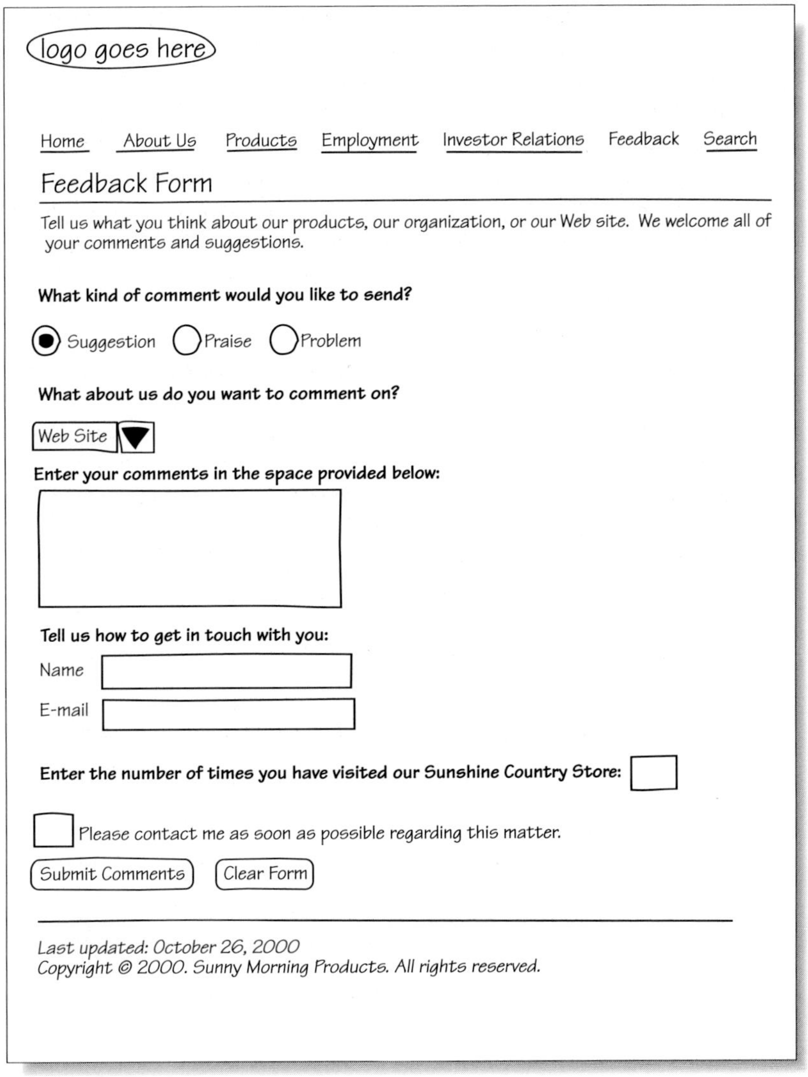

> (logo goes here)
>
> Home   About Us   Products   Employment   Investor Relations   Feedback   Search
>
> Feedback Form
> _____
>
> Tell us what you think about our products, our organization, or our Web site. We welcome all of your comments and suggestions.
>
> **What kind of comment would you like to send?**
>
> ● Suggestion   ○ Praise   ○ Problem
>
> **What about us do you want to comment on?**
>
> [Web Site ▼]
>
> **Enter your comments in the space provided below:**
>
> [   ]
>
> **Tell us how to get in touch with you:**
>
> Name [   ]
>
> E-mail [   ]
>
> **Enter the number of times you have visited our Sunshine Country Store:** [   ]
>
> [ ] Please contact me as soon as possible regarding this matter.
>
> (Submit Comments)   (Clear Form)
> _____
>
> Last updated: October 26, 2000
> Copyright © 2000. Sunny Morning Products. All rights reserved.

Before you add form fields to a Web page, you need to create a form Web page. Rather than starting with a blank page and typing all the necessary text, Amanda created some of the feedback form on the Feedback Web page for you. Now, you will create the necessary form fields, including specifying their properties. Begin by opening this page and including it in the current sunny Web.

To include a partially completed page using FrontPage Editor:

1. Click the **FrontPage Editor** program button on the taskbar to switch to that program.

2. Click the **Open** button 🗁 on the Standard toolbar to open the Open dialog box, and then click the **Select a file on your computer** button 🖳 to open the Select File dialog box.

3. Make sure the drive that contains your Student Disk appears in the Look in text box, double-click the **Tutorial.06** folder, click the **feedback.htm** file, and then click the **OK** button. The partially completed Feedback Web page opens in FrontPage Editor.

   Now, you are ready to save the file in your open Web.

> **4.** Click **File** on the menu bar, click **Save As** to open that dialog box, make sure a:\wwwroot\sunny appears in the Look in text box, click the **OK** button to open the Save Embedded Files dialog box, and then click the **OK** button to save the file in the images folder.
>
> **TROUBLE?** If the folder is not set to images/ in the Save Embedded Files text box, then click the Change Folder button to open that dialog box, click the images folder, and then click the OK button to return to the Save Embedded Files dialog box. Click the OK button to continue.

Now, you are ready to modify the existing Feedback Web page so that it contains a form for entering data. No matter which type of form field you are adding to a Web page, you follow the same procedure of inserting the desired field and then changing its properties.

REFERENCE window	**ADDING FORM FIELDS**
	▪ Place the insertion point where you want the form field to appear on your Web page. ▪ Click the desired form field toolbar button on the Forms toolbar to select the desired form field and place it on your form. *or* ▪ Click Insert on the menu bar, point to Form Field, and then click the desired form field. ▪ Right-click the form field object to select it and open its properties dialog box. ▪ Enter the appropriate values for the field's properties. ▪ Click the OK button.

Although you can place form fields on Web page in any order, Amanda wants you to begin by adding radio buttons.

Adding Radio Buttons

Radio buttons, or **option buttons**, are easily arranged on a Web page in groups or series that share a common group name. A **group name** is used to identify a related series of radio buttons. Within a group of radio buttons, only one button can be selected at a time—selecting a different button deselects a previously selected radio button. You label radio buttons by typing the appropriate text next to them. For example, a Web page form might have a section with the group name of "Age" with corresponding radio button labels consisting of "Under 25," "25–40," "41–65," and "Over 65." Radio buttons commonly are used when only a few choices are available. Keep in mind that a form can contain several radio button groups. In addition, the first radio button you add to a form will be selected automatically when you run the form, unless you change the default settings.

When you create radio button groups on a form, keep in mind the following design suggestions:

- Use radio buttons when you want to limit the user to one of a few related and mutually exclusive choices.

- The minimum number of radio buttons in a group is two, and the recommended maximum is seven.

- Label each radio button clearly.

- Use a heading or other feature to identify the group name for the radio buttons.

Continue to develop the Feedback Web page by adding the radio button form field as your first form field. Amanda already included the text for the radio button labels in the partially completed Web page and asks you to insert the radio buttons to the left of these labels. First, Amanda wants you to display the Forms toolbar to make it easy to add the form fields to the Web page. The Forms toolbar contains buttons that let you add the most frequently used form fields to your Web page. Figure 6-10 describes the Forms toolbar buttons and their uses.

Figure 6-10 ◀
Forms toolbar
buttons

Button Name	Button	Function
One-Line Text Box	[abl]	Lets the user enter a single line of text data.
Scrolling Text Box		Lets the user enter multiple lines of text data.
Check Box	☑	Lets the user select one or more choices from a group, independent of other selections.
Radio Button	◉	Lets the user select a single choice from a group of two or more mutually exclusive choices.
Drop-Down Menu		Lets the user select a choice from a list of scrollable items.
Push Button	▭	Processes a command to submit data to a server or clear data from a form when clicked.

To display the Forms toolbar and add a radio button:

1. Click **View** on the menu bar, and then click **Forms Toolbar**. The Forms toolbar displays in your window below the Format toolbar. See Figure 6-11.

Figure 6-11 ◀
Feedback Web
page with
Forms toolbar
displayed

Forms toolbar
(yours might appear
in a different
location)

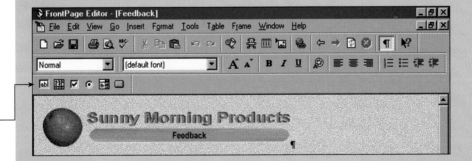

TROUBLE? If the Forms Toolbar doesn't appear, then it already was checked on the View menu and displayed in your window. Clicking this selection caused it to disappear. Repeat Step 1.

With the Forms toolbar displayed, now you can add the appropriate radio buttons to the Feedback Web page.

2. Scroll down the Feedback Web page until you see the "Suggestion Praise Problem" text that you will use as the labels for your radio buttons. See Figure 6-12.

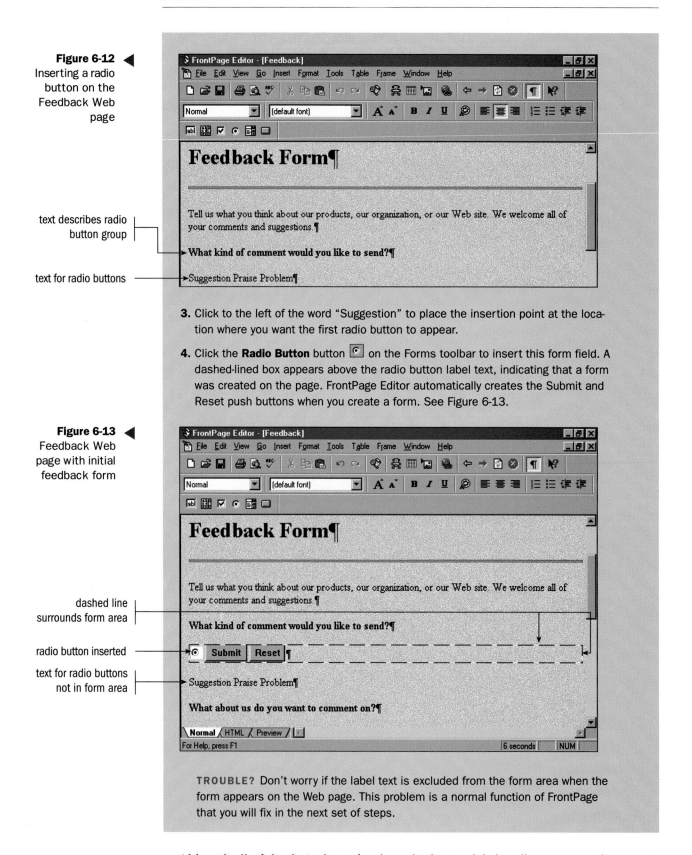

Figure 6-12 ◄
Inserting a radio
button on the
Feedback Web
page

text describes radio
button group

text for radio buttons

3. Click to the left of the word "Suggestion" to place the insertion point at the location where you want the first radio button to appear.

4. Click the **Radio Button** button ⊙ on the Forms toolbar to insert this form field. A dashed-lined box appears above the radio button label text, indicating that a form was created on the page. FrontPage Editor automatically creates the Submit and Reset push buttons when you create a form. See Figure 6-13.

Figure 6-13 ◄
Feedback Web
page with initial
feedback form

dashed line
surrounds form area

radio button inserted

text for radio buttons
not in form area

TROUBLE? Don't worry if the label text is excluded from the form area when the form appears on the Web page. This problem is a normal function of FrontPage that you will fix in the next set of steps.

Although all of the desired text for the radio button labels still appears on the page, it is not included in the form you just created. You can use the Cut and Paste commands to move this text, as well as the rest of the text Amanda included for the form, to the form area of your Web page.

To place existing text in the form area of a Web page:

1. Click and drag the pointer to select the text beginning with "**Suggestion**" through "**Please contact me**" and include the two blank lines immediately above the horizontal line at the bottom of the page. Do *not* select the horizontal line.

2. Click the **Cut** button ✂ on the Standard toolbar to delete this text from the Feedback Web page and place it on the Clipboard.

3. Click immediately to the right of the radio button in the form area of the page to place the insertion point at the location where you want the text to appear. Make sure that you see the insertion point, instead of selection handles around the form area or radio button.

4. Click the **Paste** button 📋 on the Standard toolbar to insert the text from the Clipboard into the form area, as indicated by the dashed line.

   There still is one line of text that you want to include in the form area.

5. Scroll up the window until you see the text "What kind of comment would you like to send?", select "**What kind of comment would you like to send?**", click ✂, and then press the **Delete** key to remove the extra paragraph.

6. If necessary, click to the left of the radio button to place the insertion point at that location, click 📋 to insert the text, and then press the **Enter** key to insert a blank line between the text and the radio button.

   You have one last change to make in order to place the radio button label immediately to the right of the button.

7. Click to the right of the radio button to place the insertion point at that location, and then press the **Delete** key. The text is included within the form area and arranged as desired. See Figure 6-14.

Figure 6-14 ◀
Feedback Web
page with
incomplete
feedback form

dashed line
surrounds form area

insertion point

form area includes
desired text

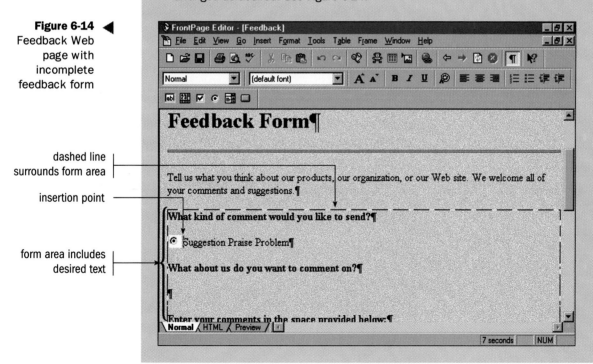

After adding the first radio button to a Web page, including the additional radio buttons is straightforward. Amanda asks you to finish adding the radio buttons to the form.

To add additional radio buttons to an existing form area of a Web page:

1. Click to the left of "P" in the word "Praise" to place the insertion point at that location.

2. Click the **Radio Button** button ⊙ on the Forms toolbar to insert this form field. Notice that this second radio button does not appear selected.

   TROUBLE? If you accidentally place the insertion point at the wrong location, click the Undo button ↶ on the Standard toolbar to remove the form field, and then repeat Steps 1 and 2.

3. Click to the left of "P" in the word "Problem" to place the insertion point at that location.

4. Click ⊙ on the Forms toolbar to insert that form field.

5. Click the **Save** button 🖬 on the Standard toolbar to save your changes.

The Suggestion, Praise, and Problem radio buttons now belong to the same group, under the group name heading of "What kind of comment would you like to send?" Keep in mind that the user can select only one of these radio buttons. After placing a form field on the form, you can change its properties from the default values to more meaningful ones. For example, the Suggestion radio button currently is assigned to a default group named R1 and has a value of V1. Because these values don't correspond well to the work that you are doing on the Feedback Web page, you want to rename the properties for this field. Amanda suggests you change the current radio button properties by naming the series of radio buttons as the MessageType group.

To change radio button properties:

1. Click the **radio button** to the left of "Suggestion" to select it. Selection handles appear at each corner of this object for the form field.

2. Right-click the selected **radio button** to display the Shortcut menu, and then click **Form Field Properties** to open the Radio Button Properties dialog box with its default values.

3. Type **MessageType** in the Group Name text box, select **V1** in the Value text box, and then type **Suggestion** in the Value text box. Notice that in the Initial State section, the Selected radio button is selected, indicating that this radio button appears selected when the Feedback page opens in the Web browser. See Figure 6-15.

Figure 6-15 ◀
Completed
Radio Button
Properties
dialog box

indicates group name

indicates Suggestion
radio button will
appear selected

selected form field
object

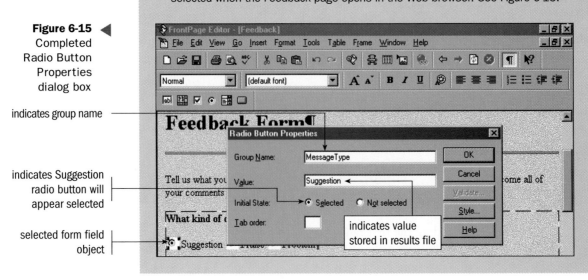

4. Click the **OK** button to complete the changes to the radio button's properties and close the dialog box.

Now you change the properties for the next two radio buttons and assign them to the same group as Suggestion.

5. Right-click the **radio button** to the left of "Praise," and then click **Form Field Properties** to open the Radio Button Properties dialog box with its default values. The default for the Praise radio button is "Not selected" because only one radio button can be selected in a group at a time.

6. Type **MessageType** in the Group Name text box, select **V2** in the Value text box, type **Praise**, and then click the **OK** button.

7. Right-click the **radio button** to the left of "Problem," and then click **Form Field Properties** to open the Radio Button Properties dialog box with its default values.

8. Type **MessageType** in the Group Name text box, select **V3** in the Value text box, type **Problem**, and then click the **OK** button.

9. Click the **Save** button 🖫 on the Standard toolbar to save the file.

You specified the MessageType radio button group to include each of the three radio button form fields you placed on the form. Now, you can continue your training by adding another type of form field—a drop-down menu.

Adding Drop-Down Menus

Although radio buttons are useful when you want a user to select from only a few choices, a drop-down menu is appropriate when you want to offer a variety of choices. A drop-down menu is scrollable so the user can choose from a lengthy list of choices. Although a user could select one or more items from a drop-down menu, usually this type of menu is organized to allow only one selection from the menu.

When you create drop-down menus on a form, keep in mind the following design suggestions:

■ Use a drop-down menu when you want the user to have a variety of choices.

■ Drop-down menus should contain a minimum of three choices.

■ Drop-down menu items either should be arranged by use, with the most commonly used entries appearing first in the list, or arranged in ascending order alphabetically, numerically, or chronologically.

■ The default choice in a drop-down menu either should be the most-used choice or the first choice in the list.

Amanda wants you to add a drop-down menu to the form as the next form field to provide a list of categories from which the user can choose when sending comments to Sunny Morning Products.

To add a drop-down menu to a form:

1. Click the line immediately below the "What about us do you want to comment on?" text to place the insertion point at that location.

2. Click the **Drop-Down Menu** button 🖳 on the Forms toolbar to insert this form field.

After adding the drop-down menu form field, you can add its choices and revise its properties from the default options to more meaningful ones. In specifying the drop-down menu properties, you also create the user's choice list. You now add the choices to the drop-down menu and revise their properties.

To add choices to a drop-down menu and change its properties:

1. Right-click the **drop-down menu** you just added to select it and display the Shortcut menu, and then click **Form Field Properties** to open the Drop-Down Menu Properties dialog box.

2. Type **Subject** in the Name text box.

3. Click the **Add** button to open the Add Choice dialog box, type **Web Site** in the Choice text box (make sure to type a space between the two words), click the **Specify Value** check box to select it, click in the Specify Value text box and type **WebSite** (as one word, without a space), and then in the Initial State section, click the **Selected** option button. Your completed Add Choice dialog box should match Figure 6-16.

Figure 6-16 ◀
Completed Add
Choice dialog
box

indicates text to
appear in menu
choices

indicates value to
store in results file

selected drop-down
menu form field

indicates that this
choice will appear
selected in menu

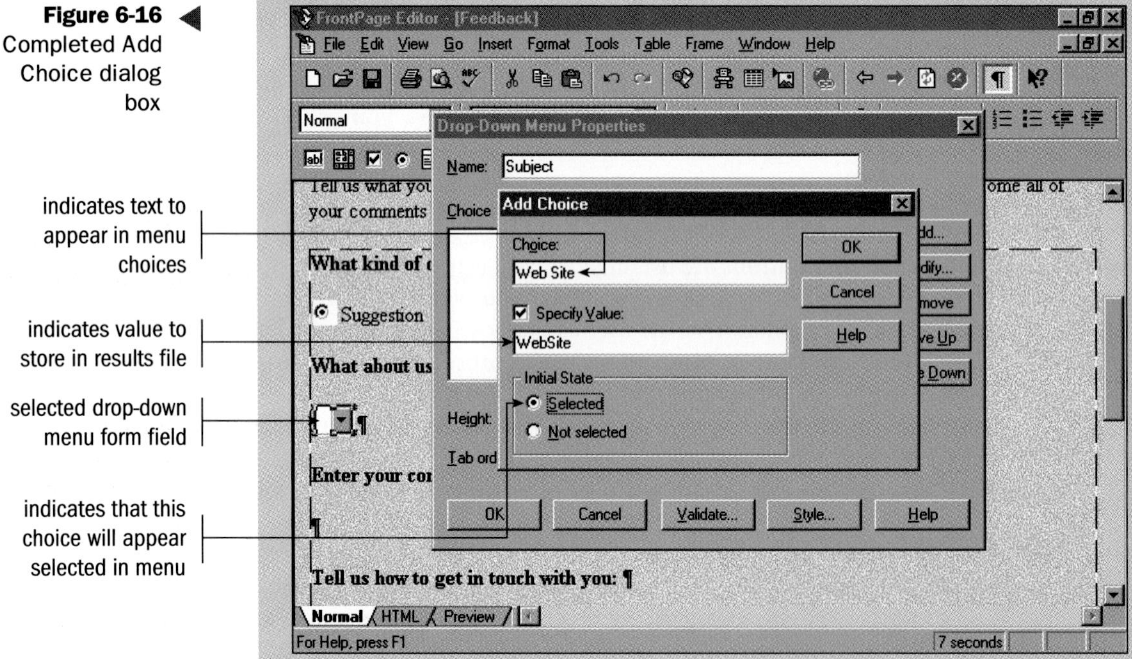

4. Click the **OK** button to complete adding this choice to the menu's available choices and to close the Add Choice dialog box.

5. Click the **Add** button in the Drop-Down Menu Properties dialog box to re-open the Add Choice dialog box, type **Company** in the Choice text box, and then click the **OK** button to close the Add Choice dialog box. Because the other default properties are acceptable, no other changes are necessary in the Add Choice dialog box.

6. Repeat Step 5 to add the **Products** choice to the drop-down menu. Your completed Drop-Down Menu Properties dialog box should match Figure 6-17.

Figure 6-17 ◀
Completed
Drop-Down
Menu
Properties
dialog box

list of items for
menu choices

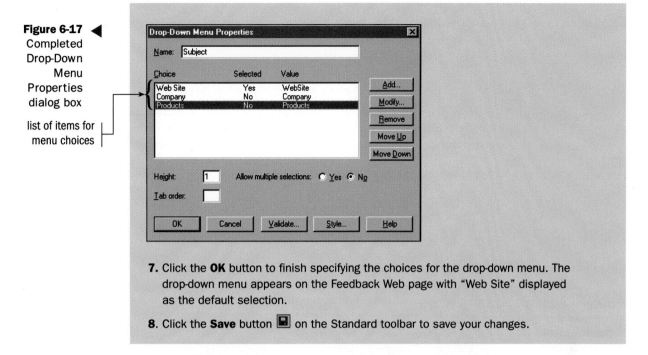

7. Click the **OK** button to finish specifying the choices for the drop-down menu. The drop-down menu appears on the Feedback Web page with "Web Site" displayed as the default selection.

8. Click the **Save** button 🖫 on the Standard toolbar to save your changes.

Although the drop-down menu and its choices are in place, clicking the drop-down menu list arrow would select this form field if it was not already selected. Otherwise, a list of the other available choices is not displayed. You must test the Web page in your Web browser window, which you will do later in this tutorial, to display the list. Your development of the Feedback Web page is going well. Next, Amanda explains how to add a one-line text box form field to your form.

Adding One-Line Text Boxes

Often, a user is required to supply nonstandard information on a form, and sometimes radio buttons or drop-down menus don't provide an effective format. Text box form fields provide users with a means of directly entering text information in a form. A **one-line text box** accepts a single line of typed information. When required, you can specify this form field as a password field in which asterisks appear when a text value is typed in the field to hide the text as it is typed.

When you create one-line text boxes on a form, keep in mind the following design suggestions:

■ Use a one-line text box when you want the user to enter a small amount of unique information.

■ A one-line text box limits the number of data characters a user enters.

In addition to being unique, a user's name and e-mail address usually consist of short information. Therefore, Amanda designed these form fields as one-line text boxes. Next, you add the Name and E-mail text boxes to the form.

To add a one-line text box to a form:

1. Scroll down the Feedback Web page until the text "Tell us how to get in touch with you:" is at the top of the document window, which is where you will place the one-line text boxes on the form.

2. Click anywhere on **Name**, and then press the **End** key to place the insertion point a few spaces to the right of this text.

3. Click the **One-Line Text Box** button ⊞ on the Forms toolbar to insert this form field on the Web page form.

4. Repeat Steps 2 and 3 to add a one-line text box for E-mail.

Now that you've added the two text box form fields to the form, you need to set their lengths. Amanda wants you to adjust their current properties so that each of these text boxes displays 35 characters, rather than their default lengths of 20 characters.

To change the properties of a one-line text box:

1. Right-click inside the **Name** text box to select it and display the Shortcut menu, and then click **Form Field Properties** to open the Text Box Properties dialog box with its default values.

2. Type **UserName** in the Name text box, select **20** (or the current value) in the Width in characters text box, and then type **35** to set the text box length to 35 characters. Your completed Text Box Properties dialog box should match Figure 6-18.

Figure 6-18 ◀
Completed Text
Box Properties
dialog box

selection for one-line
text box field object

new width of text box

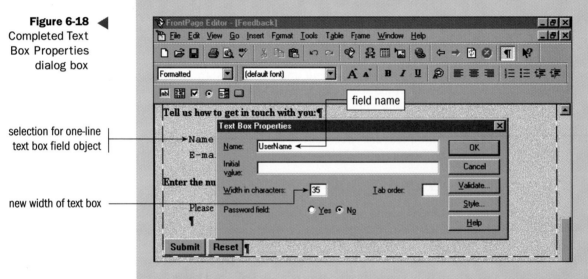

3. Click the **OK** button. The Name text box now extends to the right for the added characters.

4. Repeat Steps 1 through 3 for the E-mail form field. Use the name **UserEmail** with the same character width of **35**.

5. Click the **Save** button ⊟ on the Standard toolbar to save your changes.

Using one-line text boxes for users to enter their names and e-mail information is effective because only a brief, single line of text is necessary for each category. However, some text information, such as user comments or problem descriptions, requires more space.

Adding Scrolling Text Boxes

A **scrolling text box** accepts multiple lines of text information. As with the information a user supplies in a one-line text box, the information in a scrolling text box usually is unique. For example, a scrolling text box often is an effective form field to use when asking a user to describe problems or complaints experienced with a particular product or service. A scrolling text box form field often is referred to as a **multi-line text box**.

When you create a scrolling text box on a form, keep in mind the following design suggestions:

- Use a scrolling text box when you want a user to supply information that might include more than one line.

- A scrolling text box accepts and displays multiple lines of unique text the user enters.

Amanda's design of the Feedback Web page includes a scrolling text box form field that allows users to enter lengthy comments. You add this form field to the current form next.

To add a scrolling text box to a form:

1. Scroll up the Feedback Web page until the text "Enter your comments in the space provided below:" is at the top of the document window, click anywhere on that text, and then press the **down arrow** key to place the insertion point on the line below this text, which is where you want to put the scrolling text box on the form.

2. Click the **Scrolling Text Box** button ▦ on the Forms toolbar to insert this form field on the form.

With the scrolling text box inserted on the form, you change the current default properties of this form field from 20 characters wide with two lines displayed to an enlarged area that is 50 characters wide with five lines displayed.

To change the properties of a scrolling text box:

1. Double-click the **scrolling text box** you just added to select it and open the Scrolling Text Box Properties dialog box.

2. Type **Comments** in the Name text box; select **20** (or the current value) in the Width in characters text box and type **50**; and then select **2** (or the current value) in the Number of lines text box and type **5**. Notice that the Initial value text box is blank, which indicates that this text box appears empty when the Feedback page first opens in the Web browser. Your completed Scrolling Text Box Properties dialog box should match Figure 6-19.

Figure 6-19 ◄
Completed
Scrolling Text
Box Properties
dialog box

field name

scrolling text box in
form area (your text
box might be
selected)

new text box width

new text box height

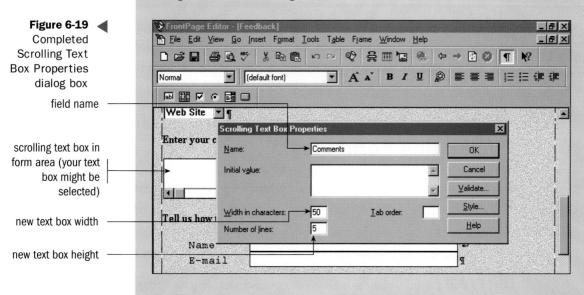

3. Click the **OK** button. The Feedback Web page re-displays in your window with the enlarged scrolling text box.

TROUBLE? If the scrolling text box form field does not appear on the form 50 characters wide as specified, this is not a problem. It will appear correctly when viewed in your browser window. Continue with the next step.

4. Click the **Save** button 💾 on the Standard toolbar.

Quick Check

1. A(n) _____ is a predesigned Web page on which you can base your own Web page.

2. Which WebBot is used to locate a text string in a page in the current Web?

3. A(n) _____ is a Web page that permits a user to enter data that is processed on the Web server.

4. A(n) _____ is the name of a form field and the value contained in the field when the user submits the form to the server.

5. True or False: A form handler is a program that is part of your Web browser and is used to process a user form.

6. True or False: In a named group of radio buttons, you can select as many buttons as you want before submitting a form for processing, but only one remains selected.

7. True or False: A text box is a form field that is used when you want to limit the user to selecting only one of two or more related and mutually exclusive choices.

8. A(n) _____ is a form field object that is used to present the user with longer lists of items from which to make a selection.

You are making good progress in specifying each of the fields for the feedback form. In the next session, you continue to add the remainder of the form fields necessary to complete the development of the Feedback Web page.

SESSION

6.2

In this session you will learn how to validate form fields in order to verify data entered by a user. You will continue adding form fields, such as check boxes and push buttons, to a form. In addition, you will specify the form handler used by the Web server, test this form on a client, and, finally, view the HTML code for forms.

Validating Form Fields

The one-line text boxes and the scrolling text box you added to the Feedback Web page allow the user to enter unique text information. However, in certain situations, you might want to edit or validate the information a user supplies in these text boxes. For example, you can specify that a text box contains a minimum or maximum number of characters and that the text must be numeric, such as testing for the year 2000, which is numeric and contains four characters. FrontPage allows you to validate form field input data. **Form field validation** is the process of performing a check on the information a user enters in one or more form fields to verify that the information is acceptable. Unacceptable data is flagged as an error, and the user must change it before the form handler on the server accepts the response. Form field validations are specified using the appropriate validation dialog box for the type of form field that is being validated. Verification of data entered in a one-line text box usually is the most frequently applied validation for a Web page form. You can specify data validation criteria when you initially specify the properties of the field, or you can edit the validation properties after adding the field to the form.

In designing the Feedback Web page, Amanda used a one-line text box in which a user enters the number of visits to the Sunshine Country Store. She wants this form field validated so the value entered is an integer between zero and 100. Another aspect of this validation is that the user is required to enter a number (even zero) in order to submit an acceptable form to the server. In other words, the user cannot skip this form field when entering data. As the next part of your training in developing the Feedback Web page, you will add the one-line text box form field for the number of visits to the Sunshine Country Store and then proceed to validate this form field.

To add a one-line text box to the form and change its properties:

1. Scroll down the Feedback Web page until the text "Tell us how to get in touch with you:" is at the top of the document window, click anywhere on the **Enter the number of times you have visited our Sunshine Country Store:** text, and then press the **End** key to place the insertion point at the location where you want this text box to appear.

2. Click the **One-Line Text Box** button 🔲 on the Forms toolbar to insert this form field.

   With the Visits text box in place on the form, you change the form field properties so that the acceptable number of visits entered is a value between zero and 100.

3. Double-click the **one-line text box** form field you just added to select it and open the Text Box Properties dialog box.

4. Type **Visits** in the Name text box, and then select **20** (or the current value) in the Width in characters text box and type **3** to limit the user to entering three characters so the maximum number of visits that can be displayed in the text box is 999.

After you have specified or changed a form field's properties, you begin the validation process by clicking the Validate button to open that dialog box. If the Validate button is dimmed, then that form field cannot be validated. Continue specifying the properties for the Visits text box by specifying that the field can accept only integers of zero to 100.

To validate a one-line text box form field:

1. Click the **Validate** button in Text Box Properties dialog box to open the Text Box Validation dialog box.

2. Click the **Data Type** list arrow, and then click **Integer** to specify that data type. Notice that you can validate numbers or text, as well.

3. In the Numeric Format section, click the **None** option button in the Grouping category.

4. In the Data Length section, click the **Required** check box to select it, click in the Min Length text box and type **1**; and then press the **Tab** key to advance to the Max Length text box and type **3**. You specified 1 as the minimum number of characters and 3 as the maximum number of characters that a user can enter in the field.

5. In the Data Value section, click the **Field Must Be** check box to select it, click the **Field Must Be** list arrow, click **Greater than or equal to**, and then click in the corresponding Value text box and type **0** (the number zero, and not the capital letter "O") to establish the minimum value for the number of visits.

6. In the Data Value section, click the **And Must Be** check box to select it, click the **And Must Be** list arrow, click **Less than or equal to**, click in the corresponding Value text box, and then type **100** to set the maximum value for the upper limit. Your completed Text Box Validation dialog box should match Figure 6-20.

Figure 6-20 ◀
Completed Text
Box Validation
dialog box

selected data type

selected text box
form field

requires user to
enter data

criteria for validating
data value

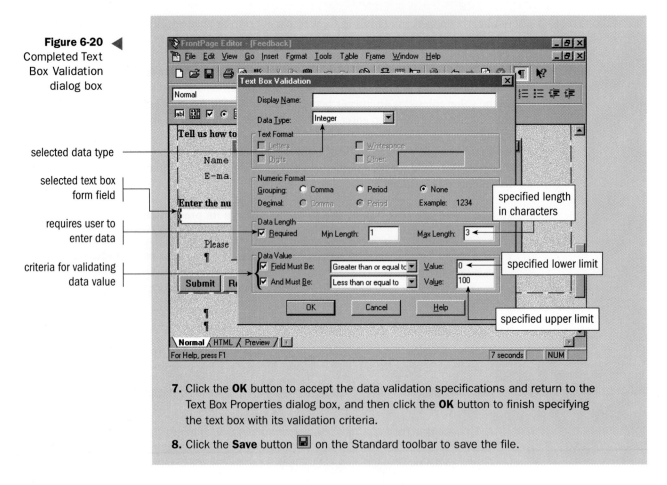

7. Click the **OK** button to accept the data validation specifications and return to the Text Box Properties dialog box, and then click the **OK** button to finish specifying the text box with its validation criteria.

8. Click the **Save** button 🖫 on the Standard toolbar to save the file.

The one-line text box for entering a numeric value that is validated is complete. Now a user can enter only an acceptable integer value between the minimum of zero and the maximum of 100. Next, Amanda wants you to add a form field that will enable Sunny Morning Products to respond to user requests.

Adding Check Boxes

You use check boxes to present a list of items, one or more of which the user can select to pick any number of items from a list. Unlike a radio button, selecting one check box does not deselect another check box. You can set the properties of each check box so it is selected or not selected when a user first accesses a form.

When you create check boxes on a form, keep in mind the following design suggestions:

- Use check boxes when you want a user to select from a series of one or more independent and nonexclusive choices.

- Set the default selection to the most frequently occurring selection.

- Label each check box.

Next, you add a check box to the feedback form that allows the user to request a response from someone at Sunny Morning Products.

To add a check box to a form:

1. Click anywhere on the "Please contact me as soon as possible regarding this matter." text, and then press the **Home** key to place the insertion point at the beginning of this text, which is where you want the check box to appear.

2. Click the **Check Box** button ☑ on the Forms toolbar to insert this form field on the form.

Now that you've added the check box to the form, you can change its default property values so the name and value of this form field are recognized easily when reviewing the user's response.

To specify the properties for the check box:

1. Double-click the **check box** form field you just added to select it and open the Check Box Properties dialog box.

2. Type **ContactMe** in the Name text box, select the current text in the Value text box, and then type **Yes**. Notice that in the Initial State section, the Not checked option button is selected, indicating that this check box will not be checked when the Feedback Web page first opens in the Web browser. Your completed Check Box Properties dialog box should match Figure 6-21.

Figure 6-21 ◀
Completed
Check Box
Properties
dialog box

indicates value to
store in results file for
checked state

selected check box
form field

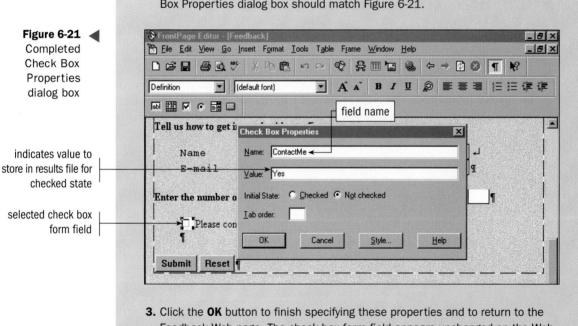

3. Click the **OK** button to finish specifying these properties and to return to the Feedback Web page. The check box form field appears unchanged on the Web page because changing the Name and Value properties has no effect on this field's appearance in FrontPage Editor or in the Web browser, although it does affect how the data are stored on the server ultimately.

You finished adding all of the form fields that collect input data from the user. To complete the development of this form, you need to supply the user with a way of sending this data to the server for processing.

Adding Push Buttons

Push buttons, or **command buttons,** allow users to submit or reset a form. When a user submits a form, its data is passed to the Web server for processing by a form handler. You will learn more about form handlers in the next section.

There are three types of push buttons—each type implements a different processing action. You use a **submit push button** to submit a form to the server for processing. A **reset push button** clears any previously entered data from the form, whereas a **normal push button** creates a push button that initiates the execution of a user-defined script (which is an advanced feature of a Web page that is beyond the scope of this tutorial). Submit and reset are the two most common push buttons used with Web forms. Initially, when you add a push button to a form, the button automatically is assigned the default name of "Submit," regardless of the type of push button you added. You must change the properties of the button to assign it the name you prefer.

When you create a new form on a Web page, FrontPage adds two push button fields to the form automatically when you place the first form field on the Web page and create the form. One of the automatically created push buttons is labeled "Submit," and the other is labeled "Reset." The submit push button automatically is associated with the FrontPage default form handler that processes the submitted form results on the Web server. Because these two buttons are automatically placed on the form, all you need to do is to edit their settings to make any required changes from the defaults set by FrontPage.

Next, Amanda wants you to edit the submit and reset push buttons on the Feedback Web page. The submit push button is used to send the form to the server for processing, whereas the reset push button is used to clear input values from all of the form fields. You begin by editing the submit push button to rename it as the "Submit Comments" push button.

To change the properties of a submit button:

1. Double-click the **Submit** push button that is included on the form to select it and open the Push Button Properties dialog box.

2. Type **Submit** in the Name text box, select the current text in the Value/Label text box, and then type **Submit Comments**. Notice in the Button type section that the Submit option button is selected as the default, which indicates the action of this button is to perform a submission of the form's data to the Web server. Your completed Push Button Properties dialog box should match Figure 6-22.

Figure 6-22 ◀
Completed Push
Button
Properties
dialog box

indicates submit
push button type

selected push button
on form

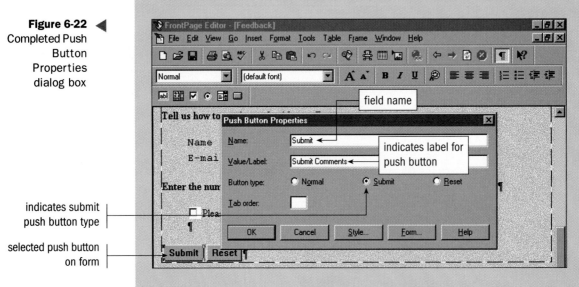

3. Click the **OK** button to finish specifying the properties for this form field and return to FrontPage Editor with the revised value of "Submit Comments" displayed as the title for this push button.

Now you can edit the second push button—the reset push button—on the form that is used to clear the data previously entered in each of the fields. Amanda wants this push button to be titled "Clear Form."

To change the properties of a reset push button:

1. Double-click the **Reset** push button that is included on the form to select it and open the Push Button Properties dialog box.

2. Type **Clear** in the Name text box, select **Reset** in the Value/Label text box, and then type **Clear Form** to name the reset push button.

3. In the Button type section, verify that the **Reset** option button is selected to specify that the action of this button is to reset the values in each form field to those displayed when the Feedback Web page first opens in the browser.

4. Click the **OK** button to finish specifying the properties for this form button. The Push Button Properties dialog box closes, and the reset push button now appears with the title "Clear Form" on the Feedback Web page.

5. Click the **Save** button 🔳 on the Standard toolbar.

You have finished placing all the form fields that collect user input data on the form and you provided a means for the user to submit this data. When the user submits this data to the server, however, the server needs to know how to handle it. Next, you will specify the type of processing the server needs to complete when it receives the user's data from the form on the Feedback Web page.

Using a Form Handler

A **form handler** is a program on a Web server that communicates between the server and the user in order to carry out the activities involved in processing data received from a form. **Form handlers,** or simply **handlers,** process the information from a form that a user submits to the Web server, including returning messages to the user. **FrontPage form handlers** are programs that distinguish a FrontPage Web from other Webs on a server. They are the part of the FrontPage program that implements interactive or dynamic Web pages. Figure 6-23 describes the four types of form handlers available in FrontPage.

Figure 6-23 ◀
FrontPage form
handlers

Form Handler	Description
Custom ISAPI, NSAPI, CGI, or ASP Scripts	Programs or scripts created by a Web site developer for specialized processing of form data on the Web server.
Discussion Form Handler	Gathers information from a form, formats it into an HTML page, stores the page on the Web server, and adds the page to a table of contents and a text index.
Registration Form Handler	Allows users to register for a service offered at the Web server site by adding a user and password to a list of users with permission to access a FrontPage Web.
Save Results Form Handler	Collects information from a user and stores it in one of several available formats for further processing or sends the results to an e-mail address.

FrontPage form handlers are installed with the FrontPage Extensions that reside on the Web server. You specify a FrontPage form handler by assigning a specific form handler in the Form Properties dialog box. Each of the five form handlers has a unique dialog box that is used to specify the distinct parameters for that form handler.

The **Save Results Form Handler**, also known in FrontPage as the **WebBot Save Results Component**, is a general data-collecting form handler that includes a user input form that is used to obtain data from a Web page and store the data values in a desired format in a file on the Web server. You have the option of sending the results to an e-mail address or storing them in a file on the server. This server-processing support is what distinguishes FrontPage from other Web development tools. As the results from a form are stored on the server, they are kept in one of several different formats that you can specify as a setting for the Save Results Form Handler. The two most popular methods of storing form information submitted to the server are either as a text file with one line for each form that was submitted to the server *or* as an HTML file with a line for each field name and value pair. In the text file method, the first entry or row in the table contains the names of the fields from which the data is obtained, whereas with the HTML file method, the field name is included as a field name/data value pair and the name is repeated with the data from each user submission. In the HTML file, the results of each submission are appended to the bottom of the previous HTML page.

In addition to storing the results in a file on the Web server, you can send the results to an e-mail address. In order to send e-mail from a Web server on which the form resides, the FrontPage Server Extensions must be configured to deliver the e-mail to e-mail transport. (This configuration is separate from installing FrontPage and is beyond the scope of this book.) You can check with your instructor or technical support person to determine if your FrontPage installation is enabled for e-mail for forms.

When you configure the Save Results Form Handler, you specify the format of your results file. Using a text file, you can collect several other pieces of data, such as the current date and Internet Protocol (IP) address of the user, in addition to the form fields you specified on the Web page. A text file of the results is stored in the _private folder of your FrontPage Web. Files in this folder are *not* available to users accessing your Web site using an Internet connection. However, if you are using the server computer where the Web is stored, you can access the file as long as you are an authorized computer user. However, it is important to remember that an HTML file is included with your other HTML files, which any user with Web privileges can access.

Recall that Andrew wants to collect information from Sunny Morning Products Web site users. This information is stored on the Sunny Morning Products' Web server computers. Amanda wants you to use the default Save Results Form Handler that will perform the server-side processing of the form data submitted by the user from the Feedback Web page.

To configure the Save Results Form Handler:

1. Right-click anywhere in the form area to display the Shortcut menu, and then click **Form Properties** to open the Form Properties dialog box. See Figure 6-24.

Figure 6-24
Form Properties
dialog box

selects FrontPage
Save Results Form
Handler

leave blank for
FrontPage default
confirmation page

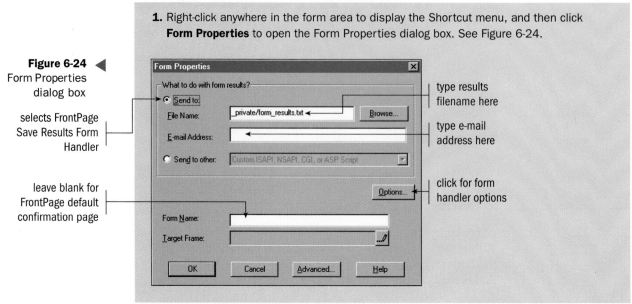

type results
filename here

type e-mail
address here

click for form
handler options

2. In the What to do with form results? section, verify that the **Send to** option button is selected. In the File Name text box, select the current value, and then type **_private/feedback.txt** as the filename. This is the folder and file where the results will be stored on the server within the Sunny Morning Web.

3. Type your e-mail address in the E-mail Address text box.

4. Click the **Options** button to open the Options for Saving Results of Form dialog box. See Figure 6-25. In the File Format list box, verify that **Text database using comma as separator** is the selected value.

> **TROUBLE?** If Text database using comma as separator is not selected as the File Format, then click the File Format list arrow and click Text database using comma as separator to select it.

Figure 6-25 ◀
File Results settings in the Options for Saving Results of Form dialog box

verify box checked for name-value pairs in results file

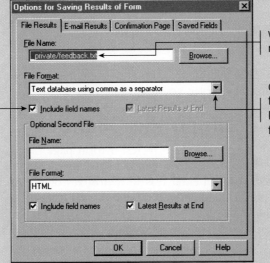

verify filename for results file

click to select format for results file from list of available formats

5. Click the **Saved Fields** tab to display those settings. See Figure 6-26. In the Additional information to save section, click the **Remote computer name** check box to select it, which will cause the user's IP address to be included in the data stored in the text database file with a field name of "Remote Name." Note that the Form Fields to Save text box displays a list of all the form fields on your feedback form and that these fields will be saved to the results file.

Figure 6-26 ◀
Saved Fields settings in the Options for Saving Results of Form dialog box

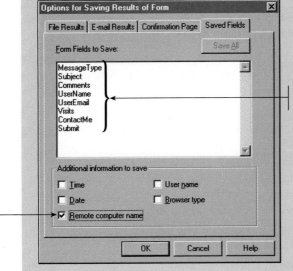

list of form fields for saving results to file

click to store IP address of remote computer in results file

6. Click the **OK** button to return to the Form Properties dialog box, and then verify that the Form Name text box contains no value for the confirmation page. When there is no Form Name, FrontPage automatically generates a default confirmation page, which is the action you want.

   TROUBLE? If a value appears in the Form Name text box, then select it and press the Delete key to remove it.

7. Click the **OK** button to finish specifying the form handler. A FrontPage Editor message box opens and displays a message indicating that the FrontPage Server Extensions have not been configured for e-mail. This message displays because the form is created on the client without a server available to check for the e-mail transport.

8. Click the **No** button to retain the e-mail address for use with the form on the server.

9. Click the **Save** button 🖫 on the Standard toolbar.

Now that you identified the form handler, including specifying the file where you want the results stored on the server, you need to test the form.

Testing a Form on the Client

Unlike other Web pages, you need to test a form page on the client *and* on the server. When testing the form on a client, you need to test each of the form fields for entering data. For example, you can enter text in text boxes or use drop-down menus to ensure they display the choices you entered. Also, you can clear all the data from the form and then re-enter it. However, any form fields that use data validation, such as the number of visits field, require access to a server to enable this verification and cannot be tested until you submit the form to a server for processing.

At this point in the development of the feedback form, Amanda wants you to test the form only on the client. Your test of the form will include reviewing the layout of data on the form and testing the operation of the form fields you added. You will finish testing the form later in the next session when you place the Web on a server.

To test a form on the client using Internet Explorer:

1. Click the **Preview in Browser** button 🔍 on the Standard toolbar to switch to Internet Explorer and open the Feedback Web page in the browser window. If necessary, maximize the window. The text **"[FrontPage Save Results Component]"** appears on the Web page because the e-mail transport could not be verified on the server with a disk-based Web.

   TROUBLE? If the FrontPage Editor message box displays a message indicating that the page contains elements that need to be saved or published to preview correctly, then click the OK button.

2. Scroll down the page until you see the form fields, and then click the **Praise** option button in the What kind of comment would you like to send? section to select it.

3. Click the **What about us do you want to comment on?** list arrow, and then click **Products**.

4. Click in the Enter your comments in the space provided below: text box, and then type **Your Olympic Gold sports drink is great stuff**.

5. Click in the Name text box, type your **first** and **last name**, (type a space in between names), press the **Tab** key to advance to the E-mail text box, and then type your e-mail address.

6. Click in the Enter the number of times you have visited our Sunshine County Store: text box, and then type **200**.

7. Click the **Please contact me as soon as possible regarding this matter** check box to select it and complete the data entry on this form.

8. Click the **Submit Comments** push button to confirm your form has a submit button rather than a reset button. The FrontPage Run-Time Component Page opens in the browser to advise you that a Web server is required for the page to function correctly. You will do that later in this tutorial.

9. Click the **Back** button ⬜ on the Internet Explorer toolbar to return to the Feedback Web page, and then click the **Clear Form** push button. The data you previously entered disappears from the form because this is a client action that does not require a server. Your test of the form using only the Web browser on the client is successful.

Although the browser on the client performs data validation, a server is required to generate any error messages. Now that your client testing is complete, you are ready to view the HTML code used by FrontPage to implement the form fields on the Feedback Web page.

Viewing HTML Code for a Form

Several HTML tags are used to compile the HTML code for a form, including special FrontPage codes to implement the server-side form processing. For example, all the form fields are nested within the FORM tag that specifies the beginning and end of the form on the Web page. The POST value for the method property specifies that the form information submitted is to be processed by or posted to the server. The WEBBOT-SELF value of the action property specifies that the POST is performed using one of the FrontPage WebBots, with the WEBBOT tag specifying the parameters for the server processing that includes the Save Results Form Handler. Each of the form field objects is implemented with the INPUT tag, except the drop-down menu, which is implemented with the SELECT tag. The different field types are distinguished by the type property within each INPUT tag. Amanda asks you to view the HTML code for the feedback form.

To view the HTML code for the Feedback Web page:

1. Click the **FrontPage Editor** program button on the taskbar to switch to that program.

2. Click the **HTML** tab to switch to that Editor view and display the HTML code for the Feedback page.

3. Scroll the page until the <FORM> tag appears in the upper-left corner of the window. See Figure 6-27. Notice the use of the <FORM>, <!--WEBBOT>, <INPUT>, and <SELECT> tags.

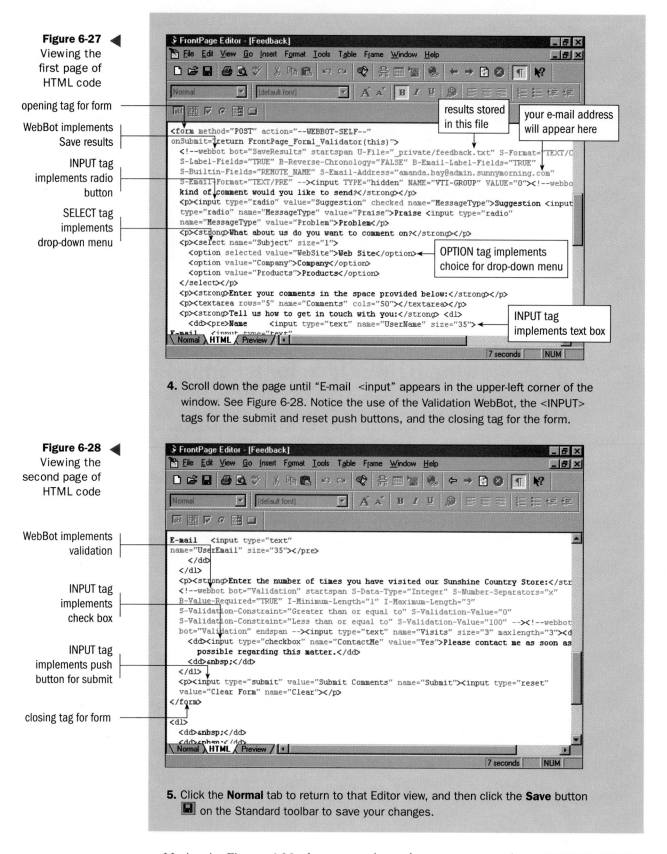

Figure 6-27
Viewing the first page of HTML code

opening tag for form

WebBot implements Save results

INPUT tag implements radio button

SELECT tag implements drop-down menu

results stored in this file

your e-mail address will appear here

OPTION tag implements choice for drop-down menu

INPUT tag implements text box

4. Scroll down the page until "E-mail <input" appears in the upper-left corner of the window. See Figure 6-28. Notice the use of the Validation WebBot, the <INPUT> tags for the submit and reset push buttons, and the closing tag for the form.

Figure 6-28
Viewing the second page of HTML code

WebBot implements validation

INPUT tag implements check box

INPUT tag implements push button for submit

closing tag for form

5. Click the **Normal** tab to return to that Editor view, and then click the **Save** button on the Standard toolbar to save your changes.

Notice in Figure 6-28 that a number of parameters, such as S-VALIDATION-CONSTRAINT and S-VALIDATION-VALUE, are included to ensure the correct implementation of the WebBot. These parameters provide the necessary data for the WebBot to carry out the desired processing on the Web server.

Quick Check

1. True or False: Variation is the process of performing a check or data edit to verify that information a user enters in a form field is in the correct format.

2. True or False: Selecting the Field Must Be and the Greater than or equal option in the Data Value section of the Text Box Validation dialog box establishes a minimum value that the user must enter.

3. A(n) _____ is a form field that can include an unlimited number of independent and nonexclusive choices.

4. What is the default action of a push button form field?

5. True or False: The reset action of a push button form field removes all user-entered data and displays the same values as when the Web page first opened in the browser window.

6. True or False: A form handler is a program on a Web server that is used to carry out the activities involved in processing data received from a form.

7. The _____ Form Handler is used to obtain data from an input form and store it in a named file on a server.

8. True or False: Creating a results file in the _private folder permits access to the file by any user accessing the Web site using an Internet connection.

Your form is taking shape. The final task is to publish the Web to a server and make sure that the server processes requests correctly. You will publish the Web as your last task in Amanda's training course.

SESSION 6.3

In this session you will use a personal Web server to access Web pages stored on a Web server. You will publish a disk-based Web to a server-based Web, process forms using a server, and examine results stored on the server. Finally, you will create a hit counter, include a banner ad, recalculate and verify hyperlinks, and then set the permissions necessary for accessing a Web.

Using a Personal Web Server

To function as a Web server, a computer connected to the WWW requires a Web server program, which is special software that works with the computer's operating system to receive and carry out requests for Web pages. In this tutorial, you will be using the **Microsoft Personal Web Server**, or **PWS**, that is included on the same CD-ROM as your FrontPage program and usually is installed when the FrontPage Explorer, FrontPage Editor, and Internet Explorer programs are loaded on your computer. Keep in mind that your installation could use a different Web server, such as the Microsoft FrontPage Personal Web Server or the Microsoft Internet Information Server. You usually can tell if the Microsoft Personal Web Server is running on your computer by the Web server icon 🖥 that displays on the Windows taskbar. However, you might have the Microsoft Personal Web Server but its icon on the taskbar might be turned off. Whether the Web server runs when Windows 95 starts is an optional property as well. The default for both of these properties is to display the icon and run the Web server when Windows 95 starts. If the Microsoft FrontPage Personal Web Server is installed on your computer, the FrontPage PWS might be included in the Windows Start folder; in this case, it would start automatically, or you might be able to start it manually using a Programs menu item or a desktop icon. The 🖥 vhttpd32.exe icon is used with the FrontPage PWS.

When you want to access a local Web server, such as PWS, you do not need to use the "www" prefix or the server type suffix in the URL; you use the computer name or the FrontPage default name of **localhost**. The primary use of a local Web server is in the development and testing of the server-side processing for your Web. Recall that a local Web server is located on the same computer as the browser. For example, you might use either localhost, mypc, or 141.209.51.60 as the URL with a default name, your computer name, or an IP address, respectively. You can use the "http://" protocol identifier because you are using the hypertext protocol, but its use is optional. Because the specification in using a PWS varies from computer to computer, it is important to work with your instructor or technical support person to determine the correct configuration for your computer. Your instructor will advise you of any differences that you might encounter as you complete the steps in this session, as well.

Figure 6-29 illustrates the differences between using a disk-based Web and a server-based Web with your Web pages. With a disk-based Web, the Web browser opens each Web page by obtaining it directly from the file stored on your disk. With a server-based Web, the Web browser uses the TCP/IP network software to send the request for a Web page to the server. The server then obtains a copy of the file stored on your disk and sends it back to the browser by way of the TCP/IP network connection, where it is opened in the browser window. Thus, with a local Web server, the same TCP/IP network software utilizing the same network processing is used to obtain the requested files as if you were connecting to another WWW server.

Figure 6-29 ◀
Comparison of file transfers for disk-based versus server-based Webs

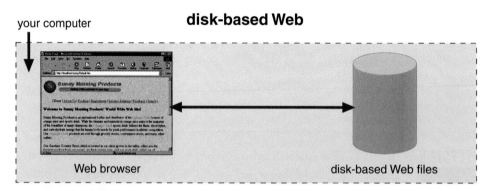

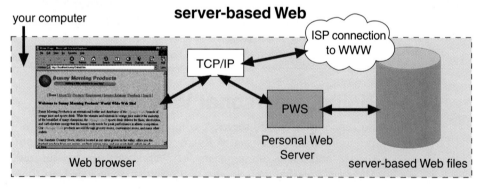

The technical support person at Sunny Morning Products installed the Microsoft PWS on Amanda's computer. The name of this computer is mypc (your computer name might be different). Next, Amanda asks you to test this PWS to make sure it is installed and operating correctly and that you can access it using your Web browser.

To test the PWS installation:

1. If you are using a URL that is different than the FrontPage default of localhost, check with your instructor or technical support person to determine the appropriate name or IP address of your computer.

2. Click the **Internet Explorer** program button on the taskbar to switch to that program.

> **TROUBLE?** If the Internet Explorer program button does not appear on the taskbar, then start Internet Explorer.

3. If necessary, click in the Address box, type **localhost** or the name provided by your instructor as the URL, and then press the **Enter** key. The Home Page for the root Web on your computer's server or the default Home Page that installs with the PWS (see Figure 6-30) opens in Internet Explorer, which confirms that the PWS or another Web server is installed and available.

Figure 6-30 ◀
Default PWS
Home Page

URL for PWS
(your URL might
be different)

default template
Home Page for PWS
(your page might
look different)

indicates local server

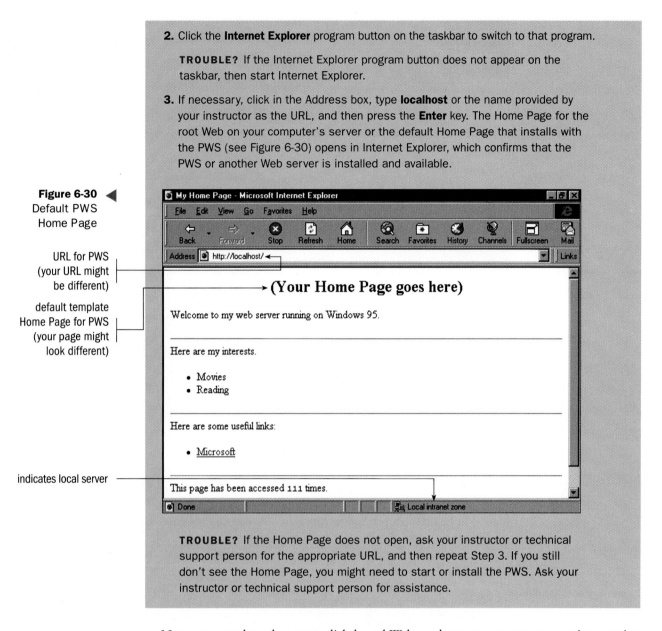

> **TROUBLE?** If the Home Page does not open, ask your instructor or technical support person for the appropriate URL, and then repeat Step 3. If you still don't see the Home Page, you might need to start or install the PWS. Ask your instructor or technical support person for assistance.

Next, you need to place your disk-based Web on the server so you can continue testing the feedback form on the Feedback Web page.

Publishing a Web

You **publish** a Web by copying the Web files to your server. A server-based Web usually is located on the same drive as the FrontPage program, but it must have a unique Web name. If you are using a shared computer, you need to make sure a conflict won't exist between the Web name you will publish to and those Webs that previously were published to your server.

The default installation of the PWS creates the webshare folder at the root level on your computer's disk drive where the PWS program is installed. If you are using the FrontPage PWS, this folder is called the FrontPage Webs folder. Within the webshare folder, the wwwroot folder (the content folder for the FrontPage PWS) is created and becomes the location of the root Web. Any other Webs that are created and published to this Web server appear as folders under the wwwroot folder (or the content folder). If you have a custom installation of PWS, the names of these folders might be different—you will need to know how your computer is organized before publishing your Web. Each Web folder contains the special FrontPage Server Extension folders and files.

PUBLISHING A WEB TO YOUR COMPUTER'S SERVER

- Make sure FrontPage Explorer is your active program and that the Web is open in Explorer.
- Click the Publish button on the FrontPage Explorer toolbar to publish the Web to your computer with the same Web name.

You can publish the active Web to your computer's server and give it the same name using the Publish button on the Standard toolbar. However, to publish the active Web to any WWW server or to change its name on your computer's server or on another server, you need to publish the Web using the Publish FrontPage Web command on the File menu.

PUBLISHING A WEB TO ANY SERVER

- Make sure FrontPage Explorer is your active program and that the Web is open in Explorer.
- Click File on the menu bar, and then click Publish FrontPage Web to open the Publish dialog box.
- Click the More Webs button to open the Publish FrontPage Web dialog box, and then type or edit the location and name of the FrontPage Web.
- Click the OK button to return to the Publish dialog box, and then click the OK button to publish the Web.

When you publish a Web to the PWS, it is placed in a folder with the Web's name within the wwwroot folder. If the Web you are publishing already exists, you can replace the Web pages. Amanda wants you to publish the sunny Web to the PWS, which will copy your disk-based Web for Sunny Morning Products to a server-based Web. Although you could do this using the Publish button, she asks you to use the Publish FrontPage Web command on the File menu so you can gain experience publishing to any server, and not just to the server on your computer.

To publish a Web to another Web server:

1. Click the **FrontPage Explorer** program button on the taskbar to switch to this program.

   TROUBLE? If the Sunny Morning Web (a:\wwwroot\sunny) on your Student Disk is not the open Web, then open that Web in FrontPage Explorer and continue with Step 2.

2. Click **File** on the menu bar, click **Publish FrontPage Web** to open the Publish dialog box, click the **Published changed pages only** check box to deselect it, and then click the **More Webs** button to open the Publish FrontPage Web dialog box. See Figure 6-31. Notice that "copy_of_sunny" appears in the text box for specifying the location for publishing the Web. FrontPage assigns this name automatically using the name of your open disk-based Web.

Figure 6-31
Publish
FrontPage Web
dialog box

current Web location
is the same as that
of your disk-based
Web with prefix
of "copy_of_"

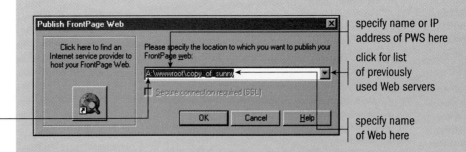

specify name or IP
address of PWS here

click for list
of previously
used Web servers

specify name
of Web here

TROUBLE? If the Publish dialog box opens but the Publish FrontPage Web dialog box opens automatically on top of the Publish dialog box, then continue with Step 3.

3. Click the **location** list arrow to display a list of known, previously used locations, click **localhost** as the name of your destination computer, and then edit the Web name by changing "copy_of_sunny" to **sunny**.

TROUBLE? If localhost or the name of your computer does not appear in the list, click the text box to close the list, select the current value in the text box, and then type either localhost or the name of your computer, followed by /sunny.

TROUBLE? If you are connected to a network server and your computer's name contains a period, then use the IP address and not the computer's name.

4. Click the **OK** button to begin publishing the Web. Several messages including "Listing pages in...," "Publishing pages: xx% completed..." and "Processing web updates ..." appear in the status bar as the Web is published to the server. The status bar displays the message "Published to http://localhost/sunny" (or a similar message with your computer's name) when the publish processing is completed and the Web has been copied successfully. Be patient—it might take several minutes to finish publishing the Web.

TROUBLE? If you click the OK button and return to the Publish dialog box, verify that http://localhost/sunny appears below the text box as the specified destination Web, and then click the OK button.

TROUBLE? If the Publishing FrontPage Components message box opens with a list of the Web pages that contain components that require a Web server for processing, then click the Continue button.

When your Web is published to the PWS, FrontPage automatically changes the filename of your home page from index.htm to default.htm. Recall that index.htm was the default name selected by FrontPage when you created your FrontPage Web. Any references to the index.htm page within the pages of the Web also are changed automatically to this filename. If you subsequently publish the Web from the server back to your Student Disk, then the filename is changed back to index.htm. You can use the Publish FrontPage Web command to make a backup copy of a Web to your server. When you use this command, all of the FrontPage Extensions and special files for the Web are copied to your disk. You make a backup copy of a Web from your computer's hard drive by opening that Web and then publishing it to a disk.

Now that you have published the sunny Web to your computer, you can open it.

To open a server-based Web:

1. Click the **Open FrontPage Web** button 🖼 on the FrontPage Explorer toolbar to open the Getting Started dialog box, click the **More Webs** button to open the Open FrontPage Web dialog box, click the **Select a Web server or disk location** list arrow, and then click **localhost** or the name of your computer to select it.

   TROUBLE? If you are referencing your computer's IP address rather than its name, type your computer's IP address in the Select a Web server or disk location text box. If your computer's name does not appear in the list, check with your instructor or technical support person and then type the appropriate name in the text box.

2. Click the **List Webs** button to display a list of available Webs in the FrontPage Webs found at location box, and then click **sunny** to select that Web.

   TROUBLE? If you are using a shared computer, make sure to select the name of the Web that you published to the server, and not sunny.

3. Click the **OK** button. After a few seconds, the sunny Web opens in FrontPage Explorer in Folders view.

You can perform the same activities using this server-based Web as you did with the disk-based Web. For example, you can select the hyperlinks in FrontPage Explorer to open any other Web pages. The main difference is that the server obtains any file you open, rather than opening an HTML file from your Student Disk. You would notice this difference in the FrontPage Explorer title bar because it displays the URL of the currently open Web.

Processing Forms on the Server

When a form is processed on the server, the user usually receives a confirmation page. A **confirmation page** contains a copy of the data that the user entered for verification purposes. This Web page can be a default confirmation page generated entirely by the FrontPage Web server or a custom page designed by the developer. With FrontPage, a custom confirmation page is developed using the Confirmation Field WebBot Component; a separate WebBot is used for each confirmed field. (Developing a custom confirmation page is beyond the scope of this tutorial.)

Amanda wants you to test the processing of the forms you created for both the Search and Feedback Web pages using the server to make sure these pages process correctly. Before testing these new pages, however, you need to create the hyperlinks from the Home Page to the new pages. You will do this first, and then you will test the processing of the Search page.

To create the hyperlinks to the Search and Feedback Web pages:

1. Click the **FrontPage Editor** program button on the taskbar to switch to that program.

2. Open the Home Page, which is now default.htm, from the sunny (local) Web that you just published to localhost.

   TROUBLE? If you don't see default.htm in the Open dialog box, then you are not looking for the Home Page in the published Web. Make sure that you are looking in your server-based Web for the file, and then repeat Step 2.

3. Select **Search** in the navigation bar on the Home Page, click the **Create or Edit Hyperlink** button 🖼 on the Standard toolbar, click the **Search.htm** page, and then click the **OK** button.

4. Repeat Step 3 to create a hyperlink from the Feedback link in the navigation bar to the Feedback.htm page in the Web.

5. Save your changes.

Now you can test the processing of the Search and Feedback Web pages.

To process Web page forms on a server using Internet Explorer:

1. Click the **Internet Explorer** program button on the taskbar to switch to that program.

2. If necessary, click in the Address box and type **localhost** or the name of your computer, followed by **/sunny/** (for example, localhost/sunny/), and then press the **Enter** key. The Sunny Morning Products Home Page opens in Internet Explorer. If necessary, refresh the page to see your changes.

3. Click the **Search** hyperlink on the navigation bar to open that Web page, scroll down the page until you see the Search for, Start Search, and Clear form fields, type **MIS** in the Search for text box, and then click the **Start Search** push button. After a few seconds, the search is completed, as indicated by the new URL in the Address box that identifies the page created by the server.

   TROUBLE? If the Security Alert dialog box opens, click the Yes button.

4. Scroll down the Search page until the Search for text box is at the top of the page. See Figure 6-32. This is the revised version of the Search page—the confirmation page—that the Web server generated that contains a list of pages with a matching text string. Every page returned in the list is a hyperlink that allows you to link to that page.

Figure 6-32 ◄
Confirmation page from search performed by Web server

search text string

number of matches found

document with matching text string obtained from search

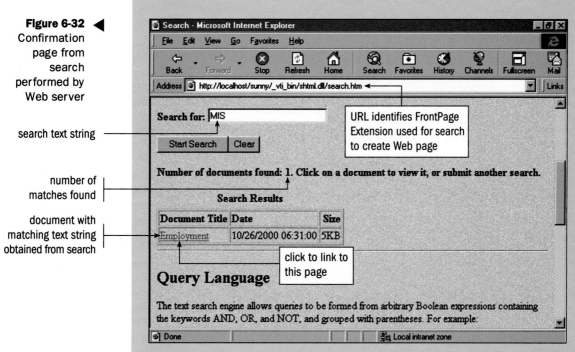

5. Click the **Back** button on the Internet Explorer toolbar to return to the Search page, and then click again to return to the Home Page. Your test of the search form is successful, so now you can test the feedback form.

6. Click the **Feedback** hyperlink on the navigation bar to open that page, and then enter the same data in this form that you used in Steps 2 through 7 in the Steps entitled "To test a form on the client using Internet Explorer" from Session 6.2 in this tutorial.

7. Click the **Submit Comments** push button. The form validation error message box opens to indicate that this data does not meet the validation condition. See Figure 6-33.

Figure 6-33 ◀
Form validation
error message
box

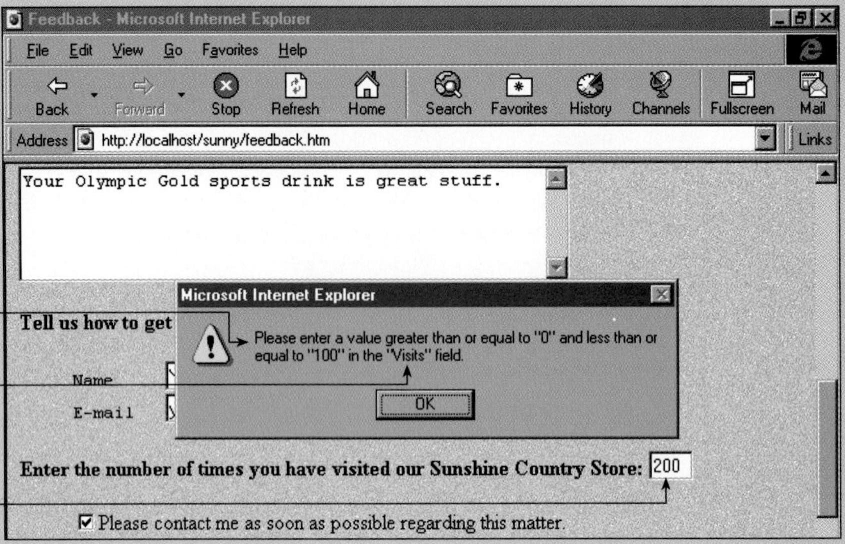

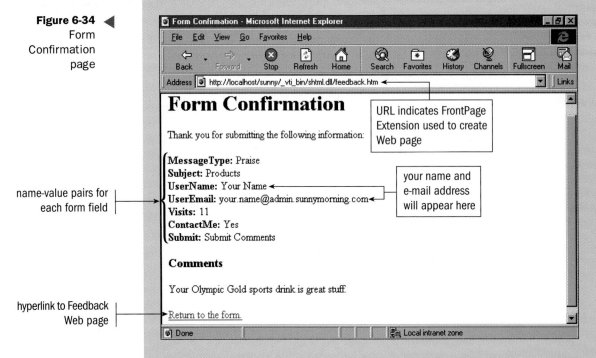

description of error

name of field
with error

value exceeds
limit for field

8. Click the **OK** button, type **11** in the visits text box, and then click the **Submit Comments** push button. It will take a few minutes for the server to process the form data. The Form Confirmation page opens with a copy of the data you entered on the form. See Figure 6-34.

Figure 6-34 ◀
Form
Confirmation
page

name-value pairs for
each form field

hyperlink to Feedback
Web page

TROUBLE? If the Security Alert message box opens, click the Yes button.

TROUBLE? If you see a blank form instead of the Form Confirmation page shown in Figure 6-34, then you probably entered a form name in the Form Name text box in the Form Properties dialog box. Return to the steps entitled "To configure the Save Results Form Handler" and clear any value in the Form Name text box, save your changes, and then repeat Steps 1-8.

TROUBLE? If a FrontPage Error page displays, then your computer and/or Web server are not configured to process sending e-mail from the form. Check with your instructor or technical support person concerning the implementation of this feature in FrontPage. After this feature is enabled, repeat Steps 6 through 8 and send the results to an e-mail address. Or, click the FrontPage Explorer program button on the taskbar, double-click feedback.htm to open that page in FrontPage Editor, right-click the form area to display the Shortcut menu, click Form Properties, select the E-mail Address value, press the Delete key, select the Form Name value, press the Delete key, click the OK button, click the Save button, click the Preview in Browser button, and then click the Refresh button. Now, repeat Steps 6 through 8 without sending the results to an e-mail address.

9. Click the **Return to the form** hyperlink to re-open the Feedback Web page in the Internet Explorer window. Your test of forms processing is complete.

When the confirmation page opened in the browser window after you submitted the form, the form's results were written to a text file for later use. For example, you could use the data collected from the feedback form in a spreadsheet program or with a special purpose program, such as one written using Visual Basic, to summarize and report this information. For example, you might select the "problem" information as a separate report to discuss with your manager.

Examining Stored Results

The data gathered from the feedback form was stored in a text file on the server because this arrangement was specified for the form's properties. Recall that when you store data in a text file, the name of each form field on your form appears in the first line of the file and each set of values for the form occupies a separate line or record in the file. When the first form results are stored to the file, the line containing the form field names is placed in the file. For subsequent storage of file data, only the results—not the form field names—are written to the file. Because the data from each additional form submission is appended to the bottom of the file, the last set of results submitted to the server is listed at the bottom of the file. Unless you submitted your form more than once, the results file that you specified for the Save Results Component WebBot only contains two lines—the field names and the result of one submission. You can examine the contents of the results file at any time on the server computer. Amanda asks you to review this file to increase your understanding of how the data submitted to the server are stored.

To examine stored results:

1. With the Feedback Web page still open in your window, click the **Start** button on the taskbar, point to **Programs**, point to **Accessories**, and then click **Notepad** to start the Notepad program. An untitled Notepad document opens in your window.

2. Click **File** on the menu bar, and then click **Open** to open the Open dialog box.

3. Make sure the drive that contains your server-based Web appears in the Look in text box, double-click the **webshare** folder, double-click the **wwwroot** folder, double-click the **sunny** folder (if you used a different Web name, then use that Web name), double-click the **_private** folder, click the **feedback.txt** file, and then click the **Open** button. The c:\webshare\wwwroot\sunny_private\feedback.txt file opens in your Notepad window. If necessary, maximize the window. See Figure 6-35.

Figure 6-35 ◀
Results file on
Web server

field names ———

data values ———

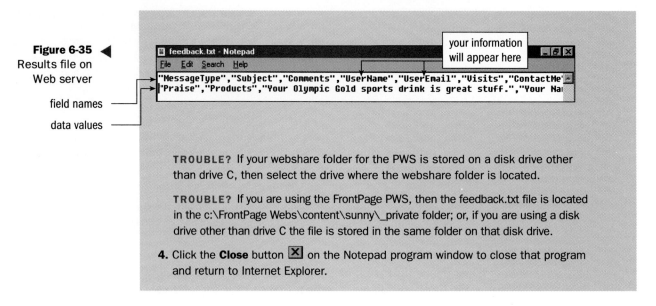

TROUBLE? If your webshare folder for the PWS is stored on a disk drive other than drive C, then select the drive where the webshare folder is located.

TROUBLE? If you are using the FrontPage PWS, then the feedback.txt file is located in the c:\FrontPage Webs\content\sunny_private folder; or, if you are using a disk drive other than drive C the file is stored in the same folder on that disk drive.

4. Click the **Close** button ☒ on the Notepad program window to close that program and return to Internet Explorer.

You verified that the results of the feedback form are stored in the feedback.txt file in the _private folder of the sunny Web. The data in this file is arranged using the name-value pairs that you specified when you created the feedback form.

Using a Hit Counter

A **hit counter** is a FrontPage component that counts the number of visitors to a Web page (usually, the Web's Home Page). Amanda discussed the idea of using a hit counter with Andrew on the Home Page of the Sunny Morning Products Web. Andrew agreed because a hit counter would help the marketing department understand the use of the site.

The hit counter is a FrontPage component that is processed on the Web server and requires a server-based Web for its implementation. Because a hit counter is a built-in FrontPage component, you just need to insert it in the appropriate location on your Web page. With FrontPage, you can set properties for the counter style and reset the counter, if desired. The counter style is a GIF image that contains the digits zero through nine that are used to display the current value of the counter on the Web page. You can use FrontPage to create a custom GIF file with a different style than that provided by FrontPage; however, you need to use a separate graphics program, such as Microsoft Image Composer, to create the GIF file. (Creating a custom hit counter is beyond the scope of this book.)

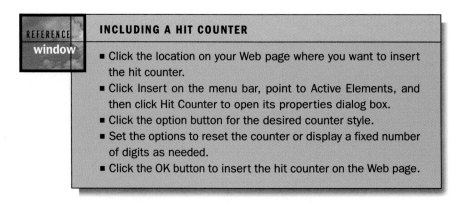

REFERENCE
window

INCLUDING A HIT COUNTER

- Click the location on your Web page where you want to insert the hit counter.
- Click Insert on the menu bar, point to Active Elements, and then click Hit Counter to open its properties dialog box.
- Click the option button for the desired counter style.
- Set the options to reset the counter or display a fixed number of digits as needed.
- Click the OK button to insert the hit counter on the Web page.

Amanda asks you to continue your training and insert a hit counter on the Home Page that starts at 1000 and always displays six digits.

To include a hit counter:

1. Click the **FrontPage Explorer** program button on the taskbar to return to that program, and then double-click default.htm in Folders view to open the Home Page in FrontPage Editor.

   TROUBLE? If Folders view is not displayed in the FrontPage Explorer, click the Folders button 📁 on the Views bar, and then double-click default.htm to open the Home Page in FrontPage Editor.

   With the Home Page open, you are ready to include the hit counter on this page.

2. Press **Ctrl + End** to scroll to the bottom of the Home Page, click the horizontal line to select it, press the **Enter** key to insert a new paragraph, and then click the **Center** button 📑 on the Format toolbar to center this paragraph on the page. This is the location for the hit counter.

3. Type **You are visitor number** as text that precedes the hit counter, and then press the **Spacebar**.

4. Click **Insert** on the menu bar, point to **Active Elements**, and then click **Hit Counter** to open the Hit Counter Properties dialog box. See Figure 6-36.

Figure 6-36 ◀
Hit Counter
Properties
dialog box

click to select this
counter style

click to enable
counter reset

click to enable
size specification

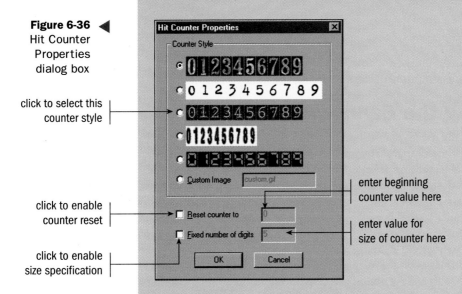

enter beginning
counter value here

enter value for
size of counter here

5. In the Counter Style section, click the option button for the third counter style to select it.

6. Click the **Reset counter to** check box to select it, and then type **1000** in its value text box. Andrew wants to start the counter at this number, rather than at zero.

7. Click the **Fixed number of digits** check box to select it, and then type **6** in its value text box so the counter will display six digits.

8. Click the **OK** button to finish specifying the hit counter and return to the Web page. The placeholder "**[Hit Counter]**" indicates that the hit counter is included on the Web page.

9. Press the **Spacebar**, and then type **to our Web site.** as the rest of the text that accompanies the hit counter.

10. Click the **Save** button 💾 on the Standard toolbar to save your changes.

Now, you are ready to test the hit counter to make sure that it operates correctly. Amanda asks you to do this next.

To test the hit counter:

1. Click the **Preview in Browser** button 🔍 on the Standard toolbar to open the Home Page in your browser, and then click the **Refresh** button 🗘 on the Internet Explorer toolbar to open the revised page in the browser.

2. Press **Ctrl + End** to scroll to the bottom of the Home Page and display the hit counter. You are visitor number 1001.

3. Click 🗘 again, and then scroll to the bottom of the Web page. Now, you are visitor number 1002. Each time the page is opened or refreshed, the hit counter is incremented by one. See Figure 6-37.

Figure 6-37 ◀
Home Page with
hit counter

hit counter with initial
value plus number of
page refreshes

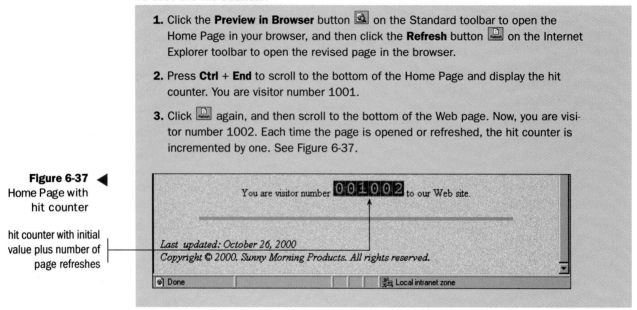

The hit counter provides Andrew with the information he wants on the number of visitors to the Sunny Morning Web. By measuring this Web traffic, he will have a better idea for future commitments to enhancing the Sunny Web site.

Using the Banner Ad Manager

Banner ads are dynamic "billboards" that display a series of images, such as images of products or company slogans. As each new image in the series appears, the Web browser applies a visual transition effect so the transition from one image to the next occurs seamlessly. If desired, you can associate a hyperlink with a banner ad. A banner ad is different from a page banner. The banner ad displays a series of different images, whereas the page banner automatically generates a page heading from the page title. You can use both presentations on the same Web page, and you can include them in a shared border.

The Banner Ad Manager is a Java applet that controls the continuous display of the series of images on the Web page. For the Banner Ad Manager to work correctly, you need to use it with a server-based Web. Although you could create a page on a disk-based Web that includes a banner ad, you would need to use a server-based Web to test it. This is similar to creating and testing a Web search or form.

Before you place a banner ad on your Web, you need to create the GIF image files that you will use in the banner ads. You can use Microsoft Image Composer as an image-editing program to create these images, or you can obtain them from some other source. (Creating images using Image Composer is beyond the scope of this book.)

Andrew wants to use a banner ad to increase the visual impact of the Sunny Morning Products Home Page.

CREATING A BANNER AD

- Click the location where you want to insert the banner ad.
- Click Insert on the menu bar, point to Active Elements, and then click Banner Ad Manager.
- Type the desired values for the Width and Height in pixels.
- In the Transition section, use the list arrow to select the desired effect and enter the time value for each image.
- Click the Add button, select the first image, and then click the Add button and select the rest of the images for the banner.
- Click the OK button to finish specifying the banner ad.

Amanda asks you to replace the current Sunny Morning Products logo on the Home Page with a banner ad. Although you can display a series of several different images, Amanda wants you to use two different images that appear repeatedly.

To include a banner ad:

1. Click the **FrontPage Editor** program button on the taskbar to return to that program and the open Home Page.

2. Scroll to the top of the page, click the **Sunny Morning Products Logo** image to select it, and then press the **Delete** key to remove this image from the Home Page. This is where you will place the banner ad.

3. Click **Insert** on the menu bar, point to **Active Elements**, and then click **Banner Ad Manager** to open that dialog box. See Figure 6-38.

Figure 6-38
Banner Ad Manager dialog box

specifies the size of the image

displays available effects

click to specify images for display

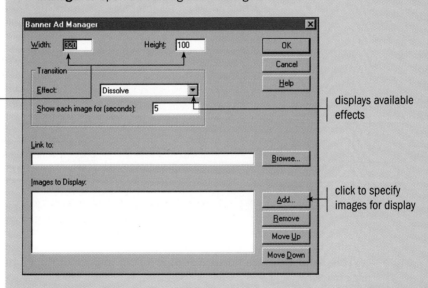

4. Select the current value in the Width text, and type **380.** Then select the current value in the Height text box, and type **65.** You will use the default values for the Transition.

Now, you need to specify the image files for the banner ad.

5. Click the **Add** button to open the Add Image to Banner Ad dialog box, click the **Select a file on your computer** button to open the Select File dialog box, make sure the drive that contains your Student Disk appears in the Look in text box, double-click the **Tutorial.06** folder, and then double-click the **Images** folder.

6. Click the **banner1.gif** file to select it as the first file, and then click the **OK** button.

7. Repeat Steps 5 and 6 to select the **banner2.gif** file as the second file. Both file-names appear in the Images to Display text box.

8. Click the **OK** button to finish specifying the banner ad. Only the first image you specified displays on the page in FrontPage Editor. Notice that the banner ad image appears with a white background because a banner ad image cannot have a transparent background. You need to make sure the images used in the banner ad contain the desired background before adding them.

9. Click the **Save** button 🖫 on the Standard toolbar to open the Save Embedded Files dialog box with the suggested filenames and folder, which should be the root folder of the Web. (The root folder is indicated by not listing any folder name in the folder column.) Click the **OK** button to accept these values and save the page with this modification.

TROUBLE? If "images/" or any folder name appears in the Folder column, click the Change Folder button to open that dialog box, click any HTM file in the list, and then click the OK button to return to the Save Embedded Files dialog box. Click the OK button to save the files in the root folder.

With the banner ad included on the Home Page, you are ready to test it to make sure that it operates correctly. Amanda asks you to do this next.

To test the Banner Ad Manager:

1. Click the **Preview in Browser** button 🔍 on the Standard toolbar to open the Home Page in your browser.

2. Click the **Refresh** button 🔃 on the Internet Explorer toolbar to display the revised page. Watch the logo as the image changes. See Figure 6-39.

Figure 6-39 ◀
Banner Ad
Manager
displays
different images

second image
displays in banner

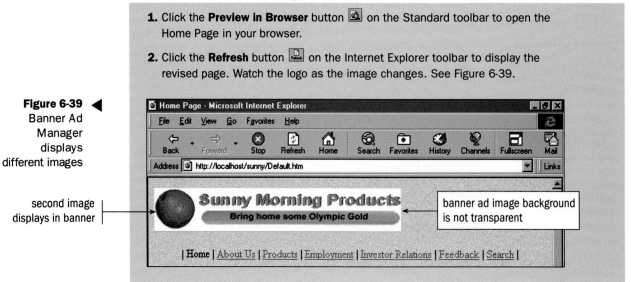

This banner ad should increase the visual impact of the Home Page, as Andrew had anticipated.

Using Drag and Drop

The FrontPage **drag and drop** feature allows you to rearrange the files within your Web by dragging files from one folder in the Web to another folder in the Web. Drag and drop is useful when you save a file in the wrong folder and want to move it to another folder. When you use drag and drop, FrontPage automatically adjusts the references to the files, including any references to them in the hyperlinks. The images for the banner ad were saved in the root directory of the Web. Because these are image files, a better organization is to keep them with the other image files in the images folders. Amanda wants you to move the files to that folder.

To use drag and drop to reorganize files within a Web:

1. Click the **FrontPage Explorer** program button on the taskbar to return to that program, and then scroll to the bottom of the list of filenames in Folders view.

   TROUBLE? If Folders view is not displayed, then click the Folders button ▣ on the Views bar.

2. Click **Banner1.gif** to select that file, and then hold down the **Ctrl** key and click **Banner2.gif** to select both files.

3. With the pointer on top of the selected files, hold down the mouse button and position the pointer on top of the images folder. The pointer changes to ▯ when the pointer is positioned on the images folder.

   TROUBLE? If the pointer changes to ⊘ when you move it on top of the images folder, then you already have saved the files in the images folder. Continue with Step 4. The files are saved in the correct location.

4. Release the mouse button. The files are moved to the images folder, and their references are renamed within all the pages of the Web where they are used.

Now that the files have been moved to the images folder, Amanda asks you to verify that their hyperlinks were changed in the Java applet of the Banner Ad Manager.

To verify the renamed file references:

1. Click the **Show FrontPage Editor** button 🔳 on the FrontPage Explorer toolbar to return to that program and the open Home Page.

2. Right-click the banner ad to display the Shortcut menu, and then click **Java Applet Properties** to open the Banner Ad Manager dialog box. In the Images to Display text box, the images/ folder is now a prefix for each of the filenames.

3. Click the **Cancel** button to return to the Home Page.

The FrontPage drag and drop feature provides a convenient means for organizing the files within a Web and maintaining the correct relationships among the hyperlinks of the reorganized Web pages.

Global Find and Replace

FrontPage Explorer allows you to find and replace text across all the pages of a Web. When you use the global find and replace command, each page of the Web is examined to locate the text string to replace. The find and replace command works on elements that can be edited in place on a Web page. For example, page titles added in the Page Properties dialog box or buttons that were added to the page by a FrontPage component are not included in the processing with the find and replace command. A text hyperlink, such as one used within a user-defined navigation bar, is text that can be replaced. You select the All pages option button in the Replace in FrontPage Web dialog box to replace the matching text string in all of the pages in your open Web.

Amanda reviewed the current Web and decided to change the "About Us" text in the user-defined navigation bar on each Web page to "Our Company." You can do this with a global find and replace action.

To perform a global find and replace:

1. Click the **FrontPage Explorer** program button on the taskbar to return to that program. The Home Page remains open in FrontPage Editor.

2. Click **Tools** on the menu bar, and then click **Replace** to open the Replace in FrontPage Web dialog box.

3. In the Find what text box, type **About Us**; in the Replace with text box, type **Our Company**; click the **Match whole word only** check box to select it; click the **Match case** check box to select it; and then notice that the **All pages** option button is selected in the Find in section. See Figure 6-40.

Figure 6-40 ◀
Replace in
FrontPage Web
dialog box

existing text ———

radio button
specifies All pages
in current Web

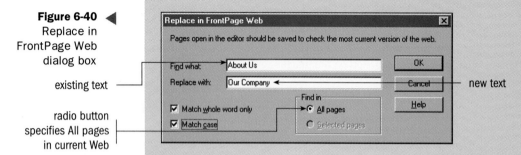

new text

4. Click the **OK** button to complete the find and replace, and wait while the Find occurrences of "About Us" dialog box opens. See Figure 6-41. This dialog box lists each page in the Web that contains the "About Us" text string.

Figure 6-41 ◀
Find
occurrences of
"About Us"
dialog box

Status indicates
replacement not
finished

summary of
Find command

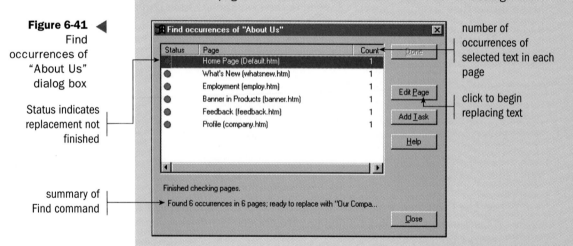

number of
occurrences of
selected text in each
page

click to begin
replacing text

5. Click the **Edit Page** button to open the first page in Editor and to open the Replace dialog box. See Figure 6-42.

Figure 6-42 ◀
Replace dialog
box

current page opened
in Editor for
text replacement
(your page might
be different)

text to replace

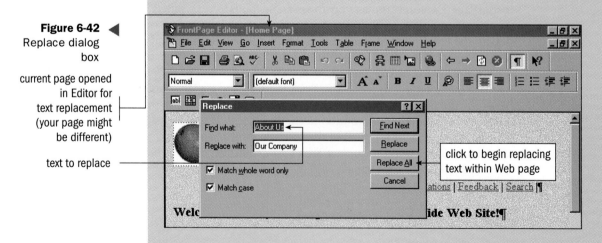

click to begin replacing
text within Web page

6. Click the **Replace All** button to perform the replace and open the Continue with next document? message box. See Figure 6-43.

Figure 6-43
Continue with
next document?
message box

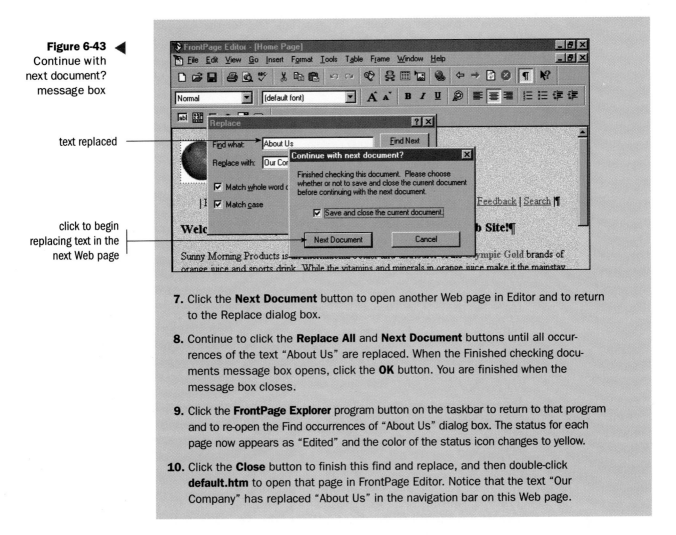

text replaced

click to begin
replacing text in the
next Web page

7. Click the **Next Document** button to open another Web page in Editor and to return to the Replace dialog box.

8. Continue to click the **Replace All** and **Next Document** buttons until all occurrences of the text "About Us" are replaced. When the Finished checking documents message box opens, click the **OK** button. You are finished when the message box closes.

9. Click the **FrontPage Explorer** program button on the taskbar to return to that program and to re-open the Find occurrences of "About Us" dialog box. The status for each page now appears as "Edited" and the color of the status icon changes to yellow.

10. Click the **Close** button to finish this find and replace, and then double-click **default.htm** to open that page in FrontPage Editor. Notice that the text "Our Company" has replaced "About Us" in the navigation bar on this Web page.

Amanda and Andrew think this change better describes the information provided by the hyperlink and are pleased with this revision to the Web site.

Changing Filenames in Folders View

After creating your Web pages, you might want to change the page filenames to have more meaningful descriptions or so the filenames more closely match the page titles or uses. Because filenames are used in the hyperlinks you created on each individual Web page, it would be a tedious and error-prone activity for you to search each hyperlink and change the filename manually. Similar to global find and replace, FrontPage Explorer does this search and replace for you across all the pages in your Web. This allows you to rename files to identify them more appropriately as changes occur to your Web site during its development. Renaming a Web page's filename in FrontPage Explorer is very similar to renaming a file in Windows Explorer. You select the current filename in Folders view and change it to the desired new name.

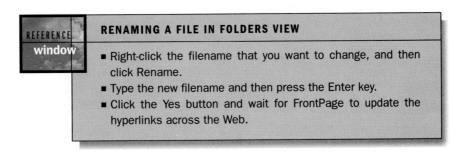

REFERENCE window

RENAMING A FILE IN FOLDERS VIEW

- Right-click the filename that you want to change, and then click Rename.
- Type the new filename and then press the Enter key.
- Click the Yes button and wait for FrontPage to update the hyperlinks across the Web.

You already have changed the hyperlink text for the "About Us" hyperlink to "Our Company." The Web page that this hyperlink references is the company.htm file with a page title of "Profile." Amanda would like you to rename the company.htm file to profile.htm so that the filename matches the page title, similar to the manner in which many of the other files are named within the Sunny Morning Products Web.

To rename a file in Folders view:

1. Click the **FrontPage Explorer** program button on the taskbar to switch to that program.

2. Click the **Folders** button [icon] on the Views bar to display that view.

3. Right-click the **company.htm** filename to display the Shortcut menu, and then click **Rename**. The current filename appears highlighted to indicate that it is selected for editing.

4. Type **profile.htm** as the new filename, and then press the **Enter** key to open the Rename dialog box, which asks if you want to update the page references so the hyperlinks will not be broken.

5. Click the **Yes** button and then wait for FrontPage to update the hyperlinks on all the pages in your Web.

   Now, Amanda wants you to verify this update by checking the hyperlink on the Home Page.

6. Press the **F5** key to refresh the display in FrontPage Explorer.

7. Double-click **default.htm** to open that page in FrontPage Editor, and then point to the **Our Company** hyperlink. Notice that "profile.htm" is the filename for the hyperlink that displays in the status bar, which confirms the update of the hyperlink.

You successfully renamed the Profile page using a new filename that matches its page title and confirmed that its hyperlinks are not broken. You agree with Amanda that this change provides a clearer identification of the Web page. But, now you wonder if there are any problems with any of the other hyperlinks.

Recalculating and Verifying Hyperlinks

After changing a Web, you need to recalculate hyperlinks to update the display of the current FrontPage Web in FrontPage Explorer. **Recalculating hyperlinks** is the process of updating the display of all views of the FrontPage Web in which you are working, including updating the text index created by a WebBot Search component. If any hyperlink in the FrontPage Web is invalid, it will display as a broken hyperlink in Hyperlinks view in FrontPage Explorer after the hyperlinks have been recalculated. You can check the hyperlinks of a Web using either a disk-based Web or a server-based Web. However, when performing recalculation using a server-based Web, the text index maintained by FrontPage Explorer for use in a text search of the pages in the Web is updated as well.

Verifying hyperlinks is the process of checking all the hyperlinks in your FrontPage Web to identify any broken hyperlinks. The Verify Hyperlinks command allows you to check both internal and external hyperlinks, where an **external hyperlink** consists of a link to a page that does not exist in your open Web and might link to an entirely different computer. The Verify Hyperlinks dialog box will list any broken hyperlinks so you can repair them. You can use the Recalculate Hyperlinks and Verify Hyperlinks commands to help you detect and repair broken hyperlinks. One of the primary differences between these two commands is in how a broken hyperlink is displayed—the Verify Hyperlinks command provides a single list of all the broken hyperlinks. Both commands provide information that is useful in locating and correcting hyperlink problems.

Recalculating Hyperlinks

Because the server-based Web is currently the open Web, Amanda asks you to recalculate the hyperlinks on the server-based Web.

To recalculate hyperlinks:

1. Click the **FrontPage Explorer** program button on the taskbar to switch to that program.

2. Click the **Hyperlinks** button ▦ on the Views bar, and then click **Home Page** in the left pane to make this page the center focus in the right pane.

3. Click **Tools** on the menu bar, and then click **Recalculate hyperlinks**. The Recalculate Hyperlinks dialog box opens. See Figure 6-44.

Figure 6-44 ◀
Recalculate Hyperlinks dialog box

click to continue recalculating hyperlinks

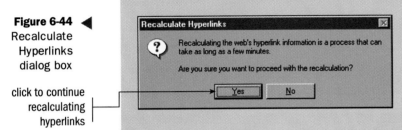

4. Click the **Yes** button. The "Updating hyperlinks and text indices..." message displays in the status bar. After a few minutes, Hyperlinks view is refreshed with the Home Page as the center focus in the right pane, and all the hyperlinks are updated.

The hyperlinks are recalculated, and their display is updated if there are any changes. No broken links are visible from the view with the Home Page.

Verifying Hyperlinks

Verifying hyperlinks will point out any problem hyperlinks located anywhere in the Web. This is useful because the page that is the center focus might not contain any broken links, but broken links might occur within another page that is buried deep in the hyperlink structure. Amanda wants you to verify the hyperlinks to determine if there are any related unknown problems in the sunny Web. If any hyperlinks need to be repaired, then they will appear in Hyperlink Status view until you repair them.

To verify hyperlinks:

1. Click **Tools** on the menu bar, and then click **Verify Hyperlinks** to switch to Hyperlink Status view and open the Verify Hyperlinks dialog box. See Figure 6-45. A broken hyperlink—custordr.htm—is listed because it uses a page that you have not created or imported into the sunny Web.

   TROUBLE? Don't worry if your list differs from Figure 6-45. The hyperlinks listed will vary according to the steps you completed in the Tutorial Assignments.

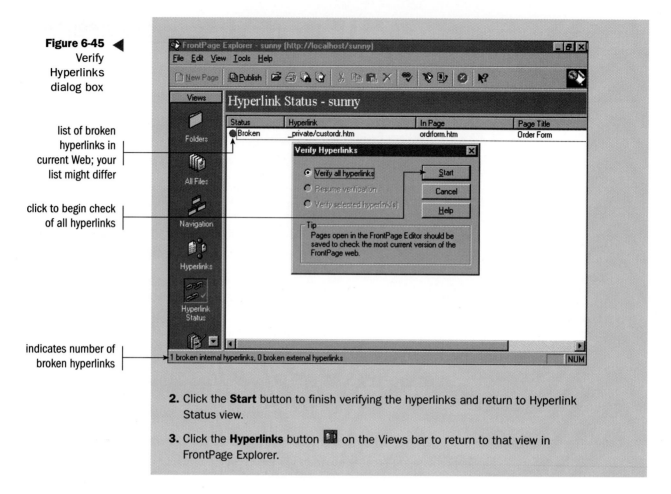

Figure 6-45 ◀
Verify
Hyperlinks
dialog box

list of broken
hyperlinks in
current Web; your
list might differ

click to begin check
of all hyperlinks

indicates number of
broken hyperlinks

2. Click the **Start** button to finish verifying the hyperlinks and return to Hyperlink Status view.

3. Click the **Hyperlinks** button 🖿 on the Views bar to return to that view in FrontPage Explorer.

Recalculating and verifying hyperlinks helped you isolate an unfinished Web page, and possibly other problems in your Web. The broken hyperlink, custordr.htm, is a custom-designed HTML page that is used to confirm a customer's order. The repair of this hyperlink will remain on the list in Hyperlink Status view to remind you to finish this task later.

Setting Permissions

Permissions allow a Web site developer to control who can browse, author, or administer a FrontPage Web. You can set permissions only for a server-based Web. You use FrontPage Explorer to administer the settings of permissions on each Web site as well as to allow specified users access to the site. If you want to control access to a disk-based Web, you need to use the tools available on your file system. For example, you can use Windows Explorer to change the sharing properties for the folder that contains the disk-based Web. When you are ready to publish your Web site to the WWW, you need to change the user permissions according to how much or how little access you want a user to have. There are three types of permissions: browsing, authoring, and administering. **Browsing permissions** authorize a user to open the Web using a Web browser, but restrict users from accessing or changing its Web pages. **Authoring permissions** allow a user to access and change a page in FrontPage Editor. Finally, **administering permissions** let a user control other users' permissions. For example, because you would not want anyone using FrontPage to be able to access and change your Web, you would set the permissions to browsing. Permissions also are hierarchical. For example, a user with administering permissions also has authoring and browsing rights, whereas authoring permissions give a user browsing rights but not administering rights.

The process of setting permissions depends on your network configuration and its authorized users. When using the Microsoft Personal Web Server or the Microsoft Internet Information Server, you cannot use FrontPage to add new users or groups or to set passwords on these Web servers. Instead, you must use the operating system's features for controlling that access. You must assign new users or groups user names and passwords for the network before you can assign them permissions to your Web.

With some versions of the Microsoft Personal Web Server, however, you cannot set permissions for users or groups of users that are known to the Web server. With these versions, all users on the network can browse your FrontPage Web and use any forms that require server processing, but authoring is permitted only from the computer on which the Web server itself is installed. In that case permissions are not used and the Permissions command is dimmed on the Tools menu. Any user can browse the Web, but authoring and administering the Web is permitted only from the computer on which the Web server itself is installed.

Where permissions are allowed, they are established for the root Web and are inherited by all other FrontPage Webs, unless you change them. You change permissions for an individual Web by using the Settings tab of the Permissions dialog box. Amanda wants you to change the permissions for the sunny Web so that users can only browse the Web.

To set permissions:

1. Click **Tools** on the menu bar, and then click **Permissions** to open that dialog box for the currently open Web.

   TROUBLE? If the Permissions command is dimmed, then this command is not available on your computer. Press the Esc key and read the following steps without executing them.

2. Click the **Use unique permissions for this web** option button to select it, and then click the **Apply** button.

3. Click the **Users** tab to display those settings, which list each user and the assigned access rights. See Figure 6-46. You can use this dialog box to add or remove users from the list and change the access rights of current users by editing them. Check with your instructor or technical support person for the user name you can change.

   TROUBLE? Don't worry if your list of names differs from Figure 6-46. This list is based on the server on your computer and varies from computer to computer.

Figure 6-46 ◀
Permissions -
sunny dialog
box

user name list (your
list might be different)

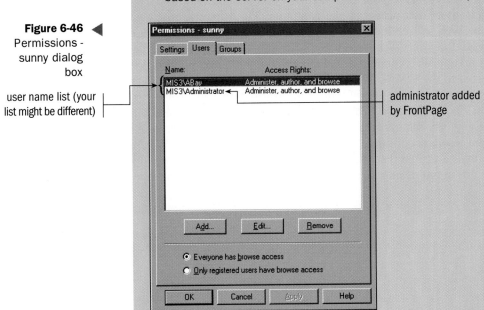

administrator added
by FrontPage

4. Click the desired user on your computer, and then click the **Edit** button to open the Edit Users dialog box. See Figure 6-47. This is where you change a user's permission.

Figure 6-47 ◄
Edit Users
dialog box

click to permit
browsing only

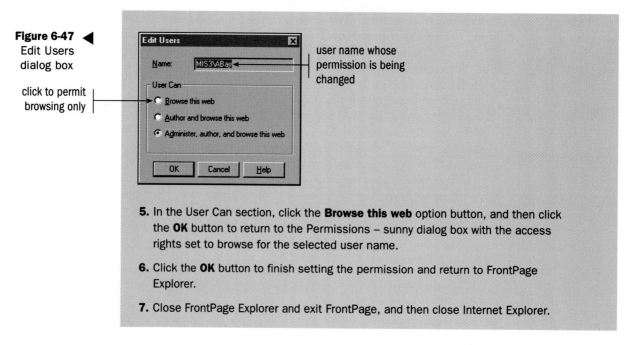

user name whose
permission is being
changed

5. In the User Can section, click the **Browse this web** option button, and then click the **OK** button to return to the Permissions – sunny dialog box with the access rights set to browse for the selected user name.

6. Click the **OK** button to finish setting the permission and return to FrontPage Explorer.

7. Close FrontPage Explorer and exit FrontPage, and then close Internet Explorer.

Now you have completed all the tasks necessary for making the sunny Web available on the WWW.

Going Live

Going live is the process of making your Web site available to WWW users, or at least to those individuals who have permission to access it on the WWW. If you developed your site locally using a personal Web server, you need to publish it to the FrontPage Web site in order for WWW users to access it. You do this in the same manner as when you published the Web from your Student Disk to the personal Web server.

Generally, an individual designated as its administrator manages a Web server. The administrator is responsible for the overall management of the server, including the management of user access to the computer. The administrator determines how and where your Web will be located on the server, based on the procedures that have been established for your Web server by your ISP. Then, as appropriate, you use the Publish FrontPage Web command in FrontPage Explorer to publish your Web to a server connected to the WWW. These procedures vary from computer to computer. When publishing your Web to a WWW site, the information you provide should be as complete as possible. In the past, "Under Construction" icons have been a popular way of bridging the gap between information that will be supplied at a later date. However, these types of icons now are considered to be inappropriate. Because all Web sites are dynamic, it generally is accepted that Web sites will be modified, revised, and updated continuously. It is best to develop and test your Web site locally and then publish it to the server.

Quick Check

1. True or False: You cannot install a Web server on a computer that has an installed Web browser.

2. True or False: You must have a connection with an Internet service provider (ISP) in order to use a Web server.

3. After you copy a disk-based Web to a server-based Web, the Web is _____.

4. A(n) _____ is a Web page that echoes the data a user enters so the user can verify the data values that were entered.

5. When storing results in a text-formatted file, what data appear in the first line of a file to identify the other data stored in that file?

6. Which command checks all the hyperlinks in a FrontPage Web and subsequently lists any broken hyperlinks?

7. Which FrontPage feature gives a Web site developer control over which users can browse, author, or administer a FrontPage Web?

You have completed all the activities in Amanda's training course. Although there are a number of other features associated with FrontPage, you are well on your way to using this tool to develop effective Web sites. Amanda is confident in your abilities to assist her with the ongoing maintenance and enhancements to the Sunny Morning Products Web site.

Tutorial Assignments

You have made significant progress in mastering the development of forms processed using the FrontPage Extensions on a Web server. Amanda wants you to practice these new skills before you begin assisting her in maintaining the Sunny Morning Products Web site. Make sure your Student Disk is in drive A or the appropriate disk drive, start FrontPage Explorer, and then do the following:

1. Open the sunny (local) Web that you published in the tutorial in FrontPage Explorer.

2. In FrontPage Editor, add a navigation bar to the Search page. (*Hint:* Copy the navigation bar from the Home Page, paste it into the Search page, and then modify the hyperlinks as necessary.) Save the page and test the hyperlinks using Internet Explorer.

3. Open the Feedback Web page in FrontPage Editor. Under the "Tell us how to get in touch with you:" entries, add two fields: (a) "Phone" with a field name of "UserPhone" and (b) "FAX" with a field name of "UserFAX." Both fields have a width of 35 characters.

4. Add two choices to the drop-down menu field form: "Employee" and "Other." The Selected parameter for each field should be set to No, and the Value parameter for each field is the same as the choice text.

5. Save the Web.

6. Change the height of the drop-down menu so two choices are visible in the menu. Test these revisions using Internet Explorer, and then print a copy of this revised page.

7. Create a custom confirmation form for the feedback form using the Confirmation Form template. Modify the form using the appropriate form field names from the feedback form. Add a Confirmation Field WebBot Component that acknowledges the number of visits to the Sunshine Country Store together with appropriate narrative text. Make any other appearance-related revisions to the form.

8. Save the new confirmation form as the confirm.htm file in the _private folder of the sunny Web on the server. Test the Confirmation Form, and then print the form from both FrontPage Editor and Internet Explorer.

9. Start Microsoft Excel, and then open the _private/feedback.txt file that contains the stored results from the feedback form. When the Text Import Wizard dialog box opens, select the delimited option button, click the Next button, select the Comma Delimiters option button, and then click the Finish button. The data are displayed as an Excel list with the field names in the top row.

10. Print the list in Step 9 from Excel, and then close Excel without saving the file.

11. Modify the Banner Ad Manager used with the Home Page by including the banner3.gif file in the images folder for Tutorial.06 as the third image used in the banner ad.

12. Open the Map page. Delete the existing hover button in the column on the right side of the table near the bottom of that page and replace it with a hover button that uses the barn.gif and bridge.gif files in the images folder of the Tutorial.06 folder. On mouse over, the barn.gif image should change to the bridge.gif image. In order for these images to work correctly, you need to open this page using a server-based Web. After clicking the hover button, the user is linked to the Recipes Web that you created in Tutorial 5. In other words, when the user clicks the hover button, the Home Page of the Recipes Web opens.

13. Test the hover button that you created in Step 12 in Internet Explorer.

14. Arrange and clearly identify the printouts and answers for all the questions in the tutorial assignments.

15. Close any open programs, and save changes to your Web files.

Case Problems

1. Constructing Search and Feedback Pages for Royal Hair Care Products Customer response to the Kuick Dry Reliable Solution has exceeded company expectations. Many customers wrote letters to Royal Hair Care Products to praise the product. Valerie meets with Nathan to share this information. They review their storyboard design of the Royal Web site and discuss how the Customer Feedback page could be designed to capture specific information from customers on how well the product works, how often they use it, and so forth. They also review the need to create a keyword search capability for their Web site. Valerie asks you to help Nathan complete the necessary design and development activities for the Search and Customer Feedback pages.

If necessary, start FrontPage Explorer, insert your Student Disk in drive A or the appropriate disk drive, and then do the following:

1. Read all the questions for this case problem, and prepare a planning analysis sheet for the enhancements to the Royal Web site.

2. Access the Royal Web. If you did not create this Web in Tutorial 2 and make changes to it in Tutorials 3, 4, and 5, then create this Web and see your instructor.

3. Open the Tasks list. If the list does not include tasks for creating the Customer Feedback page and the Keyword Search page, then add these tasks to the list. Print the list.

4. Create a Keyword Search page using the FrontPage Search Page template as a starting point. Include either the royal01.gif or royal02.gif file from the Tutorial.02\Royal folder as an image for the logo on this page. Copy the navigation bar from the Home Page, and then place it in approximately the same location as the one on the Home Page. Modify the hyperlinks as necessary for the navigation bar on the Search page. Save the page, and then test it using Internet Explorer.

5. Design and create the Customer Feedback page based on the following information:

   - There are three types of comments or feedback: testimonial, suggestion, or problem.
   - Ask the customer to indicate a preference for either the gel or liquid spray form of the product.
   - Ask the customer for the average number of applications of Kuick Dry Reliable Solution each week. This number should not exceed 15.
   - Ask where the customer purchases the product most often (for example, drug store, discount store, department store, beauty salon, supermarket, variety store, or other). If the customer selects other, then the type of store should be entered in a separate text box.
   - Accept customer comments or feedback information as narrative text input.
   - Ask for the customer's contact information, including the customer's name, street address, city, state, postal code, e-mail address, home phone number, and fax number.
   - Provide a method for requesting additional information.
   - Provide a method of requesting a product sample.

You determine the specific use of each of radio button, drop-down menu, one-line text box, scrolling text box, and check box form fields for this feedback form. Use the royal01.gif or royal02.gif file from the Tutorial.02\Royal folder on your Student Disk as the page header logo. The Customer Feedback page must include a navigation bar similar to the one used on the Home Page. Save the results you collect from this form as comma-delimited text in the feedback.txt file in the _private folder of your Royal Web. Save this Web page.

6. Print the HTML code for the Customer Feedback page. Circle the FORM, SELECT, and INPUT tags, and then circle the code that implements the Save Results WebBot on the hardcopy.

7. Publish the Royal Web to your Web server, open the published Web in FrontPage Explorer, and then verify all the hyperlinks.

8. Repair any broken hyperlinks. Make the Feedback page the center focus in Hyperlinks view, and then print the Hyperlinks view using WordPad or your word-processing program.

9. Test the Keyword Search page using the Web that you published to the server. Use a search text string that returns a match for at least one page in the Web. Print a copy of the search page returned from the server that shows the list of pages where the text string matches were found.

10. Test the Customer Feedback page using realistic data that you create. Print the form with the data entered in it. Print the default confirmation form that echoes the user input data. Enter data for at least three different users.

11. Print the feedback.txt file that contains the results the user entered.

12. Add a hit counter to the Home Page with your choice of specifications and location.

13. Replace the logo file at the top of the Home Page with a banner ad of the royal01.gif and royal02.gif files from the Tutorial.02\images folder on your Student Disk. Select an appropriate effect and duration for the images.

14. Use global find and replace to change the "Keyword Search" text in the navigation bar to "Search."

15. Recalculate the hyperlinks in the Web site and list any broken links.

16. Verify the hyperlinks in the Web site, and list any identified problems.

17. Arrange and clearly identify the printouts and answers for all the questions in the case.

18. Close FrontPage Editor, FrontPage Explorer, and Internet Explorer.

2. Preparing a Contact Page for Buffalo Trading Post Recently, many Buffalo Trading Post (BTP) customers told sales associates that they like the Buffalo Web site and would like to be able to use it to request additional information or to be added to a mailing list. During Donna's most recent Web site development update meeting, the sales associates encouraged her to develop a Contact Web page for customers. The sales associates agreed that the page's design should include a way to obtain customer information so the customer could be added to the mailing list. Customers also should be able to send comments directly to BTP about items they would like to either buy or sell as well as to indicate their primary interest among the categories of women's clothing, children's clothing, and accessories. The sales associates also were interested in finding out how many times a customer visited the store and how frequently they visit BTP. Donna organized the ideas from the meeting and then met with Karla to review the Contact page requirements. Karla wants you to assist Donna to create this Contact page for the BTP Web site.

If necessary, start FrontPage Explorer, insert your Student Disk in drive A or the appropriate disk drive, and then do the following:

1. Read all the questions in this case problem, and prepare a planning analysis sheet for the Buffalo Web site enhancements.

2. Open the Buffalo Web. If you did not create this Web in Tutorial 2 and make changes to it in Tutorials 3, 4, and 5, then create this Web and see your instructor.

3. Open the Tasks list. If the list does not include tasks for creating the Contact page and the Where page, then add these tasks to the list. Print the list.

4. Determine the types of form fields the Contact page should contain to allow users to provide the necessary information to BTP. Include at least one radio button group, one drop-down menu, one one-line text box, one scrolling text box, and one check box form field. Apply an appropriate validation to at least one of the form fields. Define the validation criteria in your design, and then implement those criteria. Use the b_contac.gif in the Tutorial.06\buffalo folder on your Student Disk as the page header logo. Save the results collected from this form as comma-delimited text in the contact.txt file in the _private folder of your Buffalo Web. Save this Web page.

5. Print the HTML code for the Contact page. Circle the FORM, SELECT, and INPUT tags, and then circle the code that implements the Save Results WebBot on the hardcopy.

6. Publish the Buffalo Web to your Web server. Open the published Web in FrontPage Explorer to verify all the hyperlinks. Repair any broken hyperlinks. Make the Contact page the center focus in Hyperlinks view, and then print the Hyperlinks view using WordPad or your word-processing program.

7. Test the Contact page using realistic data that you create, and then print the form with the data entered in it. Print the default confirmation form that echoes the user input data. Enter data for at least three different users.

8. Print the contact.txt file that contains the user's results.

9. Create a custom confirmation form that acknowledges the user's contact information. Include a navigation bar to the other Buffalo Web pages. Save this form as the confirm.htm file in the _private folder of the Buffalo Web on the server.

10. Test your custom confirmation form, print the form from FrontPage Editor, and then print the HTML code for that page. Circle the HTML code entries that implement the confirmation fields.

11. Design and create a "Where" Web page that provides information on the nearest BTP store location. Use the b_where.gif in the Tutorial.06\buffalo folder on your Student Disk as the page header logo. Include a navigation bar with links to the other pages in the Web.

12. Add a hit counter to the Home Page of the Web. You determine the appropriate style and location.

13. Design and create a banner ad using the Banner Ad Manager. Select the page where you will use the banner ad. You create the GIF files that are used for the banner ad. Use at least three different images with the banner ad. If you cannot create the images for the banner, then use at least two images that are saved on your Student Disk.

14. (*Optional*) Use the Help system to learn more about creating a discussion group. Use the Discussion Web Wizard to create a discussion Web that is *added* to the current Buffalo Web. Modify each of the discussion pages so they share a common background with the Home Page. Make any other appropriate enhancements to these pages. Print each of these pages from either FrontPage Editor or Internet Explorer.

15. Draw a final sketch of the Buffalo Web site that shows the Web pages and their hyperlinks.

16. Arrange and clearly identify the printouts and answers for all the questions in the case.

17. Close all open programs, and save changes to your Web files.

3. Developing Search and Feedback Pages for Pardon My Garden   Nolan is pleased with Shannon's progress on the Pardon My Garden Web site. The two of them just completed a review of their storyboard design and explained the Customer Feedback page to Samantha Wyman in the marketing department. Samantha believes this page provides a great opportunity to gather customer information. Shannon noted that in addition to the Customer Feedback page, she and Nolan also have a Keyword Search page and a Franchise Information page that remain to be completed as part of their planned Web site development. Nolan agrees with Shannon's assessment of the remaining work. He asks you to assist Shannon in developing these Web pages.

If necessary, start FrontPage Explorer, insert your Student Disk in drive A or the appropriate disk drive, and then do the following:

1. Read all the questions for this case problem, and prepare a planning analysis sheet for these revisions to the Garden Web site.

2. Access the Garden Web. If you did not create this Web in Tutorial 2 and make changes to it in Tutorials 3, 4, and 5, then create this Web and see your instructor.

3. Create a Keyword Search page using the FrontPage template as your starting point. Include either the garden01.gif or garden02.gif file from the Tutorial.02\Garden folder as an inline image for the logo on this page. Copy the navigation bar from the Home Page, and place it in approximately the same location as the one on the Home Page. Then modify the hyperlinks as necessary for this navigation bar. Save the page, and then test it using Internet Explorer.

4. Design and create the Customer Feedback page, and determine the information the user will provide. Include at least one radio button group, one drop-down menu, one one-line text box, one scrolling text box, and one check box group form field. Use validation with at least two of the form fields. Define the validation criteria in your design, and then implement those criteria. The garden01.gif and garden02.gif files in the Tutorial.02\Garden folder on your Student Disk are available for your use as the inline image logo for this page. Save the results that you collect from this form as comma-delimited text in the feedback.txt file in the _private folder of your Garden Web. Save this Web page.

5. Print the HTML code for the Customer Feedback page. Circle the FORM, SELECT, and INPUT tags, and then circle the code that implements the Save Results WebBot on the hardcopy.

6. Publish the Garden Web to your Web server, open the published Web in FrontPage Explorer, and then verify all the hyperlinks.

7. Repair any broken hyperlinks. Make the Customer Feedback page the center focus in Hyperlinks view. Print Hyperlinks view using WordPad or your word-processing program.

8. Test the Keyword Search page using the Web that you published to the server. Use an appropriate search text string that returns a match with at least one page in the Web. Print a copy of the search page returned from the server that shows the list of pages where the text string matches were found.

9. Modify the Customer Feedback page so the Save Results WebBot places the results in a second file named feedback.htm in the _private folder of the Garden Web that is stored in HTML format. Specify the second results file using the Advanced tab.

10. Test the Customer Feedback page using realistic data that you create. Print the form with the data entered in it. Print the default confirmation form that echoes the user input data. Enter data for at least three different users.

11. Print the feedback.txt file that contains the results the user entered.

12. Use Internet Explorer to open the feedback.htm file located in the _private folder of the Garden Web. Print this Web page.

13. Design and create the franchise information page that provides information about applying for and managing a Pardon My Garden franchise. This page should include a navigation bar with links to the other pages in the Web. Use one of the GIF files from the Tutorial.02\Garden folder for the logo on this page. Save the page, test it, and then print the page from either FrontPage Editor or Internet Explorer.

14. Add a hit counter to the Home Page of the Garden Web and a second hit counter to the Customer Feedback page.

15. Design and create a banner ad using the Banner Ad Manager. Select the page where you will use the banner ad. Create the GIF files that are used for the banner ad. Use at least three different images with the banner ad. If you cannot create the images, then use FrontPage clip art images or images that are saved on your Student Disk.

16. Start Microsoft Excel, and then open the _private\feedback.txt file that contains the stored results from the Customer Feedback page. Use the comma-delimited options to open this file. The data should display as an Excel list. Select one of the fields, and sort the list using that field. Do *not* include the field names in the sort.

17. Print the list from Step 16 from Excel. Save the file as feedback.xls in the Tutorial.06\Garden folder. Write a short paragraph describing other potential uses for this data.

18. Arrange and clearly identify the printouts and answers for all the questions in the case.

19. Close any open programs, and save changes to your Web files.

4. Producing Search and Feedback Pages for Replay Music Factory Many of Replay Music Factory's satisfied customers have swapped their old CDs for different ones. Based on the success of the Specials page, Bob Gustafson in marketing asked to meet with Mary Kay to review further development of their Web site. Mary Kay described her plan to include a Keyword Search page, and Bob discussed how information from a customer feedback form could help him make sound marketing decisions. Bob is particularly interested in receiving information from customers about CDs they would like to acquire that Replay does not currently stock. This information should include different categories of music and performers, as well as specific titles of interest to customers. Mary Kay reviews her notes on requirements for the Web pages and then asks you to assist Justin with these enhancements to their Web.

If necessary, start FrontPage Explorer, insert your Student Disk in drive A or the appropriate disk drive, and then do the following:

1. Read all the questions for this case problem, and prepare a planning analysis sheet for the modifications to the Replay Web site.

2. Access the Replay Web. If you did not create this Web in Tutorial 2 and change it in Tutorials 3, 4, and 5, then create this Web and see your instructor for any additional Web pages that might be available for use with this Web.

3. Create a Keyword Search page using the FrontPage template as your starting point. Include an appropriate page heading and logo. Create a navigation bar similar to the one used on the Home Page, and place it in approximately the same location as the one on the Home Page. Implement all the hyperlinks for the navigation bar. Save the page, and test it using Internet Explorer.

4. Design and create the Feedback page based on information you determine the user will provide. Use at least one radio button, drop-down menu, one-line text box, scrolling text box, and check box form field. Use validation with at least two of the form fields. Define the validation criteria in your design, and then implement those criteria. Your design should include a sketch of this page. Include a page heading and logo on this page similar to the one used in Step 3. Save the results you collect from this form as comma-delimited text in the feedback.txt file in the _private folder and as HTML format in the feedback.htm file in the _private folder of your Replay Web. Save this Web page.

5. Print the HTML code for the Feedback page. Circle the FORM, SELECT, and INPUT tags, and then circle the code that implements the Save Results WebBot.

6. Publish the Replay Web to your Web server, open the published Web in FrontPage Explorer, and then verify all the hyperlinks.

7. Repair any broken hyperlinks. Make the Feedback page the center focus in Hyperlinks view. Print the Hyperlinks view using WordPad or your word-processing program.

8. Test the Keyword Search page using the Web that you published to the server. Use a search text string that returns a match with at least one page in the Web. Print a copy of the search page returned from the server that shows the list of pages where the text string matches were found.

9. Create a custom confirmation form that acknowledges the feedback information the user entered. This page should include a navigation bar and background similar to the other pages in the Replay Web. Save this page as the feedback.htm file in the _private folder of the Replay Web on the server.

10. Print the custom confirmation form from FrontPage Editor, and then print the HTML code for that page. Circle the HTML code entries that implement the confirmation fields.

11. Test the Feedback page using realistic data that you have created. Print the form with the data entered in it. Print the custom confirmation form that echoes the user input data. Enter data for at least three different users.

12. Print the feedback.txt file that contains the user's results.

13. Use Internet Explorer to open the feedback.htm file located in the _private folder of the Replay Web. Print this page.

14. Use the Frequently Asked Questions template to create a new page in the Replay Web. Include several questions that Replay customers might ask. Make the pages similar to the other pages in the Replay Web. Save the pages, and print them from Internet Explorer.

15. If there are any other pages in your Web site design that have not been created, then create each of these pages, save them, test them, and print a copy of each one from either FrontPage Editor or Internet Explorer. These pages should include a navigation bar with links to the other Web pages.

16. Add a hit counter to at least two different pages in the Web. Which pages have the hit counter? Why did you select these pages?

17. Start Microsoft Excel, and then open the _private\feedback.txt file that contains the stored results from the Feedback page. Use the comma-delimited option to open this file. The data should display as an Excel list. Select one of the fields, and sort the list using that field. Make sure not to include the field names in the sort. Print this list from Excel. Save the page as feedback.xls in the Tutorial.06\Garden folder. Write a short paragraph describing what else you might do with this data.

18. Design and create a banner ad using the Banner Ad Manager. Select the page where you will use the banner ad. Create the GIF files that are used for the banner ad. Use at least three different images with the banner ad. If you cannot create the images, then use FrontPage clip art images or images that are saved on your Student Disk.

19. If all the images are not in your images folder, then reorganize the files of your Web by moving all image files to the images folder.

20. Prepare a final sketch of the Replay Web site that shows the Web pages created and their hyperlinks.

21. Arrange and clearly identify the printouts and answers for all the questions in the case.

22. Close any open programs, and save changes to your Web files.

Answers to Quick Check Questions

SESSION 1.1

1 The Internet is a network of connected computers; the WWW provides for the storage and retrieval of information among those connected computers.

2 The Web browser requests and receives information. This information is obtained from the Web server.

3 URL

4 hyperlink or link

5 site

6 Disk-based Web files are obtained from a disk without the use of a server program. Server-based Web files require a server program for accessing the Web files.

7 home

SESSION 1.2

1 It creates all of the HTML codes for you.

2 FrontPage Explorer

3 FrontPage Editor

4 Hyperlinks

5 WebBots

6 More than one hyperlink to the same page from another page.

7 A word-processing program

SESSION 1.3

1 FrontPage Editor

2 Using View HTML from FrontPage Editor or using View Source from Internet Explorer.

3 Using FrontPage Editor

4 Opening indicates the start of a feature, such as <BODY>, and closing turns off the feature, such as </BODY> where the / character indicates that the tag is a closing tag.

5 <B> to open and </B> to close; also, <STRONG> and </STRONG>.

6 <A> tag with the HREF property

7 False

SESSION 2.1

1 Analyze/define the problem, design the Web site, build the Web pages, and test the Web site

2 Analyze/define the problem

3 interactive

4 True

5 False

6 True

7 home page

SESSION 2.2

1 Format menu, Shortcut menu, or Format toolbar buttons

2 H1

3 left, center, and right

4 style

5 True

6 False

7 False

SESSION 2.3

1 To organize the multimedia files for your Web

2 background

3 True

4 marquee

5 To include a logo that identifies a company or other organization

6 To make a Web page more appealing or exciting

7 META tags

SESSION 3.1

1 True

2 bulleted

3 defined term and definition

4 nested

5 True

6 Increase Indent

SESSION 3.2

1 location

2 icon

3 Use the Preview tab or browser.

4 Image Properties dialog box

5 GIF

6 hotspot

7 Type it and then press the Spacebar.

SESSION 3.3

1 Tasks list

2 Just add a web task

3 column label button

4 broken link

5 Do Task

6 marked as complete

SESSION 4.1

1 cell

2 Cell padding

3 True

4 17 rows by 12 columns

5 False

6 Click the left border or click and drag the insertion point across the row.

7 Splitting

SESSION 4.2

1 frame set

2 template

3 True

4 FrontPage Editor

5 edit

6 _top

7 False

SESSION 5.1

1 thumbnail

2 any three: black and white, reverse, flip, rotate left, rotate right, change brightness, washout, or bevel

3 False

4 mouse over

5 True

6 page transition

7 True

SESSION 5.2

1 shared border

2 True

3 False

4 False

5 theme

6 False

7 Editor

SESSION 6.1

1 template

2 search

3 form

4 name-value pair

5 False

6 True

7 False

8 drop-down menu

SESSION 6.2

1 False

2 True

3 check box

4 submit

5 True

6 True

7 Save Results

8 False

SESSION 6.3

1 False

2 False

3 published

4 Confirmation page

5 field names

6 Verify Hyperlinks

7 permissions

Glossary/Index

Microsoft FrontPage 98 **Task Reference**

TASK	PAGE #	RECOMMENDED METHOD	WHERE USED
Animation, add	FP 5.13	Click object to select it, click Format, point to Animation, click desired effect	FrontPage Editor
Background color, change	FP 2.23	See Reference Window: "Changing the Background Color"	FrontPage Editor
Background image, select	FP 2.25	See Reference Window: "Selecting a Background Image"	FrontPage Editor
Background sound, add	FP 2.33	See Reference Window: "Adding a Background Sound"	FrontPage Editor
Banner ad, create	FP 6.43	See Reference Window: "Creating a Banner Ad"	FrontPage Editor
Bookmark, create	FP 3.13	Select bookmark text or location, click Edit, click Bookmark, type bookmark name in Bookmark Name text box, click OK	FrontPage Editor
Bulleted list, create	FP 3.10	Click paragraph for list, click ▤	FrontPage Editor
Cell contents, align	FP 4.15	Select cells for aligning contents, right-click selected cells, click Cell Properties, specify Horizontal Alignment and Vertical Alignment, click OK	FrontPage Editor
Cells, merge in table	FP 4.13	Select cells to merge, click ▦ on Table toolbar	FrontPage Editor
Cells, split in table	FP 4.12	Select cells to split, click ▦ on Table toolbar, click desired split, specify number of rows or columns, click OK	FrontPage Editor
Column, delete	FP 4.11	Select column, click ▦	FrontPage Editor
Column, insert in table	FP 4.9	Click top border of table to select column insertion location, click ▦ on Table toolbar	FrontPage Editor
Column, select	FP 4.11	Click top border of table to select column	FrontPage Editor
Definition list, create	FP 3.8	Click location for list, click Change Style list arrow, click Defined Term	FrontPage Editor
E-mail link, create	FP 3.31	Click location for address, type Internet e-mail address, press the Spacebar	FrontPage Editor
Filename, rename in Folders view	FP 6.47	Right-click filename, click Rename, type new filename, press Enter	FrontPage Explorer
Form field, add	FP 6.10	Click location for field, click button of desired field object on the Forms toolbar, right-click form object, click Form Field Properties, specify properties for form object, click OK	FrontPage Editor
Form handler, assign	FP 6.26	Right-click anywhere on form area, click Form Properties, select desired form handler, click OK	FrontPage Editor
Form stored results, examine	FP 6.39	Click File, click Open, locate *.txt file in the _private folder of your Web, click Open	Notepad
Frame set, create	FP 4.26	Click File, click New, click Frames tab, click desired frame layout, click OK	FrontPage Editor

Microsoft FrontPage 98 **Task Reference**

TASK	PAGE #	RECOMMENDED METHOD	WHERE USED
Global find and replace	FP 6.45	Click Tools, click Replace, specify find text, specify replace text, specify desired options, click OK, click Edit Page, click Replace All, click Next Document, repeat until finished, click OK	FrontPage Explorer
Heading, create	FP 2.14	Click paragraph to change, click Change Style list arrow, click desired heading	FrontPage Editor
Hit counter, include	FP 6.40	Click location for hit counter, click Insert, point to Active Elements, click Hit Counter, click option button for desired style, enter desired settings, click OK	FrontPage Editor
Horizontal line, add to Web page	FP 2.31	Click location to add line, click Insert, click Horizontal Line	FrontPage Editor
Horizontal line, change properties	FP 2.32	Right-click horizontal line, click Horizontal Line Properties, change settings, click OK	FrontPage Editor
Hover button, change component properties	FP 5.11	Right-click hover button, click Java Applet Properties, change settings, click OK	FrontPage Editor
Hover button, create	FP 5.8	Click location for button, click Insert, point to Active Elements, click Hover Button, specify settings for hover button, click OK	FrontPage Editor
Hover button, resize	FP 5.10	Click hover button to select it, drag any corner to resize the button	FrontPage Editor
HTML code, view	FP 1.40	Click the HTML tab	FrontPage Editor
HTML code, view	FP 1.41	Click View, click Source	Internet Explorer
Hyperlink to another Web page, create	FP 3.21	Select text for hyperlink, click 🔲, select destination page, click OK	FrontPage Editor
Hyperlink to bookmark, create	FP 3.16	Select text or image for bookmark, click 🔲, click Bookmark list arrow, click desired bookmark, click OK	FrontPage Editor
Hyperlink, create using drag and drop	FP 3.22	See Reference Window: "Creating a Hyperlink Using Drag and Drop"	FrontPage Explorer and FrontPage Editor
Hyperlinks, recalculate	FP 6.49	Click Tools, click Recalculate Hyperlinks, click Yes	FrontPage Explorer
Hyperlinks, verify	FP 6.49	Click Tools, click Verify Hyperlinks, click Start	FrontPage Explorer
Hyperlinks view, display	FP 1.30	Click 🔲 on Views bar	FrontPage Explorer
Image characteristics, change	FP 5.5	Click image to select it, click button of desired image characteristic on the Image toolbar	FrontPage Editor
Image, convert to GIF or JPEG	FP 3.25	See Reference Window: "Converting Images to GIF or JPEG Format"	FrontPage Editor

Microsoft FrontPage 98 **Task Reference**

TASK	PAGE #	RECOMMENDED METHOD	WHERE USED
Image hotspots, create	FP 3.28	Click image to select it, click button for desired hotspot shape on the Image toolbar, specify the desired location of the hotspot, click hyperlink destination, click OK	FrontPage Editor
Images, convert format	FP 3.25	Right-click image, click Image Properties, click General tab, click conversion option button in Type section, click OK	FrontPage Editor
Initial pages for frames, setting	FP 4.29	Click Set Initial Page button in desired frame, double-click the desired filename	FrontPage Editor
Inline image, add	FP 2.28	See Reference Window: "Adding an Inline Image"	FrontPage Editor
Mailto address, create	FP 3.31	See E-mail link, create	FrontPage Editor
Marquee, create	FP 2.36	Click location for marquee, click Insert, point to Active Elements, click Marquee, specify marquee properties, click OK	FrontPage Editor
META tag, add	FP 2.37	Right-click anywhere on page, click Page Properties, click Custom tab, click Add button in User Variables section, specify Name in text box, enter Value in text box, click OK, click OK	FrontPage Editor
Nested list, create	FP 3.12	Press Enter to insert paragraph in existing list, click ⊞, click ⊟ or ⊟ to create nested list	FrontPage Editor
Numbered list, create	FP 3.11	Click paragraph for list, click ⊟	FrontPage Editor
Page banner, create	FP 5.27	Click location for page banner, click ⊞, click Page Banner, click OK, click OK	FrontPage Editor
Page, delete from Navigation structure	FP 5.28	Right-click page icon in Navigation pane, click Delete, click Remove this page from all navigation bars option button, click OK	FrontPage Explorer
Page, replace	FP 4.3	Click ⊞, click ⊞, select the desired file, click OK, click File, click Save As, click OK	FrontPage Editor
Page transition, apply	FP 5.12	Click Format, click Page Transition, click Event list arrow, click desired event, specify duration, click desired transition effect, click OK	FrontPage Editor
Permissions, set on a server-based Web	FP 6.51	Click Tools, click Permissions, click Use unique permissions for this web, click Apply, click Users, click desired user, click Edit, specify desired permission in the User Can section, click OK, click OK	FrontPage Explorer
Repeated hyperlinks, display	FP 1.33	Click ⊞	FrontPage Explorer
Row, delete from table	FP 4.11	Select row, click ⊞	FrontPage Editor
Row, insert in table	FP 4.9	Click left border of table to select row at insertion location, click ⊞	FrontPage Editor
Row, select in table	FP 4.9	Click left border of table to select row	FrontPage Editor

Microsoft FrontPage 98 **Task Reference**

TASK	PAGE #	RECOMMENDED METHOD	WHERE USED
RTF file, include in a Web page	FP 3.7	Click location for text, click Insert, click File, select desired file, click Open button	FrontPage Editor
Shared border, edit	FP 5.23	Click desired shared border to select it, make edit changes to border, click 🖫	FrontPage Editor
Shared border, turn off for an individual page	FP 5.25	Click Tools, click Shared Borders, click Set for this page only option button, click check boxes for border location to deselect, click OK	FrontPage Editor
Special characters, insert	FP 2.16	Click Insert, click Symbol, click desired symbol, click Insert, click Close	FrontPage Editor
Table, align	FP 4.8	Right-click anywhere on table, click Table Properties, click Alignment list arrow, click desired alignment, click OK	FrontPage Editor
Table caption, add	FP 4.18	Click anywhere on table to select it, click Table, click Insert Caption, type desired caption	FrontPage Editor
Table, insert	FP 4.5	Click location for table, click 🏛, click a table button in the lower-right corner to specify table size or drag corner to increase table size	FrontPage Editor
Table properties, change	FP 4.6	Right-click anywhere on table, click Table Properties, specify settings for properties, click OK	FrontPage Editor
Table properties, setting	FP 4.19	Right-click anywhere on table, click Table Properties, change desired table properties, click OK	FrontPage Editor
Task, delete from Tasks list	FP 3.45	In Tasks view, click task to select it, click 🗙, click Yes	FrontPage Explorer
Task, reassign	FP 3.46	In Tasks view, double-click task to select it and open dialog box, enter new value in the Assign To text box, click OK	FrontPage Explorer
Tasks list, add new Web page	FP 3.38	See Reference Window: "Creating a New Web Page and Adding It to a Tasks List"	FrontPage Editor
Tasks list, add task	FP 3.40	See Reference Window: "Adding a Task to a Tasks List"	FrontPage Explorer
Tasks list, sort	FP 3.41	In Tasks view, click Task column label button	FrontPage Explorer
Template, create Web page from	FP 6.3	Click File, click New, click desired template, click OK	FrontPage Editor
Text, align	FP 2.15	Click paragraph to align, click desired alignment button on the Format toolbar	FrontPage Editor
Text color, change	FP 2.17	Select text, click 🖻, select color, click OK	FrontPage Editor
Text over image, add	FP 5.6	Click image to select it, click 🅰 on the Image toolbar, type desired text, press Enter, click anywhere on Web page to complete specification	FrontPage Editor

Microsoft FrontPage 98 **Task Reference**

TASK	PAGE #	RECOMMENDED METHOD	WHERE USED
Theme, apply to entire Web	FP 5.29	Click 🔲 on Views bar, click Use Selected Theme option button, click the desired theme, click Apply button, click Yes	FrontPage Explorer
Theme, apply to single Web page	FP 5.32	Click Format, click Theme, click Use Selected Theme option button, click desired theme, click OK	FrontPage Editor
Theme, change for entire Web	FP 5.31	Click 🔲, click the desired theme, click Apply button	FrontPage Explorer
Thumbnail image, create	FP 5.4	Click image to select it, click Tools, click Auto Thumbnail	FrontPage Editor
Transparent image, create	FP 3.26	Click image to select it, click 🔲, click the color on the image to make transparent	FrontPage Editor
URL, open	FP 1.12	Click Address box, type desired URL, press Enter	Internet Explorer
Web page, add in Navigation view	FP 5.18	Click Web page of parent for new page, click 🔲New Page	FrontPage Explorer
Web page, import	FP 3.3	Click File, click Import, click Add File, select desired file, click Open button, click OK	FrontPage Explorer
Web page, link to	FP 1.13	Click the desired hyperlink	Internet Explorer
Web page, open in FrontPage Editor	FP 2.22	Click 🔲, click filename, click OK	FrontPage Editor
Web page, print	FP 1.22	Click File, click Print, click OK	Internet Explorer
Web page, print	FP 2.20	Click 🔲	FrontPage Editor
Web page, rename in Navigation view	FP 5.17	Right-click page icon, click Rename, type new title for page, press Enter	FrontPage Explorer
Web page, save	FP 2.12	Click 🔲	FrontPage Editor
Web page, spell check	FP 2.18	Click 🔲	FrontPage Editor
Web page, test in browser	FP 2.19	Click 🔲	FrontPage Editor
Web, publish to any server	FP 6.34	Click File, click Publish FrontPage Web, click More Webs button, type or edit the location and name of the FrontPage Web, click OK, click OK	FrontPage Explorer
Web site, create	FP 2.7	Click Create a New FrontPage Web button, click option button for type of Web, type name of Web in Choose a title text box, click OK	FrontPage Explorer